Business P720

MW00965933

TABLE OF CONTENTS
& ACKNOWLEDGEMENTS

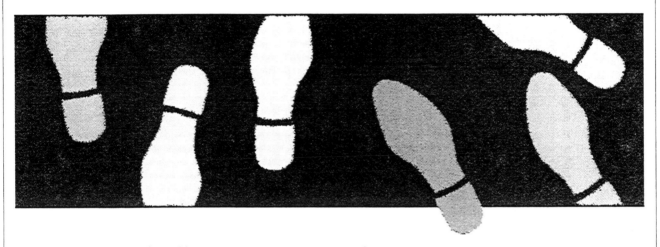

I. Operational Effectiveness Is Not Strategy

For almost two decades, managers have been learning to play by a new set of rules. Companies must be flexible to respond rapidly to competitive and market changes. They must benchmark continuously to achieve best practice. They must outsource aggressively to gain efficiencies. And they must nurture a few core competencies in the race to stay ahead of rivals.

Positioning – once the heart of strategy – is rejected as too static for today's dynamic markets and changing technologies. According to the new dogma, rivals can quickly copy any market position, and competitive advantage is, at best, temporary.

But those beliefs are dangerous half-truths, and they are leading more and more companies down the path of mutually destructive competition. True, some barriers to competition are falling as regulation eases and markets become global. True, companies have properly invested energy in becoming leaner and more nimble. In many industries, however, what some call *hypercompetition* is a self-inflicted wound, not the inevitable outcome of a changing paradigm of competition.

The root of the problem is the failure to distinguish between operational effectiveness and strat-

What Is Strategy?

by Michael E. Porter

egy. The quest for productivity, quality, and speed has spawned a remarkable number of management tools and techniques: total quality management, benchmarking, time-based competition, outsourcing, partnering, reengineering, change management. Although the resulting operational improvements have often been dramatic, many companies have been frustrated by their inability to translate those gains into sustainable profitability. And bit by bit, almost imperceptibly, management tools have taken the place of strategy. As managers push to improve on all fronts, they move farther away from viable competitive positions.

Operational Effectiveness: Necessary but Not Sufficient

Operational effectiveness and strategy are both essential to superior performance, which, after all, is the primary goal of any enterprise. But they work in very different ways.

Michael E. Porter is the C. Roland Christensen Professor of Business Administration at the Harvard Business School in Boston, Massachusetts.

A company can outperform rivals only if it can establish a difference that it can preserve. It must deliver greater value to customers or create comparable value at a lower cost, or do both. The arithmetic of superior profitability then follows: delivering greater value allows a company to charge higher average unit prices; greater efficiency results in lower average unit costs.

Ultimately, all differences between companies in cost or price derive from the hundreds of activities required to create, produce, sell, and deliver their products or services, such as calling on customers, assembling final products, and training employees. Cost is generated by performing activities, and cost advantage arises from performing particular activities more efficiently than competitors. Similarly, differentiation arises from both the choice of activities and how they are performed. Activities, then, are the basic units of competitive advantage. Overall advantage or disadvantage results from all a company's activities, not only a few.[1]

Operational effectiveness (OE) means performing similar activities *better* than rivals perform them. Operational effectiveness includes but is not limited to efficiency. It refers to any number of practices that allow a company to better utilize its inputs by, for example, reducing defects in products or developing better products faster. In contrast, strategic positioning means performing *different* activities from rivals' or performing similar activities in *different ways*.

Differences in operational effectiveness among companies are pervasive. Some companies are able

A company can outperform rivals only if it can establish a difference that it can preserve.

to get more out of their inputs than others because they eliminate wasted effort, employ more advanced technology, motivate employees better, or have greater insight into managing particular activities or sets of activities. Such differences in opera-

This article has benefited greatly from the assistance of many individuals and companies. The author gives special thanks to Jan Rivkin, the coauthor of a related paper. Substantial research contributions have been made by Nicolaj Siggelkow, Dawn Sylvester, and Lucia Marshall. Tarun Khanna, Roger Martin, and Anita McGahan have provided especially extensive comments.

Operational Effectiveness Versus Strategic Positioning

high / low — Nonprice buyer value delivered

Productivity Frontier (state of best practice)

high / low — Relative cost position

tional effectiveness are an important source of differences in profitability among competitors because they directly affect relative cost positions and levels of differentiation.

Differences in operational effectiveness were at the heart of the Japanese challenge to Western companies in the 1980s. The Japanese were so far ahead of rivals in operational effectiveness that they could offer lower cost and superior quality at the same time. It is worth dwelling on this point, because so much recent thinking about competition depends on it. Imagine for a moment a *productivity frontier* that constitutes the sum of all existing best practices at any given time. Think of it as the maximum value that a company delivering a particular product or service can create at a given cost, using the best available technologies, skills, management techniques, and purchased inputs. The productivity frontier can apply to individual activities, to groups of linked activities such as order processing and manufacturing, and to an entire company's activities. When a company improves its operational effectiveness, it moves toward the frontier. Doing so may require capital investment, different personnel, or simply new ways of managing.

The productivity frontier is constantly shifting outward as new technologies and management approaches are developed and as new inputs become available. Laptop computers, mobile communications, the Internet, and software such as Lotus Notes, for example, have redefined the productivity frontier for sales-force operations and created rich possibilities for linking sales with such activities as order processing and after-sales support. Similarly, lean production, which involves a family of activities, has allowed substantial improvements in manufacturing productivity and asset utilization.

For at least the past decade, managers have been preoccupied with improving operational effectiveness. Through programs such as TQM, time-based competition, and benchmarking, they have changed how they perform activities in order to eliminate inefficiencies, improve customer satisfaction, and achieve best practice. Hoping to keep up with shifts in the productivity frontier, managers have embraced continuous improvement, empowerment, change management, and the so-called learning organization. The popularity of outsourcing and the virtual corporation reflect the growing recognition that it is difficult to perform all activities as productively as specialists.

As companies move to the frontier, they can often improve on multiple dimensions of performance at the same time. For example, manufacturers that adopted the Japanese practice of rapid changeovers in the 1980s were able to lower cost and improve differentiation simultaneously. What were once believed to be real trade-offs – between defects and costs, for example – turned out to be illusions created by poor operational effectiveness. Managers have learned to reject such false trade-offs.

Constant improvement in operational effectiveness is necessary to achieve superior profitability. However, it is not usually sufficient. Few companies have competed successfully on the basis of operational effectiveness over an extended period, and staying ahead of rivals gets harder every day. The most obvious reason for that is the rapid diffusion of best practices. Competitors can quickly imitate management techniques, new technologies, input improvements, and superior ways of meeting customers' needs. The most generic solutions – those that can be used in multiple settings – diffuse the fastest. Witness the proliferation of OE techniques accelerated by support from consultants.

OE competition shifts the productivity frontier outward, effectively raising the bar for everyone. But although such competition produces absolute improvement in operational effectiveness, it leads to relative improvement for no one. Consider the $5 billion-plus U.S. commercial-printing industry. The major players – R.R. Donnelley & Sons Company, Quebecor, World Color Press, and Big Flower Press – are competing head to head, serving all types of customers, offering the same array of printing technologies (gravure and web offset), investing heavily in the same new equipment, running their presses faster, and reducing crew sizes. But the resulting major productivity gains are being captured by customers and equipment suppliers, not retained in superior profitability. Even industry-

Japanese Companies Rarely Have Strategies

The Japanese triggered a global revolution in operational effectiveness in the 1970s and 1980s, pioneering practices such as total quality management and continuous improvement. As a result, Japanese manufacturers enjoyed substantial cost and quality advantages for many years.

But Japanese companies rarely developed distinct strategic positions of the kind discussed in this article. Those that did – Sony, Canon, and Sega, for example – were the exception rather than the rule. Most Japanese companies imitate and emulate one another. All rivals offer most if not all product varieties, features, and services; they employ all channels and match one anothers' plant configurations.

The dangers of Japanese-style competition are now becoming easier to recognize. In the 1980s, with rivals operating far from the productivity frontier, it seemed possible to win on both cost and quality indefinitely. Japanese companies were all able to grow in an expanding domestic economy and by penetrating global markets. They appeared unstoppable. But as the gap in operational effectiveness narrows, Japanese companies are increasingly caught in a trap of their own making. If they are to escape the mutually destructive battles now ravaging their performance, Japanese companies will have to learn strategy.

To do so, they may have to overcome strong cultural barriers. Japan is notoriously consensus oriented, and companies have a strong tendency to mediate differences among individuals rather than accentuate them. Strategy, on the other hand, requires hard choices. The Japanese also have a deeply ingrained service tradition that predisposes them to go to great lengths to satisfy any need a customer expresses. Companies that compete in that way end up blurring their distinct positioning, becoming all things to all customers.

This discussion of Japan is drawn from the author's research with Hirotaka Takeuchi, with help from Mariko Sakakibara.

leader Donnelley's profit margin, consistently higher than 7% in the 1980s, fell to less than 4.6% in 1995. This pattern is playing itself out in industry after industry. Even the Japanese, pioneers of the new competition, suffer from persistently low profits. (See the insert "Japanese Companies Rarely Have Strategies.")

The second reason that improved operational effectiveness is insufficient – competitive convergence – is more subtle and insidious. The more benchmarking companies do, the more they look alike. The more that rivals outsource activities to efficient third parties, often the same ones, the more generic those activities become. As rivals imitate one another's improvements in quality, cycle times, or supplier partnerships, strategies converge and competition becomes a series of races down identical paths that no one can win. Competition based on operational effectiveness alone is mutu-

ally destructive, leading to wars of attrition that can be arrested only by limiting competition.

The recent wave of industry consolidation through mergers makes sense in the context of OE competition. Driven by performance pressures but lacking strategic vision, company after company has had no better idea than to buy up its rivals. The competitors left standing are often those that outlasted others, not companies with real advantage.

After a decade of impressive gains in operational effectiveness, many companies are facing diminishing returns. Continuous improvement has been etched on managers' brains. But its tools unwittingly draw companies toward imitation and homogeneity. Gradually, managers have let operational effectiveness supplant strategy. The result is zero-sum competition, static or declining prices, and pressures on costs that compromise companies' ability to invest in the business for the long term.

II. Strategy Rests on Unique Activities

Competitive strategy is about being different. It means deliberately choosing a different set of activities to deliver a unique mix of value.

Southwest Airlines Company, for example, offers short-haul, low-cost, point-to-point service between midsize cities and secondary airports in large cities. Southwest avoids large airports and does not fly great distances. Its customers include business travelers, families, and students. Southwest's frequent departures and low fares attract price-sensitive customers who otherwise would travel by bus or car, and convenience-oriented travelers who would choose a full-service airline on other routes.

Most managers describe strategic positioning in terms of their customers: "Southwest Airlines serves price- and convenience-sensitive travelers,"

The essence of strategy is choosing to perform activities differently than rivals do.

for example. But the essence of strategy is in the activities – choosing to perform activities differently or to perform different activities than rivals. Otherwise, a strategy is nothing more than a marketing slogan that will not withstand competition.

A full-service airline is configured to get passengers from almost any point A to any point B. To reach a large number of destinations and serve passengers with connecting flights, full-service airlines employ a hub-and-spoke system centered on major airports. To attract passengers who desire more comfort, they offer first-class or business-class service. To accommodate passengers who must change planes, they coordinate schedules and check and transfer baggage. Because some passengers will be traveling for many hours, full-service airlines serve meals.

Southwest, in contrast, tailors all its activities to deliver low-cost, convenient service on its particular type of route. Through fast turnarounds at the gate of only 15 minutes, Southwest is able to keep planes flying longer hours than rivals and provide frequent departures with fewer aircraft. Southwest does not offer meals, assigned seats, interline baggage checking, or premium classes of service. Automated ticketing at the gate encourages customers to bypass travel agents, allowing Southwest to avoid their commissions. A standardized fleet of 737 aircraft boosts the efficiency of maintenance.

Southwest has staked out a unique and valuable strategic position based on a tailored set of activities. On the routes served by Southwest, a full-

4

service airline could never be as convenient or as low cost.

Ikea, the global furniture retailer based in Sweden, also has a clear strategic positioning. Ikea targets young furniture buyers who want style at low cost. What turns this marketing concept into a strategic positioning is the tailored set of activities that make it work. Like Southwest, Ikea has chosen to perform activities differently from its rivals.

Consider the typical furniture store. Showrooms display samples of the merchandise. One area might contain 25 sofas; another will display five dining tables. But those items represent only a fraction of the choices available to customers. Dozens of books displaying fabric swatches or wood samples or alternate styles offer customers thousands of product varieties to choose from. Salespeople often escort customers through the store, answering questions and helping them navigate this maze of choices. Once a customer makes a selection, the order is relayed to a third-party manufacturer. With luck, the furniture will be delivered to the customer's home within six to eight weeks. This is a value chain that maximizes customization and service but does so at high cost.

In contrast, Ikea serves customers who are happy to trade off service for cost. Instead of having a sales associate trail customers around the store, Ikea uses a self-service model based on clear, in-store displays. Rather than rely solely on third-party manufacturers, Ikea designs its own low-cost, modular, ready-to-assemble furniture to fit its positioning. In huge stores, Ikea displays every product it sells in room-like settings, so customers don't need a decorator to help them imagine how to put the pieces together. Adjacent to the furnished showrooms is a warehouse section with the products in boxes on pallets. Customers are expected to do their own pickup and delivery, and Ikea will even sell you a roof rack for your car that you can return for a refund on your next visit.

Although much of its low-cost position comes from having customers "do it themselves," Ikea offers a number of extra services that its competitors do not. In-store child care is one. Extended hours are another. Those services are uniquely aligned with the needs of its customers, who are young, not wealthy, likely to have children (but no nanny), and, because they work for a living, have a need to shop at odd hours.

The Origins of Strategic Positions

Strategic positions emerge from three distinct sources, which are not mutually exclusive and often overlap. First, positioning can be based on

Finding New Positions: The Entrepreneurial Edge

Strategic competition can be thought of as the process of perceiving new positions that woo customers from established positions or draw new customers into the market. For example, superstores offering depth of merchandise in a single product category take market share from broad-line department stores offering a more limited selection in many categories. Mail-order catalogs pick off customers who crave convenience. In principle, incumbents and entrepreneurs face the same challenges in finding new strategic positions. In practice, new entrants often have the edge.

Strategic positionings are often not obvious, and finding them requires creativity and insight. New entrants often discover unique positions that have been available but simply overlooked by established competitors. Ikea, for example, recognized a customer group that had been ignored or served poorly. Circuit City Stores' entry into used cars, CarMax, is based on a new way of performing activities — extensive refurbishing of cars, product guarantees, no-haggle pricing,

sophisticated use of in-house customer financing – that has long been open to incumbents.

New entrants can prosper by occupying a position that a competitor once held but has ceded through years of imitation and straddling. And entrants coming from other industries can create new positions because of distinctive activities drawn from their other businesses. CarMax borrows heavily from Circuit City's expertise in inventory management, credit, and other activities in consumer electronics retailing.

Most commonly, however, new positions open up because of change. New customer groups or purchase occasions arise; new needs emerge as societies evolve; new distribution channels appear; new technologies are developed; new machinery or information systems become available. When such changes happen, new entrants, unencumbered by a long history in the industry, can often more easily perceive the potential for a new way of competing. Unlike incumbents, newcomers can be more flexible because they face no trade-offs with their existing activities.

producing a subset of an industry's products or services. I call this *variety-based positioning* because it is based on the choice of product or service varieties rather than customer segments. Variety-based positioning makes economic sense when a company can best produce particular products or services using distinctive sets of activities.

Jiffy Lube International, for instance, specializes in automotive lubricants and does not offer other

Strategic positions can be based on customers' needs, customers' accessibility, or the variety of a company's products or services.

car repair or maintenance services. Its value chain produces faster service at a lower cost than broader line repair shops, a combination so attractive that many customers subdivide their purchases, buying oil changes from the focused competitor, Jiffy Lube, and going to rivals for other services.

The Vanguard Group, a leader in the mutual fund industry, is another example of variety-based positioning. Vanguard provides an array of common stock, bond, and money market funds that offer predictable performance and rock-bottom expenses. The company's investment approach deliberately sacrifices the possibility of extraordinary performance in any one year for good relative performance in every year. Vanguard is known, for example, for its index funds. It avoids making bets on interest rates and steers clear of narrow stock groups. Fund managers keep trading levels low, which holds expenses down; in addition, the company discourages customers from rapid buying and selling because doing so drives up costs and can force a fund manager to trade in order to deploy new capital and raise cash for redemptions. Vanguard also takes a consistent low-cost approach to managing distribution, customer service, and marketing. Many investors include one or more Vanguard funds in their portfolio, while buying aggressively managed or specialized funds from competitors.

The people who use Vanguard or Jiffy Lube are responding to a superior value chain for a particular type of service. A variety-based positioning can serve a wide array of customers, but for most it will meet only a subset of their needs.

A second basis for positioning is that of serving most or all the needs of a particular group of cus-

tomers. I call this *needs-based positioning*, which comes closer to traditional thinking about targeting a segment of customers. It arises when there are groups of customers with differing needs, and when a tailored set of activities can serve those needs best. Some groups of customers are more price sensitive than others, demand different product features, and need varying amounts of information, support, and services. Ikea's customers are a good example of such a group. Ikea seeks to meet all the home furnishing needs of its target customers, not just a subset of them.

A variant of needs-based positioning arises when the same customer has different needs on different occasions or for different types of transactions. The same person, for example, may have different needs when traveling on business than when traveling for pleasure with the family. Buyers of cans – beverage companies, for example – will likely have different needs from their primary supplier than from their secondary source.

It is intuitive for most managers to conceive of their business in terms of the customers' needs they are meeting. But a critical element of needs-based positioning is not at all intuitive and is often overlooked. Differences in needs will not translate into meaningful positions unless the best set of activities to satisfy them *also* differs. If that were not the case, every competitor could meet those same needs, and there would be nothing unique or valuable about the positioning.

In private banking, for example, Bessemer Trust Company targets families with a minimum of $5 million in investable assets who want capital preservation combined with wealth accumulation. By assigning one sophisticated account officer for every 14 families, Bessemer has configured its activities for personalized service. Meetings, for example, are more likely to be held at a client's ranch or yacht than in the office. Bessemer offers a wide array of customized services, including investment management and estate administration, oversight of oil and gas investments, and accounting for racehorses and aircraft. Loans, a staple of most private banks, are rarely needed by Bessemer's clients and make up a tiny fraction of its client balances and income. Despite the most generous compensation of account officers and the highest personnel cost as a percentage of operating expenses, Bessemer's differentiation with its target families produces a return on equity estimated to be the highest of any private banking competitor.

Citibank's private bank, on the other hand, serves clients with minimum assets of about $250,000 who, in contrast to Bessemer's clients, want convenient access to loans–from jumbo mortgages to deal financing. Citibank's account managers are primarily lenders. When clients need other services, their account manager refers them to other Citibank specialists, each of whom handles prepackaged products. Citibank's system is less customized than Bessemer's and allows it to have a lower manager-to-client ratio of 1:125. Biannual office meetings are offered only for the largest clients. Both Bessemer and Citibank have tailored their activities to meet the needs of a different group of private banking customers. The same value chain cannot profitably meet the needs of both groups.

The third basis for positioning is that of segmenting customers who are accessible in different ways. Although their needs are similar to those of other customers, the best configuration of activities to reach them is different. I call this *access-based positioning*. Access can be a function of customer geography or customer scale – or of anything that requires a different set of activities to reach customers in the best way.

Segmenting by access is less common and less well understood than the other two bases. Carmike Cinemas, for example, operates movie theaters exclusively in cities and towns with populations under 200,000. How does Carmike make money in markets that are not only small but also won't support big-city ticket prices? It does so through a set of activities that result in a lean cost structure. Carmike's small-town customers can be served through standardized, low-cost theater complexes requiring fewer screens and less sophisticated pro-jection technology than big-city theaters. The company's proprietary information system and management process eliminate the need for local administrative staff beyond a single theater manager. Carmike also reaps advantages from centralized purchasing, lower rent and payroll costs (because of its locations), and rock-bottom corporate overhead of 2% (the industry average is 5%). Operating in small communities also allows Carmike to practice a highly personal form of marketing in which the theater manager knows patrons and promotes attendance through personal contacts. By being the dominant if not the only theater in its markets–the main competition is often the high school football team – Carmike is also able to get its pick of films and negotiate better terms with distributors.

Rural versus urban-based customers are one example of access driving differences in activities. Serving small rather than large customers or densely rather than sparsely situated customers are other examples in which the best way to configure marketing, order processing, logistics, and after-sale service activities to meet the similar needs of distinct groups will often differ.

Positioning is not only about carving out a niche. A position emerging from any of the sources can be broad or narrow. A focused competitor, such as Ikea, targets the special needs of a subset of customers and designs its activities accordingly. Focused competitors thrive on groups of customers who are overserved (and hence overpriced) by more broadly targeted competitors, or underserved (and hence underpriced). A broadly targeted competitor–for example, Vanguard or Delta Air Lines – serves a wide array of customers, performing a set of activities designed to meet their common needs. It

The Connection with Generic Strategies

In *Competitive Strategy* (The Free Press, 1985), I introduced the concept of generic strategies – cost leadership, differentiation, and focus – to represent the alternative strategic positions in an industry. The generic strategies remain useful to characterize strategic positions at the simplest and broadest level. Vanguard, for instance, is an example of a cost leadership strategy, whereas Ikea, with its narrow customer group, is an example of cost-based focus. Neutrogena is a focused differentiator. The bases for positioning – varieties, needs, and access – carry the understanding of those generic strategies to a greater level of specificity. Ikea and Southwest are both cost-based focusers, for example, but Ikea's focus is based on the needs of a customer group, and Southwest's is based on offering a particular service variety.

The generic strategies framework introduced the need to choose in order to avoid becoming caught between what I then described as the inherent contradictions of different strategies. Trade-offs between the activities of incompatible positions explain those contradictions. Witness Continental Lite, which tried and failed to compete in two ways at once.

7

ignores or meets only partially the more idiosyncratic needs of particular customer groups.

Whatever the basis – variety, needs, access, or some combination of the three – positioning requires a tailored set of activities because it is always a function of differences on the supply side; that is, of differences in activities. However, positioning is not always a function of differences on the demand, or customer, side. Variety and access positionings, in particular, do not rely on *any* customer differences. In practice, however, variety or access differences often accompany needs differences. The tastes – that is, the needs – of Carmike's small-town customers, for instance, run more toward comedies, Westerns, action films, and family entertainment. Carmike does not run any films rated NC-17.

Having defined positioning, we can now begin to answer the question, "What is strategy?" Strategy is the creation of a unique and valuable position, involving a different set of activities. If there were only one ideal position, there would be no need for strategy. Companies would face a simple imperative – win the race to discover and preempt it. The essence of strategic positioning is to choose activities that are different from rivals'. If the same set of activities were best to produce all varieties, meet all needs, and access all customers, companies could easily shift among them and operational effectiveness would determine performance.

III. A Sustainable Strategic Position Requires Trade-offs

Choosing a unique position, however, is not enough to guarantee a sustainable advantage. A valuable position will attract imitation by incumbents, who are likely to copy it in one of two ways.

First, a competitor can reposition itself to match the superior performer. J.C. Penney, for instance, has been repositioning itself from a Sears clone to a more upscale, fashion-oriented, soft-goods retailer. A second and far more common type of imitation is straddling. The straddler seeks to match the benefits of a successful position while maintaining its existing position. It grafts new features, services, or technologies onto the activities it already performs.

For those who argue that competitors can copy any market position, the airline industry is a perfect test case. It would seem that nearly any competitor could imitate any other airline's activities. Any airline can buy the same planes, lease the gates, and match the menus and ticketing and baggage handling services offered by other airlines.

Continental Airlines saw how well Southwest was doing and decided to straddle. While maintaining its position as a full-service airline, Continental also set out to match Southwest on a number of point-to-point routes. The airline dubbed the new service Continental Lite. It eliminated meals and first-class service, increased departure frequency, lowered fares, and shortened turnaround time at the gate. Because Continental remained a full-service airline on other routes, it continued to use travel agents and its mixed fleet of planes and to provide baggage checking and seat assignments.

But a strategic position is not sustainable unless there are trade-offs with other positions. Trade-offs occur when activities are incompatible. Simply put, a trade-off means that more of one thing necessitates less of another. An airline can choose to serve meals – adding cost and slowing turnaround time at the gate – or it can choose not to, but it cannot do both without bearing major inefficiencies.

Trade-offs create the need for choice and protect against repositioners and straddlers. Consider Neutrogena soap. Neutrogena Corporation's variety-based positioning is built on a "kind to the skin," residue-free soap formulated for pH balance. With a large detail force calling on dermatologists, Neutrogena's marketing strategy looks more like a drug company's than a soap maker's. It advertises in medical journals, sends direct mail to doctors, attends medical conferences, and performs research at its own Skincare Institute. To reinforce its positioning, Neutrogena originally focused its distribution on drugstores and avoided price promotions. Neutrogena uses a slow, more expensive manufacturing process to mold its fragile soap.

In choosing this position, Neutrogena said no to the deodorants and skin softeners that many customers desire in their soap. It gave up the large-volume potential of selling through supermarkets and using price promotions. It sacrificed manufacturing efficiencies to achieve the soap's desired attributes. In its original positioning, Neutrogena made a whole raft of trade-offs like those, trade-offs that protected the company from imitators.

Trade-offs arise for three reasons. The first is inconsistencies in image or reputation. A company known for delivering one kind of value may lack credibility and confuse customers – or even undermine its reputation – if it delivers another kind of value or attempts to deliver two inconsistent things at the same time. For example, Ivory soap, with its position as a basic, inexpensive everyday soap would have a hard time reshaping its image to match Neutrogena's premium "medical" reputation. Efforts to create a new image typically cost tens or even hundreds of millions of dollars in a major industry–a powerful barrier to imitation.

Second, and more important, trade-offs arise from activities themselves. Different positions (with their tailored activities) require different product configurations, different equipment, different employee behavior, different skills, and different management systems. Many trade-offs reflect inflexibilities in machinery, people, or systems. The more Ikea has configured its activities to lower costs by having its customers do their own assembly and delivery, the less able it is to satisfy customers who require higher levels of service.

However, trade-offs can be even more basic. In general, value is destroyed if an activity is overdesigned or underdesigned for its use. For example, even if a given salesperson were capable of providing a high level of assistance to one customer and none to another, the salesperson's talent (and some of his or her cost) would be wasted on the second customer. Moreover, productivity can improve when variation of an activity is limited. By providing a high level of assistance all the time, the salesperson and the entire sales activity can often achieve efficiencies of learning and scale.

Finally, trade-offs arise from limits on internal coordination and control. By clearly choosing to compete in one way and not another, senior management makes organizational priorities clear. Companies that try to be all things to all customers, in contrast, risk confusion in the trenches as employees attempt to make day-to-day operating decisions without a clear framework.

Positioning trade-offs are pervasive in competition and essential to strategy. They create the need for choice and purposefully limit what a company offers. They deter straddling or repositioning, because competitors that engage in those approaches undermine their strategies and degrade the value of their existing activities.

Trade-offs ultimately grounded Continental Lite. The airline lost hundreds of millions of dollars, and the CEO lost his job. Its planes were delayed leaving congested hub cities or slowed at the gate by baggage transfers. Late flights and cancellations generated a thousand complaints a day. Continental Lite could not afford to compete on price and still pay standard travel-agent commissions, but neither could it do without agents for its full-service business. The airline compromised by cutting commissions for all Continental flights across the board. Similarly, it could not afford to offer the same frequent-flier benefits to travelers paying the much lower ticket prices for Lite service. It compromised again by lowering the rewards of Continental's entire frequent-flier program. The results: angry travel agents and full-service customers.

Continental tried to compete in two ways at once. In trying to be low cost on some routes and full service on others, Continental paid an enormous straddling penalty. If there were no trade-offs between the two positions, Continental could have succeeded. But the absence of trade-offs is a dangerous half-truth that managers must unlearn. Quality is not always free. Southwest's convenience, one kind of high quality, happens to be consistent with low costs because its frequent departures are facilitated by a number of low-cost practices – fast gate turnarounds and automated ticketing, for example. However, other dimensions of airline quality – an assigned seat, a meal, or baggage transfer – require costs to provide.

In general, false trade-offs between cost and quality occur primarily when there is redundant or wasted effort, poor control or accuracy, or weak coordination. Simultaneous improvement of cost and differentiation is possible only when a company begins far behind the productivity frontier or when the frontier shifts outward. At the frontier, where

Trade-offs are essential to strategy. They create the need for choice and purposefully limit what a company offers.

companies have achieved current best practice, the trade-off between cost and differentiation is very real indeed.

After a decade of enjoying productivity advantages, Honda Motor Company and Toyota Motor Corporation recently bumped up against the frontier. In 1995, faced with increasing customer resistance to higher automobile prices, Honda found that the only way to produce a less-expensive car was to skimp on features. In the United States, it replaced the rear disk brakes on the Civic with lower-cost drum brakes and used cheaper fabric for the back seat, hoping customers would not notice. Toyota tried to sell a version of its best-selling Corolla in Japan with unpainted bumpers and cheaper seats. In Toyota's case, customers rebelled, and the company quickly dropped the new model.

For the past decade, as managers have improved operational effectiveness greatly, they have internalized the idea that eliminating trade-offs is a good thing. But if there are no trade-offs companies will never achieve a sustainable advantage. They will have to run faster and faster just to stay in place.

As we return to the question, What is strategy? we see that trade-offs add a new dimension to the answer. Strategy is making trade-offs in competing. The essence of strategy is choosing what *not* to do. Without trade-offs, there would be no need for choice and thus no need for strategy. Any good idea could and would be quickly imitated. Again, performance would once again depend wholly on operational effectiveness.

IV. Fit Drives Both Competitive Advantage and Sustainability

Positioning choices determine not only which activities a company will perform and how it will configure individual activities but also how activities relate to one another. While operational effectiveness is about achieving excellence in individual activities, or functions, strategy is about *combining* activities.

Southwest's rapid gate turnaround, which allows frequent departures and greater use of aircraft, is essential to its high-convenience, low-cost positioning. But how does Southwest achieve it? Part of the answer lies in the company's well-paid gate and ground crews, whose productivity in turnarounds is enhanced by flexible union rules. But the bigger part of the answer lies in how Southwest performs other activities. With no meals, no seat assignment, and no interline baggage transfers, Southwest avoids having to perform activities that slow down other airlines. It selects airports and routes to avoid congestion that introduces delays. Southwest's strict limits on the type and length of routes make standardized aircraft possible: every aircraft Southwest turns is a Boeing 737.

Fit locks out imitators by creating a chain that is as strong as its strongest link.

What is Southwest's core competence? Its key success factors? The correct answer is that everything matters. Southwest's strategy involves a whole system of activities, not a collection of parts. Its competitive advantage comes from the way its activities fit and reinforce one another.

Fit locks out imitators by creating a chain that is as strong as its *strongest* link. As in most companies with good strategies, Southwest's activities complement one another in ways that create real economic value. One activity's cost, for example, is lowered because of the way other activities are performed. Similarly, one activity's value to customers can be enhanced by a company's other activities. That is the way strategic fit creates competitive advantage and superior profitability.

Types of Fit

The importance of fit among functional policies is one of the oldest ideas in strategy. Gradually, however, it has been supplanted on the management agenda. Rather than seeing the company as a whole, managers have turned to "core" competencies, "critical" resources, and "key" success factors. In fact, fit is a far more central component of competitive advantage than most realize.

Fit is important because discrete activities often affect one another. A sophisticated sales force, for example, confers a greater advantage when the company's product embodies premium technology and its marketing approach emphasizes customer assistance and support. A production line with high levels of model variety is more valuable when combined with an inventory and order processing system that minimizes the need for stocking finished goods, a sales process equipped to explain and encourage customization, and an advertising theme that stresses the benefits of product variations that meet a customer's special needs. Such complementarities are pervasive in strategy. Although some fit among activities is generic and applies to many companies, the most valuable fit is strategy-specific because it enhances a position's uniqueness and amplifies trade-offs.[2]

There are three types of fit, although they are not mutually exclusive. First-order fit is *simple consistency* between each activity (function) and the overall strategy. Vanguard, for example, aligns all activities with its low-cost strategy. It minimizes portfolio turnover and does not need highly compensated money managers. The company distributes its funds directly, avoiding commissions to brokers. It also limits advertising, relying instead on public relations and word-of-mouth recommendations. Vanguard ties its employees' bonuses to cost savings.

Consistency ensures that the competitive advantages of activities cumulate and do not erode or cancel themselves out. It makes the strategy easier to communicate to customers, employees, and shareholders, and improves implementation through single-mindedness in the corporation.

Second-order fit occurs when *activities are reinforcing*. Neutrogena, for example, markets to upscale hotels eager to offer their guests a soap recommended by dermatologists. Hotels grant Neutrogena the privilege of using its customary packaging while requiring other soaps to feature the hotel's name. Once guests have tried Neutrogena in a luxury hotel, they are more likely to purchase it at the drugstore or ask their doctor about it. Thus Neutrogena's medical and hotel marketing activities reinforce one another, lowering total marketing costs.

In another example, Bic Corporation sells a narrow line of standard, low-priced pens to virtually all major customer markets (retail, commercial, promotional, and giveaway) through virtually all available channels. As with any variety-based positioning serving a broad group of customers, Bic emphasizes a common need (low price for an acceptable pen) and uses marketing approaches with a broad reach (a large sales force and heavy television advertising). Bic gains the benefits of consis-

Mapping Activity Systems

Activity-system maps, such as this one for Ikea, show how a company's strategic position is contained in a set of tailored activities designed to deliver it. In companies with a clear strategic position, a number of higher-order strategic themes (in dark purple) can be identified and implemented through clusters of tightly linked activities (in light purple).

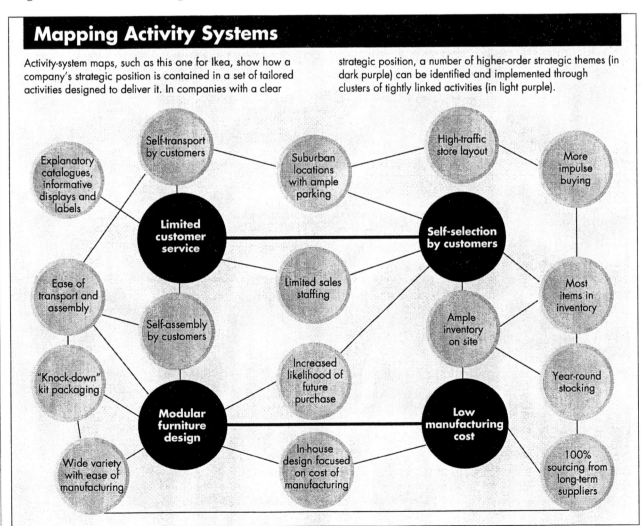

11

Vanguard's Activity System

Activity-system maps can be useful for examining and strengthening strategic fit. A set of basic questions should guide the process. First, is each activity consistent with the overall positioning – the varieties produced, the needs served, and the type of customers accessed? Ask those responsible for each activity to identify how other activities within the company improve or detract from their performance. Second, are there ways to strengthen how activities and groups of activities reinforce one another? Finally, could changes in one activity eliminate the need to perform others?

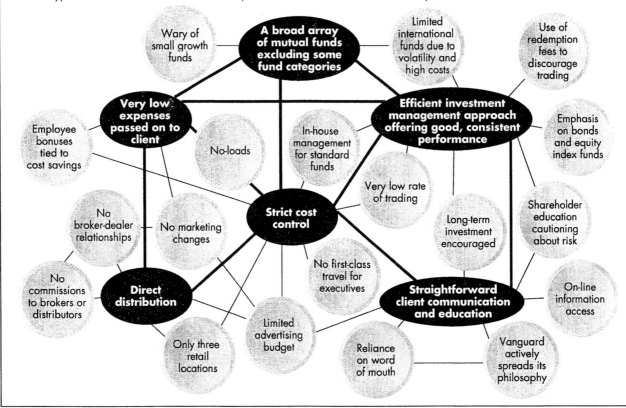

tency across nearly all activities, including product design that emphasizes ease of manufacturing, plants configured for low cost, aggressive purchasing to minimize material costs, and in-house parts production whenever the economics dictate.

Yet Bic goes beyond simple consistency because its activities are reinforcing. For example, the company uses point-of-sale displays and frequent packaging changes to stimulate impulse buying. To handle point-of-sale tasks, a company needs a large sales force. Bic's is the largest in its industry, and it handles point-of-sale activities better than its rivals do. Moreover, the combination of point-of-sale activity, heavy television advertising, and packaging changes yields far more impulse buying than any activity in isolation could.

Third-order fit goes beyond activity reinforcement to what I call *optimization of effort*. The Gap, a retailer of casual clothes, considers product availability in its stores a critical element of its strategy. The Gap could keep products either by holding store inventory or by restocking from warehouses. The Gap has optimized its effort across these activities by restocking its selection of basic clothing almost daily out of three warehouses, thereby minimizing the need to carry large in-store inventories. The emphasis is on restocking because the Gap's merchandising strategy sticks to basic items in relatively few colors. While comparable retailers achieve turns of three to four times per year, the Gap turns its inventory seven and a half times per year. Rapid restocking, moreover, reduces the cost of implementing

The competitive value of individual activities cannot be separated from the whole.

the Gap's short model cycle, which is six to eight weeks long.[3]

Coordination and information exchange across activities to eliminate redundancy and minimize wasted effort are the most basic types of effort optimization. But there are higher levels as well. Product design choices, for example, can eliminate the need for after-sale service or make it possible for customers to perform service activities themselves. Similarly, coordination with suppliers or distribution channels can eliminate the need for some in-house activities, such as end-user training.

In all three types of fit, the whole matters more than any individual part. Competitive advantage grows out of the *entire system* of activities. The fit among activities substantially reduces cost or increases differentiation. Beyond that, the competitive value of individual activities–or the associated skills, competencies, or resources – cannot be decoupled from the system or the strategy. Thus in competitive companies it can be misleading to explain success by specifying individual strengths, core competencies, or critical resources. The list of strengths cuts across many functions, and one strength blends into others. It is more useful to think in terms of themes that pervade many activities, such as low cost, a particular notion of customer service, or a particular conception of the value delivered. These themes are embodied in nests of tightly linked activities.

Fit and Sustainability

Strategic fit among many activities is fundamental not only to competitive advantage but also to the sustainability of that advantage. It is harder for a rival to match an array of interlocked activities than it is merely to imitate a particular sales-force approach, match a process technology, or replicate a set of product features. Positions built on systems of activities are far more sustainable than those built on individual activities.

Consider this simple exercise. The probability that competitors can match any activity is often

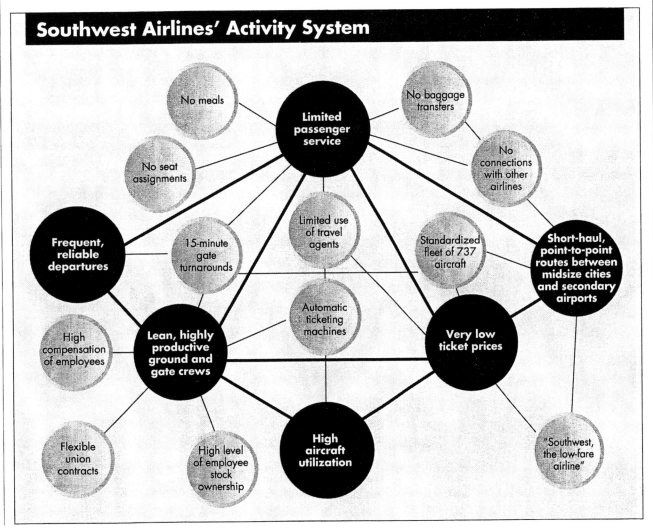

Southwest Airlines' Activity System

less than one. The probabilities then quickly compound to make matching the entire system highly unlikely (.9×.9= .81; .9×.9×.9×.9= .66, and so on). Existing companies that try to reposition or straddle will be forced to reconfigure many activities.

Strategic positions should have a horizon of a decade or more, not of a single planning cycle.

And even new entrants, though they do not confront the trade-offs facing established rivals, still face formidable barriers to imitation.

The more a company's positioning rests on activity systems with second- and third-order fit, the more sustainable its advantage will be. Such systems, by their very nature, are usually difficult to untangle from outside the company and therefore hard to imitate. And even if rivals can identify the relevant interconnections, they will have difficulty replicating them. Achieving fit is difficult because it requires the integration of decisions and actions across many independent subunits.

A competitor seeking to match an activity system gains little by imitating only some activities and not matching the whole. Performance does not improve; it can decline. Recall Continental Lite's disastrous attempt to imitate Southwest.

Finally, fit among a company's activities creates pressures and incentives to improve operational effectiveness, which makes imitation even harder. Fit means that poor performance in one activity will degrade the performance in others, so that weaknesses are exposed and more prone to get at-

tention. Conversely, improvements in one activity will pay dividends in others. Companies with strong fit among their activities are rarely inviting targets. Their superiority in strategy and in execution only compounds their advantages and raises the hurdle for imitators.

When activities complement one another, rivals will get little benefit from imitation unless they successfully match the whole system. Such situations tend to promote winner-take-all competition. The company that builds the best activity system – Toys R Us, for instance – wins, while rivals with similar strategies – Child World and Lionel Leisure – fall behind. Thus finding a new strategic position is often preferable to being the second or third imitator of an occupied position.

The most viable positions are those whose activity systems are incompatible because of trade-offs. Strategic positioning sets the trade-off rules that define how individual activities will be configured and integrated. Seeing strategy in terms of activity systems only makes it clearer why organizational structure, systems, and processes need to be strategy-specific. Tailoring organization to strategy, in turn, makes complementarities more achievable and contributes to sustainability.

One implication is that strategic positions should have a horizon of a decade or more, not of a single planning cycle. Continuity fosters improvements in individual activities and the fit across activities, allowing an organization to build unique capabilities and skills tailored to its strategy. Continuity also reinforces a company's identity.

Conversely, frequent shifts in positioning are costly. Not only must a company reconfigure individual activities, but it must also realign entire sys-

Alternative Views of Strategy

The Implicit Strategy Model of the Past Decade

☐ One ideal competitive position in the industry
☐ Benchmarking of all activities and achieving best practice
☐ Aggressive outsourcing and partnering to gain efficiencies
☐ Advantages rest on a few key success factors, critical resources, core competencies
☐ Flexibility and rapid responses to all competitive and market changes

Sustainable Competitive Advantage

☐ Unique competitive position for the company
☐ Activities tailored to strategy
☐ Clear trade-offs and choices vis-à-vis competitors
☐ Competitive advantage arises from fit across activities
☐ Sustainability comes from the activity system, not the parts
☐ Operational effectiveness a given

14

tems. Some activities may never catch up to the vacillating strategy. The inevitable result of frequent shifts in strategy, or of failure to choose a distinct position in the first place, is "me-too" or hedged activity configurations, inconsistencies across functions, and organizational dissonance.

What is strategy? We can now complete the answer to this question. Strategy is creating fit among a company's activities. The success of a strategy depends on doing many things well—not just a few—and integrating among them. If there is no fit among activities, there is no distinctive strategy and little sustainability. Management reverts to the simpler task of overseeing independent functions, and operational effectiveness determines an organization's relative performance.

V. Rediscovering Strategy

The Failure to Choose

Why do so many companies fail to have a strategy? Why do managers avoid making strategic choices? Or, having made them in the past, why do managers so often let strategies decay and blur?

Commonly, the threats to strategy are seen to emanate from outside a company because of changes in technology or the behavior of competitors. Although external changes can be the problem, the greater threat to strategy often comes from within. A sound strategy is undermined by a misguided view of competition, by organizational failures, and, especially, by the desire to grow.

Managers have become confused about the necessity of making choices. When many companies operate far from the productivity frontier, trade-offs appear unnecessary. It can seem that a well-run company should be able to beat its ineffective rivals on all dimensions simultaneously. Taught by popular management thinkers that they do not have to make trade-offs, managers have acquired a macho sense that to do so is a sign of weakness.

Unnerved by forecasts of hypercompetition, managers increase its likelihood by imitating everything about their competitors. Exhorted to think in terms of revolution, managers chase every new technology for its own sake.

The pursuit of operational effectiveness is seductive because it is concrete and actionable. Over the past decade, managers have been under increasing pressure to deliver tangible, measurable performance improvements. Programs in operational effectiveness produce reassuring progress, although superior profitability may remain elusive. Business publications and consultants flood the market with information about what other companies are doing, reinforcing the best-practice mentality. Caught up in the race for operational effectiveness, many managers simply do not understand the need to have a strategy.

Companies avoid or blur strategic choices for other reasons as well. Conventional wisdom within an industry is often strong, homogenizing competition. Some managers mistake "customer focus" to mean they must serve all customer needs or respond to every request from distribution channels. Others cite the desire to preserve flexibility.

Organizational realities also work against strategy. Trade-offs are frightening, and making no choice is sometimes preferred to risking blame for a bad choice. Companies imitate one another in a type of herd behavior, each assuming rivals know something they do not. Newly empowered employees, who are urged to seek every possible source of improvement, often lack a vision of the whole and the perspective to recognize trade-offs. The failure to choose sometimes comes down to the reluctance to disappoint valued managers or employees.

The Growth Trap

Among all other influences, the desire to grow has perhaps the most perverse effect on strategy. Trade-offs and limits appear to constrain growth. Serving one group of customers and excluding others, for instance, places a real or imagined limit on revenue growth. Broadly targeted strategies emphasizing low price result in lost sales with customers sensitive to features or service. Differentiators lose sales to price-sensitive customers.

Managers are constantly tempted to take incremental steps that surpass those limits but blur a company's strategic position. Eventually, pressures to grow or apparent saturation of the target market lead managers to broaden the position by extending product lines, adding new features, imitating competitors' popular services, matching processes, and even making acquisitions. For years, Maytag Corporation's success was based on its focus on reliable, durable washers and dryers, later extended to include dishwashers. However, conventional wis-

Reconnecting with Strategy

Most companies owe their initial success to a unique strategic position involving clear trade-offs. Activities once were aligned with that position. The passage of time and the pressures of growth, however, led to compromises that were, at first, almost imperceptible. Through a succession of incremental changes that each seemed sensible at the time, many established companies have compromised their way to homogeneity with their rivals.

The issue here is not with the companies whose historical position is no longer viable; their challenge is to start over, just as a new entrant would. At issue is a far more common phenomenon: the established company achieving mediocre returns and lacking a clear strategy. Through incremental additions of product varieties, incremental efforts to serve new customer groups, and emulation of rivals' activities, the existing company loses its clear competitive position. Typically, the company has matched many of its competitors' offerings and practices and attempts to sell to most customer groups.

A number of approaches can help a company reconnect with strategy. The first is a careful look at what it already does. Within most well-established companies is a core of uniqueness. It is identified by answering questions such as the following:

☐ Which of our product or service varieties are the most distinctive?

☐ Which of our product or service varieties are the most profitable?

☐ Which of our customers are the most satisfied?

☐ Which customers, channels, or purchase occasions are the most profitable?

☐ Which of the activities in our value chain are the most different and effective?

Around this core of uniqueness are encrustations added incrementally over time. Like barnacles, they must be removed to reveal the underlying strategic positioning. A small percentage of varieties or customers may well account for most of a company's sales and especially its profits. The challenge, then, is to refocus on the unique core and realign the company's activities with it. Customers and product varieties at the periphery can be sold or allowed through inattention or price increases to fade away.

A company's history can also be instructive. What was the vision of the founder? What were the products and customers that made the company? Looking backward, one can reexamine the original strategy to see if it is still valid. Can the historical positioning be implemented in a modern way, one consistent with today's technologies and practices? This sort of thinking may lead to a commitment to renew the strategy and may challenge the organization to recover its distinctiveness. Such a challenge can be galvanizing and can instill the confidence to make the needed trade-offs.

dom emerging within the industry supported the notion of selling a full line of products. Concerned with slow industry growth and competition from broad-line appliance makers, Maytag was pressured by dealers and encouraged by customers to extend its line. Maytag expanded into refrigerators and cooking products under the Maytag brand and acquired other brands – Jenn-Air, Hardwick Stove, Hoover, Admiral, and Magic Chef – with disparate positions. Maytag has grown substantially from $684 million in 1985 to a peak of $3.4 billion in 1994, but return on sales has declined from 8% to 12% in the 1970s and 1980s to an average of less than 1% between 1989 and 1995. Cost cutting will improve this performance, but laundry and dishwasher products still anchor Maytag's profitability.

Neutrogena may have fallen into the same trap. In the early 1990s, its U.S. distribution broadened to include mass merchandisers such as Wal-Mart Stores. Under the Neutrogena name, the company expanded into a wide variety of products – eye-makeup remover and shampoo, for example – in which it was not unique and which diluted its image, and it began turning to price promotions.

Compromises and inconsistencies in the pursuit of growth will erode the competitive advantage a company had with its original varieties or target customers. Attempts to compete in several ways at once create confusion and undermine organizational motivation and focus. Profits fall, but more revenue is seen as the answer. Managers are unable to make choices, so the company embarks on a new round of broadening and compromises. Often, rivals continue to match each other until desperation breaks the cycle, resulting in a merger or downsizing to the original positioning.

Profitable Growth

Many companies, after a decade of restructuring and cost-cutting, are turning their attention to growth. Too often, efforts to grow blur uniqueness,

16

create compromises, reduce fit, and ultimately undermine competitive advantage. In fact, the growth imperative is hazardous to strategy.

What approaches to growth preserve and reinforce strategy? Broadly, the prescription is to concentrate on deepening a strategic position rather than broadening and compromising it. One approach is to look for extensions of the strategy that leverage the existing activity system by offering features or services that rivals would find impossible or costly to match on a stand-alone basis. In other words, managers can ask themselves which activities, features, or forms of competition are feasible or less costly to them because of complementary activities that their company performs.

Deepening a position involves making the company's activities more distinctive, strengthening fit, and communicating the strategy better to those customers who should value it. But many companies succumb to the temptation to chase "easy" growth by adding hot features, products, or services without screening them or adapting them to their strategy. Or they target new customers or markets in which the company has little special to offer. A company can often grow faster – and far more profitably – by better penetrating needs and varieties where it is distinctive than by slugging it out in potentially higher growth arenas in which the company lacks uniqueness. Carmike, now the largest theater chain in the United States, owes its rapid growth to its disciplined concentration on small markets. The company quickly sells any big-city theaters that come to it as part of an acquisition.

Globalization often allows growth that is consistent with strategy, opening up larger markets for a focused strategy. Unlike broadening domestically,

At general management's core is strategy: defining a company's position, making trade-offs, and forging fit among activities.

expanding globally is likely to leverage and reinforce a company's unique position and identity.

Companies seeking growth through broadening within their industry can best contain the risks to strategy by creating stand-alone units, each with its own brand name and tailored activities. Maytag has clearly struggled with this issue. On the one hand, it has organized its premium and value brands into

separate units with different strategic positions. On the other, it has created an umbrella appliance company for all its brands to gain critical mass. With shared design, manufacturing, distribution, and customer service, it will be hard to avoid homogenization. If a given business unit attempts to compete with different positions for different products or customers, avoiding compromise is nearly impossible.

The Role of Leadership

The challenge of developing or reestablishing a clear strategy is often primarily an organizational one and depends on leadership. With so many forces at work against making choices and trade-offs in organizations, a clear intellectual framework to guide strategy is a necessary counterweight. Moreover, strong leaders willing to make choices are essential.

In many companies, leadership has degenerated into orchestrating operational improvements and making deals. But the leader's role is broader and far more important. General management is more than the stewardship of individual functions. Its core is strategy: defining and communicating the company's unique position, making trade-offs, and forging fit among activities. The leader must provide the discipline to decide which industry changes and customer needs the company will respond to, while avoiding organizational distractions and maintaining the company's distinctiveness. Managers at lower levels lack the perspective and the confidence to maintain a strategy. There will be constant pressures to compromise, relax trade-offs, and emulate rivals. One of the leader's jobs is to teach others in the organization about strategy – and to say no.

Strategy renders choices about what not to do as important as choices about what to do. Indeed, setting limits is another function of leadership. Deciding which target group of customers, varieties, and needs the company should serve is fundamental to developing a strategy. But so is deciding not to serve other customers or needs and not to offer certain features or services. Thus strategy requires constant discipline and clear communication. Indeed, one of the most important functions of an explicit, communicated strategy is to guide employees in making choices that arise because of trade-offs in their individual activities and in day-to-day decisions.

Emerging Industries and Technologies

Developing a strategy in a newly emerging industry or in a business undergoing revolutionary technological changes is a daunting proposition. In such cases, managers face a high level of uncertainty about the needs of customers, the products and services that will prove to be the most desired, and the best configuration of activities and technologies to deliver them. Because of all this uncertainty, imitation and hedging are rampant: unable to risk being wrong or left behind, companies match all features, offer all new services, and explore all technologies.

During such periods in an industry's development, its basic productivity frontier is being established or reestablished. Explosive growth can make such times profitable for many companies, but profits will be temporary because imitation and strategic convergence will ultimately destroy industry profitability. The companies that are enduringly successful will be those that begin as early as possible to define and em-body in their activities a unique competitive position. A period of imitation may be inevitable in emerging industries, but that period reflects the level of uncertainty rather than a desired state of affairs.

In high-tech industries, this imitation phase often continues much longer than it should. Enraptured by technological change itself, companies pack more features – most of which are never used – into their products while slashing prices across the board. Rarely are trade-offs even considered. The drive for growth to satisfy market pressures leads companies into every product area. Although a few companies with fundamental advantages prosper, the majority are doomed to a rat race no one can win.

Ironically, the popular business press, focused on hot, emerging industries, is prone to presenting these special cases as proof that we have entered a new era of competition in which none of the old rules are valid. In fact, the opposite is true.

Improving operational effectiveness is a necessary part of management, but it is *not* strategy. In confusing the two, managers have unintentionally backed into a way of thinking about competition that is driving many industries toward competitive convergence, which is in no one's best interest and is not inevitable.

Managers must clearly distinguish operational effectiveness from strategy. Both are essential, but the two agendas are different.

The operational agenda involves continual improvement everywhere there are no trade-offs. Failure to do this creates vulnerability even for companies with a good strategy. The operational agenda is the proper place for constant change, flexibility, and relentless efforts to achieve best practice. In contrast, the strategic agenda is the right place for defining a unique position, making clear trade-offs, and tightening fit. It involves the continual search for ways to reinforce and extend the company's position. The strategic agenda demands discipline and continuity; its enemies are distraction and compromise.

Strategic continuity does not imply a static view of competition. A company must continually improve its operational effectiveness and actively try to shift the productivity frontier; at the same time, there needs to be ongoing effort to extend its uniqueness while strengthening the fit among its activities. Strategic continuity, in fact, should make an organization's continual improvement more effective.

A company may have to change its strategy if there are major structural changes in its industry. In fact, new strategic positions often arise because of industry changes, and new entrants unencumbered by history often can exploit them more easily. However, a company's choice of a new position must be driven by the ability to find new trade-offs and leverage a new system of complementary activities into a sustainable advantage.

---

1. I first described the concept of activities and its use in understanding competitive advantage in *Competitive Advantage* (New York: The Free Press, 1985). The ideas in this article build on and extend that thinking.

2. Paul Milgrom and John Roberts have begun to explore the economics of systems of complementary functions, activities, and functions. Their focus is on the emergence of "modern manufacturing" as a new set of complementary activities, on the tendency of companies to react to external changes with coherent bundles of internal responses, and on the need for central coordination – a strategy – to align functional managers. In the latter case, they model what has long been a bedrock principle of strategy. See Paul Milgrom and John Roberts, "The Economics of Modern Manufacturing: Technology, Strategy, and Organization," *American Economic Review* 80 (1990): 511-528; Paul Milgrom, Yingyi Qian, and John Roberts, "Complementarities, Momentum, and Evolution of Modern Manufacturing," *American Economic Review* 81 (1991) 84-88; and Paul Milgrom and John Roberts, "Complementarities and Fit: Strategy, Structure, and Organizational Changes in Manufacturing," *Journal of Accounting and Economics*, vol. 19 (March-May 1995): 179-208.

3. Material on retail strategies is drawn in part from Jan Rivkin, "The Rise of Retail Category Killers," unpublished working paper, January 1995. Nicolaj Siggelkow prepared the case study on the Gap.

Reprint 96608   To place an order, call 1-800-545-7685.

7

Strategy in High-Technology Industries

 Opening Case

Extending the Wintel Monopoly to Wireless

Microsoft and Intel are co-owners of the dominant Wintel standard, based on the combination of a Microsoft operating system and an Intel microprocessor that is used in over 90 percent of the world's PCs. ("Wintel" was coined because Microsoft's Windows operating system is designed to run on an Intel microprocessor.) This fact has helped to make Microsoft and Intel the two most valuable companies in the global computer industry. Now the duo is trying to extend their standard and make it the dominant one in the wireless phone industry. The focus of their attention is next-generation wireless phones, or 3G phones, which will increasingly come to resemble computers. They will have color screens; a full range of personal information management applications such as address and date books; and the ability to browse the Internet, send and receive text-based email, and run a variety of applications, including pocket-sized versions of Microsoft's popular Office suite.

The strategy that Microsoft and Intel are pursuing is to create a reference design, or template, for making 3G wireless phones that they will license to electronics companies that wish to manufacture these devices. Microsoft will supply the operating system, which will be based on its Pocket PC operating system, a Windows-based operating system for small digital devices. Intel will supply key elements of the onboard microprocessor technology. Both companies will work together to produce the reference design, which is a set of standard specifications outlining how to build a handset using Microsoft and Intel technology. In creating this design, Microsoft and Intel claim that their main motive is to "demystify and democratize the wireless industry, so that more companies can break into the market. We want to enable one of them to become the next Nokia," said a Microsoft spokesman. (Nokia is the global leader in the market, with a 40 percent share of all wireless handset sales.) More generally, the idea is to try to accelerate the adoption of 3G wireless technology.

If all goes well, the Microsoft-Intel reference design will be licensed to a number of electronics companies that will use it to make wireless handsets. These companies will no longer have to invest in creating the design themselves, enabling them to cut R&D expenses and hence handset prices. As cheap handsets reach the market, probably in 2003–2004, demand will start to expand. As the installed base of Microsoft-Intel phones grows, more applications will be written to run on those phones. In addition, software companies will write web-based applications that reside on servers and can be accessed by consumers with a Microsoft-Intel phone over a wireless connection. These two developments will increase the value of owning a Microsoft-Intel phone, as opposed to a phone based on a different reference design. As the value increases, more consumers will buy phones based on the Microsoft-Intel design, as opposed to phones made by companies like Nokia, and the installed base of Microsoft-Intel phones will expand further, creating an incentive to develop more software for those phones, and so on. In other words, through the operation of a positive feedback loop, the reference design now being developed by Microsoft and Intel could become the de facto standard in the wireless handset market.

If this occurs, Microsoft and Intel will have extended their dominant position in PCs to the wireless handset market. They should be able to profit from this by charging a licensing fee for the reference design and by developing and selling complementary products, such as additional applications that run on a wireless handset or reside on servers that consumers with handsets can access via wireless connections to the Web.

The eventual outcome is less clear than the strategy. For one thing, several other companies are promoting alternative and potentially incompatible reference designs and operating systems for wireless handsets. These include Qualcomm, Nokia, Ericsson, and Motorola, all heavyweights in the wireless market. For another, it is still not clear that the wireless handset market has the same imperatives for standardization as the personal computer market does. If it does, however, the market will probably hone in on a single reference design. Whether that design is the one promoted by Microsoft and Intel or by another competitor depends in large part on the differential success of the strategies these different companies are pursuing as they try to win this emerging format war.

Sources: D. Pringle, "Wintel Duo Targets the Cellphone," *Wall Street Journal,* February 19, 2002, p. E2. A Doland, "Looking Beyond the Basic Cell Phone," *Columbian,* February 19, 2002, p. E2. B. McDonough, "Microsoft Jostles for Mobile Market Position," Wireless .Newsfactor.com, February 19, 2002.

Overview

In this chapter, we look at the nature of competition and strategy in high-technology industries. **Technology** refers to the body of scientific knowledge used in the production of goods or services. **High-technology (high-tech) industries** are those in which the underlying scientific knowledge that companies in the industry use is advancing rapidly, and by implication so are the attributes of the products and services that result from its application. The computer industry is often thought of as the quintessential example of a high-technology industry. Other industries often considered high tech are telecommunications, where new technologies based on wireless and the Internet have proliferated in recent years; consumer electronics, where the digital technology underlying products from DVD players to video game terminals and digital cameras is advancing rapidly; pharmaceuticals, where new technologies based on cell biology, recombinant DNA, and genomics are revolutionizing the process of drug discovery; power generation, where new technologies based on fuel cells and cogeneration may change the economics of the industry; and aerospace, where the combination of new composite materials, electronics, and more efficient jet engines may give birth to a new era of near-supersonic commercial aircraft, such as Boeing's planned sonic cruiser.

This chapter focuses on high-technology industries for a number of reasons. First, technology is accounting for an ever larger share of economic activity. Estimates suggest that roughly 15 percent of total economic activity in the United States is accounted for by information technology industries.[1] This figure actually underestimates the true impact of technology on the economy, because it ignores the other high-technology areas we just mentioned. Moreover, as technology advances, many low-technology industries are becoming more high tech. For example, the development of biotechnology and genetic engineering transformed the production of seed corn, long considered a low-technology business, into a high-technology business. Moreover, high-technology products are making their way into a wide range of businesses; today a Ford Taurus contains more computing power than the multimillion dollar mainframe computers used in the Apollo space program, and the competitive advantage of physical stores, such as Wal-Mart, is based on their use of information technology.[2] The circle of high-technology industries is both large and expanding, and even in industries not thought of as high tech, technology is revolutionizing aspects of the product or production system.

Although high-tech industries may produce very different products, when it comes to developing a business model and strategies that will lead to a competitive advantage and superior profitability, they face a similar situation. This chapter examines the competitive features found in many high-tech industries and the kinds of strategies that companies must adopt to build business models that will allow them to achieve superior performance and profitability.

By the time you have completed this chapter, you will have an understanding of the nature of competition in high-tech industries and strategies that companies can pursue to succeed in those industries.

Technical Standards and Format Wars

Especially in high-tech industries, ownership of **technical standards**—a set of technical specifications that producers adhere to when making the product or a component of it—can be an important source of competitive advantage.[3] *Indeed, the source of product differentiation is based on the technical standard.* Often, only one standard will come to dominate a market, so many battles in high-tech industries revolve around companies competing to be the one that sets the standard.

Battles to set and control technical standards in a market are referred to as **format wars;** they are essentially battles to control the source of differentiation and thus the value that such differentiation can create for the customer. Because differentiated products often command premium prices and are often expensive to develop, the competitive stakes are enormous. The profitability and very survival of a company may depend on the outcome of the battle, for example, the outcome of the battle now being waged over the establishment and ownership of the reference design for next-generation wireless handsets will help to determine which companies will be the leaders in the decades to come.

Examples of Standards

A familiar example of a standard is the layout of a computer keyboard. No matter what keyboard you buy, the letters are all in the same pattern.[4] The reason is quite obvious. Imagine if each computer maker changed the ways the keys were laid out—

if some started with QWERTY on the top row of letters (which is indeed the format used and is known as the QWERTY format), some with YUHGFD, and some with ACFRDS. If you learned to type on one layout, it would be irritating and time-consuming to have to relearn on a YUHGFD layout. So we have this standard format (QWERTY) because it makes it easy for people to move from computer to computer because the input medium, the keyboard, is set out in a standard way.

Another example of a technical standard concerns the dimensions of containers used to ship goods on trucks, railcars, and ships: all have the same basic dimensions—the same height, length, and width—and all make use of the same locking mechanisms to hold them onto a surface or to bolt against each other. Having a standard ensures that containers can easily be moved from one mode of transportation to another—from trucks, to railcars, to ships, and back to railcars. If containers lacked standard dimensions and locking mechanisms, it would suddenly become much more difficult to ship containers around the world. Shippers would have to make sure that they had the right kind of container to go on the ships and trucks and railcars scheduled to carry a particular container around the world—very complicated indeed.

Consider, finally, the personal computer. Most share a common set of features: an Intel or Intel-compatible microprocessor, random access memory (RAM), a Microsoft operating system, an internal hard drive, a floppy disk drive, a CD drive, a keyboard, a monitor, a mouse, a modem, and so on. We call this set of features the dominant design for personal computers (a **dominant design** refers to a common set of features or design characteristics). Embedded in this design are several technical standards (see Figure 7.1). For example, there is the Wintel technical standard based on an Intel microprocessor and a Microsoft operating system. Microsoft and Intel own that standard, which is central to the personal computer. Developers of software applications, component parts, and peripherals such as printers adhere to this standard when developing their own products because this guarantees that their products will work well with a personal computer based on the Wintel standard. Another technical standard for connecting peripherals to the PC is the Universal Serial Bus (or USB), established by an industry standards-setting board. No one owns it; the standard is in the public domain. A third technical standard is for communication between a PC and the Internet via a modem. Known as TCP/IP, this standard was also

FIGURE 7.1

Technical Standards
for Personal
Computers

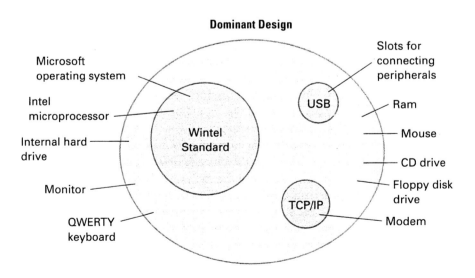

Dominant Design

Microsoft operating system

Intel microprocessor

Internal hard drive

Monitor

QWERTY keyboard

Wintel Standard

USB

TCP/IP

Slots for connecting peripherals

Ram

Mouse

CD drive

Floppy disk drive

Modem

set by an industry association and is in the public domain. Thus, as with many other products, the PC is actually based on several technical standards. It is also important to note that when a company owns a standard, as Microsoft and Intel do with the Wintel standard, it may be a source of competitive advantage and high profitability.

Benefits of Standards

Standards emerge because there are economic benefits associated with them. First, having a technical standard helps to guarantee *compatibility* between products and their complements, other products used with them. For example, containers are used with railcars, trucks, and ships, and PCs are used with software applications. Compatibility has tangible economic benefits of reducing the costs associated with making sure that products work well with each other.

Second, having a standard can help to *reduce confusion* in the minds of consumers. A few years ago, several consumer electronics companies were vying with each other to produce and market the first DVD players, and they were championing different variants of the basic DVD technology—different standards—that were incompatible with each other; a DVD disc designed to run on a DVD player made by Toshiba would not run on a player made by Sony, and vice versa. The companies feared that selling these incompatible versions of the same technology would produce confusion in the minds of consumers, who would not know which version to purchase and might decide to wait and see which technology ultimately dominated the marketplace. With lack of demand, the technology might fail to gain traction in the marketplace and would not be successful. To avoid this possibility, the developers of DVD equipment established a standard-setting body for the industry, the DVD Forum, which established a common technical standard for DVD players and discs that all companies adhered to. The result was that when DVDs were introduced, there was a common standard and no confusion in consumers' minds. This helped to boost demand for DVD players, making this one of the fastest-selling technologies of the late 1990s and early 2000s. First introduced in 1997, by 2001 some 13 million DVD players were sold in the United States, and they are now in one in four homes in the country.[5] However, so far the DVD Forum has not been able to agree on a common standard for the next version of DVDs, DVD recorders., which is slowing diffusion and adoption of the technology (see Strategy in Action 7.1).

Third, the emergence of a standard can help to *reduce production costs*. Once a standard emerges, products based on that standard design can be mass-produced, enabling the manufacturers to realize substantial economies of scale and lower their cost structures. The fact that there is a central standard for PCs (the Wintel standard) means that the component parts for a PC can be mass-produced. A manufacturer of internal hard drives, for example, can mass-produce drives for Wintel PCs, enabling it to realize substantial scale economies. If there were several competing and incompatible standards, each of which required a unique type of hard drive, production runs for hard drives would be shorter, unit costs would be higher, and the cost of PCs would go up.

Fourth, the emergence of standards can help to reduce the *risks associated with supplying complementary products* and thus increase the supply for those complements. Consider the risks associated with writing software applications to run on personal computers. This is a risky proposition, requiring the investment of considerable sums of money for developing the software before a single unit is sold. Imagine what would occur if there were ten different operating systems in use for PCs, each with only 10 percent of the market, rather than the current situation, where 95 percent of the world's PCs adhere to the Wintel standard. Software developers would be faced with the need to write ten different versions of the same software applica-

Strategy in Action   7.1

Where Is the Standard for DVD Recorders?

A few years ago, the 200-member DVD Forum achieved something of a coup when it managed to broker an agreement among some of its most important members on a common set of standards for DVD players. This common standard reduced consumer confusion and helped to propel DVD players into a mass market phenomenon, now replacing analog VHS video players in many living rooms. Nevertheless, current technology lacks one attribute of VHS technology: it cannot record. It's not that a technology for making DVD recorders does not exist; in fact, several do, and therein lies the problem. The DVD Forum has been unable to get some of its most powerful members to agree on a common technical standard for DVD recorders, primarily because different companies want to see their variant of the technology become the industry standard.

There are at least three versions of DVD recorders now on offer: Hewlett Packard is pushing one format, Sony and Philips are sponsoring another, and Matsushita yet another. And most important, DVD discs recorded using one format may not play on widely used DVD players or on computers that use another recording format.

First introduced in 1999, by 2001 some 350,000 DVD recorders had sold, many of them incorporated into new personal computers. But industry observers feel that sales could have been much higher had there been harmonization of standards. By way of comparison, some 40 million CD recorders were sold in 2001, making CD recording technology solidly mainstream (DVDs can hold ten times

as many data as CDs and are thus better suited to recording video). One reason for the slow takeup of DVD recorders has been the confusion over standards, and it's not just consumers who are confused. Many retailers are hesitant about stocking the technology until the battle over standards is resolved.

Another reason for the slow market growth has been the high price of DVD recorders. As of mid-2002, a stand-alone DVD recorder still cost around $1,500, putting the technology out of the reach of most people. However, DVD-recordable drives built into personal computers had fallen to $400 per unit, bringing them close to the price point at which a mass market develops. For the price to fall lower, producers need to be able to manufacture in high volume and realize significant scale economies. But here lies the catch: to generate significant demand to support mass production and bring prices down, it may first be necessary to harmonize standards and reduce consumer confusion—and that is something that the producers currently seem unwilling to do. For the time being, the different companies are continuing to push their own proprietary standard in the hope that they establish it as the leading standard in the industry and reap the associated gains.

Sources: E. Ramstad, "DVD Makers Battle over Tech Standard," *Wall Street Journal,* November 9, 2000, p. B6. B. Dudley, "Dueling DVD-Recorder Formats Make Playing Discs a Challenge," *Seattle Times,* January 9, 2002, p. C3.

tion, each for a much smaller market segment. This would change the economics of software development, increase its risks, and reduce potential profitability. Moreover, because of their higher cost structure and fewer economies of scale, the price of software programs would increase.

Thus, although many people complain about the consequences of Microsoft's near monopoly of PC operating systems, that monopoly does have at least one good effect: it substantially reduces the risks facing the makers of complementary products and the costs of those products. In fact, standards lead to both low-cost and differentiation advantages for individual companies and can help raise the level of industry profitability.

Establishment of Standards   Standards emerge in an industry in three main ways. First, recognizing the benefits of establishing a standard, companies in an industry might lobby the government to mandate an industry standard. In the United States, for example, the Federal

Communication Commission (FCC), after detailed discussions with broadcasters and consumer electronics companies, has mandated a single technical standard for digital television broadcast (DTV) and is requiring broadcasters to have capabilities in place for broadcasting digital signals based on this standard by 2006. The FCC took this step because it believed that without government action to set the standard, the rollout of DTV would be very slow. With a standard set by the government, consumer electronics companies can have greater confidence that a market will emerge, and this should encourage them to develop DTV products.

Second, technical standards are often set by cooperation among businesses, without government help, often through the medium of an industry forum, such as the DVD Forum. Companies cooperate in this way when they decide that competition among them to create a standard might be harmful because of the uncertainty that it would create in the minds of consumers.

When standards are set by the government or an industry association, they fall into the **public domain,** meaning that anyone can freely incorporate the knowledge and technology on which the standard is based into their products. For example, no one owns the QWERTY format, and therefore no one company can profit from it directly. Similarly, the language that underlies the presentation of text and graphics on the Web, hypertext markup language (HTML), is in the public domain; it is free for all to use. The same is true for TCP/IP, the communications standard used for transmitting data on the Internet.

Often, however, the industry standard is selected competitively by the purchasing patterns of customers in the marketplace—that is, by *market demand*. In this case, the strategy and business model a company has developed for promoting its technological standard is of critical importance because ownership of an industry standard that is protected from imitation by patents and copyrights is a valuable asset—a source of sustained competitive advantage and superior profitability. Microsoft and Intel, for example, both owe their competitive advantage to their ownership of Format wars, which exist between two or more companies competing against each other to get their designs adopted as the industry standard, are common in high-tech industries because of the high stakes. The Wintel standard became the dominant standard for PCs only after Microsoft and Intel won format wars against Apple Computer's proprietary system and later against IBM's OS/2 operating system. Microsoft and Real Networks are currently competing head to head in a format war to establish rival technologies—Windows Media Player and RealPlayer—as the standard for streaming video and audio technology on the Web. The *Opening Case* tells how Microsoft and Intel are also engaged in a format war in the wireless business as they try to get their standard for 3G wireless phones established as the industry standard.

Network Effects, Positive Feedback, and Lockout

There has been a growing realization that when standards are set by competition between companies promoting different formats, network effects are a primary determinant of how standards are established.[6] **Network effects** arise in industries where the size of the "network" of *complementary* products is a primary determinant of demand for an industry's product. For example, the demand for automobiles early in the twentieth century was an increasing function of the *network* of paved roads and gas stations. Similarly, the demand for telephones is an increasing function of the number of other numbers that can be called with that phone; that is, of the size of the telephone network (i.e., the telephone network is the complementary product). When the first telephone service was introduced in New York City, only a hundred numbers could be called. The network was very small because of the limited number of wires and telephone switches, which made the telephone a relatively useless piece of equipment. As more and more people got telephones and as the network of wires and switches expanded, the value of a telephone connection increased. This led to an increase in demand for telephone lines, which further increased the value of owning a telephone, setting up a positive feedback loop. The same type of positive feedback loop is now at work in the Internet.

To understand why network effects are important in the establishment of standards, consider the classic example of a format war: the battle between Sony and Matsushita to establish their respective technology for videocassette recorders (VCRs) as the standard in the marketplace. Sony was first to market with its Betamax technology, followed by Matsushita with its VHS technology. Both companies sold VCR recorder-players, and movie studios issued films prerecorded on VCR tapes for rental to consumers. Initially, all tapes were issued in Betamax format to play on Sony's machine. Sony *did not* license its Betamax technology, preferring to make all of the player-recorders itself. When Matsushita entered the market, it realized that to make its VHS format players valuable to consumers, it would have to encourage movie studios to issue movies for rental on VHS tapes. The only way to do that, Matsushita's managers reasoned, was to increase the installed base of VHS players as rapidly as possible. They believed that the greater the installed base of VHS players, the greater the incentive would be for movie studios to issue movies for rental on VHS format tapes. The more prerecorded VHS tapes were available for rental, the greater the value of a VHS player became to consumers, and therefore, the greater the demand would be VHS players (see Figure 7.2). Matsushita wanted to exploit a positive feedback loop.

To do this, Matsushita chose a licensing strategy under which any consumer electronics company was allowed to manufacture VHS format players under license. The strategy worked. A large number of companies signed on to manufacture VHS players, and soon far more VHS players were available for purchase in stores than Betamax players. As sales of VHS players started to grow, movie studios issued more films for rental in VHS format, and this stoked demand. Before long, it was clear to anyone who walked into a video rental store that there were more and more VHS tapes available for rent and fewer and fewer Betamax tapes. This served to reinforce the positive feedback loop, and ultimately Sony's Betamax technology was shut out of the market. The pivotal difference between the two companies was strategy: Matsushita chose a licensing strategy, and Sony did not. As a result, Matsushita's VHS technology became the de facto standard for VCRs, while Sony's Betamax technology was locked out.

FIGURE 7.2

Positive Feedback in the Market for VCRs

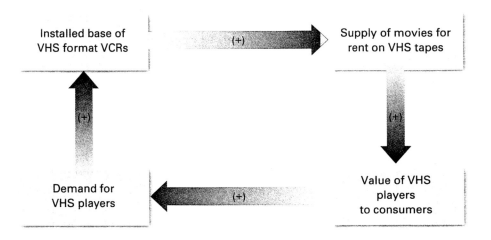

The general principle that emerges from this example is that when two or more companies are competing with each other to get their technology adopted as a standard in an industry, and when network effects and positive feedback loops are important, the company that wins the format war will be the one whose strategy best exploits positive feedback loops. It turns out that this is a very important strategic principle in many high-technology industries, particularly computer hardware, software, telecommunications, and consumer electronics. Microsoft is where it is today because it exploited a positive feedback loop. So did Dolby (see Strategy in Action 7.2).

An important implication of the positive feedback process is that as the market settles on a standard, companies promoting alternative standards can become **locked out** of the market when consumers are unwilling to bear the switching costs required for them to abandon the established standard and adopt the new standard. In this context, **switching costs** are the costs that consumers must bear to switch from a product based on one technological standard to a product based on another.

For illustration, imagine that a company developed an operating system for personal computers that was both faster and more stable (crashed less) than the current standard in the marketplace, Microsoft Windows. Would this company be able to gain significant market share from Microsoft? Only with great difficulty. Consumers buy personal computers not for their operating system but for the applications that run on that system. A new operating system would initially have a very small installed base, so few developers would be willing to take the risks in writing word processing programs, spreadsheets, games, and other applications for that operating system. Because there would be very few applications available, consumers who did make the switch would have to bear the switching costs associated with giving up some of their applications—something that they might be unwilling to do. Moreover, even if applications were available for the new operating system, consumers would have to bear the costs of purchasing those applications, another source of switching costs. In addition, they would have to bear the costs associated with learning to use the new operating system, yet another source of switching costs. Thus, many consumers would be unwilling to switch even if the new operating system performed better than Windows, and the company promoting the new operating system would be locked out of the market.

Consumers *will* bear switching costs if the benefits of adopting the new technology outweigh the costs of switching. For example, in the late 1980s and early 1990s, millions of people switched from analog record players to digital CD players even though the switching costs were significant: they had to purchase the new player technology, and many people purchased duplicate copies of their favorite music recordings. They nevertheless made the switch because for many people, the perceived benefit—the incredibly better sound quality associated with CDs—outweighed the costs of switching.

As this process started to get under way, a positive feedback started to develop, with the growing installed base of CD players leading to an increase in the number of music recordings issued on CDs, as opposed to or in addition to vinyl records. Past some point, the installed base of CD players got so big that music companies started to issue recordings only on CDs. Once this happened, even those who did not want to switch to the new technology were required to if they wished to purchase new music recordings. The industry standard had shifted: the new technology had locked in as the standard, and the old technology was locked out. It follows that despite its dominance, the Wintel standard for personal computers could one day be superseded

Strategy in Action

How Dolby Became the Standard in Sound Technology

7.2

Inventor Ray Dolby's name has become synonymous with superior sound in homes, movie theaters, and recording studios. The technology produced by his company, Dolby Laboratories, is part of nearly every music cassette and cassette recorder, prerecorded videotape, and, most recently, DVD movie disc and player. Since 1976, close to 1 billion audio products that use Dolby's technology have been sold worldwide. More than 29,000 movie theaters now show films in Dolby Digital Surround Sound, and some 10 million Dolby Digital home theater receivers have been sold since 1999. Dolby technology has become the industry standard for high-quality sound in the music and film industry. Any company that wants to promote its products as having superior technology licenses sound technology from Dolby. How did Dolby build this technology franchise?

The story goes back to 1965 when Dolby Laboratories was founded in London by Ray Dolby (the company's headquarters moved to San Francisco in 1976). Dolby, who had a Ph.D in physics from Cambridge University in England, had invented a technology for reducing the background hiss in professional tape recording without compromising the quality of the material being recorded. Dolby manufactured the sound systems incorporating his technology, but sales to professional recording studios were initially slow. Then in 1968 Dolby had a big break. He met Henry Kloss, whose company, KLH, was a highly regarded American producer of audio equipment (record players and tape decks) for the consumer market. Dolby reached an agreement to license his noise-reduction technology to KLH, and soon other manufacturers of consumer equipment started to approach Dolby to license the technology. Dolby briefly considered manufacturing record players and tape decks for the consumer market, but as he later commented, "I knew that if we entered that market and tried to make something like a cassette deck, we would be in competition with any licensee that we took on. . . . So we had to stay out of manufacturing in that area in order to license in that area."

Dolby adopted a licensing business model and then had to determine what licensing fee to charge. He knew his technology was valuable, but he also understood that charging a high licensing fee would encourage manufacturers to invest in developing their own noise-reduction technology. He decided to charge a modest fee to reduce the incentive that manufacturers would have to develop

their own technology. Then there was the question of which companies to license to. Dolby wanted the Dolby name associated with superior sound, so he needed to make sure that licensees adhered to quality standards. Therefore, the company set up a formal quality control program for its licensees' products. Licensees have to agree to have their products tested by Dolby, and the licensing agreement states that they cannot sell products that do not pass Dolby's quality tests. By preventing products with substandard performance from reaching the market, Dolby has maintained the quality image of products featuring Dolby technology and trademarks. Today, Dolby Laboratories tests samples of hundreds of licensed products every year under this program. By making sure that the Dolby name is associated with superior sound quality, Dolby's quality assurance strategy has increased the power of the Dolby brand, making it very valuable to license.

Another key aspect of Dolby's strategy was born in 1970 when Dolby began to promote the idea of releasing prerecorded cassettes encoded with Dolby noise-reduction technology so that they would have low noise when played on players equipped with Dolby noise-reduction technology. Dolby decided to license the technology on prerecorded tapes for free, instead collecting licensing fees just from the sales of tape players that used Dolby technology. This strategy was hugely successful and set up a positive feedback loop that helped to make Dolby technology ubiquitous. Growing sales of prerecorded tapes encoded with Dolby technology created a demand for players that contained Dolby technology, and as the installed base of players with Dolby technology grew, the proportion of prerecorded tapes that were encoded with Dolby technology surged, further boosting demand for players incorporating Dolby technology. By the mid-1970s, virtually all prerecorded tapes were encoded with Dolby noise-reduction technology. This strategy remains in effect today for all media recorded with Dolby technology and encompasses not only videocassettes but video games and DVD releases encoded with Dolby Surround or Dolby Digital.

As a result of its licensing and quality assurance strategies, Dolby has become the standard for high-quality sound in the music and film industries. Although the company is small—its revenues were around $125 million in 2001—its influence is large. It continues to push the boundaries of sound-reduction technology (it has been a leader in digital sound since the mid-1980s) and has successfully extended its noise-reduction franchise, first into films, then into DVD and video game technology, and most recently onto the Web, where it has licensed its digital technology to a wide range of media companies for digital music delivery and digital audio players, such as those built into personal computers and devices like Compaq's popular iPAQ hand-held computer.

Sources: M. Snider, "Ray Dolby, Audio Inventor," *USA Today,* December 28, 2000, p. D3. D. Dritas, "Dealerscope Hall of Fame: Ray Dolby," *Dealerscope* (January 2002): 74–76. J. Pinkerton, "At Dolby Laboratories: A Clean Audio Pipe," *Dealerscope* (December 2000): 33–34. Company history archived at www.dolby.com.

if a competitor finds a way of providing sufficient benefits that enough consumers are willing to bear the switching costs associated with moving to a new operating system.

Strategies for Winning a Format War

From the perspective of a company pioneering a new technological standard in a marketplace where network effects and positive feedback loops operate, the key question becomes, "What strategy should we pursue to establish our format as the dominant one?"

The various strategies that companies should adopt to win format wars revolve around *finding ways to make network effects work in their favor and against their competitors.* Winning a format war requires a company to build the installed base for its standard as rapidly as possible, thereby leveraging the positive feedback loop, inducing consumers to bear switching costs, and ultimately locking the market into its technology. It requires the company to jump-start and then accelerate demand for its technological standard or format such that it becomes established as quickly as possible as the industry standard, thereby locking out competing formats. There are a number of key strategies and tactics that can be adopted to try and achieve this.[7]

Ensure a Supply of Complements

It is important for the company to make sure that in addition to the product itself, there is an adequate supply of complements. For example, no one will buy the Sony PlayStation II unless there is an adequate supply of games to run on that machine. And no one will purchase a Palm hand-held computer unless there are enough software applications to run on it. Companies normally take two steps to ensure an adequate supply of complements.

First, they may diversify into the production of complements and seed the market with sufficient supply to help jump-start demand for their format. Before Sony produced the original PlayStation in the early 1990s, it established its own in-house unit to produce video games for the PlayStation. When it launched the PlayStation, Sony also simultaneously issued sixteen games to run on the machine, giving consumers a reason to purchase the format. Second, they may create incentives or make it easy for independent companies to produce complements. Sony also licensed the right to produce games to a number of independent game developers, charged the developers a lower royalty rate than they had to pay to competitors such as Nintendo and Sega, and provided them with software tools that made it easier for them to develop the games. Thus, the launch of the Sony PlayStation was accompanied by the simultaneous launch of thirty or so games, which quickly helped to stimulate demand for the machine.

Leverage Killer Applications

Killer applications are applications or uses of a new technology or product that are so compelling that they persuade customers to adopt the new format or technology in droves, thereby "killing" demand for competing formats. Killer applications often help to jump-start demand for the new standard. For example, in the late 1990s, hand-held computers based on the Palm operating system became the dominant format in the market for personal digital assistants (PDA). The killer applications that drove adoption of the Palm format were the personal information management functions and a pen-based input medium (based on **Graffiti**) that Palm bundled with its original PalmPilot, which it introduced in 1996. There had been PDAs before the PalmPilot, including Apple Computer's ill-fated Newton, but it was the applications and ease of use of the PalmPilot that persuaded many consumers to enter this market. Within eighteen months of its initial launch, more than 1 million PalmPilots had been launched, making for a faster demand ramp-up than the first cell phones and pagers. Similarly, the killer applications that induced consumers to sign up to online services such as AOL were email, chatroom, and the ability to browse the Web.

Ideally, the company promoting a technological standard will want to develop the killer applications itself—that is, develop the appropriate complementary products—as Palm did with the PalmPilot. However, it may also be able to leverage the applications that others develop. For example, the early sales of the IBM PC following its 1981 introduction were driven primarily by IBM's decision to license two important software programs for the PC, VisiCalc (a spreadsheet program) and Easy Writer (a word processing program), both developed by independent companies. IBM saw that they were driving rapid adoption of rival personal computers, such as the Apple II, so it quickly licensed them, produced versions that would run on the IBM PC, and sold them as complements to the IBM PC, a strategy that was to prove very successful.

Aggressively Price and Market

A common tactic to jump-start demand is to adopt a **razor and blade strategy:** pricing the product (razor) low in order to stimulate demand and increase the installed base, and then trying to make high profits on the sale of complements (razor blades), which are priced relatively high. This strategy owes its name to the fact that it was pioneered by Gillette to sell its razors and razor blades. Many other companies have followed this strategy—for example, Hewlett Packard typically sells its printers at cost but makes significant profits on the subsequent sale of its replacement cartridges. In this case, the printer is the "razor," and it is priced low to stimulate demand and induce consumers to switch from their existing printer, while the cartridges are the "blades," which are priced high to make profits. The inkjet printer represents a proprietary technological format because only Hewlett Packard cartridges can be used with the printers, and not cartridges designed for competing inkjet printers, such as those sold by Canon. A similar strategy is used in the video game industry: manufacturers price video game consoles at cost to induce consumers to adopt their technology, while making profits on the royalties they receive from the sales of games that run on their system.

Aggressive marketing is also a key factor in jump-starting demand to get an early lead in installed base. Substantial up-front marketing and point-of-sales promotion techniques are often used to try to get potential early adopters to bear the switching costs associated with adopting the format. If these efforts are successful, they can be the start of a positive feedback loop. Again, the Sony PlayStation provides a good example. Sony co-linked the introduction of the PlayStation with nationwide television advertising aimed at its primary demographic (eighteen to thirty-four-year-olds) and in-store displays that allowed potential buyers to play games on the machine before making a purchase. More recently, Microsoft earmarked $500 million for marketing its new X-Box in 2002. Successful marketing can set the ball rolling and create a positive feedback loop.

Cooperate with Competitors

Companies have been close to simultaneously introducing competing and incompatible technological standards a number of times. A good example is the compact disc. Initially four companies—Sony, Philips, JVC, and Telefunken—were developing CD players using different variations of the underlying laser technology. If this situation had persisted, they might have ultimately introduced incompatible technologies into the marketplace, so a CD made for a Philips CD player would not play on a Sony CD player. Understanding that the near-simultaneous introduction of such incompatible technologies can create significant confusion among consumers and often leads them to delay their purchases, Sony and Philips decided to join forces with each other and cooperate on developing the technology. Sony contributed its error correction technology, and Philips contributed its laser technology. The result of this cooperation was that momentum among other players in the industry shifted toward the Sony-Philips alliances; JVC and Telefunken were left with little support. Most important, recording labels announced that they would support the Sony-Philips format but not the Telefunken or JVC format. Telefunken and JVC subsequently decided to abandon their efforts to develop CD technology. The cooperation between Sony and Philips was important because it reduced confusion in the industry and allowed a single format to rise to the fore, which speeded up adoption of the technology. The cooperation was a win-win situation for both Philips and Sony, which eliminated the competitors and were able to share in the success of the format.

License the Format

Another strategy often adopted is to license the format to other enterprises so that they can produce products based on it. The company that pioneered the format gains from the licensing fees that flow back to it and from the enlarged supply of the product, which can stimulate demand and help accelerate market adoption. This was the strategy that Matsushita adopted with its VHS format for the videocassette recorder. In addition to producing VCRs at its own factory in Osaka, Matsushita let a number of other companies produce VHS format players under license (Sony decided not to license its competing Betamax format and produced all Betamax format players itself), and so VHS players were more widely available. More people purchased VHS players, which created an incentive for film companies to issue more films on VHS tapes (as opposed to Betamax tapes), which further increased demand for VHS players, and hence helped Matsushita to lock in VHS as the dominant format in the marketplace. Sony, ironically the first to market, saw its position marginalized by the reduced supply of the critical complement, prerecorded films, and ultimately withdrew Betamax players from the consumer marketplace.

Dolby, we saw in Strategy in Action 7.2, adopted a similar licensing strategy to get its noise-reduction technology adopted as the technological standard in the music and film industries. By charging a modest licensing fee for use of the technology in recording equipment and forgoing licensing fees on media recorded using Dolby technology, Dolby deliberately sought to reduce the financial incentive that potential competitors might have to develop their own, possibly superior, technology. Dolby calculated that its long-run profitability would be maximized by adopting a licensing strategy that limited the incentive of competitors to enter the market (this can be thought of as an example of limit pricing; see Chapter 6).

The correct strategy to pursue in a particular scenario requires that the company consider all of these different strategies and tactics and pursue those that seem most appropriate given the competitive circumstances prevailing in the industry and the likely strategy of rivals. Although there is no one best mix of strategies and tactics, of

31

critical importance is keeping the goal of rapidly increasing the installed base of products based on its standard at the front of its mind. By helping to jump-start demand for its format, a company can induce consumers to bear the switching costs associated with adopting its technology and leverage any positive feedback process that might exist. Also important is not pursuing strategies that have the opposite effect. For example, pricing high to capture profits from early adopters, who tend not to be as price sensitive as later adopters, can have the unfortunate effect of slowing demand growth and letting a more aggressive competitor pick up share and establish its format as the industry standard.

Costs in High-Technology Industries

In many high-tech industries, the fixed costs of developing the product are very high, but the costs of producing one extra unit of the product are very low. This is most obvious in the case of software. For example, it reportedly cost Microsoft $1 billion to develop Windows XP, the latest version of its Windows operating system, but the costs of producing one more copy of Windows XP is virtually zero. Once Windows XP was completed, Microsoft produced master disks that it sent out to PC manufacturers, such as Dell Computer, which then loaded a copy of Windows XP onto every PC it sells. The cost to Microsoft was effectively zero, and yet it receives a significant licensing fee for each copy of Windows XP installed on a PC.[8] For Microsoft, the *marginal cost* of making one more copy of Windows XP is close to zero, although the *fixed costs* of developing the product are $1 billion.

Many other high-technology products have similar cost economics: very high fixed costs and very low marginal costs. Most software products share these features, although if the software is sold through stores, the costs of packaging and distribution will raise the marginal costs, and if it is sold by a sales force direct to end users, this too will raise the marginal costs. Many consumer electronics products have the same basic economics. The fixed costs of developing a DVD player or a video game console can be very expensive, but the costs of producing an incremental unit are very low. The costs of developing a new drug, such as Viagra, can run to over $500 million, but the marginal costs of producing each additional pill is at most a few cents.

Comparative Cost Economics

To grasp why this cost structure is strategically important, it must be understood that in many industries, marginal costs *rise* as a company tries to expand output (economist call this the *law of diminishing returns*). To produce more of a good, a company has to hire more labor and invest in more plant and machinery. At *the margin*, the additional resources used are not as productive, so this leads to increasing marginal costs. However, the law of diminishing returns often does not apply in many high-tech settings, such as the production of software or sending one more bit of data down a digital telecommunications network.

Consider two companies, α and β (see Figure 7.3). Company α is a conventional producer and faces diminishing returns, so as it tries to expand output, its marginal costs rise. Company β is a high-tech producer, and its marginal costs do not rise at all as output is increased. Note that in Figure 7.3, Company β's marginal cost curve is drawn as a straight line near to the horizontal axis, implying that marginal costs are close to zero and do not vary with output, whereas Company α's marginal costs rise as output is expanded, illustrating diminishing returns. Company β's flat and low marginal cost curve means that its average cost curve will fall continuously over all ranges of output as it spreads its fixed costs out over greater volume. In contrast, the

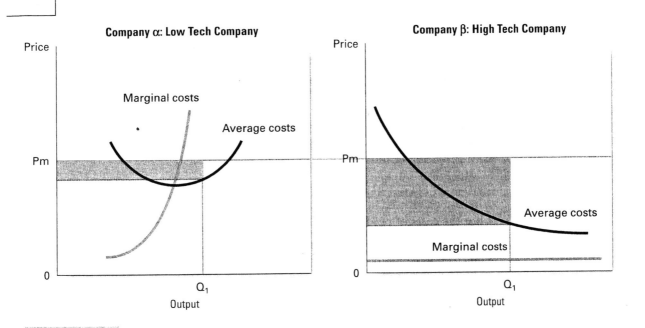

FIGURE 7.3

Cost Structures in High-Technology Industries

rising marginal costs encountered by Company α mean that its average cost curve is the **U**-shaped curve familiar from basic economics texts. For simplicity, assume that both companies sell their product at the same price, P_m, and both sell exactly the same quantity of output, $0 - Q_1$. You will see from Figure 7.3 that at an output of Q_1, Company β has much lower average costs than Company α and as a consequence is making far more profit (profit is the shaded area in Figure 7.3).

Strategic Significance If a company can shift from a cost structure where it encounters increasing marginal costs to one where fixed costs may be high but marginal costs are much lower, its profitability may increase. In the consumer electronics industry, such a shift has been playing out for two decades. Music recordings used to be based on analog technology where marginal costs rose as output expanded due to diminishing returns (as in the case of Company α in Figure 7.3). Since the 1980s, digital systems such as CD players have replaced analog systems. Digital systems are software based, and this implies much lower marginal costs of producing one more copy of a recording. As a result, the music labels have been able to lower prices, expand demand, and see their profitability increase (their production system that has more in common with Company β in Figure 7.3).

This process is still unfolding. The latest technology for making copies of music recordings is based on distribution over the Internet (for example, by downloading onto an MP3 player). Here, the marginal costs of making one more copy of a recording are lower still. In fact, they are close to zero and do not increase with output. The only problem is that the low costs of copying and distributing music recordings have created a major copyright problem that the major music labels have yet to solve (we discuss this in more detail shortly when we consider intellectual property rights). The same shift is now beginning to affect other industries. Some companies are building their strategies around trying to exploit and profit from this shift. For an example, Strategy in Action 7.3 looks at SonoSite.

Strategy in Action   7.3

Lowering Costs Through Digitalization

The ultrasound unit has been an important piece of diagnostic equipment in hospitals for some time. Ultrasound units use the physics of sound to produce images of soft tissues in the human body. They can produce detailed three-dimensional color images of organs and, by using contrast agents, track the flow of fluids through an organ. A cardiologist, for example, can use an ultrasound in combination with contrast agents injected into the bloodstream to track the flow of blood through a beating heart. In additional to the visual diagnosis, ultrasound also produces an array of quantitative diagnostic information of great value to physicians.

Modern ultrasound units are sophisticated instruments that cost around $250,000 to $300,000 each for a top-line model. They are fairly bulky instruments, weighing some 300 pounds, and are wheeled around hospitals on carts.

A few years back, a group of researchers at ATL, one of the leading ultrasound companies, came up with an idea for reducing the size and cost of a basic unit. They theorized that it might be possible to replace up to 80 percent of the solid circuits in an ultrasound unit with software, in the process significantly shrinking the size and reducing the weight of machines and thereby producing portable ultrasound units. Moreover, by digitalizing much of the ultrasound, replacing hardware with software, they could considerably drive down the marginal costs of making additional units, allowing them to make a good profit at much lower price points.

They reasoned that a portable and inexpensive ultrasound unit would find market opportunities in totally new niches. For example, a small, inexpensive ultrasound unit could be placed in an ambulance or carried into battle by an army medic, or purchased by family physicians for use in their offices. Although they realized that it would be some time, perhaps decades, before such small, inexpensive machines could attain the image quality and diagnostic sophistication of top-of-the-line machines, they saw the opportunity in terms of creating market niches that previously could not be served by ultrasound companies due to the high costs and bulk of the product.

The researchers ultimately became a project team within ATL and were then spun out of ATL as an entirely new company, SonoSite. In late 1999, they introduced their first portable product, weighing just six pounds and costing around $25,000. SonoSite targeted niches that full-sized ultrasound products could not reach: ambulatory care and foreign markets that could not afford the more expensive equipment. In 2001, the company sold $46 million worth of its product. In the long run, SonoSite plans to build more features and greater image quality into the small hand-held machines, primarily by improving the software. This could allow the units to penetrate U.S. hospital markets that currently purchase the established technology, much as client-server systems based on PC technology came to replace mainframes for some functions in business corporations.

Sources: Interviews by Charles W. L. Hill. SonoSite 10K for 2001.

Another implication of its cost structure is that when a high-tech company faces high fixed costs and low marginal costs, its strategy should emphasize the low-cost option: deliberately drive prices down to drive volume up. Look again at Figure 7.3 and you will see that *the high-tech company's average costs fall rapidly as output expands.* This implies that prices can be reduced to stimulate demand, and so long as prices fall less rapidly than average costs, per unit profit margins will expand as prices fall. This is a consequence of the fact that the firm's marginal costs are low and do not rise with output. This strategy of pricing low to drive volume and reap wider profit margins is central to the business model of some very successful high-technology companies, including Microsoft. When Microsoft founder Bill Gates was called into a U.S. Senate hearing during the Microsoft antitrust investigation in 2000, he explained to the bemused senators that Microsoft did not behave like a classic monopolist, raising prices and restricting output to maximize profits. Rather, he said, Microsoft cut prices to stimulate sales and thus increase its profit margins. Gates claimed the strategy was good for consumers—they got cheaper software—and good for Microsoft's profit margins. It was clear from the questioning that the senators had trouble believing this explanation, but for Gates and his company, it has been a central aspect of their strategy since the early 1980s.

Managing Intellectual Property Rights

Ownership of a technology can be a source of sustained competitive advantage and superior profitability, particularly when the company owns a technology that is the standard in an industry, such as Microsoft and Intel's Wintel standard for personal computers and Dolby's ownership of the standard for noise-reduction technology in the music and film recording industries. Even if a technology is not standard but is valued by a sufficient numbers of consumers, ownership of that technology can still be very profitable. Apple's current personal computer technology is by no means the standard in the marketplace, much as Apple would like it to be. In fact, the company's iMac technology accounts for less than 10 percent of the personal computers sold every year. But that small slice of a very large market is still a valuable niche for Apple.

Intellectual Property Rights

Because new technology is the product of intellectual and creative effort, we call it intellectual property. The term **intellectual property** refers to the product of any intellectual and creative effort and includes not only new technology but also a wide range of intellectual creations, including music, films, books, and graphic art. As a society, we value the products of intellectual and creative activity. Intellectual property is seen as a very important driver of economic progress and social wealth.[9] But it is also often expensive, risky, and time-consuming to create intellectual property.

For example, a new drug to treat a dangerous medical condition such as cancer can take twelve to sixteen years to develop and cost $500 million. Moreover, only 20 percent of new drugs that are tested in humans actually make it to the market.[10] The remainder fail because they are found to be unsafe or ineffective. Given the costs, risks, and time involved in this activity, few companies would be willing to embark on the road required to develop a new drug and bring it to market unless they could be reasonably sure that if they were successful in developing the drug, their investment would be profitable. If the minute they introduced a successful cancer drug, their competitors produced imitations of that drug, no company would even consider making the initial investment.

To make sure that this does not happen, we grant the creators of intellectual property certain rights over their creation. These rights, which stop competitors from copying or imitating the creation for a number of years, take the legal forms of patents, copyrights, and trademarks, which all serve the same basic objective: to give individuals and companies an incentive to engage in the expensive and risky business of creating new intellectual property.

The creation of intellectual property is a central endeavor in high-technology industries, and the management of intellectual property rights has moved to center stage in many of these companies. Developing strategies to protect and enforce intellectual property rights can be an important aspect of competitive advantage. For many companies, this amounts to making sure that their patents and copyrights are respected. It is not uncommon, therefore, to see high-technology companies bringing lawsuits against their competitors for patent infringement. In general, companies often use such lawsuits not only to sanction those they suspect of violating the company's intellectual property rights, but also to signal to potential violators that the company will aggressively defend its property. Legal action alone suffices to protect intellectual property in many industries, but in others, such as software, the low costs of illegally copying and distributing intellectual property call for more creative strategies to manage intellectual property rights.

Digitalization and Piracy Rates

Protecting intellectual property has become more complicated in the past few decades because of **digitalization,** that is, the rendering of creative output in digital form. This can be done for music recordings, films, books, newspapers, magazines, and computer software. Digitalization has dramatically lowered the cost of copying and distributing digitalized intellectual property or digital media. As we have seen, the marginal cost of making one more copy of a software program is very low, and the same is true for any other intellectual property rendered in digital form. Moreover, digital media can be distributed at a very low cost (again, almost zero), for example, by distributing over the Internet. Reflecting on this, one commentator has described the Internet as a "giant out-of-control copying machine."[11] The low marginal costs of copying and distributing digital media have made it very easy to sell illegal copies of such property. In turn, this has helped to produce a high level of piracy (in this context, **piracy** refers to the theft of intellectual property).

In the software industry, estimates suggest that in 2000, some 37 percent of all software used around the world was pirated, costing software companies close to $12 billion in lost revenues. The piracy rate ranged from 94 percent in China to 24 percent in the United States. As a region, Asia had the highest piracy rate at 51 percent and North America had the lowest piracy rate at 25 percent. The piracy rate in Western Europe was 34 percent. Although North America had the lowest rate of software piracy, because of the size of the market, the loss to companies was still huge, amounting to almost $3 billion.[12] The problem of piracy is also endemic in the music industry. The International Federation of the Phonographic Industry estimates that in 2000, some 36 percent of all CDs around the globe were illegally produced and sold, costing the music recording industry some $4.1 billion in lost revenues.[13]

The scale of this problem is so large that simply resorting to legal tactics to enforce intellectual property rights has amounted to nothing more than a partial solution to the piracy problem. Many companies now build sophisticated encryption software into their digital products, which can make it more difficult for pirates to copy digital media and thereby raise the costs of stealing. But the pirates too are sophisticated and often seem to be able to find their way around encryption software. This raises the question of whether there are additional strategies that can be adopted to manage digital rights, and thereby limit piracy.

Strategies for Managing Digital Rights

One strategy is simply to recognize that while the low costs of copying and distributing digital media make some piracy inevitable, the same attributes can be used to the company's advantage. The basic strategy here represents yet another variation of the basic razor and razor blades principle: give something away for free in order to boost the sales of a complementary product. A familiar example concerns Adobe Acrobat Reader, the software program for reading documents formatted by Adobe Acrobat (i.e., PDF formatted documents). Adobe developed Adobe Acrobat to allow people to format documents in a manner that resembled a high-quality printed page and to display and distribute these documents over the Web. Moreover, Adobe documents are formatted in a read-only format, meaning that they cannot be altered by individuals nor can parts of those documents be copied and pasted to other documents. Its strategy has been to give away Adobe Acrobat Reader for free and then make money by selling its Acrobat software for formatting documents. The strategy has worked extremely well. Anyone can download a copy of Acrobat Reader from Adobe's web site. Because the marginal costs of copying and distributing this software over the Web are extremely low, the process is almost costless for both Adobe and its customers. The result is that the Acrobat Reader has diffused very rapidly and is now the dominant format for viewing high-quality documents distributed and downloaded over the Web. As the installed base of Acrobat Readers has grown, sales of Adobe Acrobat software have soared as more and more organizations and individuals realize that formatting their digital documents in Acrobat format makes sense.

Another strategy is to take advantage of the low costs of copying and distributing digital media to drive down the costs of purchasing those media, thereby reducing the incentive that consumers have to steal. When coupled with encryption software that makes piracy more difficult and vigorous legal actions to enforcement of intellectual property regulations, this can slow the piracy rate and generate incremental revenues that cost little to produce.

Several music companies are now experimenting with variants of this strategy. Roxio, a manufacturer of software for copying, or "burning," music onto CDs, has begun to partner with several music labels to develop just such a strategy.[14] In 2001, Roxio's Easy CD Creator and Toast software accounted for 70 percent of the CD burning software sold. The software is now preloaded onto most new personal computers. However, Roxio's sales growth has been hampered by opposition from music labels, which argue that Roxio's software is promoting music piracy and hurting CD sales. In response, Roxio has persuaded several music companies to start experimenting with a service that allows users to burn music onto CDs. In January 2002, Pressplay, a service backed by Sony, Universal Music, and EMI, began to allow users to download songs digitally and burn them onto CDs. Users pay $25 a month to burn twenty songs, although they can burn only two tracks from a single artist each month. This business model allows subscribers to customize a CD, which is what many do anyway when pirating CDs by burning them. However, in theory, the service saves customers money because they do not have to purchase the original CDs. Pressplay and Roxio hope that the strategy will reduce piracy rates, while generating incremental revenues that cost very little to produce due to the extremely low marginal costs of copying and distributing music in this manner.

Capturing First-Mover Advantages

In high-technology industries, companies often compete by striving to be the first to develop revolutionary new products, that is, to be a **first mover.** By definition, the first mover with regard to a revolutionary product is in a monopoly position. If the new product satisfies unmet consumer needs and demand is high, the first mover can capture significant revenues and profits. Such revenues and profits signal to potential rivals that there is money to be made by imitating the first mover. As illustrated in Figure 7.4, in the absence of strong barriers to imitation, this implies that imitators will rush into the market created by the first mover, competing away the first mover's monopoly profits and leaving all participants in the market with a much lower level of returns.

Despite imitation, some first movers have the ability to capitalize on and reap substantial **first-mover advantages**—the advantages of pioneering new technologies and products that lead to an enduring competitive advantage. Intel introduced the world's first microprocessor in 1971 and today still dominates the microprocessor

FIGURE 7.4

The Impact of
Imitation on Profits of
a First Mover

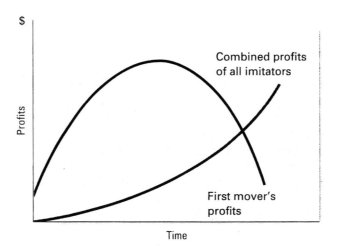

segment of the semiconductor industry. Xerox introduced the world's first photo-copier and for a long time enjoyed a leading position in the industry. Cisco introduced the first Internet protocol network router in 1986 and still dominates the market for that equipment today. Some first movers can reap substantial advantages from their pioneering activities that lead to an enduring competitive advantage. They can, in other words, limit or slow the rate of imitation.

But there are plenty of counterexamples suggesting that first-mover advantages might not be easy to capture and, in fact, that there might be **first mover disadvantages**—the competitive *disadvantages* associated with being first. For example, Apple Computer was the first company to introduce a hand-held computer, the Apple Newton, but the product failed; a second mover, Palm, succeeded where Apple had failed. In the market for commercial jet aircraft, DeHavilland was first to market with the Comet, but it was the second mover, Boeing, with its 707 jetliner, that went on to dominate the market.

Clearly being a first mover does not by itself guarantee success. As we shall see, the difference between innovating companies that capture first-mover advantages and those that fall victim to first-mover disadvantages in part turns on the strategy that the first mover pursues. Before considering the strategy issue, however, we need to take a closer look at the nature of first-mover advantages and disadvantages.[15]

First-Mover Advantages

There are five main sources of first-mover advantages.[16] First, the first mover has an opportunity to *exploit network effects* and positive feedback loops, locking consumers into its technology. In the VCR industry, Sony could have exploited network effects by licensing its technology, but instead the company ceded its first-mover advantage to the second mover, Matsushita.

Second, the first mover may be able to establish significant *brand loyalty,* which is expensive for later entrants to break down. Indeed, if the company is successful in this endeavor, its name may become closely associated with the entire class of products, including those produced by rivals. People still talk of "Xeroxing" when they are going to make a photocopy or "FedExing" when they are going to send a package by overnight mail.

Third, the first mover may be able to ramp up sales volume ahead of rivals and thus reap cost advantages associated with the realization of *scale economies and learning effects* (see Chapter 4). Once the first mover has these cost advantages, it can respond to new entrants by cutting prices in order to hold on to its market share and still earn significant profits.

Fourth, the first mover may be able to create *switching costs* for its customers that subsequently make it difficult for rivals to enter the market and take customers away from the first mover. Wireless service providers, for example, will give new customers a "free" wireless phone, but customers must sign a contract agreeing to pay for the phone if they terminate the service contract within a specified time period, such as a year. Because the real cost of a wireless phone may run $100 to $200, this represents a significant switching cost that later entrants have to overcome.

Finally, the first mover may be able to *accumulate valuable knowledge* related to customer needs, distribution channels, product technology, process technology, and so on. This accumulated knowledge gives it a knowledge advantage that later entrants might find difficult or expensive to match. Sharp, for example, was the first mover in the commercial manufacture of active matrix liquid crystal displays used in laptop computers. The process for manufacturing these displays is very difficult, with a high reject rate for flawed displays. Sharp has accumulated such an advantage with regard to production processes that it has been very difficult for later entrants to match it on product quality, and thus costs.

First-Mover Disadvantages Balanced against these first-mover advantages are a number of disadvantages. First, the first mover has to bear significant *pioneering costs* that later entrants do not. The first mover has to pioneer the technology, develop distribution channels, and educate customers about the nature of the product. All of this can be expensive and time-consuming. Later entrants, by way of contrast, might be able to *free-ride* on the first mover's investments in pioneering the market and customer education.

Related to this, first movers are more prone to *make mistakes* because there are so many uncertainties in a new market. Later entrants may be able to learn from the mistakes made by first movers, improve on the product or the way in which it is sold, and come to market with a superior offering that captures significant market share from the first mover. For example, one of the reasons that the Apple Newton failed was that the handwriting software in the hand-held computer failed to recognize human handwriting. The second mover in this market, Palm, learned from Apple's error. When it introduced the PalmPilot, it used software that recognized letters written in a particular way, Graffiti, and then persuaded customers to learn this method of inputting data into the hand-held computer.

Third, first movers run the risk of *building the wrong resources and capabilities* because they are focusing on a customer set that is not going to be characteristic of the mass market. This is the *crossing the chasm* problem that we discussed in the previous chapter. You will recall that the customers in the early market—those we categorized as innovators and early adopters—have different characteristics from the first wave of the mass market, the early majority. The first mover runs the risk of gearing its resources and capabilities to the needs of innovators and early adopters and not being able to switch when the early majority enters the market. As a result, first movers run a greater risk of plunging into the chasm that separates the early market from the mass market.

Finally, the first mover may invest in *inferior or obsolete technology*. This can happen when its product innovation is based on underlying technology that is advancing rapidly. By basing its product on an early version of the technology, it may lock itself into something that rapidly becomes obsolete. In contrast, later entrants may be able to leapfrog the first mover and introduce products that are based on later versions of the underlying technology. This happened in France during the 1980s when, at the urging of the government, France Telecom introduced the world's first consumer online service, Minitel. France Telecom distributed crude terminals to consumers for free, which they could hook up to their phone line and use to browse phone directories. Other simple services were soon added, and before long the French could carry out online shopping, banking, travel, weather, and news—all years before the Web was invented. The problem was that by the standards of the Web, Minitel was very crude and inflexible, and France Telecom, as the first mover, suffered. The French were very slow to adopt personal computers and then the Internet primarily because Minitel had such a presence. As late as 1998, only a fifth of French households had a computer, compared with two-fifths in the United States, and only 2 percent of households were connected to the Internet compared to over 30 percent in the United States. As the result of a government decision, France Telecom, and indeed an entire nation, was slow to adopt a revolutionary new online medium, the Web, because they were the first to invest in a more primitive version of the technology.[17]

Strategies for Exploiting First-Mover Advantages

The task facing a first mover is how to exploit its lead in order to capitalize on first-mover advantages and build a sustainable long-term competitive advantage while simultaneously reducing the risks associated with first mover disadvantages, There are three basic strategies available: (1) develop and market the innovation itself, (2) develop and market the innovation jointly with other companies through a strategic alliance or joint venture, and (3) license the innovation to others and let them develop the market.

The optimal choice of strategy depends on the answers to three questions:

1. Does the innovating company have the *complementary assets* to exploit its innovation and capture first-mover advantages?

2. How difficult is it for imitators to copy the company's innovation? In other words, what is the *height of barriers to imitation?*

3. Are there *capable competitors* that could rapidly imitate the innovation?

Complementary Assets. Complementary assets are the assets required to exploit a new innovation and gain a competitive advantage.[18] Among the most important complementary assets are competitive manufacturing facilities capable of handling rapid growth in customer demand while maintaining high product quality. State-of-the-art manufacturing facilities enable the first mover to move quickly down the experience curve without encountering production bottlenecks or problems with the quality of the product. The inability to satisfy demand because of these problems, however, creates the opportunity for imitators to enter the marketplace. For example, in 1998, Immunex was the first company to introduce a revolutionary new biological treatment for rheumatoid arthritis. Sales for this product, Enbrel, ramped up very rapidly, hitting $750 million in 2001. However, Immunex had not invested in sufficient manufacturing capacity. In mid-2000, it announced that it lacked the capacity to satisfy demand and that bringing additional capacity on line would take at least two years. This manufacturing bottleneck gave the second mover in the market, Johnson & Johnson, the opportunity to expand demand for its product rapidly, which by early 2002 was outselling Enbrel. Immunex's first-mover advantage had been partly eroded because it lacked an important complementary asset, the manufacturing capability required to satisfy demand.

Complementary assets also include marketing know-how, an adequate sales force, access to distribution systems, and an after-sales service and support network. All of these assets can help an innovator build brand loyalty and help the innovator achieve market penetration more rapidly.[19] In turn, the resulting increases in volume facilitate more rapid movement down the experience curve and the attainment of a sustainable cost-based advantage due to scale economies and learning effects. One of the reasons that EMI, the first mover in the market for CT scanners, ultimately lost out to established medical equipment companies, such as GE Medical Systems, was that it lacked the marketing know-how, sales force, and distribution systems required to compete effectively in the world's largest market for medical equipment, the United States.

Developing complementary assets can be very expensive, and companies often need large infusions of capital for this purpose. That is the reason first movers often lose out to late movers that are large, successful companies, often established in other industries, with the resources to develop a presence in the new industry quickly. Microsoft and 3M exemplify companies that can move quickly to capitalize on the opportunities when other companies open up new product markets, such as compact discs or floppy disks. For example, although Netscape pioneered the market for Internet browsers with the Netscape Navigator, Microsoft's Internet Explorer ultimately dominated the market for Internet browsers.

Height of Barriers to Imitation. Recall from Chapter 3 that **barriers to imitation** are factors that prevent rivals from imitating a company's distinctive competencies and innovations. Although ultimately any innovation can be copied, the higher the barriers are, the longer it takes for rivals to imitate, and the more time the first mover has to build an enduring competitive advantage.

Barriers to imitation give an innovator time to establish a competitive advantage and build more enduring barriers to entry in the newly created market. Patents, for example, are among the most widely used barriers to imitation. By protecting its photocopier technology with a thicket of patents, Xerox was able to delay any significant imitation of its product for seventeen years. However, patents are often easy to "invent around." For example, one study found that this happened to 60 percent of patented innovations within four years.[20] If patent protection is weak, a company might try to slow imitation by developing new products and processes in secret. The most famous example of this approach is Coca-Cola, which has kept the formula for Coke a secret for generations. But Coca-Cola's success in this regard is an exception. A study of 100 companies has estimated that proprietary information about a company's decision to develop a major new product or process is known to its rivals within about twelve to eighteen months of the original development decision.[21]

Capable Competitors. **Capable competitors** are companies that can move quickly to imitate the pioneering company. Competitors' capability to imitate a pioneer's innovation depends primarily on two factors: (1) R&D skills and (2) access to complementary assets. In general, the greater the number of capable competitors with access to the R&D skills and complementary assets needed to imitate an innovation, the more rapid imitation is likely to be.

In this context, R&D skills refer to the ability of rivals to reverse-engineer an innovation in order to find out how it works and quickly develop a comparable product. As an example, consider the CT scanner. GE bought one of the first CT scanners produced by EMI, and its technical experts reverse-engineered it. Despite the product's technological complexity, GE developed its own version, which allowed it to imitate EMI quickly and ultimately to replace EMI as the major supplier of CT scanners.

With regard to complementary assets, the access that rivals have to marketing, sales know-how, or manufacturing capabilities is one of the key determinants of the rate of imitation. If would-be imitators lack critical complementary assets, not only do they have to imitate the innovation, they may also have to imitate the innovator's complementary assets. This is expensive, as AT&T discovered when it tried to enter the personal computer business in 1984. AT&T lacked the marketing assets (sales force and distribution systems) necessary to support personal computer products. The lack of these assets and the time it takes to build them partly explain why four years after it entered the market, AT&T had lost $2.5 billion and still had not emerged as a viable contender. It subsequently pulled out of this business.

Three Innovation Strategies. The way in which these three factors—complementary assets, height of barriers to imitation, and the capability of competitors—influence the choice of innovation strategy is summarized in Table 7.1. The competitive strategy of *developing and marketing the innovation alone* makes most sense when (1) the innovator has the complementary assets necessary to develop the innovation, (2) the barriers to imitating a new innovation are high, and (3) the number of capable competitors is limited. Complementary assets allow rapid development and promotion of the innovation. High barriers to imitation buy the innovator time to establish a competitive advantage and build enduring barriers to entry through brand loyalty or experience-based cost advantages. The fewer the capable competitors there are, the less likely it is that any one of them will succeed in circumventing barriers to imitation and quickly imitating the innovation.

The competitive strategy of *developing and marketing the innovation jointly with other companies through a strategic alliance or joint venture* makes most sense when (1) the innovator lacks complementary assets, (2) barriers to imitation are high, and (3) there are several capable competitors. In such circumstances, it makes sense to enter into an alliance with a company that already has the complementary assets—in other words, with a capable competitor. Theoretically, such an alliance should prove to be mutually beneficial, and each partner can share in high profits that neither could earn on its own. Moreover, such a strategy has the benefit of co-opting a potential rival. For example, had EMI teamed up with a capable competitor to develop the market for CT scanners, such as GE Medical Systems, instead of going it alone, the company might not only have been able to build a more enduring competitive advantage, it would also have co-opted a potentially powerful rival into its camp.

TABLE 7.1

Strategies for Profiting from Innovation

Strategy	Does the Innovator Have the Required Complementary Assets?	Likely Height of Barriers to Imitation	Number of Capable Competitors
Going it alone	Yes	High	Very few
Entering into an alliance	No	High	Moderate number
License the innovation	No	Low	Many

The third strategy, *licensing*, makes most sense when (1) the innovating company lacks the complementary assets, (2) barriers to imitation are low, and (3) there are many capable competitors. The combination of low barriers to imitation and many capable competitors makes rapid imitation almost certain. The innovator's lack of complementary assets further suggests that an imitator will soon capture the innovator's competitive advantage. Given these factors, because rapid diffusion of the innovator's technology through imitation is inevitable, the innovator can at least share in some of the benefits of this diffusion by licensing out its technology.[22] Moreover, by setting a relatively modest licensing fee, the innovator may be able to reduce the incentive that potential rivals have to develop their own competing, and possibly superior technology. This seems to have been the strategy Dolby adopted to get its technology established as the standard for noise reduction in the music and film businesses (see Strategy in Action 7.2).

Technological Paradigm Shifts

Technological paradigm shifts occur when new technologies come along that revolutionize the structure of the industry, dramatically alter the nature of competition, and require companies to adopt new strategies in order to survive. A good example of a paradigm shift that is currently unfolding is the shift from chemical to digital photography (another example of *digitalization*). For over half a century, the large incumbent enterprises in the photographic industry such as Kodak and Fuji film have generated most of their revenues from selling and processing film using traditional silver halide technology. The rise of digital photography is a huge threat to their business models. Digital cameras do not use film, the mainstay of Kodak's and Fuji's business. Moreover, these cameras are more like specialized computers than conventional cameras and are thus based on scientific knowledge that Kodak and Fuji have little knowledge of. Although both Kodak and Fuji are investing heavily in the development of digital cameras, they are facing intense competition from companies such as Sony, Canon, and Hewlett Packard, which have developed their own digital cameras, from software developers such as Adobe and Microsoft, which make the software for manipulating digital images, and from printer companies such as Hewlett Packard and Canon, which are making the printers that consumers can use to print out their own high-quality pictures at home. As digital substitution gathers speed in the photography industry, it is not clear that the traditional incumbents will be able to survive this shift; the new competitors might well rise to dominance in the new market.

If Kodak and Fuji do decline, they will not be the first large incumbents to be felled by a technological paradigm shift in their industry. In the early 1980s, the computer industry was revolutionized by the arrival of personal computer technology, which gave rise to client-server networks that replaced traditional mainframe and minicomputers for many business uses. Many incumbent companies in the mainframe era, such as Wang, Control Data, and DEC, ultimately did not survive, and even IBM went through a decade of wrenching changes and large losses before it reinvented itself as a provider of e-business solutions. In their place, new entrants such as Microsoft, Intel, Dell, and Compaq rose to dominance in this new computer industry.

Examples such as these raise four questions:

1. When do paradigm shifts occur, and how do they unfold?

2. Why do so many incumbents go into decline following a paradigm shift?

3. What strategies can incumbents adopt in order to increase the probability that they will survive a paradigm shift and emerge the other side of the market abyss created by the arrival of new technology as a profitable enterprise?

4. What strategies can new entrants into a market adopt in order to profit from a paradigm shift?

We shall answer each of these questions in the remainder of this chapter.

Paradigm Shifts and the Decline of Established Companies

Paradigm shifts appear to be more likely to occur in an industry when one, or both, of the following conditions are in place.[23] First, the established technology in the industry is mature and approaching or at its "natural limit," and second, a new "disruptive technology" has entered the marketplace and is taking root in niches that are poorly served by incumbent companies using the established technology.

The Natural Limits to Technology. Richard Foster has formalized the relationship between the performance of a technology and time in terms of what he calls the technology S-curve (see Figure 7.5).[24] This curve shows the relationship over time of *cumulative* investments in R&D and the performance (or functionality) of a given technology. Early in its evolution, R&D investments in a new technology tend to yield rapid improvements in performance as basic engineering problems are solved. After a time, diminishing returns to cumulative R&D begin to set in, the rate of improvement in performance slows, and the technology starts to approach its natural limit, where further advances are not possible. For example, one can argue that there was more improvement in the first fifty years of the commercial aerospace business following the pioneering flight by the Wright Brothers than there has been in the second fifty years. Indeed, the world's largest commercial jet aircraft, the Boeing 747, is based on a 1960s design, as is the world's fastest commercial jet aircraft, the Concorde. In commercial aerospace, therefore, we are now in the region of diminishing returns and may be approaching the natural limit to improvements in the technology of commercial aerospace.

Similarly, it can be argued that we are approaching the natural limit to technology in the performance of silicon-based semiconductor chips. Over the past two decades, the performance of semiconductor chips has been increased dramatically by packing ever more transistors onto a single small silicon chip. This process has helped to increase the power of computers, lower their cost, and shrink their size. But we are starting to approach limits to the ability to shrink the width of lines on a chip and therefore pack ever more transistors onto a single chip. The limit is imposed by the natural laws of physics. Light waves are used to help etch lines onto a chip, and one cannot etch a line that is smaller than the wavelength of light being used. Semiconductor companies are already using light with very small wavelengths, such as extreme ultraviolet, to etch lines onto a chip, but there are limits to how far this

FIGURE 7.5

The Technology S-Curve

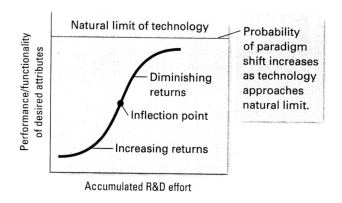

technology can be pushed, and many believe that we will reach those limits within the decade. Does this mean that our ability to make smaller, faster, cheaper computers is coming to an end? Probably not. It is more likely that we will find another technology to replace silicon-based computing and enable us to continue building smaller, faster, cheaper computers. In fact, several exotic competing technologies are already being developed that may replace silicon-based computing. These include self-organizing molecular computers, three-dimensional microprocessor technology, quantum computing technology, and using DNA to perform computations.[25]

What does all of this have to do with paradigm shifts? According to Foster, when a technology approaches its natural limit, research attention turns to possible alternative technologies, and sooner or later one of those alternatives might be commercialized and replace the established technology. That is, the probability that a paradigm shift will occur increases. Thus, sometime in the next decade or two, another paradigm shift might shake the very foundations of the computer industry as exotic computing technology replaces silicon-based computing. If history is any guide, if and when this happens, many of the incumbents in today's computer industry will go into decline, and new enterprises will rise to dominance.

Foster pushes this point a little further, noting that initially, the contenders for the replacement technology are not as effective as the established technology in producing the attributes and features that consumers demand in a product. For example, in the early years of the twentieth century, automobiles were just starting to be produced. They were valued for their ability to move people from place to place, but so was the horse and cart (the established technology). When automobiles originally appeared, the horse and cart was still quite a bit better than the automobile at doing this (see Figure 7.6). After all, the first cars were slow, noisy, and prone to breakdown. Moreover, they needed a network of paved roads and gas stations to be really useful, and that network didn't exist, so for most applications, the horse and cart was still the preferred mode of transportation—to say nothing of the fact that it was cheaper.

However, this comparison ignored the fact that in the early twentieth century, automobile technology was at the very start of its S-curve and was about to experience dramatic improvements in performance as major engineering problems were solved (and those paved roads and gas stations were built). In contrast, after 3,000 years of continuous improvement and refinement, the horse and cart was almost definitely at the end of its technological S-curve. The result was that the rapidly improv-

FIGURE 7.6

Established and Successor Technologies

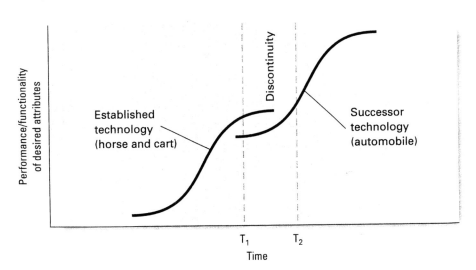

ing automobile soon replaced the horse and cart as the preferred mode of transportation. At time T_1 in Figure 7.6, the horse and cart was still superior to the automobile. By time T_2, the automobile had surpassed the horse and cart.

Foster notes that because the successor technology is initially less efficient than the established technology, established companies and their customers often make the mistake of dismissing it, only to be taken off-guard by its rapid performance improvement. A final point here is that often there is not one potential successor technologies but a swarm of potential successor technologies, only one of which might ultimately rise to the fore (see Figure 7.7). When this is the case, established companies are put at a disadvantage. Even if they recognize that a paradigm shift is imminent, they may not have the resources to invest in all the potential replacement technologies. If they invest in the wrong one, something that is easy to do given the uncertainty that surrounds the entire process, they may be locked out of subsequent development.

Disruptive Technology. Clayton Christensen has built on Foster's insights and his own research to develop a theory of disruptive technology that has become very influential in high-technology circles.[26] Christensen uses the term **disruptive technology** to refer to a new technology that gets its start away from the mainstream of a market and then, as its functionality improves over time, invades the main market. Such technologies are disruptive because they revolutionize industry structure and competition, often causing the decline of established companies. They cause a technological paradigm shift.

Christensen's greatest insight is that established companies are often aware of the new technology but do not invest in it because they listen to their customers, and their customers do not want it. Of course, this arises because the new technology is early in its development, and thus only at the beginning of the S-curve for that technology. Once the performance of the new technology improves, customers *do* want it, but by this time it is new entrants, as opposed to established companies, that have accumulated the knowledge required to bring the new technology into the mass market. Christensen supports his view by several detailed historical case studies, one of which is summarized in Strategy in Action 7.4.

FIGURE 7.7

Swarm of Successor
Technologies

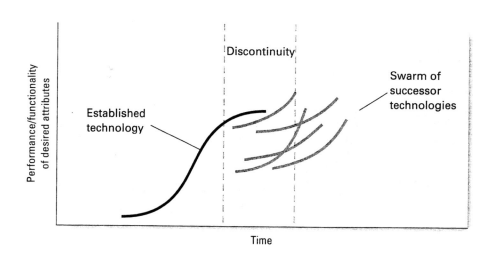

Strategy in Action   7.4

Disruptive Technology in Mechanical Excavators

Excavators are used to dig out foundations for large buildings, trenches to lay large pipes for sewers and the like, and foundations and trenches for residential construction and farm work. Prior to the 1940s, the dominant technology used to manipulate the bucket on a mechanical excavator was based on a system of cables and pulleys. Although these mechanical systems could lift large buckets of earth, the excavators themselves were quite large, cumbersome, and expensive. Thus, they were rarely used to dig small trenches for house foundations, irrigation ditches for farmers, and the like. In most cases, these small trenches were dug by hand.

In the 1940s, a new technology made its appearance: hydraulics. In theory, hydraulic systems had certain advantages over the established cable and pulley systems. Most important, their energy efficiency was higher: for a given bucket size, a smaller engine would be required using a hydraulic system. However, the initial hydraulic systems also had drawbacks. The seals on hydraulic cylinders were prone to leak under high pressure, effectively limiting the size of bucket that could be lifted using hydraulics. Notwithstanding this drawback, when hydraulics first appeared, many of the incumbent firms in the mechanical excavation industry took the technology seriously enough to ask their primary customers whether they would be interested in products based on hydraulics. Since the primary customers of incumbents needed excavators with large buckets to dig out the foundations for buildings and large trenches, their reply was negative. For this customer set, the hydraulic systems of the 1940s were not reliable or powerful enough. Consequently, after consulting with their customers, these established companies in the industry made the strategic decision not to invest in hydraulics. Instead, they continued to produce excavation equipment based on the dominant cable and pulley technology.

It was left to a number of new entrants, which included J. I. Case, John Deere, J. C. Bamford, and Caterpillar, to pioneer hydraulic excavation equipment. Because of the limits on bucket size imposed by the seal problem, these companies initially focused on a poorly served niche in the market that could make use of small buckets: residential contractors and farmers. Over time, these new entrants were able to solve the engineering problems associated with weak hydraulic seals, and as they did this, they manufactured excavators with larger buckets. Ultimately, they invaded the market niches served by the old-line companies: general contractors that dug the foundations for large buildings, sewers, and so on. At this point, Case, Deere, Caterpillar, and their kin rose to dominance in the industry, while the majority of established companies from the prior era lost share. Of the thirty or so manufacturers of cable-actuated equipment in the United States in the late 1930s, only four survived to the 1950s.

Source: M. Christensen, *The Innovator's Dilemma* (Boston: Harvard Business School Press, 1997).

In addition to listening too closely to their customers, Christensen also identifies a number of other factors that make it very difficult for established companies to adopt a new disruptive technology. He notes that many established companies declined to invest in new disruptive technologies because initially they served such small market niches that it seemed unlikely that they would have an impact on the company's revenues and profits. As the new technology started to improve in functionality and invade the main market, their investment was often hindered by the fact that exploiting the new technology required a new business model totally different from the company's established model, and thus very difficult to implement.

Both of these points can be illustrated by reference to one more example: the rise of online discount stockbrokers during the 1990s such as Ameritrade and E*Trade, which made use of a new technology, the Internet, to allow individual investors to trade stocks for a very low commission fee, whereas full-service stockbrokers, such as

Merrill Lynch, where orders had to be placed through a stockbroker who earned a commission for performing the transaction, did not. (This story is told in more detail in the *Closing Case* in Chapter 5.)

Christensen also notes that a new network of suppliers and distributors typically grows up around the new entrants. Not only do established companies initially ignore disruptive technology, so do their suppliers and distributors. This creates an opportunity for new suppliers and distributors to enter the market to serve the new entrants. As the new entrants grow, so does the associated network. Ultimately, Christensen suggests, the new entrants and their network may replace not only established enterprises, but also the entire network of suppliers and distributors associated with established companies. Taken to its logical extreme, this view suggests that disruptive technologies may result in the demise of the entire network of enterprises associated with established companies in an industry.

The established companies in an industry that is being rocked by a technological paradigm shift often have to cope with internal inertia forces that limit their ability to adapt, but the new entrants do not and thereby have an advantage. They do not have to deal with an established and conservative customer set and an obsolete business model. Instead, they can focus on optimizing the new technology, improving its performance, and riding the wave of disruptive technology into new market segments until they invade the main market and challenge the established companies, by which time they may be well equipped to beat them.

Strategic Implications for Established Companies

Although Christensen has uncovered an important tendency, it is by no means written in stone that all established companies are doomed to fail when faced with disruptive technologies, as we have seen with IBM and Merrill Lynch. Established companies must meet the challenges created by the emergence of disruptive technologies.

First, having access to the knowledge about how disruptive technologies can revolutionize markets is itself a valuable strategic asset. Many of the established companies that Christensen examined failed because they took a myopic view of the new technology and asked their customers the wrong question. Instead of asking, "Are you interested in this new technology?" they should have recognized that the new technology was likely to improve rapidly over time and instead have asked, "Would you be interested in this new technology if it improves its functionality over time?" If they had done this, they may have made very different strategic decisions.

Second, it is clearly important for established enterprises to invest in newly emerging technologies that may ultimately become disruptive technologies. Companies have to hedge their bets about new technology. As we have noted, at any time, there may be a swarm of emerging technologies, any one of which might ultimately become a disruptive technology. Large, established companies that are generating significant cash flows can and often should establish and fund central R&D operations to invest in and develop such technologies. In addition, they may wish to acquire newly emerging companies that are pioneering potentially disruptive technologies or enter into alliances with them to develop the technology jointly. The strategy of acquiring companies that are developing potentially disruptive technology is one that Cisco Systems, a dominant provider of Internet network equipment, is famous for pursuing. At the heart of this strategy must be a recognition on the part of the incumbent enterprise that it is better for the company to develop disruptive technology and then cannibalize its established sales base than to have that sales base taken away by new entrants.

However, Christensen makes the very important point that even when established companies do undertake R&D investments in potentially disruptive technologies, they often fail to commercialize those technologies because of internal forces that suppress change. For example, managers in the parts of the business that are currently generating the most cash may claim that they need the greatest R&D investment to maintain their market position and may lobby top management to delay investment in a new technology. Early on in the S-curve, when it is very unclear what the long-term prospects of a new technology may be, this can be a powerful argument. The consequence, however, may be that the company fails to build a competence in the new technology and will suffer accordingly.

In addition, Christensen argues that the commercialization of new disruptive technology often requires a radically different value chain with a completely different cost structure—a new business model. For example, it may require a different manufacturing system, a different distribution system, and different pricing options and involve very different gross margins and operating margins. Christensen argues that it is almost impossible for two distinct business models to coexist within the same organization. When they try to do that, almost inevitably the established business model will suffocate the business model associated with the disruptive technology.

The solution to this problem is to separate out the disruptive technology and place it in its own autonomous operating division. For example, during the early 1980s Hewlett Packard (HP) built a very successful laser jet printer business. Then along came ink jet technology. Some in the company believed that ink jet printers would cannibalize sales of laser jets and consequently argued that HP should not produce ink jets. Fortunately for HP, senior management at the time saw ink jet technology for what it was: a potential disruptive technology. Far from not investing in it, they allocated significant R&D funds toward its commercialization. Furthermore, when the technology was ready for market introduction, they established an autonomous ink jet division at a different geographic location with its own manufacturing, marketing, and distribution activities. They accepted that the ink jet division might take sales away from the laser jet division and decided that it was better to have an HP division cannibalize the sales of another HP division than have those sales cannibalized by another company. Happily for HP, it turns out that ink jets cannibalize sales of laser jets only on the margin and that both have profitable market niches. This felicitous outcome, however, does not detract from the message of the story: if your company is developing a potentially disruptive technology, the chances of success will be enhanced if it is placed in a stand-alone product division and given its own mandate.

Strategic Implications for New Entrants

This stream of work also holds implications for new entrants. The new entrants, or attackers, have several advantages over established enterprises. Pressures to continue the existing out-of-date business model do not hamstring new entrants, which do not have to worry about product cannibalization issues. They do not have to worry about their established customer base or relationships with established suppliers and distributors. Instead, they can focus all their energies on the opportunities offered by the new disruptive technology, ride the S-curve of technology improvement, and grow rapidly with the market for that technology. This does not mean that the new entrants have no problems to solve. They may be constrained by a lack of capital or have to manage the organizational problems associated with rapid growth; most important, they may need to find a way to take their technology from a small out-of-the-way niche into the mass market.

Perhaps one of the most important issues facing new entrants is the choice of whether to partner with an established company or go it alone in their attempt to develop and profit from a new disruptive technology. Although a new entrant may enjoy all of the advantages of the attacker, it may lack the resources required to exploit them fully. In such a case, it might want to consider forming a strategic alliance with a larger, established company to gain access to those resources. The main issues here are the same as those that we discussed earlier when examining the three strategies that companies can pursue to capture first-mover advantages: go it alone, enter into a strategic alliance, or license its technology.

Summary of Chapter

1. Technical standards are important in many high-tech industries: they guarantee compatibility, reduce confusion in the minds of customers, allow for mass production and lower costs, and reduce the risks associated with supplying complementary products.

2. Network effects and positive feedback loops often determine which standard comes to dominate a market.

3. Owning a standard can be a source of sustained competitive advantage.

4. Establishing a proprietary standard as the industry standard may require the company to win a format war against a competing and incompatible standard. Strategies for doing this include producing complementary products, leveraging killer applications, aggressive pricing and marketing, licensing the technology, and cooperating with competitors.

5. Many high-tech products are characterized by high fixed costs of development but very low or zero marginal costs of producing one extra unit of output. These cost economics create a presumption in favor of strategies that emphasize aggressive pricing to increase volume and drive down average total costs.

6. Many digital products suffer from very high piracy rates due to the low marginal costs of copying and distributing such products. Piracy can be reduced by the appropriate combination of strategy, encryption software, and vigorous defense of intellectual property rights.

7. It is very important for a first mover to develop a strategy to capitalize on first-mover advantages. A company can choose from three strategies: develop and market the technology itself, to do so jointly with another company, and license the technology to existing companies. The choice depends on the complementary assets required to capture a first-mover advantage, the height of barriers to imitation, and the capability of competitors.

8. Technological paradigm shifts occur when new technologies come along that revolutionize the structure of the industry, dramatically alter the nature of competition, and require companies to adopt new strategies in order to survive.

9. Technological paradigm shifts are more likely to occur when progress in improving the established technology is slowing due to diminishing returns and a new disruptive technology is taking root in a market niche.

10. Established companies can deal with paradigm shifts by hedging their bets with regard to technology or setting up a stand-alone division to exploit the technology.

Discussion Questions

1. What is different about high-tech industries? Were all industries once high tech?

2. Why are standards so important in many high-tech industries? What are the competitive implications of this?

3. You work for a small company that has the leading position in an embryonic market. Your boss believes that the company's future is assured because it has a 60 percent share of the market, the lowest cost structure in the industry, and the most reliable and highest-valued product. Write a memo to him outlining why his assumptions might be incorrect.

4. You are working for a small company that has developed an operating system for PCs that is faster and more stable than Microsoft's Windows operating system. What strategies might the company pursue to unseat Windows and establish its new operating system as the dominant technical standard in the industry?

5. You are a manager for a major music record label. Last year, music sales declined by 10 percent, primarily due to very high piracy rates for CDs. Your boss has asked you to develop a strategy for reducing piracy rates. What would you suggest that the company do?

Practicing Strategic Management

SMALL-GROUP EXERCISE: BURNING DVDs

Break up into groups of three to five people, and appoint one group member as a spokesperson who will communicate your findings to the class.

You are a group of managers and software engineers at a small start-up that has developed software that enables customers with PCs to copy films from one DVD to another (i.e., to "burn" DVDs).

1. How do you think that the market for this software is likely to develop? What factors might inhibit adoption of software?
2. Can you think of a strategy that your company might pursue in combination with film studios that will enable your company to increase revenues and the film companies to reduce piracy rates?

ARTICLE FILE 7

Find an example of an industry that has undergone a technological paradigm shift in recent years. What happened to the established companies as that paradigm shift unfolded?

STRATEGIC MANAGEMENT PROJECT: MODULE 7

This module requires you to analyze the industry environment in which your company is based and determine if it is vulnerable to a technological paradigm shift. With the information you have at your disposal, answer the following questions:

1. What is the dominant product technology used in the industry in which your company is based?
2. Are technical standards important in your industry? If so, what are they?
3. What are the attributes of the majority of customers purchasing the product of your company (for example, early adopters, early majority, late majority)? What does this tell you about the strategic issues that the company is likely to face in the future?
4. Did the dominant technology in your industry diffuse rapidly or slowly? What drove the speed of diffusion?
5. Where is the dominant technology in your industry on its S-curve? Are alternative competing technologies being developed that might give rise to a paradigm shift in your industry?
6. Are intellectual property rights important to your company? If so, what strategies is it adopting to protect those rights? Is it doing enough?

EXPLORING THE WEB
Visiting Kodak

Visit the web site of Kodak (**http://www.kodak.com**), and search it to find out what Kodak is doing in the area of digital photography. Use this information to answer the following questions:

1. How important do you think digital photography is in Kodak's total revenues?
2. How is this likely to change over the next decade?
3. Where is digital photography on the S-curve? Where is traditional photography? What are the implications of this comparison for Kodak?
4. Identify Kodak's competitors in (a) its traditional film business and (b) the digital photography business. What are the implications of the change in the set of competitors confronting Kodak?
5. How does the switch from traditional to digital photography change the economics of the photography business?
6. Do you think that Kodak is pursuing the correct strategies to deal with digital substitution? What do you think is the long-term outlook for Kodak's business if it continues pursuing its current strategies? Do you think the company should make some changes? If so, what?

General Task: Search the Web for information that allows you to assess the current state of competition in the market for hand-held computers such as those produced by Palm, Handspring, and Compaq. Use that information to perform an analysis of the market in the United States. Answer the following questions:

1. What is the leading standard for operating systems in this market?
2. How did this standard emerge to become the market leader?
3. How secure is this standard? Could it be supplanted by another standard over the next few years?

Closing Case

The Evolution of IBM

IBM is in many ways a remarkable organization. Founded in 1911 from the merger of two companies, the early IBM sold mechanical clocks, scales, and punch-card tabulating equipment. By 2001, it was the largest technology company on the planet with earnings of $7.7 billion on revenues of $86 billion, almost twice as much as any other technology company. In its ninety-year history, IBM has survived several paradigm shifts in technology that led to the decline and bankruptcy of many of its peers.

During the 1930s, IBM was a leader in the production of mechanical tabulators using punch-card technology. When this technology was ultimately replaced by electronic calculators and computers, many manufacturers of mechanical tabulating equipment went the way of the dinosaur. IBM, however, had begun to build capabilities in electronics during the 1930s. In 1933, it acquired a producer of electric typewriters. This led to the 1935 introduction of IBM's first electric typewriter, a technology that was to transform the typewriter industry where most incumbent enterprises sold mechanical typewriters. More important, the acquisition gave IBM access to knowledge of electronics, which it ultimately put to use elsewhere in the company. In 1947, IBM introduced its first "electronic multiplier," a calculator with electronic, as opposed to mechanical, working elements. More significant, IBM's electronic knowledge underlay its introduction in 1952 of its first production computer, the IBM 701.

In the ensuing decades, IBM rode the wave of disruptive technology. Its revolutionary System 360 computer, introduced in 1964, began to replace mechanical and simple electronic systems for performing scientific and business calculations. Its System 370 computer, introduced in 1970, solidified this trend. By the mid-1980s, IBM had emerged as the largest manufacturer of mainframe computers in the world and at the time had the dominant computing technology, with a virtual lock on the market. But by this time, a new technology was taking root that was to threaten IBM's very survival: the personal computer.

Personal computer technology was developed in the mid-1970s by a number of small start-up enterprises, including MITS and Apple. In 1980, William Lowe, the lab director at IBM's Entry Level Systems (ELS) unit in Boca Raton, Florida, pushed IBM management to give him authorization to try and develop a personal computer. Top management was initially reluctant. Its two previous attempts to introduce a PC had ended in total failure. Lowe ultimately got permission to produce a PC but with an almost unrealistic deadline of one year to complete the job. He recruited another IBM insider, Don Estridge, to head the project team. Estridge was soon persuaded that the only way to meet the deadline was for IBM to purchase off-the-shelf components, such as an Intel microprocessor and a Microsoft operating system, and to adopt an open systems design, where technical specifications were published. This would allow developers to write software applications that would run on the PC. Strategically, this approach represented a radical departure for IBM, which had tended to make the majority of its own components and software in-house and had adopted a closed systems approach. The countercultural strategy was possible only because the ELS unit was outside IBM's business mainstream, geographically separated from the company's center of operations, staffed by a maverick group of engineers and managers, and protected from IBM's bureaucracy by its CEO, Frank Cary.

Introduced in August 1981, the IBM PC was a dramatic success. However, the use of open systems architecture and off-the-shelf components soon gave rise to a thriving industry of companies that made IBM-compatible machines, or clones, such as Compaq Computer. By the mid-1980s, these clone makers were starting to eat into IBM's market share. Moreover, PC architecture based on an Intel microprocessor and Microsoft operating system went on to revolutionize the computer industry. In many companies, client-server systems based on PC technology replaced mainframe and midrange computers. As this occurred, sales of IBM mainframes slumped, and by 1993 IBM was awash in red ink. It lost $8 billion on shrinking sales as the PC technology it had given birth to cannibalized its profitable mainframe computers. Many observers were already writing IBM's obituary.

At this juncture, Lou Gerstner became CEO. A former management consultant and CEO of the tobacco company R. J. Reynolds with no computer industry experience, most observers thought that Gerstner, who knew little about computing technology, was poorly equipped to be IBM's CEO. However, Gerstner soon realized that IBM's computer business was rapidly becoming commoditized. Having given up control over microprocessor technology to Intel and software to Microsoft, IBM had no proprietary advantage. His strategy was to take IBM out of the commoditization game by emphasizing its service business. He believed that if IBM could solve the information technology problems of large corporations, the company would win big sales with recurring sales revenues spread out over years and margins that were a lot better than those IBM could get by competing only at the product level.

Not only has this strategy been very successful, it has given IBM a way to exploit the latest disruptive technology, the Internet. As Internet-centric computing has grown in importance, IBM has reinvented itself as a dominant provider of e-business solutions and services. Now if a company wishes to establish an intranet or use the Internet to execute business transactions, IBM is one of the vendors it turns to first. Although IBM still produces and sells its own computer hardware, it will now recommend the hardware of other companies if it suits the clients' needs better. It has become an e-business solutions company, ideally positioning itself to profit from the spread of web-based technology into every nook and cranny of the modern business corporation.

Case Discussion Questions

1. How many paradigm shifts has IBM survived in its history?

2. Describe how IBM was able to survive each of these paradigm shifts.

3. What does the history of IBM tell you about the strategies that incumbent companies must pursue to survive paradigm shifts?

4. In many ways, the IBM PC launched the personal computer into the mass market. How was a large incumbent enterprise able to develop what was a revolutionary product?

5. With the benefit of hindsight, could IBM have done anything different in the development of the IBM PC that would have not allowed control over the dominant standard in the market to be captured by Microsoft and Intel?

Sources: D. Kirkpatrick, "The Future of IBM," *Fortune,* February 18, 2002, pp. 60–68. P. Freiberger and M. Swaine, *Fire in the Valley* (New York: McGraw-Hill, 2000). "Follow That," *Economist,* February 2, 2002, p. 64. History of IBM from www.ibm.com.

9B11M006

THE CHINESE FIREWORKS INDUSTRY

Ruihua Jiang wrote this case under the supervision of Professor Paul W. Beamish solely to provide material for class discussion. The authors do not intend to illustrate either effective or ineffective handling of a managerial situation. The authors may have disguised certain names and other identifying information to protect confidentiality.

Version: 2014-07-18

In February 2009, Jerry Yu was spending the Chinese New Year holidays in Liuyang (lee-ou-yang), a city known as "the home of firecrackers and fireworks," located in Hunan Province in China. Jerry was an ABC (America-Born-Chinese). With an MBA, he was running a small family-owned chain of gift stores in Brooklyn, New York. Liuyang was his mother's hometown. During his visit, his relatives invited him to invest in a fireworks factory that was owned by a village. Mr. Yu had been impressed by the extravagant fireworks shows he had seen during the festival; however, he wanted to assess how attractive the Chinese fireworks industry was before he even looked at the financial details of the factory.

HISTORY OF FIREWORKS AND FIRECRACKERS

Fireworks referred to any devices designed to produce visual or audible effects through combustion or explosion. The art of making fireworks was formally known as pyrotechnics. Firecrackers were a specific kind of fireworks, usually in the form of a noisemaking cylinder. Firecrackers were often strung together and fused consecutively, a staple of Chinese New Year celebrations, weddings, grand openings, births, deaths and other ceremonial occasions.

The main ingredients of fireworks had remained almost the same over the past thousand years: 75 parts-by-weight potassium nitrate, 15 parts charcoal and 10 parts sulfur. It burned briskly when lighted, but did not erupt or make any noise. When it was found that a projectile could be thrust out of a barrel by keeping the powder at one end and igniting it, black powder became known as gunpowder. Today, smokeless powder has replaced black powder as the propellant in modern weaponry, but black powder remains a main ingredient in fireworks, both as a propellant and as a bursting charge.

It was generally believed that the Chinese were the first makers of fireworks. The Chinese made war rockets and explosives as early as the sixth century. One legend said that a Chinese cook, while toiling in a field kitchen, happened to mix together sulfur, charcoal and saltpetre, and noticed that the pile burned with a combustible force when ignited. He further discovered that when these ingredients were enclosed in a length of bamboo sealed at both ends, it would explode rather than burn, producing a loud crack. This was the origin of firecrackers. In fact, the Chinese word for firecrackers — *bao-zhu* — literally means "exploded bamboo."

The loud reports and burning fires of firecrackers and fireworks were found to be perfect for frightening off evil spirits and celebrating good news at various occasions. For more than a thousand years, the Chinese had been seeing off past years and welcoming in new ones by firing firecrackers.

Fireworks made their way first to Arabia in the seventh century, then to Europe sometime in the middle of the 13th century. By the 15th century, fireworks were widely used for religious festivals and public entertainment. Most of the early pyrotechnicians in Europe were Italians. Even today, the best-known names in the European and American fireworks industry were Italian in origin. From the 16th to the 18th century, Italy and Germany were the two best known areas in the European continent for fireworks displays.

In 1777, the United States used fireworks in its first Independence Day celebration, and fireworks have become closely associated with July Fourth celebrations ever since.

Up until the 1830s, the colors of the early fireworks were limited, but by 2009, there were six basic colors used in fireworks.

LIUYANG — THE HOMETOWN OF FIRECRACKERS AND FIREWORKS

According to historical records in China, firecrackers and fireworks "emerged during the Tang dynasty (618-907 AD), flourished during the Song Dynasty (960-1279 AD), and originated in Liuyang." For more than 1,000 years, Liuyang had been known as the "hometown of firecrackers and fireworks of China," a title that was officially conferred to Liuyang by the State Council of China in 1995. As early as 1723, Liuyang fireworks were chosen as official tributes to the imperial family and were sold all over the country. Exports started early: by 1875, firecrackers and fireworks were being shipped to Japan, Korea, India, Iran, Russia, Australia, England, the U.S., and other countries. In China, the name Liuyang had become almost synonymous with firecrackers and fireworks. Liuyang-made firecrackers and fireworks won numerous awards over its long history of fireworks making.

The long history and tradition had made fireworks more than just a livelihood for the Liuyang people. Almost every native person in the area knew something about fireworks making, or had actually made firecrackers or fireworks in their lifetime. As a result, Liuyang claimed an impressive pool of skilled labor. Firecrackers and fireworks had become the pillar industry of Liuyang, accounting for nearly 50 per cent of all jobs or about one-third of the total population in the Liuyang District (including Liuyang City and the surrounding counties). In 2008, Liuyang claimed 2,702 fireworks manufacturers with an additional 2,144 in the surrounding area. In total, there were 6,458 fireworks producers in China. While there has been some trend towards consolidation in the industry, most factories were still owned either by villages or families. Among them, about a dozen or so were medium to large factories with employment between 100 to 500 workers. The rest were small workshops employing anywhere from 10 to 50 people, depending on market demand.

Liuyang was the top fireworks exporter in the world, making up 60 per cent of global production. The trademarked brand "Red Lantern" had become well known to fireworks-lovers around the world. China now accounted for 89 per cent of worldwide fireworks exports with the vast majority of that coming from Liuyang. In addition, over the past ten years, China had become the largest market for fireworks. The ratio of domestic use to exports was 6:4, and Chinese imports of fireworks were negligible.

The increase in demand in the Chinese market had only intensified the competition. All new demand was more than met by the Chinese fireworks industry. Thus, instead of seeing increased margins, the profit margins for many small manufacturers had shrunk over the past decade. In order to make up the difference, manufacturers were cutting corners. However, some of these cost cutting efforts came at the expense of safety. A 2007 factory explosion that left 11 workers dead was blamed primarily on decreased safety standards, which were blamed on a lack of money due to cut throat competition. In response, the government and company officials from Luiyang and surrounding areas agreed to regulate the price of fireworks with the hope of increasing profit margins. With higher profit margins, company officials vowed to increase workers safety.

The Product

Fireworks could be classified into two categories: display fireworks and consumer fireworks. The display fireworks, such as aerial shells, maroons, and large Roman candles, were meant for professional (usually licensed) pyrotechnicians to fire during large public display shows. They were devices that were designed to produce certain visual or audio effect at a greater height above the ground than the consumer fireworks, which the general public could purchase in convenience stores and enjoy in their own backyards. Display fireworks were known as Explosives 1.3 (Class B prior to 1991) in the U.S. The consumer fireworks belonged to Explosives 1.4 (Class C prior to 1991). The difference lay mainly in the amount of explosive components contained in the product. Canada had a similar classification system. In the U.K., it was more carefully divided into four categories: indoor fireworks; garden fireworks; display fireworks; and display fireworks for professionals only.

There were many varieties of fireworks. Liuyang made 13 different types with more than 3,000 varieties. The major types included fountains, rockets, hand-held novelties, nail and hanging wheels, ground-spinning novelties, jumping novelties, floral shells, parachutes and firecrackers.

Historically, firecrackers made up 90 per cent of the total production and sales. Over the past 50 years or so, however, there had been a shift away from firecrackers to fireworks. In 2009, firecrackers made up less than 20 per cent of the total sales. The skill levels of fireworks-making had been greatly improved. For instance, the old-day fireworks could reach no more than 20 metres into the sky, while the new ones could go as high as 400 metres.

Not much had changed in fireworks-making. Over the last few decades, numerous novelties were added to the fireworks family. However, innovation had never reached beyond product variations. The ingredients had remained more or less the same. The process technology had not changed much either, although some manual processes, such as cutting the paper, rolling the cylinders, mixing powder, and stringing the cylinders could now be done by machines.

Safety Issues

The fact that fireworks were made with gunpowder and listed under explosives brought about the issue of safety. Numerous accidents related with fireworks had resulted in tragic human injuries and considerable property damages. As a result, fireworks had become heavily regulated in most countries.

According to the manufacturers, fireworks were the most dangerous during the production process. Powder mixing and powder filling, in turn, were the two most dangerous procedures. The workers had to abide by strict safety measures. Even a tiny spark caused by the dropping of a tool on the floor or the dragging of a chair could start a major explosion. The quality of the ingredients was also of significant importance. Impure ingredients could greatly increase the possibility of accidents. In Liuyang, almost every year, there would be one or more accidents that resulted in deaths and damages. With an ever increasing number of firms entering the industry, safety was an ongoing concern.

Once the fireworks were made, they were relatively safe to transport and store. Even in firing, good quality fireworks rarely caused any problems if everything was done properly. Most of the fireworks-related accidents occurred during private parties or street displays, and quite often involved children playing with fireworks that needed to be handled by adults, or adults firing shells that required professional expertise. Most accidents were linked to consumer backyard events rather than to public displays.

According to the United States Consumer Products Safety Commission's (CPSC) data, injuries related to fireworks had declined substantially, even though their use had increased (see Exhibit 2). For 2009, there were an estimated 5,244 fireworks-related injuries, 30 per cent of which were caused by firecrackers and bottle rockets. Of all the injuries related to firecrackers and fireworks, most were treated in the emergency department. Eight per cent of patients had to be admitted to hospital, and 7 people died due to sustained injuries.

Children from ages five to 14 were the most frequently involved in fireworks-related injuries. However, fireworks were not the only consumer product that might cause injuries to this age group. According to a 2008 CPSC Injury Surveillance Report, fireworks were actually safer than swing sets and baseballs. However, fireworks-related injuries were usually the most dramatic and the most widely publicized accidents, which partly explained the fact that fireworks was the only category among the products listed in Exhibit 3, for which prohibition, instead of education and adult supervision, was often urged.

In the United States, multiple government agencies were involved in regulating fireworks. The Bureau of Alcohol Tobacco and Firearms (BATF) controlled the manufacture, storage, sales and distribution of explosives, i.e., Class B fireworks. The CPSC regulated Class C consumer fireworks, and the Department of Transportation dealt with the transportation of fireworks. Although at the federal level, fireworks and firecrackers were allowed as long as the safety features were up to the standard, local governments would have their own different regulations regarding fireworks consumption. Out of the 50 states, one would allow only novelty fireworks, 5 had banned all consumer fireworks but allowed professional pyrotechnics, and 4 allowed customers only wire or wood stick sparklers and other novelty items. However, the remaining 40 would allow essentially all consumer fireworks. For display fireworks, permits would have to be obtained from federal and local authorities and fire departments.

All legal consumer fireworks offered for sale in the United States had been tested for stability by the Bureau of Explosives and approved for transportation by the U.S. Department of Transportation. Because of the limited amount of pyrotechnic composition permitted in each individual unit, consumer fireworks would not ignite spontaneously during storage, nor would they mass-explode during a fire. Therefore, no special storage was required.

In most of Europe, similar regulations were in place for safety considerations, only the requirements were regarded as less stringent. In Canada, however, regulations were extremely restrictive. However, over the past decade Chinese fireworks companies had made great strides in the Canadian market. In 1999, there were no Chinese companies allowed to sell fireworks in Canada. By 2009, over 75% of all fireworks imports to Canada were from China.

THE FIRECRACKERS AND FIREWORKS INDUSTRY IN CHINA

The firecrackers and fireworks industry in China was dominated by small family-owned-and-operated workshops. It was essentially a low-tech, highly labor-intensive industry. After 1949, government-run factories replaced the family-owned workshops. The increased scale and government funds made possible the automation of some processes. However, the key processes like installing powder, mixing color ingredients, and putting in fuses, were still manually done by skilled workers.

The factories themselves were made up of small workshops that stood away from each other, so that in case of an accident the whole factory would not explode. For the same safety consideration, the workshops were usually located near a water source and in sparsely populated rural areas, to reduce the noise and explosion hazard.

After the reform towards a market economy started in 1979, most of the factories were broken up and became family-run units of production again. It was hoped that this privatization might help to motivate people to increase their productivity and raise output. However, this move also served to restrict further technological innovations. There were hardly any research and development (R&D) facilities, nor human and capital resources allocated to R&D in most fireworks companies. The few resources that were available were all spent on product varieties. Even in Liuyang, out of the 400,000 or so people working in the industry, very few were engineers with advanced professional training.

In response, the Hunan and other local governments began initiatives aimed at upgrading the traditional fireworks industry. Substantial amounts of money were spent on R&D. The Liuyang Firecrackers and Fireworks Authority reported that they had spent RMB 2,000 million in projects with the Beijing University of Technology and the Nanjing University of Science. Among these initiatives were environmentally friendly fireworks, which used cold flame fireworks technology.

The majority of the manufacturing workers were regular farmers who had learned how to make fireworks just by watching and following their elders. They would come to work in fireworks workshops when there were jobs to be done, and return to till their fields if there were none. In Liuyang, for instance, few factories operated year-round. Most workshops would operate as orders came in. Since the fireworks-making communities were very concentrated geographically and had lasted for generations, only a few places (like Liuyang) could claim a large pool of skilled fireworks-makers.

Although Liuyang was by far the most well-known place for making fireworks in China, it faced increasing competition within the country. Also located in Hunan Province, Liling was another major manufacturing community of fireworks. Liling fireworks did not enjoy the same reputation and variety as Liuyang products, but they were fierce in price competition. In the neighboring Jiangxi Province, Pingxiang and Wanzai fireworks had become strong competitors both in price and quality, especially on the low- and medium-priced market. In the high-end product market, especially in large-type display fireworks and export market, Dongguan in Guangdong Province, had taken advantage of its closeness to Hong Kong and more sophisticated management and marketing practices, and snatched market share from Liuyang. By 2009, however, more than one third of all firms and 60 per cent of Chinese production remained in Luiyang.

The initial capital requirement for starting a fireworks-manufacturing facility was relatively low. To set up a factory with the necessary equipment for making large display shells would require around RMB1,250,000.[1] However, setting up a small family workshop making consumer firecrackers and fireworks would require less than RMB125,000. Consequently, the number of small manufacturers mushroomed after the government started to encourage private business ventures.

While labor costs in the area were still low, they were steadily increasing. As a result of Chinese economic growth, wages had almost doubled over the past 5 years. This was in part because many workers were moving into less dangerous occupations. Skilled workers engaged in major processes would earn an average of RMB1,200 to RMB1,800 per month. A non-skilled worker would be paid only RMB500 to RMB700 every month. In larger factories, labor costs were between 20 and 30 per cent of total costs.

The main raw materials for fireworks were gunpowder, color ingredients, paper, fuse and clay soil. None would be difficult to procure. However, because of the growth in the Chinese domestic fireworks market, costs of raw materials were steadily rising. Another possible problem in supply was quality. Major manufacturers would usually establish long-term relationships with their suppliers to guarantee the quality of the materials. The small workshops would often go with the lowest prices, sometimes at the cost of quality, which could lead to fatal results.

The number of small companies intensified competition. The private workshops were flexible and quick in responding to market demand. They did not entail much administrative cost. Compared to government-owned or some collectively-owned factories, they did incur the costs of providing health care, retirement benefits and housing. They usually did not do any product research or design. Oblivious to intellectual property protection, they would copy any popular product design and sell it for much less. The resulting price drop had become a serious problem for the whole industry. As the profit margin kept shrinking, some workshops would hire cheap unskilled workers, and use cheap equipment and raw materials to cut down on cost. The results could be disastrous.

THE DOMESTIC MARKET

Firecrackers and fireworks had long been an integral part of any ceremonies held in China. Until recently, demand had been stable, but had risen in the past three decades because of increased economic development and living standards. Economically, market reform and unprecedented growth had given rise to the daily appearance of multitudes of new companies and new stores. As people's income level and living standards kept rising, fancier and pricier fireworks and firecrackers were desired over the cheap simple firecrackers, thereby creating more profit opportunities for fireworks manufacturers. Almost every household would spend at least a couple of hundred RMB on firecrackers and fireworks during the Spring Festival.

However, during the 1990s, increased concerns over environmental pollution and safety of human life and property led more and more cities to regulate the consumption of fireworks and firecrackers. Every year, high profile fireworks-related accidents were reported and emphasized on mass media before and after the traditional Spring Festival. Some articles even condemned firecrackers and fireworks as an old, uncivilized convention that created only noise, pollution and accidents. In a wave of regulations, city after city passed administrative laws regarding the use of fireworks. By 1998, one-third of the cities in China had completely banned the use of firecrackers and fireworks. Another one-third only allowed fireworks in designated places. This led to a decline in domestic market demand.

---

[1] In 2009, the exchange rate was around 6.60 yuan per US$1.00.

However, all this began to change in the mid 2000s. Demand began to soar when Beijing lifted a 12-year ban on fireworks in 2005. Other cities followed suit. In 2005, 106 cities eased restrictions on fireworks; in 2006 another 54 cities eased restrictions. This was followed by 40 cities in 2007 and another 79 cities in 2009. All this lead to an explosion in the Chinese domestic fireworks market.

In the meantime, domestic competition grew intensely. The reform towards a market economy made it possible for numerous family-run workshops to appear. They competed mainly on price. Almost every province had some fireworks-making workshops or factories, many set up and run with the help of skilled workers who had migrated from Liuyang. These small establishments usually were located in rural, underdeveloped areas where labor cost was low. The manufacturing was done manually, sometimes without safety measures, using cheap raw materials and simplified techniques. The products were sold locally at low prices, making it difficult for Liuyang fireworks to sell in those areas. To make things worse, these products would often copy any new or popular product designs coming out of Liuyang or other traditional fireworks communities, even using their very brand names.

In the past, fireworks were sold through the government-run general merchandise companies. Eventually, private dealers took over a large part of the business. Overall, the distribution system was rather fragmented. The old government-run channels were not very effective, especially for general merchandise. In the new distribution channels, wholesale dealers would get shipments directly from the manufacturers, and then resell to street peddlers and convenience stores.

In the countryside, wholesale markets would appear in focal townships, with wholesale dealers and agents of the manufacturers setting up booths promoting their products. Small peddlers in the surrounding areas would get supplies from the market and then sell them in small towns or villages. The wholesale markets in China were important outlets for distributing general merchandise like fireworks.

In the display fireworks market, the buyers were often central and local governments, who would purchase the product for public shows on national holidays or special celebrations. Obviously, a local company would have advantages in supplying to local government in its area. Large fireworks shows usually would use invited bidding to decide on suppliers. The amount of fireworks used could range from RMB100,000 to several million yuan, depending on the scale of a fireworks show.

Account receivables and bad debt control was a problem not just for fireworks manufacturers, but for all businesses in China. Bad debts and lack of respect for business contracts had created a credit crisis in China. The bad debt problem greatly increased transaction costs, slowed down the cash turnover, and had become a headache for fireworks manufacturers. Some had chosen to withdraw from selling in the domestic market, although the profit margin was higher than in the export market.

Legal restrictions, local protectionism, cutthroat price competition, hard-to-penetrate distribution channels and bad debt were impacting negatively on the domestic sales of Liuyang fireworks. In 1997, seeing the decline of its fireworks sales, Liuyang Firecrackers and Fireworks Industry Department, the government agency in charge of the overall development of the pillar industry, decided to start an offensive strategy. First, it opened local offices in most of the 29 provinces, major cities and regions to promote Liuyang fireworks. Second, it regulated the prices that Liuyang fireworks companies could quote and sell in export sales. Third, it resorted to a government-to-government relationship in order to secure contracts for large public fireworks displays in each province. One year after introducing the offensive strategy, Liuyang fireworks sales had increased. By 2009, they controlled an estimated 60 per cent of the global market.

Over the next ten years, many legal restrictions were lifted. One of the most notable legal restrictions to be eased was foreign direct investment. With huge growth in both the Chinese domestic market and with China nearing a virtual lock on export market, the Chinese Fireworks industry had become a magnet for foreign investors. Liuyang remained the center of the Chinese fireworks industry and an attractive region for foreigners and foreign firms looking at controlling the entire fireworks value chain.

THE EXPORT MARKET

Since the opening of the Chinese economy in 1979, exporting had become a major market for the Chinese fireworks industry. As one of the most celebrated products out of China, export sales of fireworks had risen dramatically between 1978 and 2009. According to independent research, the recorded exports of firecrackers and fireworks reached US$675 million in 2009. This was up from an estimated US$143 million in 1994.

The products from China were rich in variety and low in price, but also had a lower reputation in quality control, packaging and timing control, compared to the products made in Japan and Korea. China-made fireworks also would wholesale for much lower prices, usually 80 per cent lower than similar products made in Japan or Korea.

There had been little overall co-ordination of export sales. As more and more companies were allowed to export directly, competition kept intensifying and the profit margins on export sales kept slipping. As a result, underpricing each other became a common practice. Therefore, despite its dominant share of the world market, the Chinese fireworks export industry enjoyed limited profitability. The export price of Chinese fireworks was between one-fifth and one-third the wholesale price in the United States.

The importers enjoyed a high markup even after paying the 2.4 per cent U.S. import duty. Of course, the importers had to absorb the cost of getting permits, shipping, storing and carrying the inventory for three to four months before making the sales. This gap pushed both domestic and foreign companies to find ways to control more of the value chain from production to retail.

Besides suffering from low profit margin, the Chinese fireworks makers were also risking losing their brand identities. Given the low cost and reasonably good quality of the Chinese fireworks, many large fireworks manufacturers and dealers in the West started to outsource the making of their brand-name fireworks. Failing to see the importance of brand equity, the Chinese fireworks manufacturers were sometimes reduced to mere manufacturing outfits for foreign companies, gradually losing their own brands. There were also fireworks merchants in Korea, Japan or Spain, who would buy the products from China, and then repackage them, or replace the fuses with better quality ones, then resell them for much higher prices.

The export market was usually divided into five blocks: Southeast Asia, North America, Europe, South America and the rest of the world. The most popular market had been Europe, where the regulations on fireworks were less stringent, and orders were of larger quantities and better prices. The United States was considered a tough market because of complex regulations and high competition, nevertheless a necessary one if a company wanted to remain a viable world-player. While in the past, the Canadian market was virtually closed to the Chinese fireworks due to its regulations, by 2009 Chinese imports dominated the entire Canadian market.

The foreign importers were powerful buyers for several reasons. First, they were very well informed, both through past dealings with China and the Internet. Second, they were able to hire agents who were very familiar with the industry in China. Third, they could deal directly with the factories that were willing to offer lower prices. Fourth, there were basically no switching costs, so they could play the suppliers against each other.

The diversity of the cultures in the destination countries greatly reduced the seasonality of the fireworks production and sales. As a result, orders evened out throughout the year. However, the peak season was still towards the end of the year. For the U.S., it was before July 4. Usually, the importers would receive the shipment two or three months beforehand. While the U.S. was still China's major export market for fireworks, other countries were also importing large quantities of Chinese made fireworks (see Exhibit 4).

The Internet had become a marketing outlet for Chinese fireworks. 20 per cent to 25 per cent of the worldwide sales were through the Internet. However, export sales were still made mainly through foreign trade companies or agents.

In recent years, foreign investments were also funneled into the fireworks industry. In Liuyang, four of the large fireworks factories had foreign investments, made mainly by the fireworks trading companies in Hong Kong. In 2009, the Liuyang Fireworks Company was listed on the Toronto Stock Exchange (TSE), a first for a Chinese fireworks manufacturer.

The Future of the Fireworks Industry in China

The managers of the Chinese fireworks companies that Jerry talked to expressed mixed feelings towards the future outlook of their industry. One pessimistic view was that fierce competition and more stringent safety regulations were killing the industry. As the Chinese economy advanced, the government was forcing more manufacturing regulations onto firms that were driving up costs. Moreover, as people became more environmentally-conscious and more distracted by the endless diversities of modern entertainment, traditional celebrations using firecrackers and fireworks would die a gradual death. As to the function of attracting public attention for promotional purposes, fireworks also faced challenges from new technologies, such as laser beams combined with sound effects.

In fact, "make-believe firecrackers" already appeared as substitutes in China. These were made of red plastic tubes strung together like firecrackers with electric bulbs installed inside the tubes. When the power was turned on, the lights would emit sparks, accompanied by crackling reports that sounded like firecrackers. These were being used at weddings and grand openings in cities where firecrackers and fireworks were banned. More interesting substitutes were spotted at some weddings in Beijing, where people paved the road with little red balloons, and made the limousine carrying the bride and groom run over the balloons to make explosive cracking sounds as well as leave behind red bits and pieces of debris. Also, more and more young couples were getting married in western styles, in a church or a scenic green meadow outdoors, where serene and quiet happiness prevailed over the traditional noisy way of celebrating. Therefore, some managers believed that firecrackers and fireworks were doomed to fade off into history.

The more optimistic view, however, was that the industry would not die at all. If the right moves were made by the industry, it could even grow. Some said that tradition would not die so easily. It was in their national character for the Chinese to celebrate with an atmosphere of noisy happiness. Moreover, even in the West, the popularity of fireworks was not suffering from all the regulations. No real substitutes could replace fireworks, which combined the sensual pleasures of visual, audio and emotional stimuli. For instance, the U.S. Congressional resolution in 1963 to use bells to replace fireworks in celebrating Independence Day never really caught on.

Fireworks were also being combined with modern technologies like laser beams, computerized firing and musical accompaniment to make the appeal of fireworks more irresistible. The safety problem was not really as serious as people were made to believe, and would only improve with new technological innovations like smokeless fireworks. With the success of the fireworks displays at the Beijing Olympics, China's brand as a world class fireworks producer was on the rise. With better management practices, perhaps margins could be increased.

However, both sides agreed that the Chinese fireworks industry would have to change its strategy, especially in international competition, to stay a viable and profitable player.

THE DECISION

While the Liuyang fireworks industry dominated the worldwide industry, Jerry had to decide whether he should invest in the industry. If he did invest, what was the best way to capitalize on the potential that remained unexploited in this industry? He wondered whether he could apply the industry analysis framework he had studied in his MBA program.

Exhibit 1

CHINA & LIUYANG FIRECRACKERS AND FIREWORKS:
TOTAL REVENUE
(US$000)

	2007	2009
Total Revenue Domestic (estimated)		
All China	742,395	1,009,757
Liuyang	450,000	757,500
Total Revenue Exports		
All China	494,930	673,171
Liuyang	300,000	505,000
Total Revenue (estimated)		
All China	1,237,325	1,682,928
Liuyang	750,000	1,262,500

Sources: International Fireworks Association;
          ICON Group Ltd "The World Market for Fireworks: A 2009 Global Trade Perspective

Notes:
  1. Domestic Revenue estimate based on a 6:4 domestic to export ratio as reported by
      http://www.articlesbase.com.
  2. Alternative sources put the Chinese domestic market much higher.
  3. 2009 data and 2007 data are from different sources. Caution should be used when making
      comparisons. Growth rates of 15 to 18 per cent per year have been reported by other news
      sources (especially: http://www.newsreelnetwork.com)

Exhibit 2

TOTAL FIREWORKS CONSUMPTION AND ESTIMATED FIREWORKS-RELATED INJURIES IN U.S.: 2000 TO 2008

Year	Fireworks Consumption, Millions of Pounds	Estimated Fireworks-Related Injuries	Injuries per 100,000 Pounds
2000	152.6	11,000	7.2
2001	161.6	9,500	5.8
2002	190.1	8,800	4.6
2003	220.8	9,700	4.4
2004	236.2	9,600	4.1
2005	281.5	10,800	3.8
2006	278.2	9,200	3.3
2007	265.5	9,800	3.7
2008	213.2	7,000	3.3

Source: American Pyrotechnics Association.

Exhibit 3

ESTIMATED EMERGENCY ROOM TREATMENT PER 100,000 YOUTHS (AGES 5 TO 14) FROM OUTDOOR ACTIVITIES (JUNE 22 TO JULY 22, 2008)

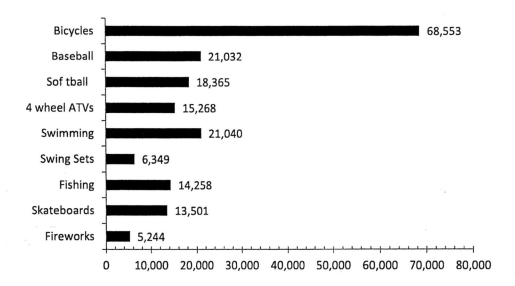

Source: American Pyrotechnics Association
As cited from the CPSC National Injury Information Clearinghouse

Exhibit 4

FIREWORKS EXPORTS FROM CHINA, 2009

Country of Destination	Rank	Value (000 US$)	% Share	Cumulative %
United States	1	301,500	44.8	44.8
Germany	2	83,553	12.4	57.2
United Kingdom	3	33,645	5.0	62.2
The Netherlands	4	32,586	4.8	67.0
Japan	5	26,764	4.0	71.0
Russia	6	16,157	2.4	73.4
Italy	7	15,967	2.4	75.8
France	8	13,574	2.0	77.8
Spain	9	13,009	1.9	79.7
Denmark	10	9,935	1.5	81.2
Canada	11	9,817	1.5	82.7
Poland	12	9,580	1.4	84.1
Taiwan	13	8,130	1.2	85.3
Finland	14	6,002	0.9	86.2
South Africa	15	5,623	0.8	87.0
Austria	16	5,488	0.8	87.8
Ukraine	17	5,445	0.8	88.7
Sweden	18	4,868	0.7	89.4
Albania	19	4,835	0.7	90.1
Argentina	20	4,793	0.7	90.8
Turkey	21	4,592	0.7	91.5
Belgium	22	4,583	0.7	92.2
Norway	23	4,336	0.6	92.8
Czech Republic	24	4,312	0.6	93.5
Venezuela	25	4,257	0.6	94.1
New Zealand	26	4,024	0.6	94.7
Switzerland	27	3,316	0.5	95.2
South Korea	28	3,104	0.5	95.6
Thailand	29	2,720	0.4	96.0
Indonesia	30	1,925	0.3	96.3
Other	31	24,731	3.7	100.0
Total		**673,171**	**100.00**	**100.00**

Source: Professor Philip M. Parker, INSEAD, copyright © 2009, www.icongrouponline.com

H A R V A R D | B U S I N E S S | S C H O O L

9-803-133
REV: MARCH 11, 2003

JAMES L. HESKETT

Southwest Airlines 2002: An Industry Under Siege

Amid Crippled Rivals, Southwest Again Tries To Spread Its Wings; Low-Fare Airline Maintains Service, Mulls Expansion In Risky Bid for Traffic
> —Front Page Headline, *The Wall Street Journal*, October 11, 2001

The Age of "Wal-Mart" Airlines Crunches the Biggest Carriers; Low-Cost Rivals Win Converts As Business Travelers Seek Alternatives to Lofty Fares
> —Front Page Headline, *The Wall Street Journal*, June 18, 2002

Vaunted Southwest Slips In On-Time Performance; Airline Famous for Reliability Now Ranks Next-to-Last
> —Page D1 Headline, *The Wall Street Journal*, September 25, 2002

Having weathered an unimaginable series of events during the past 15 months, the top management team at Southwest Airlines engaged in a series of discussions late in 2002 intended to insure sound strategic decisions in the face of industry setbacks, volatile responses on the part of competitors, the preservation of a culture formed around a charismatic founder/leader who had turned over the CEO's job to a successor, and a series of government directives that made it increasingly difficult for Southwest to implement an operating strategy that had differentiated it from its competition. As Colleen Barrett, president and chief operating officer, put it at one gathering of the top management team, "Recent events have made it increasingly difficult to live up to the promise to customers in our ads that 'You are now free to move about the country.'"

Changes in the airline operating environment after the terrorist attacks of September 11, 2001 were thought by some on Southwest's management team to make it more difficult for the airline to maintain its distinctive competitive position. For example, industry bailout efforts by Congress were intended to help Southwest's competitors that were in the worst financial condition. The need to respond to constantly changing security directives made it harder for employees to create and convey the Southwest SPIRIT. More recently, Southwest's organization had increased efforts to maintain its relatively high on-time arrival performance levels while its competitors' levels had risen. Southwest's managers attributed this largely to the addition of time to competitors' flight schedules, but it was creating the perception that Southwest's service levels were declining in relation to those of its competitors.

A series of important management decisions had positioned Southwest to resume its pre-9/11 growth. Just what form that growth might take was subject to discussion.

The Southwest Story

Southwest Airlines was founded in 1967 by Rollin King and Herb Kelleher in response to a need for increased capacity on major travel routes between major Texas cities. Although the routes were served by large "through" carriers such as American Airlines and Braniff International, often there were insufficient seats on flights making intermediate stops in Texas while arriving from cities outside Texas or departing for destinations outside the state. Because of the demand for seats on the intrastate legs of those flights, fares were high.

The Founding Strategy

Because federal regulation of the airline industry made it difficult to start an airline providing interstate service, Southwest's founders decided to create an intrastate carrier connecting Dallas, Houston, and San Antonio, Texas, roughly an hour's flying time apart from one another. Their strategy was centered around costs low enough to enable Southwest to establish fares below the cost of driving a vehicle over the same route. With three new Boeing 737s bought at favorable prices because of overproduction, Southwest finally flew its first flights on June 18, 1971 on two legs of what would become a triangular route connecting the three metro areas. Based at Love Field in Dallas and with a need to get attention, the airline's new president, Lamar Muse, adopted the "love" theme in executing its strategy. As a result, drinks served on board were called "love potions," ticket machines were called "love machines," and cabin "hostesses" (there were no males at that time) were selected for their striking appearance and dressed in suits with "hot pants" and boots (the fashion rage at the time). The hostesses were featured in what today would be called highly sexist ads extolling the distinctive features of the airline, such as stewardesses with seductive voices intoning "what you get at Southwest is me."

Southwest's point-to-point service enabled it to achieve high levels of on-time service. Its frequent departures enabled passengers to catch a later flight if they happened to miss one, a feature valued by frequent business fliers to whom Southwest hoped to cater. And its selection of older, less congested airports located more conveniently for business travelers allowed Southwest to achieve faster turnaround times at lower costs.

To achieve frequent departures with just four planes and three cities, turnaround times had to be minimized. This required that employees be given the latitude to do whatever might be necessary to get a plane turned around in the targeted time of 15 minutes; thus, early union contract job descriptions were negotiated with the open-ended clause "and whatever else might be needed to perform the service," a practice that remained in succeeding years.

All of this was done with an emphasis on fun for employees and travelers. Ground and in-flight personnel were encouraged to be creative in the way they delivered required announcements to passengers. Some sang the messages; others delivered them in dialect (such as an Arnold Schwarzenegger-like "You vill sit back. You vill relax. You vill enjoy this flight. Hasta la vista, baby") or in Donald Duck-speak. On early flights, passengers who could produce the largest holes in their socks were recognized and rewarded. In-flight contests were conducted to see how many passengers could be fitted into the bathroom at one time. And holidays were celebrated with costumes and giveaways. This emphasized the selection of employees who could be empathetic and bring pleasing personalities to the job.

Competitive Response

Southwest's principal competitors, Braniff International Airways and Trans Texas Airways (later Texas International Airlines), responded immediately. They first asked the Texas courts to enjoin issuance of Southwest's intrastate operating certificate. Then they lobbied and litigated to get the local and federal government (and courts) to force Southwest to abandon Love Field near downtown Dallas and move with other airlines to the newly opened Dallas-Fort Worth International Airport much farther from downtown Dallas. On yet another front, they initiated low-price fare "sales" intended to make it difficult for Southwest to get a foothold in the market. They failed on all three initiatives.

In one pivotal incident, on February 1, 1973, before Southwest had achieved profitability, Braniff International initiated a 60-day "half-price sale" of tickets between Dallas and Houston, offering tickets at $13 (substantially below the full cost of the service) as opposed to Southwest's $26 fare. With little knowledge of whether the sale would be extended until Southwest might be forced to discontinue service, Southwest's management countered with an ad proclaiming that "nobody's going to shoot Southwest out of the sky for a lousy $13" and offering customers an unusual alternative. They could ask to pay either $26 or $13 for exactly the same seats on Southwest flights. Those requesting $26 tickets were rewarded with gifts such as ice buckets or fifths of whiskey. The ploy worked. Fully 80% of customers requested $26 tickets. The first day of the offer generated the most traffic on Southwest up to that point. Barrett remarked, "At least for one month, we became Chivas Regal's biggest distributor." Within days, Braniff announced the discontinuance of its sale. Yet another of the legends for which the company would become known was forged.

Southwest's Takeoff

When Congress passed the Airline Deregulation Act in 1978, making it possible for airlines to begin flying new interstate routes without regulatory permission, Southwest was ready to extend its route network. Its only constraint would prove to be the so-called Wright Amendment, attached to the International Air Transportation Competition Act of 1979. It restricted interstate flights out of Love Field to the four states contiguous to Texas and was supported by those who had sought unsuccessfully to force Southwest earlier to move its operations to Dallas-Fort Worth International Airport. When Southwest did initiate service to noncontiguous states in 1982, it was from its Texas stations other than Love Field, a practice that it continued to follow subsequently.

Shortly after deregulation, however, a policy was adopted that, in spite of expansion opportunities, an effort would be made to manage the annual growth rate in aircraft capacity to about 10% to 15%. This was done to insure that the organization could maintain a strong balance sheet and, as senior managers often said, "manage in good times in order to survive in bad times."

In its only significant departure from its growth policy, in 1993 Southwest acquired Morris Air, a regional carrier based in Salt Lake City established on the Southwest model, and retained seven of Morris's operating stations, all new to the Southwest network. The routes of the two airlines were complementary and enabled Southwest to extend its service for the first time into the Northwest. The acquisition did, however, require the consolidation of two organizations with somewhat different management philosophies. For example, Morris Air's leadership had been successful in its efforts to avoid unionization while Southwest, embracing the idea of partnering with unions, had become the most heavily unionized airline in the industry and the most strike free.[1] Morris Air was only the

---

[1] Few of Morris's senior management people remained with Southwest. June Morris joined Southwest's board of directors. The only other Morris senior officer who joined Southwest was David Neeleman. He remained only a few months. After

second acquisition Southwest had made at that time, the other having been the acquisition of Muse Air in 1985, which was operated for a short time as a separate and independent company.

Southwest's growth was steady in the face of increasing requests from cities hoping to experience what had become known in government circles as "the Southwest effect." This effect inevitably resulted from Southwest's policy of pricing its service to compete with auto travel. It required that a fare structure be established that was often 70% below that being offered by other airlines at the time of Southwest's entry into a market. The result was often a 1,000% increase in traffic on the newly served city-pair markets in one year or less. Even at a time when the list of cities requesting the airline's service had grown to more than 50, Southwest chose to enter only two or three new cities each year in addition to filling out its existing network of point-to-point flights. (**Exhibit 1** contains a 2002 route map along with information about markets served by the airline.)

Southwest's strategy created a winning model for profits as well. After breaking even less than two years after its founding in 1971, the airline had enjoyed 30 consecutive years of profit beginning in 1973, a record unmatched by any airline in the world. (Financial and related information can be found in **Exhibits 2** and **3**.) Its stock, floated in an initial over-the-counter offering in 1971 and later on the American and New York Stock Exchanges with the trading symbol LUV, turned in, according to *Money* Magazine, the best performance of any stock in the Standard & Poor's 500 during that time.

This performance was bound to attract other airlines founded on some of the same beliefs. One such airline was People Express, based in Newark, New Jersey and established in 1980 with a lean organization including almost no staff. It was designed to provide a low-fare, bare-bones service aimed at college students and other pleasure travelers who were willing to pay for all amenities such as checked baggage and on-board refreshments in return for the lowest fares in markets served by the airline. The company grew rapidly both through internal growth and the acquisition of other struggling airlines. However, its failure to meet profit goals led to an unsuccessful effort to reposition the airline for business travelers at about the same time that full-fare competitors began to use their sophisticated reservation and yield-management systems to price services more competitively. While People's leadership blamed larger competitors for its subsequent demise, others felt that management had sown the seeds of its own destruction through simultaneous efforts to grow through acquisition, revamp its information systems, and reposition itself in the marketplace.

Although Southwest had been dismissed as a niche player and was able to "fly under the radar" for a number of years, by the mid-1990s major airlines were responding with the equivalent of lower-fare "fighting brands" such as Continental Lite in the southeast United States, the United Shuttle on the West Coast, and Delta Express and US Airways MetroJet on the East Coast. As they spread their routes, competition from these airlines temporarily depressed Southwest's profitability in 1995. However, it was thought that because they were spawned by full-service airlines with attendant problems of inherited management beliefs, cultures, and labor policies or route structures designed in part to connect through parents' hubs, lower-fare rivals created by the largest airlines were unable to achieve acceptable levels of profit. Southwest's management was so proud of its employees' culture that it periodically hosted "best practice" teams from all industries that wanted to discuss hiring,

---

serving out his five-year noncompete with the merged airlines, he formed JetBlue Airline in 1999. The best-financed start-up in airline history, JetBlue became profitable just six months after it began operations and was thought by some to be a potential future Southwest competitor. JetBlue, a nonunion organization operating substantially longer flights than Southwest, sought to differentiate customer service and high aircraft and labor productivity through extensive use of technology. For example, everything from passenger ticketing and check-in to in-flight entertainment was based on technological solutions. Similarly, information technology was used extensively as a substitute for front-line coordination of the efforts of ground crews to achieve "the perfect 30-minute turnaround" (later abandoned in favor of 35 to 55 minutes, depending on the nature of the flight). Some jobs, such as those of flight attendant, were designed to be short term in nature. For a comparison of Southwest and JetBlue, see Jody Hoffer Gittell, *The Southwest Airlines Way* (New York: McGraw-Hill, 2003).

4

training, and employee-relations practices. More recently, Barrett had discontinued the practice because, in her words, "I felt that we were devoting too much time, energy, attention, and resources educating the outside world about our culture—as opposed to devoting that time, energy, attention, and resources internally on enhancing and enriching our own culture."

In the 1990s other airlines around the world began to model their strategies around Southwest's, often after a visit by their managements to Dallas. The most successful of these included RyanAir, Easy Jet, and GO in Europe as well as Air Asia in the Far East.

Strategy

Important elements of the Southwest strategy, some of which were a reflection of the constraints the company faced early in its existence, included a number of things that Southwest did not do. For example, it did not employ the hub-and-spoke route system adopted by many other airlines. Hub-and-spoke systems were designed to feed large volumes of passengers into hubs where they could be redistributed to connecting flights, all of which was intended to increase average load factors (available seats utilized) and revenues per available seat mile flown. However, they were considered less convenient for passengers who preferred point-to-point flying. And they exacerbated the "domino effect" that one late flight could have on several others. Just as important, they were more costly to staff because of the extreme peaks and valleys in the traffic through each hub at "connect" times, an effect that also increased crowding and confusion for connecting passengers.

A point-to-point route system also enabled Southwest to speed the turnaround of its aircraft not required to wait for connecting flights and thereby gain greater utilization from a fleet containing only Boeing 737s. The newest of these were purchased for something less than the list price of $41 million under a contract with Boeing signed in June 2000 for as many as 436 Boeing 737s to be delivered through 2012 (on the schedule shown in **Exhibit 4**).

By mid-2001, Southwest's turnaround time had grown to an average of 24 minutes, a figure that was thought to be at least 30 minutes faster than the average for the industry as a whole. Contributing to Southwest's performance on turnaround time, in addition to its route system, were (1) an absence of meals on all Southwest flights, (2) a limited amount of checked luggage on Southwest's typically 60- to 90-minute flights, (3) a near-uniform configuration for all of its 737 aircraft, (4) a team-oriented approach to ground services with team measures for turning around planes and employees willing to do whatever necessary to get a plane pushed off on time, (5) a high-speed boarding process (described below), (6) a "handoff" of flights from one ground crew to another involving detailed information about numbers of passengers and bags as well as special passenger needs so that the receiving ground crew could make preparations in advance of a flight's arrival, and (7) the utilization of agents with the latitude to bring a wide variety of resources to bear on the flight-servicing process.

Southwest neither connected with other airlines nor sold "interline" tickets. Because it targeted business and pleasure fliers with relatively simple itineraries and short trips, these features were not thought necessary. Further, it did not assign seats. Instead, passengers were issued colorful reusable plastic boarding passes numbered so that 30 passengers could be boarded at a time in the sequence of their numbers. Once on board, passengers took any available seat, thus providing an incentive for an early arrival at the gate. This routine eliminated the time-consuming reconciliation of the double assignment of seats on full flights. And it allowed Southwest agents to keep the plane doors open for last-minute arrivals at the gate. But it led to what Barrett described as "the number one complaint about Southwest's service, particularly among the uninitiated," the absence of assigned seats.

Rather than spread its flights thinly over an extensive system, Southwest's strategy for opening markets was to limit markets served and provide high-frequency departures each day to a given destination. The intensity of this schedule reduced the consequences of a missed flight and enabled Southwest to retain tardy passengers.

Southwest was a maverick in its ticketing processes. Although its flight information was displayed in four computer reservation and ticketing systems operated by other airlines in the early 1990s, it paid $1 per booking only to the SABRE system, the only one with sufficient clout to demand payment. This allowed travel agents using SABRE to print tickets, even though a booking still necessitated a telephone call by an agent booking the ticket. Travel agents hated it because of the extra work for less commission on a lower-priced ticket. But the policy was thought to save the airline in excess of $30 million per year in computer reservation booking fees paid to airline ticketing systems and increased direct business resulting from travel agents advising customers to book Southwest flights themselves. In 1994, Southwest was ejected from all systems except SABRE. In response, the company's management was compelled to innovate new means of protecting its own ticket-distribution system over the following eight years. For example, it implemented a highly successful "ticketless" (paperless) travel program and later the development of Southwest.com as a means of using the Internet to sell travel directly to customers. These innovations had the combined effect of increasing sales and further lowering overall distribution costs.

Southwest's frequent-flier program was the simplest in the industry—fly eight flights, get one free. It had been preceded by a discount ticket program in the early 1970s in which purchasers of 10 flights received a booklet with 11 tickets, often cited by Kelleher as "the world's first frequent-flier program."

By mid-2001, Southwest's operations had grown to encompass 32,500 employees (more than 1,000 married to one another), operating a total of 360 Boeing 737 aircraft (with an average daily utilization of nearly 12 hours per aircraft) connecting 58 airports with 2,650 flights per day. It realized 7.5% of revenue passenger miles flown by the eight largest U.S. airlines and supplied an estimated 90% of all available seat miles in the "low-fare" segment of the market. It was the only airline to have been first in on-time performance, lowest in lost baggage, and highest in customer satisfaction for the same year, according to statistics maintained by the U.S. Department of Transportation, having achieved the feat five years in a row. And it had achieved an enviable financial performance. Chairman Kelleher commented: "Most people think of us as this flamboyant airline, but we're really very conservative from the fiscal standpoint. We have the best balance sheet in the industry. We've always made sure that we never overreached ourselves. We never got dangerously in debt, and never let costs get out of hand. And that gave us a real edge."[2]

Leadership, Values, and Culture

A visit to Southwest Airlines' headquarters at Love Field yielded vivid impressions of the company's leadership, values, and culture. The walls of the three-story building (with a five-story addition) were covered with literally thousands of framed photos and awards, many of them showing Southwest employees in their party cloths ranging from black tie and formals to jeans. Many others portrayed employees engaged in community activities together in their free time, often at Ronald McDonald houses for children across the country.

---

[2] Katrina Booker, "The Chairman of the Board Looks Back," *Fortune*, May 28, 2001.

6

In the hallways, jeans, Texas greetings, and hugs were the order of the day. As one of his colleagues put it, "Jim [executive vice president of operations] Wimberly's idea of dressing up is to wear socks." In response to the question, "What's the most enjoyable thing about your job?" posed by the casewriter, one staffer replied after a moment's thought, "I guess just coming to work every day." The response reflected the fact that Southwest Airlines had placed in the top five employers in *Fortune* Magazine's "100 Best Places to Work in the U.S." every year it had competed for the award.

Leadership

Many of the framed photos at headquarters included Kelleher, one of the founders, who had gained fame for his unorthodox but effective style of leadership at Southwest over the years. He could be seen on a customized Harley-Davidson presented to him by his pilot group, at an arm wrestling contest with the executive of another company in order to settle litigation over the use of an advertising slogan, or at the maintenance hangar (by his account, at 2 a.m.) dressed in a long dress with a purple boa and large purple hat to settle a performance challenge made to the maintenance crew. Kelleher's style of leadership was so charismatic and infectious that many claimed his retirement would present a serious challenge to his successors and to Southwest's culture.

By June 2001, Kelleher had turned the day-to-day operating responsibilities over to Jim Parker, former vice president–general counsel and now CEO; Barrett, his long-time associate, former executive vice president–customers, and now president and chief operating officer; and a team of other senior executives, most with long service with the airline. (**Exhibit 5** contains an organization chart as of late 2002.) Less visible to the general public, Kelleher nevertheless retained the position of chairman, with oversight responsibilities for growth strategies and government and airline industry relations. In the transition, responsibility for Southwest's unique culture remained with Barrett.

Parker had been persuaded by Kelleher to join his law firm and later (in 1986) to come to work at Southwest. He was described by one account as "modest and easygoing. Workplace colleagues say he brews the office coffee in the morning, makes his own photocopies, wears khakis and golf shirts to work."[3] In addition to devoting his time to strategic issues, he assumed personal responsibility for the negotiation of numerous labor contracts.

Barrett, who had joined Southwest with Kelleher, had begun her career as Kelleher's secretary, gradually taking on responsibility for "customers" (passengers and marketing as well as employees) and, in a way, anchoring the leadership team behind the scenes while Kelleher performed a much more public role. Shy and unassuming, Barrett spent most of her waking moments engaged in Southwest business. Little was done on the internal or external customer service front without her tacit approval.

Values and Culture

For years, Southwest had been operated on "The Basic Principles" of (1) focus on the situation, issue, or behavior, not on the person; (2) maintain the self-confidence and self-esteem of others; (3) maintain constructive relationships with your employees, peers, and managers; (4) take initiative to make things better; and (5) lead by example. Its core values were profitability, low cost, family, fun, love, hard work, individuality, ownership, legendary service, egalitarianism, common sense/ good judgment, simplicity, and altruism.

---

[3] Micheline Maynard, "Southwest, Without the Stunts," *The New York Times*, July 7, 2002, Section 3, p. 2.

In 1990, an informal group organized years before by Barrett became the core of a committee formed to plan the airline's 20th anniversary celebration. It rapidly evolved into what became known as the Culture Committee. Before, according to Donna Conover, who was named executive vice president–customer service as part of the June 2001 transition plan, "Colleen [Barrett] was the Culture Committee." Championed by Barrett and headed by a member of her staff, Susan (Sunny) Stone in 2002, the committee's goal was to "help create the Southwest Spirit and Culture where needed; to enrich it and make it better where it already exists; and to liven it up in places where it might be 'floundering.' In short, this group's goal is to do WHATEVER IT TAKES to create, enhance, and enrich the special Southwest Sprit and Culture that has made this such a wonderful Company/Family."

The committee comprised 96 employees nominated by their peers from all levels and locations in the Southwest organization, each with responsibility for attending three meetings annually to plan various events as well as for actively participating in three of the events. These ranged from employee appreciation events throughout the system to flight/operations "midnight madness" parties and breakfasts to a Christmas SPIRIT packing exercise in which goody packages were prepared for employees who had to work on Christmas. After several years, members graduated to "alumni" status and retained responsibility for attending two events each year. By 2002, there were more than 250 Culture Committee alumni. The biggest problem apparently was in finding members willing to transition to alumni status.

The biggest companywide event of the year was the annual awards banquet, for which employees from all over the system were brought to Dallas and honored for their length of service. As Conover put it, "People sort of need to come home once in awhile." In addition, the Culture Committee sponsored a Heroes of the Heart celebration at headquarters on February 14 each year. Awards were made to groups nominated by others in the organization that had gone "above and beyond" to deliver Southwest service.

The company's values and culture infused everything that it did. For example, Southwest had become well known for its efforts in partnering with unions (essentially invited into Southwest by its management), airports, and suppliers. Negotiations with unions, including the Teamsters and other national organizations, were entered with the idea of providing the best possible pay and benefits in return for flexible work rules. Efforts were made to maintain good working relations at airports from the top management to the staff in the control towers, where Southwest managers regularly appeared with donuts and coffee. Joint problem solving had become more important as problems with airport security had grown. And Southwest engaged in joint problem-solving exercises with those supplying everything from fuel to the peanuts served on planes.

The work of the Culture Committee increased in importance with the growth of the airline. For example, in contrast to the extensive preparations for Halloween at headquarters (described below), the casewriter observed few decorations on the same day at Southwest's Baltimore gates but more as he approached Dallas through Houston.

Organization

A small management team headed up Southwest's organization (as shown in **Exhibit 5**). At the very top, the team consisted of Kelleher, Parker, and Barrett, plus three executive vice presidents responsible for operations (Wimberly), customer service (Conover), and corporate staff services (Gary Kelly). Reporting to this team of six were those managing such functions as marketing, government relations, human resources (called People Department), schedule planning, legal, and others. Top

8

managers spent an unusual amount of time with one another, making decisions on a cross-functional basis. This philosophy pervaded the organization.

In contrast to competitors, the organization was staffed more heavily with managers responsible for coordinating all functions at the front-line operating level. All personnel involved in turning a plane around could be asked by them to help out wherever needed. Failure to do so according to schedule resulted in a "team late." Rather than assess individual responsibility, teams were then tasked to figure out how to avoid the problem in the future. As a result, pilots sometimes handled baggage or helped cabin attendants in picking up the cabin while gate attendants might be seen putting provisions on board for the departing flight. The theme driving this effort, according to Conover, was "doing whatever it takes" instead of "it's not my job." As she put it, "You can talk later about who should have done what."

The idea of dedicating an operations agent to each flight was somewhat unusual in the industry; other airlines regarded it as an extra expense, even though Southwest's gate crews, even including the operations agents, were among the most productive in the industry (as suggested by data in **Exhibit 6**). Employees typically became operations agents after serving in customer service or ramp positions. They could then become prime candidates for other front-line management jobs.

Throughout the organization, stress was placed on the value of "family" in the organization. This led to unusual practices in hiring new recruits, a process that Kelleher once described as "a near-religious experience." Southwest was well known, for example, for its group interviews, involving groups of 30 or more candidates for entry-level positions. Candidates were often asked to stand and describe such things as their most embarrassing moment. The interview team then watched both the presenter and those in the audience for signs of interest, concern, and empathy for the presenter. The interview team often included frequent-flier customers as well, particularly when customer-contact people were being selected. As one such customer put it when asked why he would take off time from his company to spend a day hiring Southwest employees, "I thought I might learn something and have a little fun doing it. And besides, it's my airline."

All of this was part of a process "to hire for attitude," in Conover's words. When asked if this policy extended to pilots, she replied, "Oh, my gosh, yes. That is such a close-knit group, but we're going to have people [other than the internal recruiter and chief pilot] look at them too. They have to have the right attitude."

All ground operations (station) employees experienced one to two weeks of technical orientation at individual stations before going to class in Dallas for a week to study everything from the use of company systems to the organization's values.

Southwest's employees received total compensation roughly equivalent to that of their counterparts in other airlines, but they typically worked more productively for it. This resulted in costs for Southwest that were substantially lower than those of other major airlines (as shown in **Exhibit 7**). In addition, all employees became members of Southwest's profit-sharing plan after the end of their six-month probation period, during which it was determined whether they represented a good fit with their peers. Contributions on their behalf began vesting after 12 months, although benefits began accruing from day one of their employment. No contribution to the plan was required of employees. Company contributions, depending on profits, ranged up to 14.7% of salary in 2000. By late 2002, the profit-sharing plan owned about 10% of Southwest's 763 million outstanding shares. Conover commented, "We don't get enough credit for the plan among our employees. After about five years, you begin to realize how important it is." Nevertheless, the turnover at all levels of the Southwest organization was significantly less than in other airlines. Other than for entry-level positions, the company hired from the outside talent pool only for specialized jobs, such as in information technology.

The Impact of the Events of 9/11

On the morning of September 11, 2001, as reports of plane crashes came in to Southwest's headquarters, senior executives assembled in the "control center," which was actually the board-room. Everyone waited as Southwest's planes one by one reached the ground safely across the United States. When Greg Wells, director of dispatch, reported that the last Southwest plane had landed safely, there was a huge sense of relief. At that moment, Kelleher commented, "We'll never be exactly the same industry again." Little did anyone know how true that would be.

Conover described the thought sequence following Kelleher's announcement:

> First you realize that we've got them on the ground. Then you ask, "Will we ever get them back in the air again?" Then the attitude quickly changed to "We've got to get back to work." There was never any talk about laying employees off. This attitude is so inbred in us that we didn't even think "it's going to be tough."

> The most important decision we made in the hours following the attacks was not to fly before Friday [three days after the tragedy]. The government was urging airlines to fly as soon as Thursday to demonstrate our resilience, and our competitors were preparing to do so. But we decided that after all that had happened, we couldn't put our employees through a ramp-up that we might have to postpone.

Immediate Responses

Perhaps the most remarkable response to 9/11 at Southwest was one that did not occur. No member of management could recall a conversation about a possible layoff of employees or a cutback in flights. This was not a trivial matter. As CFO Kelly pointed out, "Even though we had roughly a billion dollars 'in the bank,' it was in commercial paper; we couldn't get at it because the markets were closed for several trading days, and we didn't know what it would be worth when the markets reopened."

Overnight, security issues made the handling of passengers, baggage, and other matters more complicated and time consuming. In a way, the challenge was proportional to the number of passengers boarded, and by September 11 Southwest was boarding more passengers than any U.S. airline except Delta. One response was to add more customer service agents to the boarding process for each flight, increasing the average of employees to staff a departure from 3.5 to 5.5. As Conover put it, "We knew we had to do it to get over the hump. For the first four or five months, when things were not pretty, customers could at least find a human being. Then we let attitude take over. As we learned how to handle the problem, employees began saying 'We've got too many people here.' At that point we let attrition get us back to our former staffing levels."

Less than 48 hours after the attacks, Joyce Rogge, Southwest's senior vice president–marketing, stressed the need to get a message in the form of a public service announcement to the general public, one that would appeal to American patriotism and resiliency while recognizing the bravery of people who had suffered through the 9/11 attacks. Late on the Sunday afternoon after the attacks, she recorded Barrett's voice on an inexpensive dictaphone machine with a message that was used as a voice-over for a hastily produced television ad showing Barrett's name and title on a typed title card in front of an American flag. It was devoid of the usual Southwest humor. Subsequent television and radio ads profiled Southwest employees, assuring the public that when they were ready to fly, Southwest would be there and ready to fly them.

Heightened Security and Regulation

An even greater challenge was faced by Southwest's governmental affairs office, led by Ron Ricks, who had logged 16 years in his position after serving at the same law firm where Kelleher, Parker, and Barrett had been employed before coming to Southwest.

In the 60 days following 9/11, Southwest received roughly 200 directives from the Federal Aviation Agency (FAA), the FBI, and the CIA. Many of these would later be consolidated under the Transportation Security Administration (TSA) created by Congress later in the year, but it did not exist during this period. As Ricks put it, "It wasn't just the sheer volume of directives. A typical directive required that we implement a new security procedure overnight. The directive would contain complex 'terms of art,' hard for a 22-year-old customer service agent to understand and act on. The alternatives were 'Do it or don't operate.'" Many directives were rescinded by later directives, some no more than 24 hours after the order they rescinded. As Wimberly put it, "Overnight, we became a branch of government."

Once the TSA was created by Congress, it was staffed with people drawn from the Secret Service, FBI, CIA, and Tobacco and Firearms agencies. This contributed to continuing confusion about directives issued by the TSA. Ricks commented, "Their perceived mandate was that they were fighting a war on terrorism. We were in a mind-set of being in a war too. And we didn't know anything about that kind of war. We just concluded that we couldn't substitute our judgment for theirs."

Dave Ridley, vice president of ground operations, held a daily call with all 59 Southwest stations. He would go over "today's directive" and how Southwest would deal with it. For example, one directive required that in the absence of baggage screening, all bags were to be opened at the counter by Southwest employees, apparently with little thought about questions of logistics, employee safety, and what to do if (nonthreatening) illegal contraband were found in the bags.

Southwest's passengers typically had less accompanying baggage than those on other major airlines. However, they carried a relatively high percentage on board. When the FAA limited carry-on luggage to one bag and a personal item, the number of bags checked per passenger began rising. This added work for Southwest's baggage handling crews and in some cases necessitated enlarging crews to meet plane turnaround schedules.

Certain security directives placed Southwest at a competitive disadvantage. For example, many of Southwest's best customers, because of the "last-second" manner of their travel, fit the profile of those most likely to be thoroughly searched. Barrett estimated that as many as 15% of Southwest's passengers were being flagged for screening, a figure much higher than for other airlines.

Several of the directives dealt with the tracking of passengers and their baggage from curb to seat. But because it had never had assigned seats, Southwest's relatively simple systems were not designed to provide more detailed information and had to be reprogrammed.

The need to identify passengers requiring detailed screening forced Southwest to abandon its distinctive, colorful, reusable plastic boarding passes in favor of paper passes on which information targeting selected passengers could be printed.

Industry Bailout and Taxation

A rapidly conceived bailout for an industry in financial as well as physical peril occupied a great deal of Kelleher's and Ricks's time as well. In the immediate wake of 9/11, Southwest's competitors, many of which had little in the way of a financial cushion, began announcing cutbacks in both service and employment. In total, roughly 20% of all flights flown by seven of the eight other largest carriers were discontinued, and more than 15% of those employed by seven of the eight other largest carriers (at least 100,000) were laid off.[4]

In response to immediate airline needs, an effort was made in the U.S. House of Representatives to pass by voice vote a hastily prepared Air Transportation Safety and Systems Stabilization Act. Southwest executives learned of it the next day. Largely based on "need" (thereby freezing Southwest out of the benefit), the bill did not pass. Ricks commented, "Southwest did not advocate a bailout but did take the position that if the government decided as a matter of public policy that economic reimbursement for our losses was a good thing, then the program should be implemented in a nondiscriminatory way." Ultimately, a bill was passed that provided for up to $10 billion in loan guarantees to airlines seeking financing assistance. In addition, it provided for $5 billion to be distributed among all aviation providers based on seat miles (one seat flown one mile) available on September 10, 2001. Out of the latter pool, Southwest received $278 million.

On another front, discussions were under way concerning various methods of taxing airlines to help defray added costs to the government for airline security, especially following the assumption of airport security staffing by the federal government in November 2001. On this front, two taxes were ultimately established. The first, a tax of $2.50 on each segment flown by a passenger, hit the lowest-fare airlines the hardest. However, as Ricks commented, "After 9/11, everyone became a low-fare carrier. Therefore, the potential for a penalty to Southwest was somewhat mitigated on this score. We think the size of the tax is a reason why traffic is slow to return to the airlines. But Congress realized that it couldn't pay for obligations it had assumed without it." (Monthly traffic trends for major U.S. airlines are shown in **Exhibit 8**.)

A second tax was assessed each airline to help pay for increased costs to the government for security. Whatever each airline was paying for security prior to the takeover was to be turned over to the government.

New Competitive Position

In spite of new challenges and taxes, the decision by Southwest's management to maintain and ultimately to increase schedules and employment after 9/11 had a profound effect on its competitive position in the industry. Market share rose immediately (as shown in **Exhibit 8**). Given the immediate plunge in the value of competitors' stock from 11% to 74%, Southwest's market value quickly became greater than that for all of the other eight largest airlines combined and maintained that position for months, in spite of the fact that its earnings had suffered substantial declines as a result of lower ticket prices, higher costs, and new taxes.

Labor Relations

Several labor contract negotiations coincided with Southwest's apparently successful emergence from the 9/11 crisis. Claims of lower wages than those paid by other airlines in the face of profitable

---

[4] Among the other eight largest U.S. airlines, only Alaska Airlines did not furlough employees following September 11, 2001.

company performance emboldened several unions to seek more favorable contracts. Stating that "There's really nothing more important that we do than have a relationship with our employees," Parker continued his personal responsibility for negotiations.[5]

In spite of the fact that unions took a tougher stance than in the past, an acceptable two-year extension of the pilots' 10-year agreement (to 2006) was achieved. The mechanics, after rejecting Southwest's first offer (in a somewhat unusual move), agreed to a second offer. Similar contracts were expected to be signed with other unions. Nevertheless, it raised a question about the degree to which growth had challenged Southwest's policy of relating closely to its employees. Observers continued to conclude that the company's labor relations were still far superior to those of its competitors. As Jonathan Weaks, president of the Southwest Airlines Pilots Association (the pilots' union), put it, "We don't want to be just another airline."[6]

Short-Term Challenges: Operating Procedures

In response to the 9/11 crisis, other airlines had increased estimated-schedule flight times to reflect increased passenger- and baggage-processing times. With disappointing load factors, many flights as a result regularly arrived 20 minutes or more before their scheduled times. Southwest's management, on the other hand, had not changed its schedules in the hope that this would continue to benefit aircraft utilization. In spite of this, average turnaround times in recent months had risen from 24 to 27 minutes, a matter of real concern to management, and Southwest's reported on-time performance had slipped below that of its rivals (as shown in **Exhibit 9**).

Southwest's management had discussed several possible responses at various meetings in late October 2002. Among these, one possibility was that of just sitting tight, essentially concentrating on doing the best possible job with the resources at hand in a price-competitive environment and despite sluggish demand for the service. The price of this alternative would be depressed profits and possibly declining morale.

A second response would be simply to reschedule the airline, building more liberal flight and turnaround times into the schedule. However, too often schedules became self-fulfilling prophecies. If this proved to be true, results could be quite costly with serious profit implications.

Third, efforts could be made to redesign passenger- and baggage-handling processes once again. Southwest's practice of boarding passengers in groups just minutes before flight time, then holding the door of the aircraft open for late arrivals, was somewhat at odds with the government directive to single out passengers for a thorough search of luggage at the gate. Southwest gate agents were instructed to encourage passengers so identified to assemble at the gate for searching as early as possible in the relatively rapid boarding process. Even so, passengers were often still being searched after everyone else had boarded. Those singled out often ended up getting inferior seats even if they arrived at the gate early in order to get a good choice. One solution to this problem, that of adding extra government security guards at Southwest's gates (probably at the airline's expense), would substantially increase boarding costs.

Fourth, passenger boarding policies could be altered. Other airlines were requiring passengers to be on hand at the gate with greater lead times before boarding in order to accommodate new security procedures. This would further restrict Southwest's passengers, a direct contradiction of its past policies and its advertising strategy of freedom "to move about the country."

---

[5] Maynard, p. 2.

[6] Ibid.

Finally, open seating could be abandoned, insuring that passengers would get a seat they had chosen when they booked the seat. This would require "retraining" regular passengers, some of whom actually preferred open seating. Further, it would likely add delays, especially to full flights on which the probability of assigning the same seat to two people would be greater.

Whatever was done would have to be implemented with customers', employees', and the government's needs in mind. Conover, in charge of customers (both travelers and employees), commented on the success of Southwest's responses to changing requirements to date: "Now, both government and our employees think we're invincible. That's great, but it's almost a disservice. It has been tough trying to maintain customer service levels and relationships in a whole new environment. We sometimes wonder if we're in control of our destiny any longer."

Long-Term Challenges: Growth Strategies

Immediately after 9/11, Southwest deferred 19 aircraft deliveries, borrowed a billion dollars, and developed a contingency operating schedule. Initially, little thought was given to strategic growth plans. The primary focus, instead, was on stabilizing operations, even though decisions were made to go ahead immediately with a previously planned opening of the Norfolk station and begin accepting in early 2002 deliveries of new aircraft. But by late 2002 questions regarding appropriate long-term growth strategies began to surface once again.

Over the years, the average flight length at Southwest had gradually increased from an average of 228 miles in the first year of operations, 1971, to about 450 miles in 1998. On Thanksgiving Day, 1998, Southwest experimented with its first nonstop transcontinental flight, between Baltimore and Oakland, necessitating a flight time of about five hours. The plane was filled with passengers who had paid $99 for the flight; almost half of the passengers had never flown Southwest before. The only problem experienced by the crew was the lack of space to store the trash that accumulated during the flight. Many observers, who attributed much of Southwest's success to the focus of its operating strategy up to that time, feared that the test might mark the first crack in the strategy.

Passenger reactions to the flight were positive. Those who typically flew multiple segments to get to a distant destination were enthusiastic about getting there two hours sooner. They provided "permission" to the airline's management to introduce other long-haul flights. By late 2002, Southwest was operating 213 flights per day over 1,200 miles in length. (**Exhibit 10** contains information about Southwest's network and flights.) Some crew members preferred to work longer flights, enough to be able to staff new flights; others, according to Pete McGlade, vice president–schedule planning, "signed on with Southwest because they like more landings and takeoffs per day of work."

Because longer flights experienced high-load factors, utilized the existing infrastructure, and did not require additional catering or on-board staffing (with only snack service, the usual three cabin attendants could serve a full planeload of 137 passengers), they generated healthy profits per passenger and operating economics at least comparable to those of shorter flights. This comparison held true only if long-haul flights were operated from cities served by a substantial number of other Southwest flights.

By mid-2002, the average aircraft stage (flight) length had grown to 550 miles. Southwest's experience with longer flights raised the question of the degree to which the airline should rely on them in its future growth plans. There were a number of opportunities to connect existing stations three or more flying hours apart on the Southwest system. The alternative would be to continue to

14

add new cities to the airline's 59-station network from among more than 100 cities that were requesting Southwest service.

Questions were raised from time to time about limits to Southwest's growth and, when growth was resumed, whether the airline could resume its 14% growth per year between 1980 and 2000. However, one Wall Street analyst, examining Southwest's route structure and the density of existing service, concluded that it could double its size without opening one new station.

A Late October Visit to Southwest Airlines Headquarters

On October 30, 2002, two appropriately contrasting events took place simultaneously during the casewriter's visit to Southwest's Love Field headquarters in Dallas. The first, a three-hour emergency exercise, was called unexpectedly by Wimberly at 8 a.m. It involved a simulated report of the crash of a Southwest flight from Houston short of the runway in New Orleans just 30 minutes earlier. The hypothetical drill specified that there were survivors and that they were being evacuated to local hospitals. (Southwest in its entire history had never experienced a fatal accident.) The resulting exercise involved hundreds of people mobilized in the form of teams responsible for care (family assistance), employee assistance, business continuation, dispatch, corporate communications, an executive office taskforce (which assembled in the board room under Wimberly's direction), family notification, manifest, medical services, mortuary assistance, purchasing, reservations, security, technical support, and building services. Many were assembled in a Go Team that boarded a plane pulled up behind corporate headquarters for a simulated flight to New Orleans, during which they were briefed once again concerning their duties upon arrival. They then departed the plane and walked through the processes and decisions for which they would be responsible in the event of a real emergency. It was one of a series of emergency exercises planned for the coming months.

At the same time, many other employees continued their preparations for the annual Halloween celebration, which had been cancelled in 2001 in deference to 9/11. Each department was busy preparing its own decorations and a skit reflecting a particular theme. The legal department was building a biker's bar from which to present its show. In the executive office, employees were rehearsing for the Rocky Horror Airport Experience presented by Transylvania Scareways. And the maintenance hangar was draped with a large sign proclaiming the name of the show to be presented there, "Hogs and Kisses," featuring the department's Harley moto-ballet team. Little work appeared to be getting done anywhere in the building. The following day employees would take hundreds of their children out of school so they could attend a full schedule of skits with their parents.

Exhibit 1   Southwest Airlines Routes and Market Data, November 2002

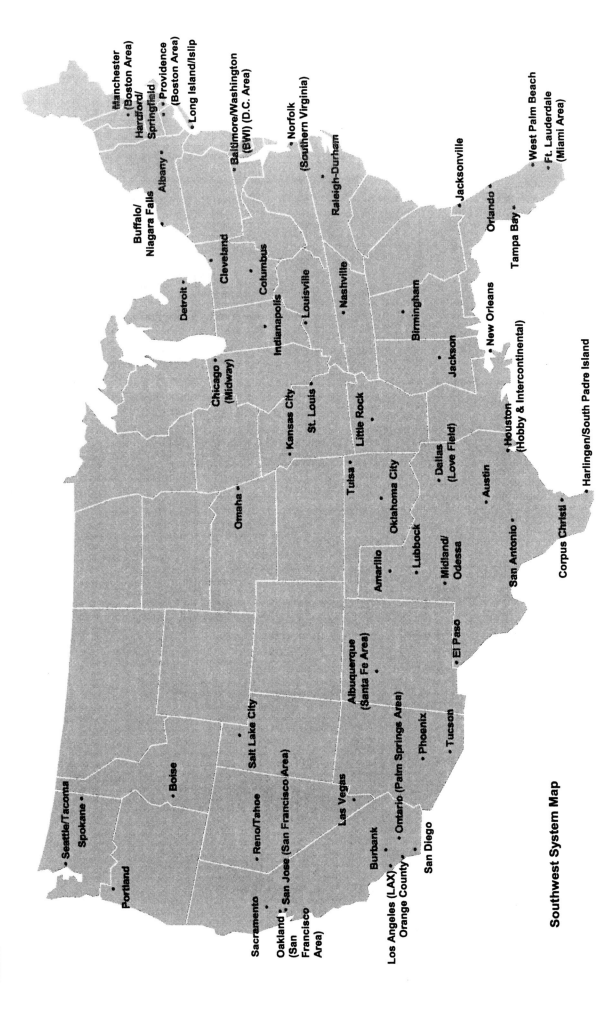

Southwest System Map

Exhibit 1 (continued)

Southwest's Market Share
Southwest's Top 100 City-Pair Markets

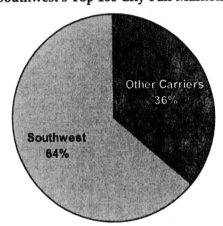

Southwest's Capacity by Region

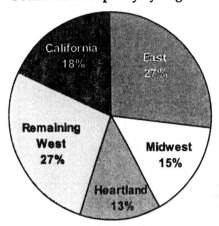

Southwest's Top 10 Airports
Daily Departures

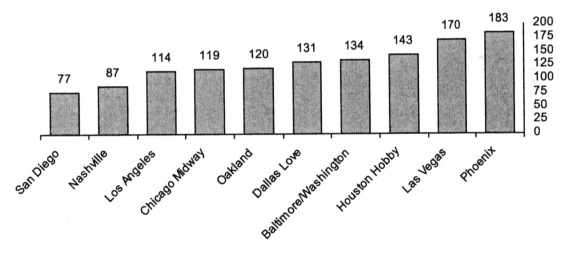

Source: Southwest Airlines Co. 2001 Annual Report.

Exhibit 2   Selected Financial and Other Information, Southwest Airlines, 1998–2001 (in thousands, except per share amounts)

	2001	2000	1999	1998
Operating revenues:				
Passenger[a]	$ 5,378,702	$ 5,467,965	$ 4,562,616	$ 4,010,029
Freight	91,270	110,742	102,990	98,500
Other[a]	85,202	70,853	69,981	55,451
Total operating revenues	5,555,174	5,649,560	4,735,587	4,163,980
Operating expenses	4,924,052	4,628,415	3,954,011	3,480,369
Operating income	631,122	1,021,145	781,576	683,611
Other expenses (income), net	(196,537)	3,781	7,965	(21,501)
Income before income taxes	827,659	1,017,364	773,611	705,112
Provision for income taxes[b]	316,512	392,140	299,233	271,681
Net income[b]	$ 511,147	$ 625,224[c]	$ 474,378	$ 433,431
Net income per share, basic[b]	$.67	$.84[c]	$.63	$.58
Net income per share, diluted[b]	$.63	$.79[c]	$.59	$.55
Cash dividends per common share	$.0180	$.0147	$.0143	$.0126
Total assets	$ 8,997,141	$ 6,669,572	$ 5,563,703	$ 4,715,996
Long-term debt	$ 1,327,158	$ 760,992	$ 871,717	$ 623,309
Stockholders' equity	$ 4,014,053	$ 3,451,320	$ 2,835,788	$ 2,397,918
Consolidated Financial Ratios[d]				
Return on average total assets	6.5%	10.1%[c]	9.2%	9.7%
Return on average stockholders' equity	13.7%	19.9%[c]	18.1%	19.7%
Consolidated Operating Statistics[e]				
Revenue passengers carried	64,446,773	63,678,261	57,500,213	52,586,400
Revenue passenger miles (RPMs, 000s)	44,493,916	42,215,162	36,479,322	31,419,110
Available seat miles (ASMs, 000s)	65,295,290	59,909,965	52,855,467	47,543,515
Passenger load factor	68.1%	70.5%	69.0%	66.1%
Average length of passenger haul	690	663	634	597
Trips flown	940,426	903,754	846,823	806,822
Average passenger fare[a]	$83.46	$85.87	$79.35	$76.26
Passenger revenue yield per RPM[a]	12.09¢	12.95¢	12.51¢	12.76¢
Operating revenue yield per ASM	8.51¢	9.43¢	8.96¢	8.76¢
Operating expenses per ASM	7.54¢	7.73¢	7.48¢	7.32¢
Fuel cost per gallon (average)	70.86¢	78.69¢	52.71¢	45.67¢
Number of employees at year end	31,580	29,274	27,653	25,844
Size of fleet at year end[f]	355	344	312	280
Common stock price range	$23.32-$11.25	$23.33-$10.00	$15.72-$9.58	$10.56-$6.81
Common stock price close[g]	$18.48	$22.35	$10.75	$10.08

Source: Southwest Airlines Co. 2001 Annual Report.

[a]Includes effect of reclassification of revenue reported in 1999 through 1995 related to the sale of flight segment credits from Other to Passenger due to the accounting change implementation in 2000.

[b]Pro forma for 1992 assuming Morris, an S-Corporation prior to 1993, was taxed at statutory rates.

[c]Excludes cumulative effect of accounting change of $22.1 million ($.03 per share).

[d]The selected consolidated financial data and consolidated financial ratios for 1992 have been restated to include the financial results of Morris Air Corporation (Morris).

[e]Prior to 1993, Morris operated as a charter carrier; therefore, no Morris statistics are included for 1992.

[f]Includes leased aircraft.

[g]The closing price on December 6, 2002 was $16.27.

18

Exhibit 3 Southwest Airlines, Consolidated Balance Sheets, December 31, 2000 and 2001 (in thousands, except per share amounts)

	December 31,	
	2001	2000
ASSETS		
Current assets:		
Cash and cash equivalents	$2,279,861	$ 522,995
Accounts and other receivables	71,283	138,070
Inventories of parts and supplies, at cost	70,561	80,564
Deferred income taxes	46,400	28,005
Prepaid expenses and other current assets	52,114	61,902
Total current assets	$2,520,219	$ 831,536
Property and equipment, at cost:		
Flight equipment	7,534,119	6,831,913
Ground property and equipment	899,421	800,718
Deposits on flight equipment purchase contracts	468,154	335,164
	8,901,694	7,967,795
Less allowance for depreciation	2,456,207	2,148,070
	6,445,487	5,819,725
Other assets	31,435	18,311
	$8,997,141	$6,669,572
LIABILITIES AND STOCKHOLDERS' EQUITY		
Current liabilities:		
Accounts payable	$ 504,831	$ 312,716
Accrued liabilities	547,540	499,874
Air traffic liability	450,407	377,061
Aircraft purchase obligations	221,840	–
Short-term borrowings	475,000	–
Current maturities of long-term debt	39,567	108,752
Total current liabilities	$2,239,185	$1,298,403
Long-term debt less current maturities	1,327,158	760,992
Deferred income taxes	1,058,143	852,865
Deferred gains from sale and leaseback of aircraft	192,342	207,522
Other deferred liabilities	166,260	98,470
Commitments and contingencies		
Stockholders' equity		
Common stock, $1.00 par value: 2,000,000 shares authorized; 766,774 and 507,897 shares issued in 2001 and 2000, respectively	766,774	507,897
Capital in excess of par value	50,409	103,780
Retained earnings	3,228,408	2,902,007
Accumulated other comprehensive income (loss)	(31,538)	–
Treasury stock, at cost: 3,735 shares in 2000	–	(62,364)
Total stockholders' equity	4,014,053	3,451,320
	$8,997,141	$6,669,572

Source: Southwest Airlines Co. 2001 Annual Report.

19

Exhibit 4   Aircraft Utilization and Fleet Size, 1997–2001, and Firm Aircraft Orders and Options as of December 31, 2001

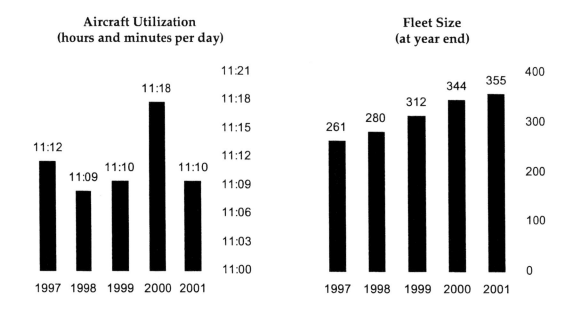

Boeing 737-700 Firm Orders and Options

Type	2002	2003	2004	2005	2006	2007	2008	2009-2012	Total
Firm orders	11	21	23	24	22	25	6	–	132
Options	–	–	13	20	20	9	25	–	87
Purchase rights	–	–	–	–	–	20	20	177	217
Total	11	21	36	44	42	54	51	177	436

Source: Southwest Airlines Co. 2001 Annual Report.

Exhibit 5   Southwest Airlines' Organization, November 2002

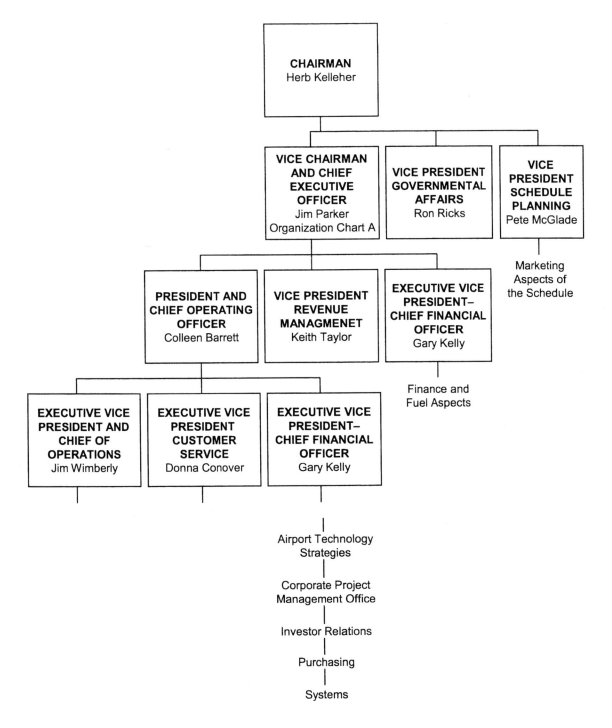

Source: Company documents.

Exhibit 6 Passengers Boarded per Employee, Major U.S. Airlines, First Quarter 2001 and 2002

Airline	First Quarter, 2001	First Quarter, 2002
Southwest	604.6	509.8
JetBlue	542.3	495.6
America West	369.8	353.2
US Air	309.9	318.8
Alaska Air	309.4	303.8
Delta	295.1	287.3
Northwest	240.6	251.2
Continental	235.1	247.4
American	194.9	241.8
United	184.6	182.2

Source: U.S. Department of Transportation.

Exhibit 7 Revenue and Cost per Passenger Seat Mile, Major U.S. Airlines, First Quarter 2001 and 2002 (in cents per mile)

Airline	First Quarter 2001			First Quarter 2002		
	Revenue/ Seat Mile[a]	Cost/Seat Mile[b]	Revenue- Cost (in cents/mile)	Revenue/ Seat Mile	Cost/Seat Mile	Revenue- Cost (in cents/mile)
Alaska Air	9.50	10.22	−.72	9.23	10.17	−.94
American	10.62	11.22	−.60	9.08	11.33	−2.25
America West	8.00	8.59	−.59	7.25	9.51	−2.26
Continental	10.04	10.39	−.35	9.12	10.73	−1.61
Delta	9.64	10.34	−.70	8.70	10.54	−1.84
JetBlue	8.54	7.41	1.13	8.22	6.82	1.40
Northwest	10.04	10.96	−.92	9.47	10.35	−.88
Southwest	8.95	7.65	1.30	7.57	7.29	.28
United	9.51	11.51	−2.00	8.48	11.41	−2.93
US Air	11.02	14.08	−3.06	9.88	14.77	−4.89

Source: U.S. Department of Transportation. The first quarter typically is the least profitable for most U.S. airlines.

[a]Revenue per seat mile is total revenue per available seat mile, occupied or not, in cents. As a result, it is a measure of both prices and capacity utilization.

[b]Cost per seat mile is total operating expenses divided by available seat miles, occupied or not, in cents.

Exhibit 8 Passenger Miles Flown, Major U.S. Airlines, First Quarter 2001 and 2002 (in billions)

Airline	First Quarter, 2001	First Quarter, 2002
American	68.6	72.1
United	74.6	64.1
Delta	62.4	56.8
Northwest	47.4	43.0
Continental	37.7	34.9
Southwest	27.8	27.0
US Air	29.6	24.8
America West	12.7	11.1
Alaska Air	7.5	7.7
JetBlue	1.6	3.4
Totals	369.9	344.9

Source: U.S. Department of Transportation.

Exhibit 9 Trends in Reported Percentage of On-Time Arrivals, Major U.S. Airlines, June 2001–July 2002

Airline	June 2001	June 2002	July 2002
Alaska Air	71.7%	77.1%	79.3%
American	78.9	81.6	81.6
America West	77.1	82.2	80.4
Continental	79.4	82.3	83.9
Delta	75.7	79.2	79.8
JetBlue	N.A.[a]	N.A.	N.A.
Northwest	81.0	80.0	80.1
Southwest	83.0	79.8	79.4
United	77.8	80.4	84.3
US Air	77.8	82.9	84.6

Source: U.S. Department of Transportation.

[a]Not available.

Exhibit 10   Southwest Airlines' Route and Flight Information, November 2002

PROFILE OF A HYPOTHETICAL NETWORK CONNECTING ALL CITIES ON THE SOUTHWEST ROUTE SYSTEM, NOVEMBER 2002

Distance	Number of Possible Route Segments[a] (city pairs)
100–400 miles	186
400–800 miles	366
800–1,200 miles	350
More than 1,200 miles	753
Total	1,655

PROFILE OF ACTUAL ROUTES SERVED BY SOUTHWEST FLIGHTS, NOVEMBER 2002

Distance	Route Segments (city pairs)	Flights
100–400 miles[b]	103	1,503
400–800 miles[c]	100	770
800–1,200 miles[d]	70	298
More than 1,200 miles[e]	65	221
Total	338	2,792

Source: Company documents.

[a]The total possible number excludes all routes under 100 miles (reflecting the shortest route actually flown between Islip, Long Island and Providence of 108 miles) and routes from Dallas Love Field, which Southwest was prohibited from flying by law (the Wright Amendment).

[b]Numbers of flights between these city pairs ranged from two per day between Austin and Harlingen, Texas (as well as many other city pairs) to 61 per day between Dallas Love Field and Houston Hobby Airport.

[c]Numbers of flights between these city pairs ranged from two per day between Albuquerque, New Mexico and Salt Lake City (as well as many other city pairs) to 32 per day between Kansas City and Chicago.

[d]Numbers of flights between these city pairs ranged from two per day between Hartford, Connecticut and Tampa, Florida (as well as many other city pairs) to 12 per day between Las Vegas and Kansas City.

[e]Numbers of flights between these city pairs ranged from two per day between Albany, New York and Las Vegas (as well as many other city pairs) to 11 per day between Phoenix and St. Louis.

24

KRISHNA PALEPU

TARUN KHANNA

INGRID VARGAS

Haier: Taking a Chinese Company Global

Only by entering the international market can we know what our competition is doing, can we raise our competitive edge. Otherwise, we'll lose the China market to foreigners.

— Zhang Ruimin, 1996[1]

All success relies on one thing in overseas markets—creating a localized brand name. We have to make Americans feel that Haier is a localized U.S. brand instead of an imported Chinese brand.

— Zhang Ruimin, 2003[2]

On December 26, 2004, Haier Group, ranked China's number-one company by the *Asian Wall Street Journal,*[3] celebrated its 20th anniversary with annual sales topping RMB 100 billion.[a] (See Exhibit 1 for Haier revenue growth.) Starting with a defunct refrigerator factory in Qingdao, Shandong province, founder and CEO Zhang Ruimin built Haier into China's largest home appliance maker.[b] Globally, Haier ranked third in white goods revenues, and was the second-largest refrigerator manufacturer (with about 6% of the global market) behind Whirlpool and ahead of Electrolux, Kenmore, and GE.[4] Zhang pledged to make Haier the world's best-selling refrigerator brand by 2006. (See Exhibit 2 for global appliance market shares.)

Haier held about a 30% share of China's RMB 129 billion white goods market,[5] and had a growing presence in "black goods" sectors such as televisions and personal computers, but margins on domestic sales were shrinking. The Haier Group's Shanghai-listed arm, Qingdao Haier, saw 2004 profit margins drop to 2.6%, from a high of 9.4% just five years earlier. (See Exhibit 3 for Qingdao Haier financials and Exhibit 4 for revenues by product.) Industry observers attributed the decline to increased competition from local firms and foreign multinationals in China. National overcapacity was estimated at 30% in televisions, washing machines, refrigerators, and other major appliances. Manufacturers were cutting prices at 10% to 15% annually.[6] In this environment, Haier was betting its future on global sales. Haier's 2004 export revenues were nearly double the previous year's, and the company was targeting $1 billion in sales to the United States alone for 2005. Could Haier

---

[a] At the time, 8.26 RMB = 1 US$.

[b] Haier, derived from the Chinese word for "sea," was pronounced "high–R," and Qingdao, "ching-dow." In Chinese, given names followed the family name. The family name Zhang was pronounced "Jong."

Professors Krishna Palepu and Tarun Khanna and Senior Researcher Ingrid Vargas, Global Research Group, prepared this case. HBS cases are developed solely as the basis for class discussion. Cases are not intended to serve as endorsements, sources of primary data, or illustrations of effective or ineffective management.

become China's first true multinational brand? In the process, would Haier be able to defend its dominant position in China against growing competition from Western and Asian multinationals?

Haier's First 20 Years

Company Origins[7]

Haier originated in 1984 when Zhang took over a failing refrigerator factory in the Chinese port city of Qingdao. At the time, Zhang was vice general manager of the household appliance division of Qingdao's municipal government, and became convinced of the latent demand for refrigerators by the sight of customers standing in line to pay cash for second-rate refrigerators as they came off the production line at Qingdao General Refrigerator Factory. The local government wanted to appoint Zhang director of the nearly bankrupt company which had to borrow from neighboring villages to pay salaries to its 800 employees, and Zhang reluctantly accepted the challenge.

The factory was a collective enterprise whose ultimate authority was the municipal government, although the workers collectively held ownership of its assets and shared any profits after the payment of local and national taxes and appropriate reinvestment in the company. Unlike the government's authority over state-owned enterprises, it did not own or have any claim—other than taxes—on a collective enterprise's assets or profits. The government could influence senior staffing and major business decisions, however. Poor performance, labor disputes, or mismanagement of funds were all grounds for the dismissal of senior managers by the local authorities.

In 1984 there were about 300 refrigerator manufacturers in China, most producing poor-quality products. Zhang believed that Chinese consumers would be willing to pay more for higher-quality products and reliable service. Inspired by the workmanship of German products that he saw during a 1984 trip to Germany, Zhang remarked "Our people aren't more stupid than Germans. Why can't we do the same as them?" and promptly entered into a technology licensing agreement with German refrigerator manufacturer Liebherr.[8] Haier later imported freezer and air conditioner production lines from Derby of Denmark and Sanyo of Japan. Joint ventures (JVs) with companies such as Japan's Mitsubishi and Italy's Merloni infused Haier with more foreign technology and designs. "First we observe and digest," Zhang explained. "Then we imitate. In the end, we understand it well enough to design it independently."[9]

One of Zhang's biggest hurdles was getting workers to understand that Haier's commitment to quality was unlike that seen at other Chinese companies. To get his message across, Zhang once pulled 76 refrigerators off the line, some for minor flaws such as scratches, and ordered staff to smash them to bits. "That got their attention," laughed Zhang. "They finally understood that I wasn't going to sell just anything, like my competitors would. It had to be the best."[10] Haier promoted personal accountability by having poorly performing workers stand on a pair of yellow painted feet on the factory floor at the end of the workday to explain their failings to assembled colleagues.

Haier made a profit of RMB 1 million in its second year, when its refrigerators sold in three major Chinese cities. Despite overwhelming market demand and soaring prices for refrigerators, Haier resisted mass production, focusing on quality and brand-building instead. In 1988, Haier won a gold medal for quality in a national refrigerator competition. In 1989 China's refrigerator market faced oversupply, but rather than cut prices as its competitors had, Haier raised them. Zhang discovered that the Haier brand commanded a 15% premium, even during a price war.[11]

By the early 1990s, oversupply was no longer an issue. "At that time, demand outstripped supply, and we didn't have a big-scale operation. So we were focused on the China market. We didn't think about building our brand in the international market yet," explained Yang Mianmian, Zhang's right hand since 1984 and later named group president. "Our target is to become a first-class brand. We need to have a fairly large scale in order to achieve this," added a Haier marketing executive. "If this brand is not of large scale, it will not be successful."

Growth and Diversification

By 1991, Haier had become China's leading refrigerator manufacturer. "Now we could let our reputation precede our new products," said Zhang. "It was time to diversify."[12] Haier found two candidates: the Qingdao Air Conditioner Factory, and the Qingdao General Freezer Factory, both stumbling due to poor management. Haier took on the debt of each firm and retained most of their employees. Introducing a new air conditioner type at the former and Haier worker discipline at the latter, within one year the new divisions had transformed a deficit of RMB 15 million into profits.

The newly expanded refrigerator, freezer, and air conditioner manufacturer was renamed Haier Group in 1992. The same year Haier acquired 500 acres of Qingdao land for a new industrial park to house corporate headquarters and the bulk of the firm's factories and subsidiaries. The land cost RMB 80 million and construction costs were estimated to exceed RMB 1 billion, while Haier's 1992 profits were just RMB 51 million.

To finance such a large capital investment, Haier was counting on promised bank loans of RMB 1.6 billion, but within a month of the land purchase, the Chinese central government tightened credit nationally in an effort to halt real estate speculation.[13] Finding no other option, Haier turned to China's nascent stock market, listing 43.7% of its refrigerator division on the Shanghai Stock Exchange in November 1993. The IPO of A shares (limited to investors from mainland China) raised RMB 369 million. "It was the first time Haier had done such a risky thing," recalled Zhang. "If we had not been successful with our IPO, Haier would have disappeared. We'd never done anything like this, and that should be the only time we do it."[14]

Acquisitions continued throughout the 1990s, sometimes under government pressure to take over poorly performing firms.[15] In 1995, the Qingdao Municipal Government pushed the nearly bankrupt Red Star washing machine company onto Haier with the obligation to take on the firm's employees and RMB 132 million in debt, the equivalent of Haier's 1993 profits.[16] Within 18 months, however, Haier had turned Red Star into the top-ranked washing machine manufacturer in China.[17] Haier added televisions and telecommunications equipment to its product mix with the 1997 acquisition of Yellow Mountain Electronics located in Anhui province. By 1997, Haier had taken over 15 companies in accordance with Haier's acquisition strategy. "We buy only those firms that have markets and good products but bad management," Zhang said. "Then we introduce our own management and quality control to turn them around."[18]

Operational Restructuring

By 1998, Haier's annual revenues had reached RMB 16.8 billion and the firm's domestic market shares for refrigerators, washing machines, and air conditioners each exceeded 30%. Haier had much to celebrate, but the long period of extraordinary growth of consumer demand in China was showing signs of slowing. Retail consumption for 1997 had grown 11.6% over the previous year, the lowest increase since 1990. Industry optimists pointed to growing income levels among rural Chinese who accounted for 72% of population, but only about 10% of rural households owned a refrigerator and 20% had a washing machine in 1998.[19] (See **Exhibit 5.**)

Haier had exported appliances on an "original equipment manufacturer" (OEM) basis since the early 1990s, and by the mid-1990s had established several overseas JVs in Asia. (See *Haier in International Markets* on 10.) Haier was anxious to focus on overseas markets, but after a decade of adding factories, the company first reorganized to achieve greater efficiency and position itself to compete effectively with multinationals both at home and abroad. Haier's many manufacturing facilities were restructured into seven product divisions: Refrigerator, Air Conditioner, Washing Machine, IT Products, Kitchen & Bath, Technology Equipment, and Direct Affiliates (including communications, housing, and biological engineering).

Before 1998, most of the acquired businesses operated independent R&D, procurement, production, and sales departments. Haier replaced the numerous service departments with four new Group-wide "Development Divisions"—Capital Flow (Finance), Commerce Flow (Sales), Material Flow (Logistics), and Overseas (Global Operations)—whose heads reported directly to the Haier Group president. These new businesses operated as independent profit centers that competed with third-party service providers for Haier's business and could sell services to external clients as well.[20] Human Resources, R&D, and Customer Relations were also joined into group-wide business centers and sold their services on a fee basis to Haier Divisions. Similarly, Total Planning Management, Total Quality Management, and Total Equipment Management centers were formed by combining these functions across divisions. In 2000, Haier added an e-commerce company serving businesses and individual customers.

Haier in Chinese Markets

By 2004, Haier had overtaken domestic rivals and defended its ground against encroaching multinationals to become the number-one appliance company in China. While several firms held a top-three position in a particular market such as washing machines or air conditioners, Haier was the only company with leading shares across white goods sectors (**Exhibit 6**). Haier was dominant in the RMB 48 billion refrigerator and freezer market, which accounted for about 38% of all white goods sales in China. In 2002, Haier's share of the country's refrigerator market was 27% by volume and 52% by revenue, and analysts estimated that the company accounted for 61% of industry profits.[21]

National Competitors

From over 100 refrigerator producers in 1989, by 1996 China had just 20 major producers remaining, with the 10 largest accounting for 80% of the market, up from 50% four years earlier. According to a Chinese industry association, refrigerator manufacturers needed to produce more than one million units annually to be profitable.[22] Only three Chinese manufacturers, together accounting for about 60% of the market, fell into this category in 1996, Haier among them.

In the 1980s, Haier's commitment to quality had been enough to distinguish it from competitors, but as the weakest Chinese firms failed or were acquired, Haier faced more formidable Chinese competitors, many specializing in just one or two product lines. Chronic price wars, especially in the refrigerator sector, hurt all of the leading players, with some selling stock at or below cost to clear inventories. According to an industry analyst, "the leading domestic players failed to reach their growth potential due to the numerous money-losing small competitors, which were being sustained in part by regional governments' budgets."[23] But Haier cited its more diversified holdings, its differentiated products, and its export strategy as protective factors that ensured continued profits.

Among Haier's domestic rivals, only Guangdon Kelon, which had once held the top position in China's white goods market, offered a full line of home appliances. Like Haier, Kelon started out as a refrigerator manufacturer in the early 1980s. In 1998, Kelon merged with a leading Chinese air conditioner manufacturer. The company listed on the Hong Kong and Shenzhen stock exchanges in the late 1990s, and Whirlpool chose Kelon to manufacture washing machines in China. In contrast to Haier's single-brand approach, Kelon followed a multibrand strategy in China. High-end appliances carried the Kelon name; the Ronshen brand was used for mid-level models; and low-cost refrigerators and air conditioners sold under the Combine brand. Because Kelon sold refrigerators and air conditioners under all three brands, each with its own assembly lines and marketing campaigns, the company cited the attainment of scale efficiency as its biggest challenge.[24]

Blaming intense competition in China's refrigerator market, Kelon reported significant losses in 2000 and 2001. An accounting scandal revealed that the listed firm and its parent group had routinely shared credit facilities and paid each other's operating expenses.[25] Another Chinese refrigeration firm, Greencool Enterprises, acquired a majority shareholding in Kelon in late 2001. Kelon's new management introduced a strategy of targeting China's rural population, selling nearly a million units of a new lower-priced brand in the first year.[26] Haier already had a strong presence in the rural markets, but had not specifically targeted this segment with specially priced products. "The future lies in the second-line and third-line markets, which is the rural population in counties and townships," said Kelon's chief executive.[27] In 2003, about 23% of rural Chinese households owned a refrigerator.[28] Kelon posted a modest profit in 2003, but reported a loss of RMB 44.7 million in 2004, citing weak sales.[29]

Foreign Entrants

China's entry into the World Trade Organization in December 2001 added pressure on Haier. "Before, our competitors were domestic brands," said Gao. "But now after China's ascension into the WTO, our competitors are Siemens, Electrolux, Samsung, LG, Matsushita, Sony, GE, and Whirlpool." Some foreign consumer appliance brands were in China even earlier. Whirlpool formed a JV with a Chinese manufacturer to produce refrigerators in a plant near Beijing as early as 1994.[30] By 1996, Zhang noted that a second generation of competition had hit the Chinese white goods market. He observed: "The Chinese market has become part of the international appliance marketplace."[31]

Most multinationals realized that penetrating the Chinese market would not be easy. "Normally, people think it's a market of 1.2 billion people and that it's going to explode," said a Siemens executive. "But in terms of saturation levels, urban areas in China are quite well equipped. The big gap is in the rural areas and smaller towns, where saturation levels are below 10%."[32] Many multinationals were banking on the emergence of a replacement market in the large cities where they targeted the high-end market. "Setting up a sales and marketing network is a big challenge," added the Siemens executive. "It is tied closely to local conditions. . . . The key point is to build an effective sales and marketing organization that can also follow changes in distribution."[33]

The media noted that multinationals tended to underestimate the Chinese manufacturers, expecting competition to come from other newly arrived foreign firms. Instead, they found themselves competing with Haier and Kelon. "Their technology was nearly as good as Whirlpool's, their prices were lower, and their styling and distribution were better suited to China," wrote *The Economist*.[34] Thinking that the China market was not ready for the latest technology, Whirlpool produced Freon refrigerators with its JV partner in 1995. Meanwhile, Chinese manufacturers began to

5

respond to consumer demand for Freon-free units. In 1996, the Whirlpool JV sold less than 60% of its newly manufactured Freon refrigerators, resulting in a loss of nearly $11 million. Realizing its mistake, Whirlpool invested in a Freon-free production line in China, but by the time it was ready 18 months later, the market was nearly saturated.[35] Whirlpool invested in refrigerator, air conditioner, washing machine, and microwave factories in the mid-1990s, and accumulated losses of over $100 million in China by 1997. The U.S. company sold most of its holdings, saving the microwave factory by focusing it on exports, and devoting its washing machine factory to production for Kelon, which marketed the washers in China under its own brand.[36] But in 2001, Whirlpool began a comeback, launching 30 new products and setting up two global research and development centers and a large production facility in China.[37]

Foreign brands were taking market share away from Chinese brands at alarming rates. Multinational-brand refrigerator unit sales represented 31% of the Chinese market in 2002, up from 26% the previous year. Foreign brands were especially strong in the automatic washing machine sector where they accounted for 38% of sales in 2002, up from 31% in 2001. Nevertheless, Yang believed that Haier would preserve its local knowledge advantage over foreign firms:

> Haier is much closer to China's consumers, so we have a grasp on their changing tastes. We design according to Chinese consumers. And we have paid a lot of attention to developing human resources in the areas of marketing and design. Foreign companies design products for China based on foreign approaches. They are not in tune with Chinese culture and values.

Retail Channels

Before 2000, Haier's customers were mostly state-owned department stores, but by 2004 appliance sales had moved out of the department stores and into individual specialized shops and private retail chains. In 2004, domestic chains such as GOME accounted for about 30% of Haier's sales. GOME was China's largest home appliance seller with over 100 outlets in 22 of China's largest cities. International chains like Wal-Mart, in China only a few years, accounted for no more than 5% of Haier's domestic revenue. In second- and third-tier cities, Haier had set up networks of licensed dealers that accounted for another 30% of sales. Independent retail shops and government purchases accounted for about 15% each, with online and telephone sales making up the rest.

The shift in retail channels since 2000 affected how Haier managed its customer relations. As Gao explained:

> A few years ago Chinese white goods customers were not very picky and it was easy for large shops to make sales. At that time all we had to do to get their orders and keep our great market share was to maintain a good relationship with these large shops and give them the goods on time. Now our distributors are the major domestic chains as well as international retailers like Wal-Mart and Carrefour. These private retailers put more emphasis on the bottom line. The old concept of sales as managing the distributor relationship through "wine and dine" is not applicable in the current market. Retailers are no longer focused on how much you can drink together, but on how much money you can make for them.

The introduction of Western retail models to China's major cities coincided with the arrival of foreign multinational appliance brands like Siemens and GE which were very familiar with these channels. The WTO-mandated opening of the rest of China to foreign retailers by the end of 2004 threatened to erase domestic firm advantages beyond the first-tier cities. However, Gao did not believe that knowledge and experience of dealing with large multinational retail chains would give foreign white goods firms enough of an edge to displace Haier. "The multinational brands together account for less than 10% of China's white goods market, so they don't have much clout with retail chains, whether domestic or international," he said. Foreign brands would fare even worse in second- and third-tier cities and in rural areas, according to Gao. He explained:

> Many foreign brands, including American ones like GE and Whirlpool, have a hard time adapting to the Chinese population and vastness. Their tried and tested sales approaches work on a more uniform population. But the diversity in geography and buying preferences in China are huge. In the rural areas, it's mostly small private enterprises that sell appliances. In one county, there may be only two or three such shops that monopolize the whole area. There are no domestic or international hypermarkets in China's rural regions.

Haier's Market Advantages

Haier executives cited the reputation of the brand and the company's creativity as the firm's main strengths for competing inside China. "Consumers recognize Haier as the number-one brand in China," said Gao. "Our prices are 20% more than our competitors', but we still have the most sales." The brand was supported by investing 5% to 7% of revenue into R&D each year. "This means we have new products each year. Our products are not made obsolete by our competitors, but by our own new products," Gao added. Haier executives would not claim any definitive operational superiority, but there were at least three areas in which Haier consistently won praise: innovative and rapid market response, superior after-sales service, and efficient distribution.

Market responsiveness "We have been successful in China because we are focused on meeting customer needs," said Zhang. "We are organized to understand what customers want and to meet those needs, which are sometimes quite differentiated."[38] Haier's 42 distribution centers throughout China operated as independent "sales companies" that needed to be responsive to the needs of customers to remain profitable.

When a customer in China's rural Sichuan province complained to Haier that his washing machine was breaking down, service technicians found the plumbing clogged with mud. Rural Chinese were using the Haier machines, meant to wash clothing, to clean sweet potatoes and other vegetables. Haier engineers modified the washer design to accommodate peasant needs. Since then, Haier washing machines sold in Sichuan were labeled, "Mainly for washing clothes, sweet potatoes and peanuts."[39]

To accommodate summer lifestyles requiring frequent changes of clothing, Haier created a tiny washing machine that cleaned a single change of clothes. The model saved on electricity and water usage, making it an instant hit in Shanghai. It was later successfully introduced to Europe. Other innovations included a washer that cleaned clothes without detergent, and a model that could wash and dry clothes in a single machine, also popular in cities where space and time were at a premium.

Haier's strategy of meeting localized market demand at home and abroad with innovative models (for example, a refrigerator with a compartment for pickling Korean kimchee cabbage) had resulted in about 96 product categories and 15,100 specifications. Haier executives maintained that these kinds of feature innovations were inexpensive to produce, but highly valued by customers. "To manage the costs of manufacturing our many different product models, our products are based on modules of components and subsystems, and on basic platforms that we can vary," said Zhang. "Periodically, we will add some new features, but the basic model is there. We don't change them randomly."[40]

Service In 1990, Haier had set up a service center in Qingdao that used a computerized system to track tens of thousands of customers. The effort soon paid off, as customers throughout China, accustomed to expecting little or no after-sales service, began to recognize Haier as a new breed of company. Stories like that of taxi driver Chu Xiaoming and his 10-year-old Haier refrigerator were repeated throughout China. In 1996, Chu half-heartedly called Haier's customer hotline, not expecting to get much help for a broken-down appliance purchased a decade earlier. One industry observer noted:

> To Chu's surprise, a uniformed serviceman showed up on his doorstep the very next day. He took the fridge back to the factory and lent Chu another for the interim. Two weeks later, Chu's old refrigerator was once again chilling his family's meats and vegetables. And best of all, the service didn't cost an arm and a leg. "They only charged me 200–300 renminbi ($24–$36) for the repairs," he said. "I'm very satisfied."[41]

By 2004, Haier had a service network of 5,500 independent contractors, one for each sales outlet. Some of these service contractors were exclusive to Haier; others serviced both Haier and competing products. Haier product owners could call a nationwide hotline to arrange for a house call by a service agent. If the appliance needed to be removed from the home for servicing, Haier provided a temporary replacement free of charge. Haier's warranty periods covering full repair costs either met or exceeded Chinese government regulations. According to Gao, customer appreciation of Haier service was one of the company's greatest competitive advantages. "In the country's ranking of service levels and after-sales service, Haier always ranks number one," he said. "Whether in quality of service or in volume, no one is able to compare to Haier at the moment."

Distribution   Haier Logistics, an independently operated company created in 1999 as part of Haier's reorganization, had become a national pioneer in the field, offering "just in time" (JIT) purchasing, raw materials delivery, and product distribution. Between 1998 and 2004, Haier had reduced the size of its main raw materials warehouse from 200,000 square meters with an inventory cycle of over 30 days, to a 20,000-square-meter distribution center with a seven-day inventory cycle. In 2004 Haier's JIT order-execution center purchased about 300,000 different components for the group's production lines from about 1000 suppliers in China and overseas, down from 2,300 suppliers before the reorganization. Logistics delivered raw materials to the production sites every two hours, on average, with inventory updates and inter-company payments made automatically using bar code scanning. Factory production usually began as soon as an order was received and took one or two days, depending on the product.

Haier required full payment in cash before completing delivery on purchase orders. Once payment had been received, Logistics delivered the goods to one of 42 Haier distribution centers located throughout China. Substantial government investments in transportation infrastructure since the late 1980s allowed Haier to take advantage of China's growing highway network. Working with over 300 transport companies which used about 16,000 vehicles across every region of China except Tibet, the network moved over 100,000 products each day, not counting small items like cellular telephones and vacuum cleaners. Haier delivered very large orders directly to retailer warehouses. Each distribution center dealt with an average of 200 customers, some with multiple retail outlets. The entire process, from initial order to final delivery of the products, took about 10 days, down from 36 days before the reorganization and introduction of information systems.

The main differentiator between Haier Logistics and domestic competitors was that Haier had reorganized logistics into a single company serving the entire group. Other Chinese companies like Midea and TCL had separate logistics operations for each product line. "Haier has very broad product lines, and Logistics makes deliveries for the entire group and for other brands besides Haier group," said logistics information center executive Zhan Li. "When transporting a refrigerator, we can also deliver a microwave, a water heater, and other products. Other companies don't really do this. This kind of scale and volume probably gives us one of the lowest logistics costs." Zhan also saw Haier's advantage over multinational companies:

> In China, there are still regulations limiting multinationals in the area of Logistics, so they have entered China on a JV basis. Multinationals have more experience than us, having gained knowledge of different approaches and practices through their worldwide operations. But in terms of logistics cost or network, they have no competitive advantage. Their staff costs must be higher than ours and they don't have a network in China. So I don't think they are very competitive in the China domestic market.

Establishing a logistics network in China was a complicated matter, requiring coverage of a vast territory, navigating widely divergent terrains, and negotiating with numerous local governments. Regulations affecting transportation could vary from location to location—for example, weight limits for trucks, making logistics a more onerous production than in developed countries. Obstacles to creating a highly integrated warehousing system like Haier's were also numerous. In large cities like Shanghai, it was difficult to find warehouse space large enough to accommodate the huge trucks required for white goods. In the most remote areas it was a challenge to connect warehouses to a company's information network. "Setting up a warehouse and delivering goods to surrounding areas in Inner Mongolia or Xinjiang Autonomous Region is difficult and expensive," said Zhan. "It's not something you can build overnight. It involves a lot of infrastructure."

Foreign multinationals could contract with one of the many independent Chinese logistics companies to handle distribution, but costs would likely be higher and coverage areas were usually limited to particular regions. "Foreign companies tend to cluster in the more developed costal areas and there are many independent logistics companies based there. These companies don't have extensive penetration of internal regions of the country, but the volume of business is not that great in those regions," explained Zhan. Multinationals that wanted China-wide coverage would have to patch together a national network using several different logistics companies. Still, many foreign companies, such as Samsung, successfully outsourced logistics to Chinese service providers. Foreign multinationals that tried to run their own distribution networks generally failed. The *China Economic Times* attributed Whirlpool's losses in the washing machine market to the multinational company's neglect of its Chinese JV partner's existing distribution network. Whirlpool tried to establish its own sales team and distribution channels, leading to high operating costs for its Chinese JV.[42]

Some Haier executives were cautious about relying on their strengths in the distribution and service networks, or even on superior knowledge of the domestic market. Gao believed that foreign companies entering China could access similar resources through third parties and become more competitive if they adapted to local market needs. He elaborated:

> They can spend money buying people who understand the China market, and they can buy the sales channels and service as well. Electrolux came into China with nothing, and they took people from Haier and quickly established a brand in China. So I don't think these are the core strengths for Haier. I think these tangible strengths are temporary. If we just sit on these strengths, sooner or later GE will catch up. I think GE and Whirlpool are great companies with a long history of over 100 years. They haven't done very well in China because they have not been very localized. If they get localized, I am sure they would do very well.

Haier in International Markets

Haier developed a formal global expansion strategy beginning in 1997 when Zhang announced his "three thirds" goal of having Haier's revenue derive in equal parts from sales of goods in three categories: one-third from goods produced and sold in China, one-third produced in China and sold overseas, and one-third produced and sold overseas. Overseas sales for 1998, largely to Europe and the United States, amounted to just over $62 million, or about 3% of total Group sales.[43] The creation of Haier's Overseas Promotion Division in 1999 signaled the beginning of rapid growth in international sales through exports and overseas production, bringing the combined figure to nearly 17% of total revenue in 2004. (See **Exhibit 1b**.)

Haier had started to venture into overseas markets as a contract manufacturer for multinational brands in the early 1990s, first exporting to the United Kingdom and Germany, and then to France and Italy. Haier also used JVs to explore foreign markets. In 1994, Mitsubishi invested $30 million for a 55% stake in a JV with Haier to set up China's largest air conditioner plant. The Qingdao factory would produce five of Mitsubishi's latest models for export to Japan.[44] In 1995, Haier became one of the first Chinese companies to engage in foreign direct investment, setting up a refrigerator and air conditioner plant in Indonesia as the majority partner in a JV with a local firm.[45] In 1997 Haier launched its first European manufacturing base, producing air conditioners in Belgrade through a JV with a Yugoslav company.[46]

Haier refrigerators sold particularly well in Germany, where they were marketed by the German appliance firm Liebherr under the "Blue Line" brand. When a blind quality test by a German magazine gave Haier's Blue Line refrigerators eight top rankings, beating Liebherr's seven, Haier decided it was time to market its own brand overseas. In 1997, Germany became the first export market for Haier-branded refrigerators. The same year, Haier formed a JV with the Philippine electronics company LKG to manufacture Haier-branded freezers, air conditioners, and washing machines in the Philippines for sale to local and regional markets.[47]

Haier continued OEM production for foreign multinationals and actively sought new OEM clients, but after 1999 the company was focused on selling Haier-branded products in overseas markets. "The objective of most Chinese enterprises is to export products and earn foreign currency. This is their only purpose," said Zhang. "Our purpose in exporting is to establish a brand reputation overseas."[48]

Typically, Chinese manufacturers exported products under an OEM client brand. For example, Kelon, Haier's largest domestic rival, had overseas sales amounting to 12.5% of total revenue in 2003,[49] but did not market its own brand overseas. At one time, Kelon-made refrigerators carrying the Magic Chef brand sold alongside Haier-branded refrigerators at U.S. Wal-Mart stores.[50] Because of the low-quality image associated with Chinese-manufactured products, said Kelon's chairman, the company preferred to manufacture products for multinational OEMs.[51]

Haier, on the other hand, was willing to bear the early costs of establishing the firm as an independent player overseas. "I predict that overseas profit growth will be a little slower than the overall company's profit growth," said Zhang. "In some mature markets we will make profits, but in entering new markets we may also at first lose money."[52]

In pursuing expansion of its brand to international markets, Haier was emulating the strategies of successful Japanese and Korean firms such as Sony, Samsung, and LG. LG Electronics, with total 2004 revenues of $24 billion (about 25% from white goods sales), was perhaps the most likely model for Haier. LG produced the first Korean refrigerator in the 1950s, and expanded into other home appliances and electronics. In the 1990s, following a makeover of its budget Lucky-Goldstar brand

10

into the higher-end LG brand, the company began its global expansion into strategic markets selected primarily on the basis of market size and expected growth, openness to foreign businesses, and intensity of competition.[53]

LG decided to focus international expansion on China and Southeast Asia. The company also established regional headquarters for Eastern Europe, Latin America, the Middle East, and Africa, which were considered secondary but high-potential markets. Seeing no competitive advantage in pursuing the developed markets of the United States, Japan, and Western Europe, LG initially maintained only a modest presence in those regions.[54] Aided by the fall of the Korean currency during the late-1990s Asian financial crisis, LG's overseas sales soared from 30% of appliance revenues before the crisis to 70% in 2001. By 2004, LG's overseas appliance sales reached about US $4 billion, and the company had made significant inroads in the U.S. market. However, while 82% of the firm's appliance sales were LG-branded, branded products accounted for just 55% of LG's U.S. sales.[55]

International Strategies

Focus on difficult markets first   Shunning conventional wisdom, Haier determined to focus on the "difficult" developed markets first, and only after proving itself in those, to go after the relatively "easy" emerging markets. In 2004, about 70% of Haier's overseas sales came from the developed markets of Europe, the United States, and Japan. Zhang explained the strategy:

> Many Chinese enterprises will first export to Southeast Asia, for instance, which has competitive markets but where there are no strong, dominant competitors. . . . We go to easier markets after we first penetrate difficult markets such as the United States and Europe. These are much bigger markets. They are also the home markets of our largest global competitors, and we believe that if we can succeed there, we can succeed in easier markets.[56]

Haier also saw going into developed markets as a way to challenge itself to meet the highest quality standards. "We chose the developed countries first because the requirements of both customers and retailers are very tough and not easy to meet," said Li Pan, Haier's brand manager for overseas markets. "For example, by entering the U.S. market, we learn the UL requirements and the difference between the U.S. customers and the Chinese customers. We learn a lot of things that we could not know if we just got into the Southeast Asian market or other developing markets."

The prestige of having a brand that sold in Europe or the United States was such that Haier could arrive in emerging markets with a ready-made reputation, thought Haier Overseas Division executives. "Customers in India or the Middle East already know our brand because when they travel they have seen our advertisements in Paris or Tokyo," said one executive. Haier also used its U.S. and European experience to convince emerging market retailers to carry Haier products. Haier found that even having a few successful products in the developed markets opened the door to introducing the full line of Haier products to developing markets, including high-end models, from the beginning.

"If we can effectively compete in the mature markets with such brand names as GE, Matsushita, and Philips, we can surely take the markets in the developing countries without much effort," reasoned Zhang. "It is just like what we did with the domestic market. After Haier refrigerators had taken Beijing and Shanghai, we met no difficulties getting into medium and small cities."[57]

Begin with niche products   Haier typically entered developed markets with just a few models to test the waters and steer clear of major competitors. "When we entered the U.S. market, we found that nobody was making competitive refrigerators for students or for offices. So we offered what the U.S. manufacturers did not make because for them the volume and prices were too low, and within three years we had over 30% market share in compact refrigerators," said Overseas Division executive Diao Yunfeng. With minimal competition, the niche products brought in high margins, added Diao. When others began to imitate, Haier added new features such as mini-fridges that doubled as computer desks, aimed at college students living in dorms.

Having a very successful product like compact refrigerators or wine cellars in the U.S. allowed Haier to get the attention of the major retail chains like Wal-Mart and Best Buy. Having developed a relationship with them, Haier was in a stronger position to get the major chains to consider Haier's major appliances. "After we were successful in the niche products, then we started to introduce regular products to the U.S. like the standard refrigerators, the apartment refrigerators, air conditioners, washing machines, and other products," said Diao.

Staff with locals   When entering a new market, "the first stage is to use the right people to establish the structure," said Li. "If we use local people, we can expand very quickly because local people know the local market very well. If we use Haier, we don't have enough human resources, especially people with an international perspective, to expand worldwide." Haier would begin by identifying a local person with experience, preferably in a leading white goods firm, to head the country operation. That person would hire a local team and develop sales and distribution channels.

"Our strategy is not just export; we want to use local people and local thinking to satisfy the needs of the customer," said Yang. "Compared to other foreign brands, we have an advantage in that we have gathered experienced people who have worked for top brands to join us." This is not the same as what multinationals entering China have done, explained Yang. "When top foreign companies come to China, they also use local Chinese, but these Chinese have not worked with major brands before. So if they are using Chinese people with no brand experience to build their brand in China, then they are in trouble."

Li believed that in time Haier would have to place its own people in key positions overseas to get better market intelligence. "We want to get more involved in the details ourselves. We have to know the information at the end terminal. You have to have your own people who will report from the field," said Li. "People are our eyes, noses, and ears. If you don't have the people, you don't know what is happening in the market. The country CEO cannot report on everything."

Yang preferred to continue sending only temporary technical support teams from China while relying on local partners to operate the business. Yang believed that U.S. consumers saw Haier as an American brand, "because Haier is produced and sold by Americans," she said. "We hope to have Haier in each country be the Haier that *they* created. For example, in the United States, we hope that it is Americans who build up Haier America," said Yang. "If Americans can create GE and Whirlpool and Electrolux, they can create Haier."

International Divisions

Haier organized overseas sales into five large regional markets: The Americas, Europe, the Middle East, Southeast Asia and East Asia. The Americas region, dominated by U.S. sales, accounted for about 30% of overseas revenue, Europe for another 30%, and the remaining regions combined made up the remaining 40%. Haier-branded products, about 80% in white goods, sold globally through 62 distributors and over 30,000 retail outlets. About 59,000 sales agents and 12,000 service personnel supported sales operations. Haier operated 18 design institutes, 13 overseas factories, and 11 industrial complexes (eight in China and one each in the U.S., Pakistan, and Jordan.)[58]

Haier's formal International Divisions included JVs on five continents. Usually Haier was the majority shareholder. In some cases, such as in the Middle East, Haier held a minority share in JVs. Launched in Dubai, United Arab Emirates in 1999, Haier Middle East developed a network of dealerships and service centers throughout the region. In 2002, Haier began manufacturing locally through JVs with firms in Iran and Algeria that produced refrigerators, washing machines, and air conditioners.[59] Haier Industrial Park in Pakistan began production in 2002. The JV with the Pakistani R Group, the country's largest dealer of household appliances, took advantage of Pakistan's largest marketing and sales network for white goods.[60] In 2001 Haier formed a JV with a Nigerian firm, Nigeria Haier Company, and in 2002 Haier New Zealand launched. As of early 2005, Haier's largest overseas operations were in Europe and the United States, with the recently launched India operation poised for rapid growth.

Haier America   Haier's entry into the U.S. market began in 1994 when Michael Jemal, a partner in a New York-based import company, Welbilt Appliances, approached the Qingdao manufacturer. At the time, just three Haier compact refrigerator models met U.S. energy and safety standards, and Jemal purchased 150,000 units to be sold in the U.S. All 150,000 sold under the Welbilt name within the year, capturing 10% of the U.S. market for compact refrigerators.

Following the success of the Welbilt line of mini-refrigerators, in 1999 Haier and Jemal formed a JV called "Haier America" to market a broader selection of products under the Haier brand. Haier America launched with rented office space in Manhattan, 17 staff people, and a $50 million sales target for the first year of operations. Jemal compared the new Haier operation to Sony's 1960 startup in a similarly dilapidated New York building. The difference was that Sony had brought 13 people from Japan to staff the new business; the Haier team was all American, except for the accountant who was sent from Qingdao.[61] Haier America later moved its headquarters into a landmark building on Broadway, which Haier purchased in 2001 for $14.5 million.

Haier established a $40 million industrial park and refrigerator factory in South Carolina. "Of course, labor costs are much higher in the United States than they are in China. They can be 10 times higher," said Zhang. "But our strategy in the U.S. market is not to manufacture cheap products, take them out of the factory, and push them into the market. We intend to manufacture quality products that we can sell at a premium."[62] Haier's U.S. factory had production capacity for 400,000 units per year. In 2002 Haier sold 80,000 full-size refrigerators in the U.S., accounting for about 2% of the market. Haier's U.S. factory, even after a planned expansion, did not have capacity for producing Haier's 10% target market share, so Haier planned to supplement with exports from China.[63]

Jemal focused on getting Haier products into the large chain retailers such as Home Depot, Best Buy, and Office Depot. (See **Exhibit 7** for U.S. distribution channels.) The most difficult one to break into was Wal-Mart, recalled Jemal. "It took us a whole year just to get an appointment." Wal-Mart finally agreed to look at Haier's room air conditioners, and after testing different products for quality and visiting Haier's manufacturing facilities in Qingdao, placed an order for 50,000 units. The next year, Wal-Mart doubled its order. In 2002, Haier sold 400,000 units of compact refrigerators, washing machines, and air conditioners to the giant retailer. In March 2005, Wal-Mart's online site listed 44 different Haier products, most targeted to the college student market. The best-sellers were a $140 compact refrigerator, a 125-can beverage center for $165, and a $200 portable clothes washer. Topping Wal-Mart's list of Haier products was a half-keg beer dispenser selling for $675.[64]

The focus on niche markets enabled Haier to avoid head-on competition with the likes of GE, Whirlpool, Maytag, and Frigidaire, which together accounted for 98% of U.S. sales of full-size refrigerators. "We don't look to compete with them, because they are much bigger than we are," said Jemal. "We believe we have our separate position in the market, and they have theirs. They can step on us anytime they want, because we are so small compared to them in the United States."[65] (See

Exhibits **8** and **9** for U.S. appliance market shares.) In 2005 *Euromonitor* reported that Haier had a 26% share for compact refrigerators, over 50% of the wine cellar market, and 17% of air conditioner sales in the United States.[66]

Haier Europe   In 2000 Haier Europe, headquartered in Varese, Italy, near the Swiss border, began coordinating sales and marketing of Haier products in 13 European countries, growing to 17 markets by 2004. Product lines included refrigerators, freezers, washing machines, dishwashers, microwave ovens, and small appliances, all designed specifically for the European market. Haier chose a former sales executive of Italy's Merloni, Europe's third-largest appliance maker, to head its European operations. The Italian executive had started his own trading company, selling GE, Whirlpool, and Siemens products, before joining Haier.[67]

In 2001, Haier invested $8 million to acquire a refrigerator plant in Padova, Italy, from Meneghetti SpA, one of Italy's largest manufacturers of built-in appliances made to match kitchen cabinetry. The new Haier plant manufactured built-in refrigerators and freezers for the expanding built-in sector, popular in the European market. In 2002, a new Italy-based company, Haier A/C Trading, began distributing Haier air conditioners in the local market.[68] By 2004 Haier had an estimated 10% share of European air conditioner sales.[69] Haier's European HQ in Varese coordinated logistics through four distribution centers in Italy, Spain, the United Kingdom, and the Netherlands.

The European appliance market was similar to the U.S. market in size and degree of development, but significant differences in distribution channels and consumer preferences across countries made it difficult for manufacturers to establish scale economies. For example, most Europeans favored front-loading washers, but in France, one of the largest markets, consumers preferred top-loaders. Independent appliance retailers dominated in Germany and Italy, while chain stores were common in France and the United Kingdom. There were few pan-European appliance retailers, and national and independent stores often favored domestic manufacturers. As a result, multinational appliance manufacturers had often found themselves at a disadvantage to local national players that tended to dominate in individual countries.[70]

Haier India   Haier earmarked India as a potential high-growth market, and invested heavily in building up production, distribution, and sales capacities in the country. In 1999 Haier formed an alliance with Indian appliance firm Fedder Lloyd Corp. to jointly produce and market refrigerators nationally. In January 2004 Haier launched a broad range of products in the Indian market, with the goal of becoming one of the top three white goods firms in India within five to seven years. A few months later, Haier announced a $200 million investment in India over four years to establish a refrigerator factory and research and development center that would serve as a production site for Southeast Asian and African markets. In June 2004, Haier India formed an alliance with Whirlpool and Voltas to manufacture refrigerators and air conditioners for the Indian market.[71]

In India, Haier discovered that the "easy" emerging markets were not so easy. The biggest challenges for Haier in India were "the environment, the economy, and especially the channels," said Li. "In the United States you can easily find the top 10 chain stores. But in India, you cannot find them." Haier found that emerging markets required an even greater reliance on locals. Haier employed a former Whirlpool India executive to head Haier India. "This key person explains the whole market to us, including how to develop the channels and how to do the marketing, and we just provide the product. He chooses the products and proposes modifications for the local market," said Li. "He also helped us to find the right factory, find the best way to assemble the product, and get it to the distributor. In India we used local human resources to help us establish the whole business."

Competing Abroad

Zhang explained his two-pronged strategy for competing with local brands on Haier's home turf:

> Consumers in the United States are used to popular brands like GE and Whirlpool, so they'll wonder why they should choose a brand they've never heard of. But large companies are established and slow moving, and we see an opportunity to compete against them in their home markets by being more customer-focused than they are. To win over those consumers we have two approaches: speed and differentiation.[72]

Product differentiation   Just as in China, Haier paid close attention to consumer needs in overseas markets and was willing to make small product modifications to please customers. "Our strategy for selling large refrigerators is the same as for compact refrigerators," said Zhang. "We send our R&D people to the United States to talk directly with our customers, or even with the salespeople in chain stores, to find out their specific needs."[73] Haier's market research resulted in simple innovations such as a freezer with a separate compartment to keep ice cream at a slightly warmer temperature, making it softer and easier to serve. "Consumers like the features we provide," said Zhang. "Large manufacturers aren't paying attention to such minor details."[74]

Response speed   Haier's 18 design centers, some in foreign markets, facilitated rapid product development. Ideas from the field could be quickly tested and made into prototypes. For example, having noted that American customers did not like deep-box freezers because items at the bottom were difficult to reach, during a visit to Qingdao, Jemal suggested to Zhang a two-level model with a drawer on the bottom. Seventeen hours later, Jemal was presented with a working model of his design. Haier executives also credited the firm's flat structure with aiding speed. Salespeople would provide market intelligence directly to model managers who, in competition with each other, would quickly assess the feasibility and profitability of a design before mobilizing resources to produce it.

The Next 20 Years

Haier faced a number of challenges in the coming years, including moving beyond niche markets in the United States to its goal of introducing a full line of products. While Haier had done well on a small scale, some industry observers doubted whether a Chinese company could break into the major leagues. "As a brand, Haier doesn't work," said a U.S. industry analyst. "People may buy a dorm refrigerator from Haier, but I don't think they'll spend a lot of money on an appliance from a company they've never heard of."[75] A Whirlpool executive believed that "one of the steps that many of the Asian companies have missed is the huge investment that's required to build brand equity."[76] But in 2005, Haier was spending about 10% of revenues on global branding and marketing, more than double the industry average.[77]

Haier would also continue to be challenged at home. Whirlpool and Electrolux had invested millions of dollars on factories and distribution in China. According to *Euromonitor*, "These companies believe that going head–to–head with Haier Group in its domestic market will prevent it from gaining the profits it might otherwise use to support its advance in the U.S."[78]

Haier's leadership was most concerned with securing the human resources needed to maintain rapid growth, especially to manage foreign markets. Haier also needed talent to develop the next generation of products. The company planned to combine its expertise in white goods with information technology, a relatively new area for Haier, to produce "intelligent" home appliances.

But above all, Haier kept its eye on developing the brand. "We are number three in the world for white goods," said Yang. "We want to be number one." Haier planned to get there one step at a time, securing market leadership at home in each sector, and then taking that product line into the global market. "In the international market, we want to get a 10% share to begin with. After that, we can expand more." Haier's long-term goal was to achieve Zhang's vision of one-third domestic sales, one-third exports, and one-third produced and sold abroad, said Yang. "Exports are about 20% now, and overseas made are at less than 10%—so the potential is great."

Exhibit 1a Haier Group Approximate Revenue and Net Profit (in RMB billions)

RMB bil	1994	1995	1996	1997	1998	1999	2000	2001	2002	2003	2004
Revenue	2.6	4.3	6.2	10.8	16.8	26.9	40.6	60.2	72.0	80.0	100.0
YoY growth	72%	69%	42%	75%	56%	60%	51%	48%	20%	11%	25%
Net profit							1.4	2.0	2.7	1.6	1.9
Net margin							3.4	3.3	3.8	2.0	1.9

Source: Company documents.

Note: Profit data for 1994–1999 was not available. Haier attributed the 2003 decline in profit to price wars in the domestic market and to increased investments in overseas markets.

Exhibit 1b Haier Group Approximate Revenue Breakdown (in US$ millions)

US$ millions	1998	1999	2000	2001	2002	2003	2004
Domestic sales	1,971	3,112	4,633	6,861	7,868	8,648	10,100
as % of total revenue	97.0	95.8	94.3	94.2	90.3	89.3	83.4
Exports from China	62	138	280	424	444	532	1,000
as % of total revenue	3.0	4.2	5.7	5.8	5.1	5.5	8.3
Overseas made & sold	<1	<1	<1	<1	400	500	1,000
as % of total revenue	na	na	na	na	4.6	5.2	8.3
Total revenue	2,033	3,250	4,913	7,284	8,712	9,680	12,100

Source: Company documents.

17

Exhibit 2a Manufacturer Global Market Shares for Large Kitchen Appliances[a] (retail volume)

Manufacturer	Base Country	2001 Volume %	2002 Volume %
Whirlpool Corp	United States	7.9	7.9
Electrolux AB	Sweden	7.3	7.1
Bosch-Siemens Hausgerate	Germany	5.8	5.7
General Electric (GE)	United States	5.3	5.4
Haier Group	China	3.2	3.8
Matsushita Ltd	Japan	3.1	3.2
Maytag Corp	United States	3.0	3.1
LG Group	Korea	2.4	2.6
Sharp Electronics	Japan	2.6	2.6
Merloni Elettrodomestici	Italy	2.3	2.5
Samsung Electronics Co	Korea	1.8	2.0
Wuxi Little Swan Co	China	1.5	2.0
Others		53.8	52.1
Total		100.0	100.0

Exhibit 2b Brand Global Market Shares for Large Kitchen Appliances[a] (retail volume)

Brand	Manufacturer	2001 Volume %	2002 Volume %
Whirlpool	Whirlpool Corp	5.2	5.2
GE	General Electric (GE)	3.7	3.8
Haier	Haier Group	3.2	3.8
Bosch	Bosch-Siemens Hausgerate	2.8	2.8
Sharp	Sharp Electronics	2.6	2.6
LG	LG Group	2.2	2.5
Maytag	Maytag Corp	1.9	2.0
Samsung	Samsung Electronics Co	1.8	2.0
Little Swan	Wuxi Little Swan Co	1.5	2.0
National	Matsushita Ltd	1.8	1.9
Siemens	Bosch-Siemens Hausgerate	1.7	1.6
Electrolux	Electrolux AB	1.5	1.6
Others		70.1	68.2
Total		100.0	100.0

Source: Euromonitor International, "The World Market for Domestic Electrical Appliances," February 2004, available from Global Market Information Database, http://www.euromonitor.com, accessed May 24, 2005.

Note: Manufacturers with more than one major brand may have a high manufacturer market share and lower brand shares.

[a]Large Kitchen Appliances included refrigerators, freezers, stoves, ovens, washers, dryers, microwave ovens, and dishwashers.

Exhibit 3a Qingdao Haier Financials in RMB millions, 2000–2004

Year ended December 31	2000	2001	2002	2003	2004
Income Statement					
Sales revenue	4,828	11,442	11,554	11,688	15,299
Operating costs	6,135	11,098	11,548	11,570	14,892
Taxes	48	201	108	100	113
Net profit	424	618	397	369	369
Balance Sheet					
Current assets	2,263	3,445	3,494	4,020	3,958
Total assets	3,934	6,942	7,324	7,373	7,107
Current liabilities	828	1,613	1,664	1,392	783
Long term debt	NA	NA	0	138	138
Total liabilities	1,123	2,010	2,065	1,984	1,389
Total equity	2,810	4,932	5,259	5,389	5,719
Cash Flows					
Operating activities	478	702	391	424	738
Investing activities	-461	-2,365	-658	206	-149
Financing activities	-126	1,914	218	-363	-704
Net change in cash	-109	250	-50	267	-115
Cash beginning balance	491	382	632	582	830
Cash ending balance	382	632	582	849	715

Exhibit 3b Qingdao Haier Financial Ratios, 2000–2004

Year ended December 31	2000	2001	2002	2003	2004
Liquidity Ratios					
Current ratio	2.7	2.1	2.1	2.9	5.1
Quick ratio	2.3	1.8	1.5	2.5	4.0
Working capital (US$ mil)	173.4	221.3	221.1	317.5	383.5
Operating Ratios					
Asset turnover	1.3	2.1	1.6	1.6	2.1
Inventory turnover	9.1	20.1	16.5	16.5	18.3
Receivables turnover	7.3	15.4	15.6	18.9	19.5
Profitability Ratios (%)					
Gross margin	18.0	16.6	12.9	14.5	13.1
Operating margin	7.7	8.6	5.6	5.2	4.1
EBITDA margin	9.7	10.1	7.2	6.8	5.5
Profit margin	8.9	5.4	3.4	3.2	2.4
Return on equity	15.7	16.0	7.8	6.9	6.7
Return on assets	11.0	11.4	5.6	5.0	5.1
SG&A expense/sales	10.4	8.2	7.6	9.5	9.1

Source: Company documents.

Exhibit 4   Qingdao Haier 2003 Revenues by Product

Product category	Revenues (as % of RMB 11.7 billion total)
Air conditioners	52
Refrigerators	28
Freezers	7
Small electrical appliances	4
Other	9

Source: Adapted from "Qingdao Haier," *China Securities Research*, November 8, 2004, available from Thomson Research/Investext, http://research.thomsonib.com, accessed April 9, 2005.

Exhibit 5   China's Household Penetration Rates for Consumer Goods

	1985	1990	1995	2000	2001	2002
Refrigerators						
Urban	6.6	42.7	66.2	80.1	81.9	87.4
Rural			5.2	12.3	13.6	14.8
Air Conditioners						
Urban		1.4	8.1	30.8	35.8	51.1
Rural			0.2	1.3	1.7	na
Washing Machines						
Urban	48.3	78.4	89.0	90.5	92.2	92.9
Rural			16.9	28.6	29.9	31.8
Color Televisions						
Urban	17.2	59.0	89.8	116.6	120.5	126.4
Rural			16.9	48.7	54.4	48.1

Source: Graham Ormerod, "Guangdong Kelon: A White Good Comeback Play," *G.K. Goh Research*, August 29, 2003, available from Thomson Research/Investext, http://research.thomsonib.com, accessed April 9, 2005.

Exhibit 6a   Refrigerator Market Shares in China (retail volume)

Company	Leading Brands	2002 (%)	2003(%)	2004(%)
Haier Group	Haier	26.7	26.2	28.2
Guangdon Kelon	Kelon, Ronshen, Combine	13.4	12.4	10.8
Henan Xinfei	Xinfei	8.5	8.5	8.9
Wuxi Bosch-Siemens	Siemens	8.4	8.4	8.5
Changsha Zhongyi Group	Electrolux	10.1	7.7	6.9
Nanjing LG Panda Appliance	LG	4.9	7.0	6.6
Hefi Meiling Group	Meiling	8.4	7.8	6.1
Suzhou Samsung	Samsung	4.2	3.9	4.4
Hefei Rongshida Group	Rongshida	2.6	3.6	4.1
Panasonic China	Panasonic	1.7	2.3	2.9
Others		11.1	12.1	12.8

Exhibit 6b   Washing Machine Market Shares in China (retail volume)

Company	Leading Brands	2002 (%)	2003(%)	2004(%)
Haier Group	Haier	25.8	25.7	30.4
Wuxi Little Swan	Little Swan	20.7	18.8	16.5
Hefei Rongshida Group	Rongshida	10.6	10.0	10.6
Nanjing LG Panda Appliance	LG	5.0	6.7	7.0
Matsushita Electric China	National	6.1	6.0	6.3
Shanghai Whirlpool	Whirlpool	4.0	4.2	4.0
Wuxi Bosch-Siemens	Siemens	3.5	3.6	3.6
Suzhou Samsung	Samsung	2.7	3.1	2.8
Hefei Royalstar	Sanyo	2.4	2.4	2.6
Jiangmen Jinling	Jinling	3.4	2.2	1.9
Others		16.0	17.4	14.2

Exhibit 6c   Air Conditioner Market Shares in China (retail volume)

Company	Leading Brands	2002 (%)	2003(%)	2004(%)
Haier Group	Haier	16.3	16.6	17.5
GD Midea Holding	Midea	10.9	10.9	11.4
Chuhai Gree	Gree	7.4	9.1	10.0
LG Electronics (Tianjin)	LG	5.5	6.4	6.4
Ningbo O	Ningbo	4.0	6.5	6.1
Qingdao Hisense	Hisense	6.2	5.7	5.6
Guangdon Kelon	Kelon, Ronshen, Combine	5.6	5.8	5.7
Chunlan Group	Chunlan	2.6	2.5	4.0
Guangdong Chigo	Chigo	1.0	1.5	3.2
TCL	TCL	1.6	1.9	3.0
Others		38.8	33.0	27.0

Source: Provided by Haier, based on data from Chinese State Statistic Bureau, China Market Monitor Company, Ltd.

Exhibit 7   United States White Goods Sales ($ millions) and Distribution Channels (%), 2003–2004

	2003	2004
Refrigerators	$5,649.4	$6,149.4
Sears	38.5	40.0
Mass merchandisers & clubs	7.5	9.0
Appliance stores	28.5	28.0
Home improvement centers	22.5	20.0
Others	3.0	3.0
Laundry appliances	$5,325.8	$5,946.2
Sears	40	42
Mass merchandisers & clubs	8	8
Appliance stores	28	27
Home improvement centers	20	18
Others	4	5
Room air conditioners	$1,655.6	$1,392.4
Sears	17	17
Mass merchandisers & clubs	31	39
Appliance stores	14	15
Home improvement centers	28	23
Others	10	6
Cooking appliances	$2,998.4	$3,276.2
Sears	36	36
Mass merchandisers & clubs	6	6
Appliance stores	32	34
Home improvement centers	23	19
Others	3	5

Source: Adapted from Gerry Beatty, "Most White Goods Rose in 2004," *HFN*, February 28, 2005, p. 44, available from Factiva, www.factiva.com, accessed March 11, 2005.

Exhibit 8   U.S. Large Household Appliance Market Shares (%)

Company	1998	1999	2000	2001	2002	2003
Whirlpool	35.7	35.6	33.1	33.0	33.7	33.3
General Electric	28.5	28.5	26.6	28.5	28.5	26.1
Maytag	17.0	18.2	17.9	19.0	16.4	14.3
Electrolux (Frigidaire)	11.9	11.8	16.6	16.7	17.7	19.7
Goodman (Amana)[a]	4.7	3.9	2.5			
Others[b]	2.2	2.0	3.3	2.8	3.7	6.6
Total	100.0	100.0	100.0	100.0	100.0	100.0

Source: Laura A. Champine and Anand Krishnan, Morgan Keegan Equity Research, "Whirlpool Corporation," March 14, 2005, available from Thomson Research/Investext, http://research.thomsonib.com, accessed April 28, 2005.

[a]Amana was acquired by Maytag in 2001.

[b]"Others" included Asian competitors such as Haier, LG, and Samsung which together accounted for much of the 2003 share increase.

Exhibit 9   Asian Manufacturers in U.S. Appliance Market, 2003

Company	Market Share	Price Range	Major Products	Other Products	Major Prod Distributor	Other Product Distributors
LG (Korean)	1.9 %	mid to high	refrigerators, washers, dryers	microwaves, A/Cs, vacuum cleaners, compact refrigerators, dehumidifiers, toasters	Best Buy	Sears, Best Buy
Samsung (Korean)	1.6 %	high	refrigerators, washers, dishwashers	microwaves, A/Cs, vacuum cleaners, dehumidifiers	Best Buy	Sears
Haier (Chinese)	1.0 %	low	refrigerators, freezers, washers, ranges	microwaves, A/Cs, compact refrigerators, wine coolers, compact dishwashers	Best Buy	Wal-Mart, Lowe's, Sears, Home Depot, Target
Daewoo (Korean)	.5 %	low	None	microwaves, A/Cs, compact refrigerators	n/a	Best Buy, Home Depot

Source: Michael Rehaut, Jonathan F. Barlow, JP Morgan North American Equity Research, "Appliance Industry: Imports, Distribution Shift Drives Negative Outlook," January 8, 2004, available from Thomson Research/Investext, http://research.thomsonib.com, accessed April 28, 2005.

23

115

Endnotes

[1] Zhang Ruimin quoted in Pamela Yatsko, "To Serve and Profit: A Chinese Fridge-Maker Wows Customers with Service," *Far Eastern Economic Review*, October 17, 1996, available from Factiva, http://www.factiva.com, accessed November 1, 2004.

[2] Zhang Ruimin quoted in Yibing Wu, "China's Refrigerator Magnate," *The McKinsey Quarterly* No. 3, 2003, available at http://www.mckinseyquarterly.com, accessed February 23, 2005.

[3] "The Asian Wall Street Journal 200 (A Special Report): How Asia's National Champion's Stack Up," *The Asian Wall Street Journal*, February 21, 2005, available from Factiva, http://www.factiva.com, accessed March 10, 2005.

[4] "Business in China—The Next Stage," *Asia Pulse*, March 17, 2005 and "Haier Ranks Second in Global Refrigerator Markets," *China Daily*, January 12, 2002, available from Factiva, http://www.factiva.com, accessed November 1, 2004.

[5] Access Asia Limited, "Refrigerators and Freezers in China: A Market Analysis," April 2005, available from ISI Emerging Markets, http://www.securities.com, accessed May 25, 2005.

[6] Dexter Roberts et al., "China's Power Brands: Bold Entrepreneurs are Producing the Mainland's Hot Consumer Products," *BusinessWeek*, November 8, 2004, available from Factiva, http://www.factiva.com, accessed March 10, 2005.

[7] This section is largely based on Lynn Sharp Paine, "The Haier Group (A)," HBS Case No. 398-101, rev. July 27, 2001, Harvard Business School Publishing, 2001.

[8] Pamela Yatsko, "To Serve and Profit."

[9] Zhang Ruimin quoted in Lynn Sharp Paine, "The Haier Group (A)," p. 7.

[10] Ibid., p. 6.

[11] Jeannie J. Yi and Shawn X. Ye, *The Haier Way: The Making of a Chinese Business Leader and a Global Brand* (Dumont, New Jersey: Homa & Sekey Books, 2003), pp. 30 and 65.

[12] Zhang Ruimin quoted in Lynn Sharp Paine, "The Haier Group (A)," p. 7.

[13] Jeannie J. Yi and Shawn X. Ye, *The Haier Way*, p. 65.

[14] Jeannie J. Yi and Shawn X. Ye, *The Haier Way*, pp. 65-66. Zhang eventually secured 240 RMB in bank loans, which together with the IPO revenue and Haier's own funds, paid for the industrial park by 1996.

[15] "Haier Group Buys Up Ailing State Firms," *South China Morning Post*, September 14, 1997, available from Factiva, http://www.factiva.com, accessed November 1, 2004.

[16] "China and the Chaebol," *The Economist*, December 20, 1997, available from ProQuest, ABI/Inform, http://www.proquest.com, accessed April 10, 2005; and Jeannie J. Yi and Shawn X. Ye, *The Haier Way*, pp. 66-67.

[17] Lynn Sharp Paine, "The Haier Group (C)," HBS Case No. 398-162, rev. July 27, 2001, Harvard Business School Publishing, 2001, p. 2.

[18] "Haier Group Buys Up Ailing State Firms," *South China Morning Post*, September 14, 1997, available from Factiva, http://www.factiva.com, accessed November 1, 2004.

[19] "End of Golden Age Brings Painful Change," *South China Morning Post*, March 12, 1998, available from Factiva, http://www.factiva.com, accessed November 1, 2004.

[20] This section is based largely on Jeannie J. Yi and Shawn X. Ye, *The Haier Way*, pp. 149-162.

[21] Access Asia Limited, "Refrigerators and Freezers in China: A Market Analysis."

[22] Scott Stevens, "Don't Blink: Household Electrical Appliances '96 Exhibition in Beijing, China," *Appliance* 39 Vol. 53, No. 10, October 1, 1996; and Li Yan, "Fridge Firms Face Tough Competition from Abroad," *Business Weekly*, February 16, 1997, both available from Factiva, http://www.factiva.com, accessed November 1, 2004.

[23] Winston Yau, "Haier's Earnings Defy Domestic Price War," *South China Morning Post*, March 30, 2002, available from Factiva, http://www.factiva.com, accessed November 1, 2004.

[24] "Online Extra: Kelon: 'We are a Multibrand Company,'" *BusinessWeek Online*, November 8, 2004, http://www.businessweekasia.com, accessed May 17, 2005.

[25] Ben Paul, "Stalking the Dragon," *The Edge* (Singapore), September 16, 2002, available from Factiva, http://www.factiva.com, accessed November 1, 2004.

[26] "China's Kelon Cuts Refrigerator Prices," *Xinhua Financial Network*, March 2, 2004, available from Factiva, http://www.factiva.com, accessed November 1, 2004.

[27] Liu Congmeng quoted in Lee Chyen Yee, "China's Guangdon Kelon Turns Inward for Growth," *Reuters News*, March 4, 2003, available from Factiva, http://www.factiva.com, accessed November 1, 2004.

[28] "Konka to Concentrate on Refrigerator," *SinoCast China IT Watch*, 26 November 2003, available from Factiva, http://www.factiva.com, accessed November 1, 2004.

[29] "HK Guangdong Kelon Electrical Hldgs FY Loss CNY44.7M," *Dow Jones Chinese Financial Wire*, April 28, 2005, available from Factiva, http://www.factiva.com, accessed May 6, 2005.

[30] "Whirlpool to Make Refrigerators in China," *Reuters News*, December 5, 1994, available from Factiva, http://www.factiva.com, accessed November 1, 2004.

[31] Zhang Ruimin quoted in Scott Stevens, "Don't Blink."

[32] Scott Stevens, "Don't Blink."

[33] Ibid.

[34] "Infatuation's End," *The Economist*, September 25, 1999, available from Factiva, http://www.factiva.com, accessed March 15, 2005.

[35] "China—Whirlpool Misunderstood China Market Experts Say," ChinaOnline, March 19, 2002, available from LexisNexis Academic, http://web.lexis-nexis.com, accessed June 8, 2005.

[36] "Infatuation's End."

[37] "Whirlpool Steps up China Comeback," *Dow Jones International News*, October 28, 2001; and "Whirlpool Relaunching Stratagem in China," *AsiaPort Daily News*, March 29, 2002; both available from Factiva, http://www.factiva.com, accessed March 15, 2005.

[38] Zhang Ruimin, quoted in Yibing Wu, "China's Refrigerator Magnate."

[39] Andrew Browne, "Haier Group Never Says 'No'," *Reuters News*, December 9, 1997, available from Factiva, http://www.factiva.com, accessed March 15, 2005.

[40] Zhang Ruimin, quoted in Yibing Wu, "China's Refrigerator Magnate."

[41] Pamela Yatsko, "To Serve and Profit."

[42] "China—Whirlpool Misunderstood China Market Experts Say," ChinaOnline, March 19, 2002, available from LexisNexis Academic, http://web.lexis-nexis.com, accessed June 8, 2005.

[43] Gao Wei, "Haier Plans Overseas Expansion," *Business Weekly*, July 4, 1999, available from Factiva, http://www.factiva.com, accessed March 15, 2005.

44 "Zhang's Qingdao Masterpiece," *Business Weekly*, June 19, 1994, available from Factiva, http://www.factiva.com, accessed November 1, 2004.

45 James Hardin, "China's Future Dragons—Successful Companies are Emerging," *Financial Times*, August 14, 1997, p. 17, available from Factiva, http://www.factiva.com, accessed November 1, 2004.

46 Jeannie J. Yi and Shawn X. Ye, *The Haier Way*, p. 199.

47 Ibid., p. 191.

48 Zhang Ruimin, quoted in Yibing Wu, "China's Refrigerator Magnate."

49 Guangdon Kelon's chairman, Gu Chujun, reported 2003 revenues of $4 billion and overseas sales of revenue of $500 in "Online Extra: Kelon: 'We are a Multibrand Company.'"

50 "Chinese Brands Out of the Shadows," *The Economist*, August 28, 1999, available from Factiva, http://www.factiva.com, accessed November 1, 2004.

51 "Online Extra: Kelon: 'We are a Multibrand Company.'"

52 Zhang Ruimin, quoted in "Online Extra: Haier: 'Local Resources' are Key Overseas," *BusinessWeek Online*, November 8, 2004, http://www.businessweekasia.com, accessed May 17, 2005.

53 J. Stewart Black, Allen J. Morrison and Young Chul Chang, "LG Group: Developing Tomorrow's Global Leaders," IVEY Case No. 9A98G009, January 22, 1999, Ivey Management Services, 1998, p. 12.

54 Ibid.

55 Moon Ihlwan, "White-Hot Goods: LG Electronics is Ringing Up Huge Overseas Sales," *BusinessWeek*, September 30, 2002, available from Factiva, http://www.factiva.com, accessed May 16, 2005.

56 Zhang Ruimin, quoted in Yibing Wu, "China's Refrigerator Magnate."

57 Zhang Ruimin, quoted in Jeannie J. Yi and Shawn X. Ye, *The Haier Way*, p. 188.

58 "Haier Group," *Euromonitor International*, January 2005, available from http://www.euromonitor.com, accessed March 28, 2005.

59 Jeannie J. Yi and Shawn X. Ye, *The Haier Way*, p. 191.

60 Ibid.

61 Ibid., pp. 205-225.

62 Zhang Ruimin quoted in Yibing Wu, "China's Refrigerator Magnate."

63 Yibing Wu, "China's Refrigerator Magnate."

64 Wal-Mart Web site, http://www.walmart.com, accessed March 17, 2005.

65 Jeannie J. Yi and Shawn X. Ye, *The Haier Way*, p. 214.

66 "Haier Group," *Euromonitor International*, January 2005, available from http://www.euromonitor.com, accessed March 28, 2005.

67 Jeannie J. Yi and Shawn X. Ye, *The Haier Way*, p. 199.

68 Ibid., p. 201.

69 "Haier Group," *Euromonitor International*.

70 Charles W.F. Baden-Fuller and John M. Stopford, "Globalization Frustrated: The Case of White Goods," *Strategic Management Journal* 12, October 1991, pp. 493-507, available from ProQuest, ABI/Inform,

http://www.proquest.com, accessed June 8, 2005; and U. Srinivasa Rangan and Jonathan Roche, "Whirlpool Corporation, 2002," Babson College case number BAB048, November 6, 2003.

[71] "Haier Group," *Euromonitor International.*

[72] Zhang Ruimin, quoted in Yibing Wu, "China's Refrigerator Magnate."

[73] Ibid.

[74] Ibid.

[75] Michael Arndt, "Can Haier Freeze Out Whirlpool and GE?" *BusinessWeek Online,* April 11, 2002, available from Factiva, http://www.factiva.com, accessed March 15, 2005.

[76] David L. Swift, executive vice president of Whirlpool Corp.'s North American region, quoted in Dexter Roberts et al., "China's Power Brands."

[77] Ben Uglow, Paloma Danjuan, and Martin Wilkie, Morgan Stanley Equity Research Europe, "Asia: Notes from Our Trip," *Capital Goods Industry Research,* January 10, 2005, p. 8, available from Thomson Research/ Investext, http://research.thomsonib.com, accessed March 10, 2005.

[78] "Haier Group," *Euromonitor International.*

9-707-433

REV: JULY 23, 2008

JOHN R. WELLS

MARINA LUTOVA

ILAN SENDER

The Progressive Corporation

"We're not in the business of auto insurance. We're in the business of reducing the human trauma and economic costs of automobile accidents—in effective and profitable ways."

—Peter Lewis. Chairman, Progressive Corporation[1]

Progressive was the number three player in the $165 billion US private passenger auto insurance industry, with net premiums written in 2006 of $14.1 billion and net income of $1.6 billion (See **Exhibit 1**). Progressive's stated consumer value proposition was "Fast, Fair, Better,"[2] and the Company was considered by many the most innovative firm in the business. Indeed, Warren Buffett, the legendary Chairman of Berkshire Hathaway, and owner of GEICO, the number four auto insurer in the US, once cited Progressive as GEICO's biggest threat.[3]

Progressive had long used sophisticated data mining techniques to price its policies, and this had proven very profitable, delivering high growth, strong underwriting profits, and a high return on equity. However, prospects for the future did not appear quite so bright. The industry leaders, State Farm[4] and Allstate[5] were adopting similar pricing techniques, and GEICO was making strong gains with its low cost direct sales approach.

A price war also loomed on the horizon. After five consecutive years of rate increases, and record levels of profitability in the industry in 2003 and 2004, premiums were flat or even in decline in 2005 and 2006, and State Farm had already cut its rates in many states.[6] Progressive, however, was determined to hold the line on pricing despite historically high margins. CEO Glenn Renwick recalled 1998 when Progressive and the industry cut prices under similar circumstances, resulting in severe underwriting losses. He feared history would repeat itself, and warned of smaller margins for the Company and the industry in 2006 and beyond.[7] He was also concerned at the mismatch between the company's high self-image in delivering consumer satisfaction and disappointing data provided by independent market research. Given the rising importance of marketing, the company's low brand awareness was also an issue. Finally, in a consolidating industry, there was the niggling question of whether Progressive could afford to ignore homeowner's insurance given the synergies with automotive, and the fact that the two leading automotive competitors held leading shares in the homeowners segment.

Auto Insurance Overview

Auto insurance was part of the Property and Casualty (P&C) sector of the insurance industry. Life and Health insurance were the other major sectors of the industry. The P&C business generated $453 billion in written premiums in the US in 2006 and the top 10 players accounted for 48% of sales (see **Exhibit 2**). The P&C insurance business was highly competitive and notorious for its cyclicality, with periods of meager underwriting profits interspersed with long periods of underwriting losses (see **Exhibit 3**). While companies typically made up for underwriting losses with income from investments, it was not uncommon for a significant percentage of firms to be declared financially impaired by ratings firms.[8]

Private passenger auto insurance accounted for $165 billion of P&C insurance, while commercial vehicle insurance added an extra $21 billion. There were approximately 280 competitors writing $5 million or more of private passenger auto insurance in the US in 2005.[9] The top four companies, State Farm, Allstate, Progressive and GEICO accounted for 43% of sales (see **Exhibit 4**). State Farm and Allstate offered a broad line of insurance products and financial services, but Progressive and GEICO focused mainly on auto insurance. Traditionally, broader line insurance players had lost money on auto insurance, but used it to win customers for more profitable products such as homeowner's insurance.[10] However, high losses due to hurricanes had caused many to review this strategy. More recently, most of the top players were making profits in auto insurance (see **Exhibit 5**).

Insurance allowed individual members of a group to pool risk and distribute losses among all members of the group.[11] Insurers collected premiums and set aside a majority of these premiums, to cover losses. Earned premiums were insurance companies' largest source of revenue.[12] Since losses were paid after the premiums were received, insurers also generated investment income from investing the premiums. They also realized gains and losses on the sale of these investments (see **Exhibit 6**).

The largest expense category for insurers was "losses" which included claims, and loss adjustment expenses, including litigation costs. The "loss ratio", an important performance metric in the industry, referred to the cost of losses divided by earned premiums. The challenge of pricing auto insurance was predicting the "frequency" of accidents an insurer could expect in a given pool of drivers and the "severity" of each accident. In 2006, the frequency of accidents in the US had been consistently falling for a number of years, faster than the industry had predicted, leading to record profits. However, some within the industry feared this trend might well reverse.[13]

Another major expense for insurers was selling costs. Insurers paid commission to an insurance broker, agent, or salesperson selling the policy. Insurers also incurred other expenses related to the underwriting process, such as salaries for actuarial staff, marketing expenses, and general administration expenses. Marketing expenditures for the top four P&C insurers were on the rise in 2006. The "expense ratio" referred to total selling and other expenses divided by earned premiums. Insurers who sold direct achieved expense ratios of the order of 20% compared to 25% for those who sold through agents. The "combined" ratio referred to the sum of all costs divided by earned premiums. A combined ratio of 100% or less indicated an underwriting profit and one more than 100% an underwriting loss.

Auto insurance was generally segmented according to risk. The "preferred" segment consisted of individuals with exemplary driving records and few risk characteristics. The "standard" segment included those with less exemplary driving records but relatively low risk profiles. The "nonstandard" segment, approximately 20% of the total market, included drivers with poor driving records or high risk profiles, young male drivers, drivers over 65, people with no prior insurance history and those driving high performance cars were all considered to be risky. Many of the established insurance players such as State Farm and Allstate had traditionally focused on the preferred and standard segments, seeking to avoid high risk customers wherever they could. However, they were expected by many state regulators to take their fair share of high risk drivers to ensure that all drivers had access to auto insurance.[14] Nevertheless, for many years, the nonstandard segment was largely left to a number of specialists such as Progressive. Progressive used sophisticated pricing strategies to assign the right rate to each policy. [15] Some of the other non-standard offers merely copied Progressive's rates.[16] Rates were high, but so were claims, and customer churn was also higher than average. In the mid-1980s the segment boundaries began to blur when Allstate focused aggressively on the nonstandard segment and Progressive finally responded in the early 1990s by entering the standard market.

Insurance was highly regulated at the state level with regulations varying considerably from one state to the next. Each state had an insurance commissioner who granted insurers operating licenses, made sure essential insurance coverage was available to all consumers, tracked insurance companies for financial stability, and ensured that policyholders were not overcharged or discriminated against. Regulation also had significant influence on what types of variables companies could use to price risk.[17] For instance, credit scores correlated with insurance risk but the use of credit scores were banned in Maryland for homeowners insurance and in California for auto insurance.[18] Many insurers chose to avoid states which they considered unfavorable from a regulatory perspective. Average auto insurance rates varied substantially from state to state based on different risks and regulatory environments (see **Exhibit 7**). Massachusetts was unique in that rates were set by the state and there was no competitive market.

Auto insurance was traditionally sold through independent agents, captive in-house agents, and direct to consumers via the telephone and the Internet. Independent agents were paid commissions of the order of 15% of premiums. They offered insurance from competing insurers. Captive agents were independent contractors and received lower commissions, but the insurer often covered some of their business office expenses and advertising. Sales direct to the consumer was small in the 1970s, under 10% of the market, but was a growing trend in the industry with the rise of the Internet.[19] The leading auto insurance players operated through a variety of distribution networks. State Farm relied on a captive sales force of 17,000 agents, Allstate on a network of 13,000 agents, Progressive on a combination of direct sales and independent agents, and GEICO on direct sales.[20]

Competitors

State Farm: Founded in 1922, in Bloomington, IL, State Farm Mutual Automobile Insurance Company was number one in the personal auto insurance industry with a market share of 18.0% in 2006.[21] State Farm generated $48.7 billion of P&C earned premiums in 2006, $30.8 billion of which were automotive and the company was the number one auto insurer in 37 US States.[22] State Farm was also the leading home insurer and provided non-medical health and life insurance through subsidiary companies.[23] Over time, State Farm had expanded into consumer lending and other investment products, but in 2006, it still generated most of its income from insurance.[24] Between 1999 and 2002 State Farm incurred heavy losses, with net worth declining by $14 billion. In an effort to improve profitability, the Company stopped writing new homeowners policies in 15 states. It also began converting to a "tiered-pricing" model based on sophisticated data-mining.[25] By 2005, State Farm had improved its underwriting performance and reduced its expense ratio. Indeed, despite net hurricane losses of $6.5 billion in 2005, the Company managed to keep P&C underwriting losses to $779 million. Strong investment income helped to deliver a pretax operating profit of $3.5 billion[26] State Farm enjoyed an A++ (superior) rating from industry rater A.M. Best, reflecting its high capitalization and conservative operating strategies.

Allstate: The Northbrook based insurer was founded in 1931 by Sears, Roebuck, and Co. and had developed into the second largest player in both personal auto and homeowners' industries with market shares of 11%-12% in each in 2006. In 2006, Allstate posted $35.8 billion in sales and pretax income of $7.2 billion. In 2005, Allstate covered $5 billon of hurricane losses, $3.6 billion from Katrina alone. Allstate, like State Farm, was positioning itself as a one-stop shop for financial services, but $29 billion of its revenues still came from P&C insurance, with $19 billion from auto. Five percent of auto premiums were nonstandard in 2006, down from 15% in 2002. Its two main business segments, Allstate Protection and Allstate Financial, sold 13 major lines of insurance including auto, homeowners', life, and commercial, along with retirement and investment products.[27] Allstate had recently introduced complex algorithms to analyze a wide range of data to generate millions of price points for its auto insurance policies,[28] and was using the same information to price home owners' policies. They argued that this approach would allow them to take on a broader range of risks. Allstate enjoyed one of the highest renewal ratios in the industry of 90%.[29]

GEICO: The Government Employees Insurance Company, (GEICO) was the fourth largest personal auto insurer in the US with a market share of 6.7% in 2006.[30] In 2006, it generated $11.1 billion of earned premiums and $1.3 billion in underwriting profits.[31] A wholly owned subsidiary of Berkshire Hathaway, it was founded in 1935 by Leo Goodwin. Goodwin focused on federal, state, and municipal employees because he believed they had fewer accidents than the general population and more stable income. He also sold direct via mail and phone, passing the savings on to customers via significant discounts.[32] GEICO grew rapidly until 1976, when under-reserving for losses almost drove the Company to insolvency.[33] Warren Buffet began investing in GEICO, and in 1996, it became a wholly owned subsidiary of Berkshire Hathaway. Thereafter, its marketing budget rose rapidly, from $31 million in 1996 to $502 million in 2004, establishing its gecko mascot in the public eye.[34] GEICO offered auto coverage, motorcycle insurance and emergency road service. Between 2004 and 2007, GEICO was repeatedly named *Fortune Magazine*'s most admired property and casualty insurance operation in the US. GEICO enjoyed the highest rating in the industry for financial strength and claims-paying ability, A++ from A.M. Best.

Progressive

After working for the state of Ohio on an insurance fraud case, Joe Lewis and fellow lawyer Jack Green started their own insurance company, Progressive.[35] Right from the start, they offered innovations such as drive-in claims service and payment by monthly installments.[36] The early years were hard but World War II proved to be particularly beneficial for Progressive since consumers had money to buy policies, but gas rationing limited the amount they could drive so there were few accidents. As a result, during the war years, Progressive built up about $400,000 in capital.[37] This helped fund growth in the post-war boom. During those early years, Joe Lewis would often take his son Peter to work with him, and Peter earned his first paycheck stuffing envelopes at Progressive when he was 12. "My entire life has been intertwined with the life of this company," he said.[38] A family tragedy made auto insurance even more significant for Peter. In 1952, his 16-year old brother Jon was killed in a driving accident while on a fishing trip. Lewis observed that his brother's death "makes every car accident an emotional experience for me. I can't take them lightly."[39]

After graduating from Princeton in 1955, Peter Lewis joined the Company in a sales role. By then, Joe Lewis had died and Jack Green was CEO. The head underwriter at the time complained that agents were trying to persuade Progressive to cover high risk customers, but Peter suggested, "They're bringing us potential business. Can't we find a way to write these people?"[40] Part of Lewis's motivation for nonstandard insurance might well have been his own driving record. "I was a serious accident waiting to happen."[41] Whatever the reason, in 1957 Progressive began writing nonstandard insurance, and wrote $86,000 worth of policies in the first year. Sales grew rapidly thereafter and turned Progressive into a major insurer. It was Peter Lewis's "first big idea at Progressive."[42] In 1965, Lewis became Chairman and CEO, and for the next 25 years, Progressive focused on the nonstandard niche, a segment of drivers that many insurers would not cover.[43]

Progressive used detailed data on drivers to price its policies, attempting to identify lower than average risks. For instance, most firms refused to insure motorists with a drunk-driving record, but Progressive discovered through its research that drunk drivers with children were least likely to re-offend.[44] Another profitable niche proved to be motorcycles which had traditionally been viewed as high risk transport for young males. Progressive identified that many Harley Davidson owners were more than 40 years old, high earners, and seldom rode their bikes. Moreover, these owners offered attractive prospects for other forms of insurance.[45] One analyst described Progressive's approach as "take the best of the worst risks, charge the average of the worst risks, and make a ton."[46] With its favorable margins, Progressive provided a top-quality claims service and was a relatively high cost operator.

Lewis set demanding targets for the organization including a 4% underwriting profit, a return on equity 15 percentage points above the rate of inflation and real growth in written premiums of at least 15% per year. In most years these targets were achieved. Meanwhile, State Farm and Allstate largely ignored the nonstandard segment, freeing Progressive to compete with smaller players.[47] According to Lewis, Progressive was dismissed as "a piddling little outfit in Ohio that does oddball things".[48] However, in 1985, Allstate, looking for growth opportunities, began aggressively competing in the nonstandard segment, and quickly passed Progressive in sales. To make matters worse, Proposition 103 became a reality.

Proposition 103 was passed on November 8, 1988 in California in response to consumer complaints of unacceptably high insurance prices. Proposition 103 mandated rate cuts of 20% in 1989, and was hotly contested in the courts. Progressive put reserves aside to cover potential rebates, and, several years later, paid out $50 million to 260,000 policyholders for business written between November 8, 1988 and November 7, 1989.[49] Meanwhile, the Company retreated rapidly from the California market which went down from 20.4 % of Progressive's premiums in 1989 to 4.1% in 1993.[50] The costs of Proposition 103 and the competitive pressure from Allstate caused a crisis at Progressive. The Company incurred small underwriting losses in 1989 and sales were flat in both 1989 and 1990. Attempts to grow in 1991 created underwriting losses.[51] Lewis was particularly concerned at Allstate's low cost structure, and fired 1,300 employees, 19% of the work force.[52] Lewis recalled, "The shock was enormous. It destroyed morale." But he felt there was no choice. "We could see that our competitors were going to kill us if we didn't do something fast."[53]

Proposition 103 also triggered Lewis to investigate how the insurance industry was really perceived by consumers. His Princeton classmate, Ralph Nader, a strong Proposition 103 supporter, invited him to Washington to meet with the heads of a number of state-level consumer groups. When Lewis tried to argue the industry's case, it was clear that no-one believed anything he said. Lewis began to understand the extent of the industry's credibility gap, and committed Progressive to "information transparency" – a policy of sharing information about prices, costs, and service with customers.[54] Lewis also concluded that "people get screwed seven ways from Sunday in auto insurance. They get dealt with adversarially, and they get dealt with slowly. Why don't we start dealing with them nicely? It would be a revolution in the business."[55] The result was a major new approach at Progressive called Immediate Response. Lewis later recalled that Proposition 103 was "the most frustrating experience" of his career. But he also called it "the best thing that ever happened to this company" because it made it what it was today.[56]

1990 -- Immediate Response

Immediate Response first launched in 1990. The core of the concept was to get an adjuster to the policyholder as soon as possible after an accident occurred to help reduce the policyholder's trauma. It also allowed Progressive to get an accurate estimate of repair costs and increased the probability of making a quick settlement without the additional cost of lawyer involvement.[57] At the accident scene, the policyholder received an assessment of damage and even a settlement check; but they might also receive a cup of coffee to settle the nerves, use of the adjuster's cell phone to reassure loved ones or arrange a ride home; whatever it took to make the experience better. Progressive's aim was to personalize its service to the needs of each claimant.[58]

Immediate Response was not without its challenges since it required extensive information flow between the customer, Progressive's central database, and the local claims offices. Initially, claims adjusters relied on cell-phones and had to call dispatchers repeatedly to get the job done. To make the whole process more efficient, four years later in 1994, Progressive launched its Immediate Response Vehicles (IRVs). The IRV's were SUVs that were fitted out with laptops linked wirelessly to the Company's mainframe, allowing adjusters to perform multiple transactions in the field.[59] Adjusters worked as a team, with some assigned to the local office and some in the field in IRV's. A damaged car or an injured person was known as a "feature" and adjusters in the IRV's dealt directly with features while those back at base handled dispatch, long-standing claims, etc. For multi-feature accidents, one adjuster took charge of the claim, and other team members helped with various features since this proved more efficient than having one adjuster do everything.[60]

In 1990 when Immediate Response was launched Progressive inspected 15% of vehicles within nine hours of the accident being reported. By 1997, this had risen to 57%. The number of claims settled with seven days had also risen markedly to 50%.[61]

One challenge of speeding the claims process was getting accident victims to report the accident earlier. Progressive set up a metric to track the time it took, and began to experiment with ways to change customer behavior.[62] The most effective idea turned out to be the Progressive Gold Card. It looked like a credit card, but with Progressive's toll-free claims number and a space to write in a policy number. It also broke in half, to allow the two parties in an accident to exchange information easier. In the six years after Progressive introduced the Gold Card, the average time it took for accident victims to report the accident approximately halved.[63]

The transition to Immediate Response was not without challenges. Lewis recalled that for the first few years, people said, "It's crazy, it's too expensive, nobody will do it." Lewis went on "And for the same three years, I sat here and said, 'We're going to do it, no matter how much it costs and no matter how much you don't like it.'"[64] Immediate Response required a wholesale change in the way people worked at Progressive. Accidents tended to occur at odd hours so Progressive needed a 24-hour claims-reporting service. The adjusters suddenly found that they virtually lived permanently on the road in their IRV's.[65] Bruce Marlow, who was made COO in 1993, said that the job of converting to a 24-hour system was "wretched." Employees accustomed to normal office hours had to accept shift work routines. Computers had to be "up" around the clock. Even accident victims didn't really understand it at first, despite the fact that Progressive's Gold Cards told them they could call at any time. Marlow commented, "Our phones didn't ring. We were like a public TV station during a fundraising drive." [66]

Progressive was always looking for improvements to the Immediate Response process. In 2002, the Company launched a 2-year review to create, according to Renwick, "the virtually perfect customer experience."[67] Renwick noted "when you stop evolving, you've got a real problem. We're always asking, 'Is there an even better way?'"[68] By 2004, Immediate Response had reduced the

6

average claims settlement cycle from 42 days to 6 days and reduced costs. Customer churn was also down by two-thirds. An unexpected additional benefit was the number of referrals from non-customers involved in accidents with Progressive clients.

1990 -- Standard and Preferred Auto Insurance

In parallel with launching Immediate Response in 1990, Lewis decided to counter Allstate's move into the nonstandard business by piloting an experiment to write standard policies. The objective was to use Progressive's data analysis skills to "out-price" its competition head-to-head. The pilot began in Florida in late 1990 and was extended to four states in 1991. The challenge turned out to be the distribution system. Progressive had to persuade the 30,000 independent agents who sold the bulk of Progressive's policies to see the Company in a new light. Progressive's agents typically didn't think of Progressive when they sold to preferred and standard drivers, but offered competitors' policies instead. Moreover, when new customers inquired about Progressive, the natural agent reaction was to assume they were high risk. Changing this behavior took many years of training and exhortation. In 1993, 4.5% of policies written by Progressive were standard.[69] By 1998, this had risen to 35%[70] and more than half of Progressive's affiliated independent agencies sold standard policies.[71] By 2005, the standard market accounted for about 60 percent of Progressive's revenues.[72] The Company continued to lead the $30-billion nonstandard insurance market, which accounted for the remaining 40 percent of its business.[73]

1993 -- Express Quote

In 1993, ostensibly to reduce the hassle of shopping for insurance, Progressive began an experiment in California called Express Quote which provided customers quotes from the top eight local competitors for a fee of $24.95.[74] Independent agents disliked the service, and customers appeared reluctant to pay for the information. In 1994, Express Quote was re-launched in Texas, Florida and Ohio as a free service by dialing 1-800-AUTOPRO, offering quotes from the top four insurers, including Progressive. Progressive often offered the lowest rate.[75] Business in the three states rose by 44% in the first year, compared with an overall gain of 30%,[76] and Progressive committed to rolling out Express Quote to other states, despite the misgivings of its agents who accused Progressive of trying to go direct.[77] Progressive got competitive price data from public rate filings, but some states didn't require insurers to publicly file their rates, so Progressive was limited in how fast it could expand the program.[78] Express Quote was an important element of Progressive's program to become a full line supplier. It also provided more opportunity to sell direct to the consumer. The next generation Express Quote service was a real-time rate quote ticker on Progressive's website, launched in early 2002.[79]

1995 -- The Internet

In 1995, Progressive became the first insurer to go online, and 2 years later, in 1997, it was the first to sell insurance over the Web.[80] In 1998, Progressive launched Personal.Progressive.com to help customers manage their policies. The system provided a wide range of data including the effect a claim might have on a consumer's insurance premium. Renwick implemented Personal.Progressive.com while he was CIO. He commented, "The site gives customers more control over the information about their policy than they've ever had. Information transparency is key at Progressive."[81] Direct sales were 11% of total in 1998, but this rose sharply to 31% by 2003 (see **Exhibit 1**). In 2003, Progressive enhanced its website to allow its 30,000 agents to obtain quotes and complete new policy applications online, 40% faster than before.[82]

With increased direct distribution, Progressive invested heavily in advertising which rose from $8 million in 1997 to $263 million in 2006. Renwick emphasized the benefits for agents. "Since we launched our direct writing initiative in 1994, we've been able to develop a brand that has real consumer appeal, and we invite independent agents to take advantage of that brand. As people begin to recognize Progressive as a leader in private passenger auto, they're more likely to call an independent agent and say... 'I feel comfortable buying that product from you.'" [83] To differentiate sales thorough agents, in 2004 Progressive launched a second brand called "Drive Insurance by Progressive". David Aaker, vice chairman of Prophet Brand Strategy, said that the Drive brand demonstrated Progressive's commitment to the independent agency channel, and provided separation and clarity with respect to the carrier's direct business.[84]

1998 -- Usage Based Charging

While executing on its Immediate Response service, its standard policy writing program and its Internet initiatives, Progressive continued to innovate with new products. In 1998, as part of the Autograph program, Progressive fitted cars in Texas with Global Positioning Satellite (GPS) devices which tracked where customers drove and when. The Company then used this information to set each customer's premium. Night driving, city driving or driving a lot cost more. Overall, customers in Houston saved an average of 25% on their policies, partly because they changed their driving habits. Transportation experts predicted that fully variable insurance premiums would lower the number of miles driven by 10% or more.[85] Autograph created some concerns about fairness and privacy. A bigger issue was the cost and availability of GPS technology, and the program was discontinued in 2002. According to Maria Henderson, the program manager "We did learn that it is technologically feasible and that customers liked it."[86]

Two years later, Progressive introduced a new program, called TripSense. In a Minnesota test, the Company put a computer chip in customers' cars to record their driving record including what time they were driving, how far they went, and how fast they drove, but had no GPS capability so could not record location. The customer was asked to upload the data onto the Web, but, for privacy purposes, was given a facility to review the data first and decide whether to send it or not. [87] In early 2006, the Company was attempting to recruit 15,000 customer volunteers to use the device for six-month period in return for $50 off their insurance policy. Progressive emphasized that the data would not be used to set rates but was purely for research purposes. [88]

Progressive also offered discounts on a trial basis to drivers who uploaded their data. In the pilot, volunteer drivers got a 5 percent discount on their insurance premiums just for logging their mileage on a secure website every six months. They got a further 10% discount if they drove less than 3000 mile in that time. "This program is just intended to help us better understand the correlation between driving behaviors and the risk of being involved in accidents," Ian Forrester, the Company's Iowa product manager, said.[89]

2000 -- Concierge Service

In 2000, Progressive began testing a new way of serving its customers better, the Concierge Service, which began operating in Cleveland Ohio. Owners could bring their damaged cars to the Concierge center for repair, and Progressive would take care of everything, including an instant replacement car while the repair was done.[90] The customer saved time, and Progressive saved money on storage and rental car costs.[91] Progressive was the first in the industry to offer this full service.[92] By 2004, Progressive had expanded the service to 18 cities.[93]

Other insurance companies also began taking greater control of the repair process. Allstate purchased a chain of auto-repair shops in 2001, and State Farm partnered with repair shops that also found rental cars for policyholders.[94] However, some consumer advocates and lawyers questioned whether such practices worked to the advantage of policyholders. Some states also had laws which prevented insurers from mandating where repairs would be performed.[95]

Progressive's next step was to introduce a service, started called Total Loss Concierge which replaced cars that had, as the name implies, been totaled.[96] By 2006, Progressive had tested the shopping service on Ohio customers for a year. Turnaround time was reduced by 35% and the Company was normally able to replace cars for under book value. Customers typically opted for a different car, and, if more expensive than the value of the totaled car, they paid the difference.[97] Customer satisfaction was high. One manager observed Thomas King, "Customers who have gone through the process, just love it."[98]

2000 -- Homeowners Insurance

In March 2000, as part of a pilot, Progressive started offering homeowner's policies in Arizona. The policies were reinsured 75% to share the risk.[99] The program aimed to attract and retain auto consumers who preferred to buy auto and home insurance from the same insurer.[100] The test was expanded to Michigan in October 2000 and then Texas and Maryland in the first quarter of 2001.[101] In August 2001, Progressive announced that it would stop accepting any new homeowners business in Texas. The Company cited increased exposure to mold related damage claims for its decision.[102] Effective May 3, 2002, the entire initiative was cancelled on the grounds that the cross selling opportunities had not materialized.[103] The major concern was that the company couldn't generate enough data to have a pricing advantage.

Management Transition

In 2000, Peter Lewis stepped down as President and CEO and Glenn Renwick took up the posts. Lewis remained as Chairman. Over the years, Lewis had certainly made his mark. Often described as "64 going on 24", 6-foot-2, with long white hair and a mischievous smile, he was irreverent and outspoken.[104] One analyst commenting on how important he was to the firm asked him about his health. He replied, "I really don't know because I don't believe in doctors. But number 1, I feel fine; number 2, I swim a mile every day; and number 3, I'm single so I get laid all the time".[105] Lewis claimed that 20 years of therapy had helped him accept that people considered him eccentric.[106] He was certainly a colorful character and caused a minor scandal in the industry when it was alleged he had smuggled pot into New Zealand on a vacation trip in 2000.[107] However, there was no questioning his creativity and ability to constantly generate ideas – a good number of which had to be "immediately and forcefully flattened"[108] according to former Progressive chief financial officer, Charles Chokel. One employee, who, like all employees had Lewis's personal telephone number reflected, "We're working for a guy who's not afraid to change things and take risks... We set the standard in the business."[109]

Soon after Renwick took over, he made a painful decision to raise insurance rates in the face of a softening market. Growth and profits were adversely affected and Wall Street criticized him. He explained his logic. "We found ourselves under-priced relative to what we saw as rapidly emerging trends. I like to think we were among the first companies to recognize these trends. ... Obviously our actions were a damper on growth. We struggled with that through 2000, and as 2001 came to a close we saw many more companies take action on rates in response to the same trends we identified."[110] Renwick's moves to slow growth were not unprecedented. "Our growth follows a step pattern," said

9

Lewis in 1990. "We will grow faster than our targeted rates for a while, then we will slow down or stop. Right now we're on the top part of the step. That's the time you identify honestly what you screwed up, and you fix it."[111]

Another key action Renwick took in 2000 was to move to 6-month policy periods rather than 12 months. "I strongly believe that we should try to make our rates as accurate as possible at all points in time," Renwick said. "When losses and loss costs take off the way they did from late 1999 into 2000, you're in a difficult position. You've sold a contract based on one set of assumptions, and now all your underlying costs are changing but you're unable to do anything about it." The move resulted in higher transaction costs, lower retention rates, and customer dissatisfaction. Renwick noted, "Our challenge is to find the right balance between maintaining accurate rates and giving customers what they want."[112]

Company Organization

Progressive's headquarters was on a rolling campus in Mayfield Village, east of Cleveland, Ohio. The complex was decked with contemporary art which Lewis began collecting in the early 1970s. "Plain-vanilla walls are uninteresting," he said. "My hope is that nonrepresentational, off-the-wall art sends a message to our people that it's okay to think outside the lines."[113]

Progressive had long maintained a relatively simple functional structure, but in the 1990s Peter Lewis restructured the Company to put general managers in charge of each state, handling agent, direct and claims. When Renwick took over as CEO he restructured the organization at the general manager level, appointing general managers responsible for each of six regions rather than single states. National business leaders were also appointed for agency sales and direct-to-consumer sales to focus marketing efforts, and a national claims business leader was created with responsibility for driving improvements in the claims process.[114] Regional and local management teams continued to be structured around the agency sales and claims functions, but direct-to-consumer sales were handled nationally. The HR, finance, and legal functions were organized nationally as shared service centers (see **Exhibit 8**).[115]

Information Technology

Progressive invested heavily in information technology and could claim many industry firsts. In 2001, Progressive topped CIO Magazine's CIO-100 list in recognition of its innovative practices and products. Progressive was the only auto insurance company to have ever received the award.[116] Progressive.com was also frequently rated the industry's best Website.[117] Renwick, a former CIO, was very technology literate. He observed, "Here at Progressive we have technology leaders working arm in arm with business leaders who view their job as solving business problems. And we have business leaders who are held accountable for understanding the role of technology in their business. Our business plan and IT are inextricably linked because their job objectives are."[118]

Human Resources

Peter Lewis attributed his company's success to his principle of "hire the best" and "pay the most." He explained: "We have the best people in the industry as measured by education, intelligence, initiative, work ethic, and work record. We find them and go after them. Then we put them through our crucible. This is a highly competitive, challenging place to work. We work harder than most companies, and that becomes sort of seductive. Many people wash out. The ones who remain are fantastic." [119] Lewis went on, "The other side of hiring good people is firing people who aren't good. We evaluate people against their objectives, which they negotiate with the Company and then put in writing. If people aren't doing their job, it's good-bye." However, Lewis went on to explain, "This is not a bloodthirsty place. It is a humane environment. But we do not suffer nonperformance."[120] Lewis was proud that he remained on good terms with the executives he fired. "I'm the best person to have been fired by or divorced from that I know."[121]

Progressive maintained strict standards for both financial results and the way they were obtained. Lewis asserted: "We make a constant effort to reward people who understand our values and objectives, and to cull those who do not."[122] The five core values were 1) integrity; 2) the Golden Rule – treat people as you would want to be treated; 3) clear objectives; 4) excellence; and 5) profit. "Progressive thrives because of its commitment to especially good people who are guided by five clear core values and are measured against unusually high standards. I thrive for the same reasons," he said.[123]

Progressive aimed to pay at the top end of industry pay scales when performance was good. The company-wide GainShare program offered profit-sharing for all employees based on the Company's underwriting performance. Each employee received a percentage of their base pay with the percentage rising significantly with seniority. Based on company growth and profit, the GainShare payout in a given year could be zero or as high as double the target amount. For entry level employees, the target bonus might amount to 8% of base pay.[124] For senior executives, it was much higher.[125] Lewis claimed he knew how well people performed, because Progressive tracked virtually every aspect of its business. "If you want to improve something, start measuring it," Lewis said. "Then attach rewards to positive measurements, or penalties to negative ones, and you'll get results."[126]

Lewis actively encouraged executives to innovate. He observed, "Anybody who challenges the status quo stands a very good chance of failing. You get nothing but resistance and criticism. But when you succeed, the resistance and criticism turn to envy and criticism."[127] This commitment to change persisted under Renwick. "We have a high tolerance for innovation and experimentation."[128] But all innovation had to be focused on the customer.[129] Testing was also part of the Company ethos. Programs could not be launched, rolled out (or expanded) until they were bug-free.[130]

When recruiting, Progressive targeted individuals that were results oriented, embraced technology and were comfortable with change. Progressive also valued the ability to deal with competing priorities, resiliency, and a willingness to make mistakes. Mistakes were considered inevitable for anyone new trying hard to get the job done.[131] Progressive believed its culture attracted the sort of people it wanted, and that employees enjoyed working with similarly minded peers. Everyone was given a lot of autonomy, and new Product Managers (entry level job for MBA level recruits) often got P & L responsibility right away. In the spring of 2005, Progressive revealed that it had intensified its recruiting at top business schools, and hired after a rigorous interview process. It also interviewed 325,000 people to hire just 6,000, and was working to eliminate unnecessary turnover.[132]

Progressive encouraged referrals in its recruiting process and, at times, had provided incentives to do so. "It's a very cost-effective way to recruit," said Jennifer Cohen, Progressive's national recruiting manager in 2001. Her aunt, sister and cousin all worked for the Company.[133]

Progressive invested a great deal in training. About half of Progressive's 28,000 employees worked in claims, and training to write repairs estimates was extensive.[134] New claim representatives attended several classes ranging in length from two days to two weeks, and existing reps returned for classes periodically throughout their Progressive careers. Class was held in a "warehouse" that could hold up to 40 damaged cars. Student teams had to estimate the damage, and compare notes with a professional assessment. Students also had to log 80 hours of online training before they got to the center.[135] IT was another strong training focus. An in-house, custom-developed curriculum offered a wide range of classes, and every one of the Company's 1,500 IT personnel took 80 hours of training a year. New employees were also put through a three-month "boot camp."[136]

Situation in 2006

In 2006, insurance rates were softening but Progressive was determined to hold prices firm. Renwick argued that the recent high industry profitability was driven by unanticipated falling accident frequencies and that this would not continue. Indeed, he recalled similar circumstances in 1998 when Progressive and the rest of the industry cut prices only to face a sharp increase in losses in subsequent years. Rather than cut price, Renwick believed that it was better for Progressive to slowly return to long term underwriting profit levels of 4% compared to 2006's 13% by allowing forecast increases in frequency and severity to erode excess profit.[137] Nor was he convinced that simply cutting prices more than the competition would drive Progressive's share. He pointed out that in one Midwestern state Progressive offered better rates than any of the competition to 35% of potential customers, but this was not reflected in market share. There might be many reasons for this; the difference in price might not be big enough; the agent may not be offering Progressive; but the important issue was that Progressive didn't know the reason. Simply cutting prices, he believed, would simply squander margin. More market research was required.[138]

He was also concerned that the consumer's perception of Progressive differed from the Company's self-perception as a champion of its customers. While Progressive's goal was to be the consumers' #1 choice for auto insurance, JD Power and Associates gave the Company a below average score for overall customer satisfaction and ranked it 14 (see **Exhibit 9**). Progressive also scored below average for collision repair satisfaction and also ranked 14.[139]

Another challenge was consumer awareness of the Progressive brand. In 2006 Progressive had achieved 57% unaided brand awareness, up from 53%. This put the brand in the top four, but well behind GEICO (79%), Allstate (69%) and State Farm (74%) who had been advertising for many years. Moreover, the leaders were increasing their advertising support aggressively.[140]

To add to these challenges, by 2006, everyone was using sophisticated data mining techniques and focusing on better claims support. Peter Lewis had once said in 1995 that he could imagine Progressive becoming number 1 in the industry.[141] Since then, Progressive had risen from 7th position to number 3. However, catching the leaders seemed a massive task, and GEICO was following closely on Progressive's heels.

Exhibit 1 Progressive Financial Performance, 1996-2006

Financial Data $ millions	1996	1997	1998	1999	2000	2001	2002	2003	2004	2005	2006
Net Premiums Earned											
Personal polices via agents	NA	NA	$4,178	$4,549	$4,643	$4,707	$5,543	$6,948	$7,894	$7,993	$7,903
Personal policies direct	NA	NA	$403	$745	$1,221	$1,787	$2,365	$3,103	$3,718	$4,076	$4,337
Total personal policies (i)	$2,916	$3,833	$4,581	$5,294	$5,864	$6,494	$7,908	$10,051	$11,612	$12,069	$12,241
Commercial policies and other sales	$283	$357	$367	$390	$484	$668	$976	$1,290	$1,558	$1,695	$1,877
Total Net Premiums Earned	**$3,199**	**$4,190**	**$4,948**	**$5,684**	**$6,348**	**$7,162**	**$8,884**	**$11,341**	**$13,170**	**$13,764**	**$14,118**
Growth in earned premiums	*17%*	*31%*	*18%*	*15%*	*12%*	*13%*	*24%*	*28%*	*16%*	*5%*	*3%*
Investment and other income	$279	$419	$344	$441	$423	$326	-$8,589	$551	$612	$539	$668
Total Revenues	**$3,478**	**$4,608**	**$5,292**	**$6,124**	**$6,771**	**$7,488**	**$294**	**$11,892**	**$13,782**	**$14,303**	**$14,786**
Underwriting expenses											
Loss and loss adjustment expenses	$2,236	$2,968	$3,376	$4,256	$5,279	$5,264	$6,299	$7,640	$8,555	$9,365	$9,395
Policy acquisition costs	$483	$608	$660	$745	$788	$865	$1,032	$1,249	$1,418	$1,448	$1,442
Other underwriting expenses	$209	$336	$496	$584	$559	$687	$874	$1,010	$1,239	$1,312	$1,403
Total underwriting expenses	**$2,927**	**$3,911**	**$4,532**	**$5,585**	**$6,627**	**$6,816**	**$8,205**	**$9,900**	**$11,212**	**$12,125**	**$12,353**
Underwriting pre-tax margin	$272	$278	$416	$98	-$278	$346	$679	$1,441	$1,958	$1,639	$1,878
% premiums of earned	*8.5%*	*6.6%*	*8.4%*	*1.7%*	*-4.4%*	*4.8%*	*7.6%*	*12.7%*	*14.9%*	*11.9%*	*13.3%*
Net Income after tax	**$313.7**	**$400.0**	**$456.7**	**$295.2**	**$46.1**	**$411.4**	**$667.3**	**$1,255.4**	**$1,648.7**	**$1,393.9**	**$1,648**

Performance Indicators	1996	1997	1998	1999	2000	2001	2002	2003	2004	2005	2006
Return on Average Equity (%)	20.5%	20.9%	19.3%	10.9%	1.7%	13.5%	19.3%	29.1%	30.0%	25.0%	25.3%
Loss Ratio (% of earned premiums)	70.2%	71.1%	68.5%	75.0%	83.2%	73.6%	70.9%	67.4%	65.0%	68.1%	66.6%
Underwriting Expense Ratio (% of earn. Prem.)	19.8%	20.7%	22.4%	22.1%	21.0%	21.1%	20.4%	18.8%	19.6%	19.3%	19.9%
Statutory Combined Ratio (% of Earned Prem.)	90.0%	91.8%	90.9%	97.1%	104.2%	94.7%	91.3%	86.2%	84.6%	87.4%	86.5%
Employees	9,557	14,126	15,735	18,753	19,490	20,442	22,974	25,834	27,085	28,336	27,778
Net premiums earned per employee $'000	$335	$297	$314	$303	$326	$350	$387	$439	$486	$486	$508
% of personal premiums via agents	NA	NA	91.2%	85.9%	79.2%	72.5%	70.1%	69.1%	68.0%	66.2%	64.6%

Source: Compiled by casewriter from company reports, analyst reports, internet sources, and casewriter estimates.

Exhibit 2   Top US Property and Casualty Writers, Net Premiums 2006

Top Property and Casualty Writers	Premiums		Top Homeowners Policy Writers	Premiums	
	$ million	% share		$ million	% share
State Farm	$48,651	10.7%	State Farm	$13,580	22.2%
American International (AIG)	$34,969	7.7%	Allstate	$7,310	11.9%
Allstate	$26,706	5.9%	Zurich	$4,281	7.0%
Berkshire Hathaway	$20,169	4.4%	Nationwide	$2,854	4.7%
Travelers	$20,062	4.4%	Travelers	$2,660	4.3%
Nationwide	$15,843	3.5%	USAA	$2,505	4.1%
Liberty Mutual	$15,367	3.4%	Liberty Mutual	$1,889	3.1%
Progressive	$14,089	3.1%	Chubb	$1,745	2.9%
Farmers	$13,253	2.9%	American Family	$1,431	2.3%
Hartford	$10,568	2.3%	Hartford	$1,048	1.7%
Top 10	**$219,677**	**48.3%**	**Top 10**	**$39,303**	**64.2%**
Other	$233,595	51.7%	Other	$21,917	35.8%
Total Industry	**$453,272**	**100.0%**	**Total Industry**	**$61,220**	**100.0%**

Source: *Best's Review*, July 2007, p 47-8.   Source: Casewriter estimates and "Facts and Statistics,"
                                                        Insurance Information Institute, www.iii.org/.

Top Personal Auto Insurance Policy Writers	Premiums		Top Commercial Auto Insurance Writers	Premiums	
	$ million	% share		$ million	% share
State Farm	$29,582	18.0%	Travelers	$2,091	6.8%
Allstate	$18,294	11.1%	Zurich	$2,011	6.6%
Progressive	$12,077	7.3%	Progressive	$1,981	6.5%
Berkshire Hathaway (GEICO)	$11,105	6.7%	American International	$1,442	4.7%
Farmers	$8,110	4.9%	Liberty Mutual	$1,316	4.3%
Nationwide	$7,490	4.5%	State Farm	$1,254	4.1%
USAA	$5,964	3.6%	Nationwide	$1,164	3.8%
American International (AIG)	$5,003	3.0%	Old Republic	$793	2.6%
Liberty Mutual	$4,251	2.6%	CAN	$789	2.6%
American Family	$3,537	2.1%	Hartford	$717	2.3%
Top 10	**$105,413**	**63.8%**	**Top 10**	**$13,558**	**37.7%**
Other	$59,811	36.2%	Other	$8,204	62.3%
Total Industry	**$165,224**	**100.0%**	**Total Industry**	**$21,762**	**100.0%**

Source: Casewriter estimates and "Facts and Statistics,"   Source: Casewriter estimates and "Facts and Statistics,"
         Insurance Information Institute, www.iii.org/.   Insurance Information Institute, www.iii.org/.

14

Exhibit 3 Property and Casualty Industry Underwriting Profits, 1990-2006

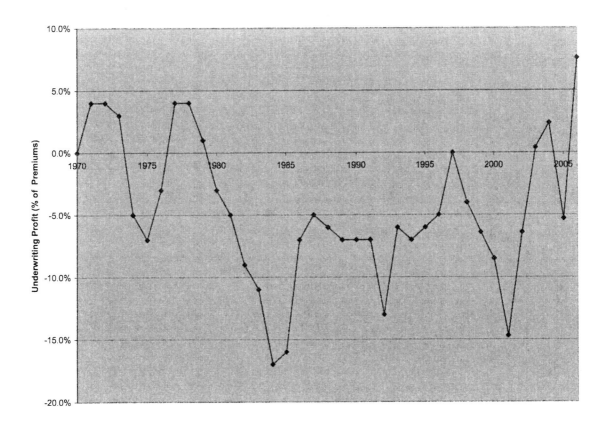

Source: Compiled by casewriter from internet sources and the *III Insurance Fact Book, 2006*, pg 23, figures based off on chart, and hence estimates, for years prior to 1998.

Exhibit 4a   Top Property/Casualty Writers 2006, Share of Premiums (%), 1996-2006

	1996	1997	1998	1999	2000	2001	2002	2003	2004	2005	2006
State Farm Group	12.5	12.6	12.3	11.8	11.0	11.6	11.3	11.3	10.9	10.9	10.7
American International	3.3	3.4	3.8	4.0	4.0	3.3	5.6	6.6	7.2	7.2	7.7
Allstate Ins Group	6.4	6.6	6.8	7.2	7.1	6.8	6.2	6.0	5.9	6.1	5.9
Berkshire Hathaway	1.4	1.7	2.7	3.0	3.4	3.3	4.0	3.8	3.8	4.0	4.4
Travelers Ins Companies	2.7	2.9	2.9	3.1	3.3	3.2	3.1	4.8	4.5	4.4	4.4
Nationwide Group	3.0	3.0	3.0	3.2	3.1	3.3	3.1	3.3	3.3	3.5	3.5
Liberty Mutual	1.8	2.1	2.6	2.8	2.9	2.7	2.8	3.0	3.0	3.2	3.4
Progressive Ins Group	1.1	1.7	1.9	2.1	2.0	2.1	2.5	2.8	3.1	3.2	3.1
Zurich-Farmers Ins Group	3.1	3.3	3.7	5.3	5.5	5.3	4.6	2.4	2.6	2.8	2.9
Hartford	2.1	2.1	2.1	2.2	2.3	1.0	2.2	2.1	2.2	2.4	2.3
Top 10	37.4	39.4	41.8	44.7	44.6	42.6	45.4	46.1	46.5	47.7	48.3
Other	62.6	60.6	58.2	55.3	55.4	57.4	54.6	53.9	53.5	52.3	51.7
Total US	100.0	100.0	100.0	100.0	100.0	100.0	100.0	100.0	100.0	100.0	100.0

Exhibit 4b   Top Private-Passenger Auto Insurance Writers 2006, Share of Premiums (%), 1996-2006

	1996	1997	1998	1999	2000	2001	2002	2003	2004	2005	2006
State Farm Group	21.4	20.5	19.7	18.9	17.9	19.0	19.3	19.0	18.2	17.7	18.0
Allstate Ins Group	12.4	12.3	12.4	12.2	11.8	11.3	10.6	10.2	10.4	11.2	11.1
Progressive Ins Group	2.8	3.7	4.2	4.8	4.7	4.9	5.8	6.7	7.3	7.5	7.3
Berkshire Hathaway	2.7	3.0	3.5	4.0	4.7	4.6	4.7	5.1	5.6	6.3	6.7
Farmers Ins Group	5.9	6.0	5.9	5.7	5.8	5.7	5.4	5.1	5.0	5.0	4.9
Nationwide Group	3.9	4.3	4.3	4.4	4.6	4.9	4.8	4.7	4.7	4.7	4.5
USAA Group	3.1	3.1	3.0	3.1	3.4	3.5	3.6	3.6	3.5	3.5	3.6
Liberty Mutual	1.7	2.2	2.3	2.2	2.3	2.8	2.9	2.9	2.9	2.6	2.6
American International	1.4	1.4	1.5	1.6	1.9	2.3	2.4	2.4	2.4	2.6	3.0
American Family	1.7	1.8	1.9	2.0	2.1	2.1	2.2	2.2	2.2	2.2	2.1
Top 10	57.0	58.3	58.7	58.9	59.2	61.1	61.7	61.9	62.2	63.3	63.8
Other	43.0	41.7	41.3	41.1	40.8	38.9	38.3	38.1	37.8	36.7	36.2
Total US	100.0	100.0	100.0	100.0	100.0	100.0	100.0	100.0	100.0	100.0	100.0

Exhibit 4c   Top Homeowners Writers 2006, Share of Premiums (%) 1996-2006

	1996	1997	1998	1999	2000	2001	2002	2003	2004	2005	2006
State Farm Group	23.4	23.0	22.7	22.5	21.4	21.9	22.3	22.4	22.4	22.2	22.2
Allstate Ins Group	11.7	11.3	11.5	11.5	11.5	11.4	11.6	11.3	11.7	12.5	11.9
Zurich Insurance Group	6.2	6.7	7.0	7.1	8.4	8.6	8.1	7.4	7.1	7.0	7.0
Nationwide Group	3.5	3.6	4.2	4.5	4.5	4.6	4.6	4.7	4.7	4.8	4.7
Travelers Ins Companies	3.6	3.5	3.6	3.8	3.8	3.6	3.5	3.6	4.0	4.3	4.3
USAA Group	3.4	3.4	3.4	3.5	3.6	3.6	3.6	3.7	3.9	4.0	4.1
Liberty Mutual	1.4	1.5	1.6	2.0	2.0	2.0	2.0	2.9	3.0	3.0	3.1
Chub & Son Group	2.1	2.1	2.2	2.3	2.4	2.6	2.8	2.8	2.8	2.8	2.9
American Family	1.7	1.8	1.9	2.1	2.1	2.2	2.3	2.6	2.7	2.5	2.3
Hartford	1.6	1.6	1.6	1.6	1.7	1.6	1.6	1.6	1.6	1.7	1.7
Top 10	58.6	58.5	59.7	60.9	61.4	62.1	62.4	63.0	63.9	64.8	64.2
Other	41.4	41.5	40.3	39.1	38.6	37.9	37.6	37.0	36.1	35.2	35.8
Total US	100.0	100.0	100.0	100.0	100.0	100.0	100.0	100.0	100.0	100.0	100.0

Source: Compiled by casewriter from various years of *Best's Review*.

Exhibit 5 Comparison of Top 4 Auto Insurance Writers, 2001-2006

	2001	2002	2003	2004	2005	2006
Premiums						
State Farm Property and Casualty	$36.9	$41.0	$45.3	$47.3	$47.5	$48.0
State Farm Auto	$25.6	$28.5	$31.0	$31.5	$30.6	$30.7
Allstate Property and Casualty	$22.2	$23.4	$24.7	$26.0	$27.0	$27.4
Allstate Auto	$15.8	$16.4	$16.8	$17.5	$18.0	$18.3
Progressive	$7.2	$8.9	$11.3	$13.2	$13.8	$12.1
GEICO	$6.1	$6.7	$7.8	$8.9	$10.1	$11.1
Loss Ratio (% of premiums)						
State Farm Property and Casualty[a]	83.4%	74.7%	63.3%	60.1%	66.6%	60.0%
State Farm Auto[a]	82.7%	76.3%	64.5%	59.8%	63.6%	60.8%
Allstate Property and Casualty	79.0%	75.6%	70.6%	68.7%	78.3%	58.5%
Allstate Auto	77.6%	74.5%	69.5%	63.2%	64.9%	61.1%
Progressive	73.6%	70.9%	67.4%	65.0%	68.1%	68.0%
GEICO	79.9%	77.0%	76.5%	71.3%	70.6%	70.1%
Expense Ratio (% of premiums)						
State Farm Property and Casualty[a]	41.2%	40.4%	37.3%	35.7%	35.1%	36.5%
State Farm Auto[a]	39.2%	38.5%	35.6%	34.4%	34.5%	35.0%
Allstate Property and Casualty	23.9%	23.3%	24.0%	24.3%	24.0%	25.1%
Allstate Auto	23.9%	23.3%	24.0%	24.3%	24.0%	24.3%
Progressive	21.0%	21.1%	20.4%	18.8%	19.6%	20.3%
GEICO	16.5%	16.8%	17.7%	17.8%	17.3%	17.5%
Combined ratio (% of premiums)						
State Farm Property and Casualty	125.1%	114.7%	100.6%	95.8%	101.6%	93.8%
State Farm	121.9%	114.8%	100.1%	94.2%	98.1%	96.0%
Allstate Property and Casualty	102.9%	98.9%	94.6%	93.0%	102.4%	83.6%
Allstate Auto	101.5%	97.8%	93.5%	87.5%	88.9%	85.4%
Progressive	94.7%	91.3%	86.2%	84.6%	87.4%	86.7%
GEICO	96.4%	93.8%	94.2%	89.1%	87.9%	88.1%
Measured Advertising ($ millions)						
State Farm	$229	$232	$207	$260	$320	$290
Allstate	$148	$174	$263	$299	$289	$350
Progressive	$113	$108	$129	$201	$252	$265
GEICO	$203	$203	$239	$286	$403	$500
Policies (millions)						
State Farm Property & Casualty (total)	65.4	66.2	65.4	65.4	66.6	67.7
State Farm Auto	39.7	40.3	39.7	39.5	40.0	40.4
Allstate Property & Casualty^	25.8	24.9	25.0	26.0	26.5	35.6
Allstate Auto (Allstate Brand total auto)	18.9	18.0	17.9	18.4	18.7	27.8
Progressive	5.1	6.9	8.2	9.1	10.0	9.9
GEICO	4.4	4.9	5.4	6.0	6.8	8.0
Premiums per Policy						
State Farm Property & Casualty+	$564	$619	$693	$723	$713	$709
State Farm Auto+	$645	$707	$781	$797	$765	$759
Allstate Property & Casualty^	$414	$478	$510	$523	$538	$562
Allstate Auto (Allstate Brand total auto)	$365	$400	$423	$427	$429	$487
Progressive+	$1,415	$1,300	$1,388	$1,447	$1,382	$1,222
GEICO+	$1,368	$1,375	$1,446	$1,482	$1,494	$1,375

Source: Compiled from annual reports, *Advertising Age*, and casewriter estimates.

[a] Not comparable with other companies. State Farm includes some loss in its expense line.

^Homeowners and Allstate Brand total auto. +Derived from premiums divided by policies in force.

Exhibit 6   Property and Casualty Revenue and Cost Structure, 2005

	Premium	% of Premium
Premiums earned	$100	100%
Investment income	$9	9%
Total Revenue	**$109**	109%
Claims		
Injuries		
Medical	$9	9%
Wage loss	$2	2%
Pain and suffering	$5	5%
Lawyers' Fees	$11	11%
Costs of settling claims	$1	1%
Total personal injuries	$28	28%
Damage to vehicles		
Property damage	$16	16%
Collision claims	$16	16%
Comprehensive claims	$7	7%
Costs of settling Claims	$1	1%
Total damage	$40	40%
Total Claims	**$68**	**68%**
Expenses		
Commissions and other selling expenses	$16	16%
General expenses	$5	5%
State premium taxes, licenses and fees	$2	2%
Dividends to policyholders	$1	1%
Total expenses	**$24**	**24%**
Claims and expense total	**$92**	92%
Pre-tax income	$14	14%
Tax	-$5	-5%
Net Income	**$9**	9%

Source: Insurance Information Institute, www.ii.org/media/facts/stats by issue/auto/.

Exhibit 7   Average Auto Expenditures and Average Auto Premiums, 2005

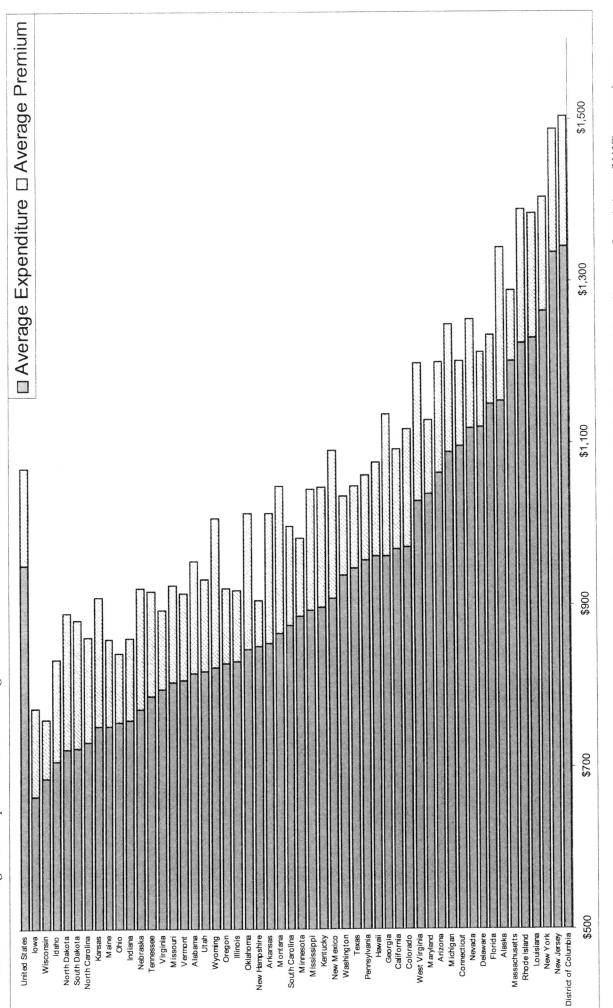

Source: Data adapted from "2005 State Expenditures and Average Premiums for Personal Automobile Insurance" by the National Association of Insurance Commissioners (NAIC), www.naic.org.

Exhibit 8   Progressive Senior Management

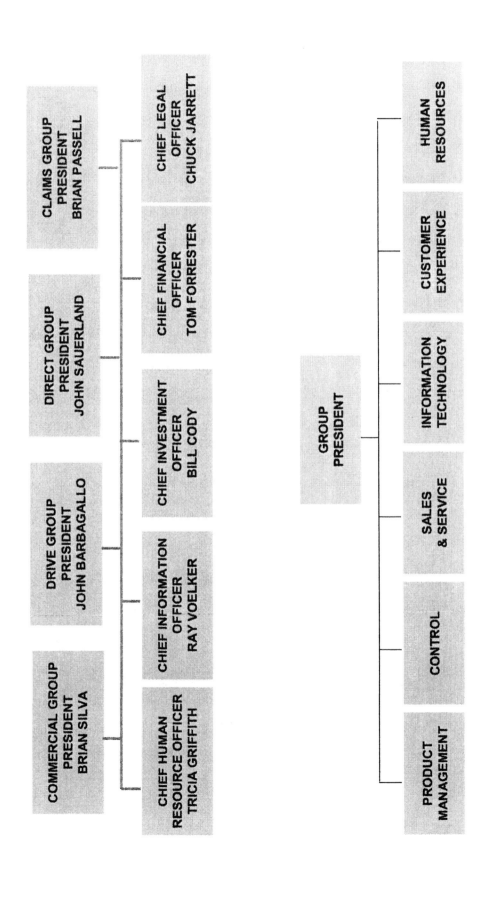

Source: Company records.

Exhibit 9 J.D. Powers Customer Satisfaction Survey

	Sales Rank	Overall Satisfaction Score	Overall Satisfaction Rank	Collision Repair Score	Collision Repair Rank
State Farm Mutual Group	1	792	4	800	3
American Family Insurance Group	10	788	5	732	16
Allstate Insurance Co. Group	2	783	8	752	13
National Indemnity Co. Group (Berkshire Hathaway)	4	783	9	765	10
Progressive Casualty Group	3	770	14	751	14
United Services Automobile Association Group	7	886	*	846	*
Nationwide Group	6	768	16	765	11
Farmers Insurance Group	5	762	19	736	15
Liberty Mutual Group	9	761	20	773	7
American International Group	8	732	25	705	19
Industry Average		781		777	

Source: "Quality of Service from Auto Insurers Trumps Brand Recognition for Customer Retention, Says J.D. Power Survey," US Insurance News, September 10, 2007 via http://www.usinsurancenews.com and "Nearly 20 Percent of Customers Consider Switching Auto Insurance Companies Following Their Most Recent Collision Claim," J.D. Power, January 9, 2007, accessed October 18, 2007 via http://www.jdpower.com/corporate/news/releases/pressrelease.aspx?ID=2007004.

*United Services Automobile Association Group (USAA) is not ranked as it only insures members of U.S. military community.

Endnotes

1 Chuck Salter, "Progressive Makes Big Claims," *Fast Company*, Issue 19, November 1998.

2 The Progressive Corporation *2005 Annual Report*, pg. 7.

3 David Stires, "Five Stocks for a Stormy Market," CNNMoney.com, *Fortune*, May 16, 2005.

4 Adrienne Carter, "A Good Neighbor Gets Better, *BusinessWeek*, June 20, 2005.

5 Adrienne Carter, "Telling the Risky from the Reliable; Will Allstate's Detailed Customer Analysis Keep the Profits from Rolling in a Price War?" *BusinessWeek*, August 1, 2005

6 Mya Frazier, "Progressive, Geico prod auto rivals into price war," *Advertising Age*, Vol. 76, Iss. 9, February 28, 2005, pg. 4-6.

7 Rick Cornejo, "Progressive to 'Hold the Line' on Pricing During Slow-Growth Auto Insurance Market," *Best's Insurance News*, March 2, 2006.

8 *Best's Review*, January, 2006, pg. 10.

9 Progressive Corp. Form 10-K (Annual Report) filed February 28, 2006, pg. 3.

10 Datamonitor, "Motor Insurance in the United State: Industry Profile," October 2005.

11 Scott P. Mason and W. James Whalen, "The Global Property and Casualty Insurance Industry," *Harvard Business School* Case no. 296-033, (1995).

12 Once the policy is issued, insurers put it on the books as written premiums. However, the net premiums written are recognized as revenue or "earned" premiums on a fractional basis. There is usually a lag of about 12 months between the moment when a policy is written and when the full premium is recognized as revenue. For more details, see Standard & Poor's, Industry Surveys: *Insurance: Property – Casualty*, January 19, 2006.

13 The Progressive Corporation, *2006 10-k*, pg. 15.

14 Allstate Corporation *Prospectus*, June 2, 1993, p 61

15 Adrienne Carter, "Telling the Risky from the Reliable; Will Allstate's Detailed Customer Analysis Keep the Profits from Rolling in a Price War?" *BusinessWeek*, August 1, 2005.

16 The Progressive Corporation, 1993 10K, p.2

17 Based on information from Standard & Poor's, Industry Surveys: *Insurance: Property – Casualty*, January 19, 2006.

18 Harriet Johnson Brackey, Knight Ridder Tribune Business News, Washington, July 13, 2006 pg.1.

19 Sylvia Nasar, "Hard road ahead for auto insurers; angry consumers demanding price regulation and spiraling costs of doing business are driving the companies to mind their customers and compete more vigorously," *Fortune Magazine*, Vol. 119, No. 10, May 8, 1989.

20 Based on Standard & Poor's, Industry Surveys: *Insurance: Property – Casualty*, January 19, 2006 and Nicolaj Siggelkow and Michael E. Porter, "Progressive Corporation," *Harvard Business School* case no.797-109 (1997).

21 *Best's Review*, October 2007.

22 A. M. Best Review, October 2005.

23 Hoover's Profile of State Farm in www.hoovers.com.

24 State Farm 2006 Annual Report.

25 Adrienne Carter, "A Good Neighbor Gets Better," *BusinessWeek*, June 20, 2005.

[26] State Farm, 2005 Year in Review, www.statefarm.com/media/2005_yearinreview.pdf, accessed July 16, 2005.

[27] Wachovia Securities, "Allstate Corporation," December 19, 2005.

[28] Adrienne Carter, "Telling the Risky from the Reliable; Will Allstate's Detailed Customer Analysis Keep the Profits from Rolling in a Price War?" *BusinessWeek*, August 1, 2005.

[29] *Business Wire*, "Allstate Reports 2005 Fourth Quarter Net Income EPS of $1.59; Fourth Quarter Operating Income EPS of $1.49; Provides Guidance on 2006," January 31, 2006.

[30] Best's Review.

[31] Company reports.

[32] Hoover's profile of GEICO in www.hoovers.com.

[33] Berkshire Hathaway, Inc., 2004 Annual Report, p. 10.

[34] Berkshire Hathaway, Inc., 2005 Annual Report, p 8.

[35] Chuck Salter, "Progressive Makes Big Claims," *Fast Company*, Issue 19, November 1998.

[36] Company website: http://www.progressive.com/progressive/history.asp, accessed July 16, 2006

[37] Chuck Salter, "Progressive Makes Big Claims," *Fast Company*, Issue 19, November 1998.

[38] Ibid.

[39] Ibid.

[40] Ibid.

[41] Ibid.

[42] Ibid.

[43] Carol J. Loomis, "Sex. Reefer? And auto insurance!," *Fortune Magazine*, Vol. 132, No. 3, August 7, 1995.

[44] Stephan Phillips, "Finance Bad Risk are this Car Insurer's Best Friends --- Progressive has scored big profits by signing up the shunned," *BusinessWeek*, November 12, 1990.

[45] Jerry Luftman, "Measure Your Business—IT Alignment – The longstanding business-IT gap can be bridged with an assessment tool to rate your efforts," *Optimize*, December 1, 2003.

[46] Sylvia Nasar, "Hard road ahead for auto insurers; angry consumers demanding price regulation and spiraling costs of doing business are driving the companies to mind their customers and compete more vigorously," *Fortune Magazine*, Vol. 119, No. 10, May 8, 1989.

[47] Joshua Mendes, "The Prince of Smart Pricing," *Fortune Magazine*, March 23, 1992.

[48] Chuck Salter, "Progressive Makes Big Claims," *Fast Company*, Issue 19, November 1998.

[49] The Progressive Corporation, 1993 10K, p12

[50] The Progressive Corporation, 1993 10K

[51] The Progressive Corporation, 1993 10K, 10 Year Financial History

[52] Brian Dumaine, "Times are Good? Create a Crisis," *Fortune Magazine*, June 28, 1993.

[53] Ibid.

[54] Chuck Salter, "Progressive Makes Big Claims," *Fast Company*, Issue 19, November 1998.

[55] Ronald Henkoff, "Service is Everybody's Business, *Fortune Magazine,* June 27, 1994.

[56] Chuck Salter, "Progressive Makes Big Claims," *Fast Company,* Issue 19, November 1998.

[57] Carol J. Loomis, "Sex. Reefer? And auto insurance!," *Fortune Magazine,* Vol. 132, No. 3, August 7, 1995.

[58] B. Joseph Pine, II and James H. Gilmore, "What business are you really in?," *Chief Executive,* October 1, 1999.

[59] Bill Davidson, "Breakthrough," *Executive Excellence,* April 1, 2004.

[60] Chuck Salter, "Progressive Makes Big Claims," *Fast Company,* Issue 19, November 1998.

[61] Ibid.

[62] Ibid.

[63] Ibid.

[64] Ibid.

[65] Carol J. Loomis, "Sex. Reefer? And auto insurance!," *Fortune Magazine,* Vol. 132, No. 3, August 7, 1995.

[66] Ibid.

[67] Elizabeth Boone, "Recipe for Success," *Rough Notes,* April 1, 2002.

[68] Dean Foust, et al, "The Best Performers," *BusinessWeek,* April 5, 2004.

[69] The Progressive Corporation, 1993 10K

[70] The Progressive Corporation, 2000 10K

[71] Chuck Salter, "What's the Hard Part? Outgrowing Your Niche," *Fast Company,* November 1998.

[72] CSFB Research Report Feb 15, 2006 – which estimated revenues divided by standard and non-standard in 2004. The firm no longer breaks them out in company reports

[73] CSFB Research Report Feb 15, 2006 – they estimate that 50% of agency sales are non-standard, and 25% of direct sales are non-standard. Agency sales are about 2/3 of the business, which implies that non-standard is 40% of the business.

[74] "New Automated Auto Insurance Information Service Puts Californians in the Driver's Seat," *PR Newswire,* February 24, 1993.

[75] Evelyn Gilbert, "Progressive's Marketing Angers Agents," National Underwriter Property & Casualty-Risk & Benefits Management, September 25, 1995.

[76] Carol J. Loomis, "Sex. Reefer? And auto insurance!," *Fortune Magazine,* Vol. 132, No. 3, August 7, 1995.

[77] Evelyn Gilbert, "Progressive's Marketing Angers Agents," National Underwriter Property & Casualty-Risk & Benefits Management, September 25, 1995.

[78] Carol J. Loomis, "Sex. Reefer? And auto insurance!," *Fortune Magazine,* Vol. 132, No. 3, August 7, 1995.

[79] "Auto Insurance Rate comparison Ticker Earns Progressive.com A Place Among Fast Company Magazine's Fast…," *PR Newswire,* February 17, 2003.

[80] Marcia Stepanek, "Rewriting the Rules of the Road," *BusinessWeek,* September 18, 2000.

[81] Julie Gallagher, "Business-Savvy CIO Turns Tech-Savvy CEO – Glenn Renwick draws from both his business and technology experience to align business and IT," *Insurance and Technology,* July 1, 2001.

[82] Robert O. Crockett, "Progressive Insurance," *BusinessWeek*, November 24, 2003.

[83] Elizabeth Boone, "Recipe for Success," *Rough Notes*, April 1, 2002.

[84] Elizabeth Boone, "Marketing," *Rough Notes*, December 1, 2004.

[85] Ira Carnahan, "Insurance by the Minute One of the nation's biggest auto insurers is using satellites to track its customers at the wheel. Is this the future of auto insurance?," *Forbes*, November 27, 2000.

[86] Gregory MacSweeney, "Risk of Being on Bleeding Edge – Progressive discontinues real-time auto insurance pilot program, *Insurance and Technology*, February 1, 2002.

[87] Louise Lee, "Can Progressive Stay In Gear? With rates falling, the car insurer is trying innovative ways to keep ahead of the pack," *BusinessWeek* August 9, 2004.

[88] Paul Herrera, "Devices to track drivers//Trip Sense; An automotive insurer is offering volunteers cash to install the gadgets in their cars," *The Press-Enterprise*, January 15, 2006.

[89] David Pitt, "Progressive insurance offers discount for exact mileage records," *Associated Press Newswires*, March 16, 2006.

[90] Pallavi Gogoi, "Online Extra: Progressive: Ahead of the Curve; Making it "all about the customer" has helped drive the car insurer to the No. 3 slot in its industry and No. 5 on the BW50," *BusinessWeek Online*, April 16, 2003.

[91] Carrie Coolidge, "The Innovator," *Forbes*, January 10 2005.

[92] "Progressive Redefining Auto Insurance Claims Process One City at a Time Launched in April 2003, Company Now has 19 One-Stop Claims Service Centers that Offer "We'll Take Care of Everything Approach" Approach to Auto Repair," *PR Newswire*, December 17, 2003.

[93] Louise Lee, "Can Progressive Stay In Gear? With rates falling, the car insurer is trying innovative ways to keep ahead of the pack," *BusinessWeek* August 9, 2004.

[94] Phil Porter, "Progressive Insurance Offers One-Stop Crash-Repair Service to Clients," *KRTBN Knight-RidderTribune Business News*: Odessa American, Texas, April 16, 2003.

[95] John Hillman, "Progressive Expands," *Best's Insurance News*, April 9, 2003.

[96] Ben Sheridan, Progressive Insurance, August 24, 2006.

[97] Stanford Group Company Research Report, June 02, 2005

[98] Louise Lee, "Can Progressive Stay In Gear? With rates falling, the car insurer is trying innovative ways to keep ahead of the pack," *BusinessWeek* August 9, 2004.

[99] The Progressive Corporation, 2000 10 K

[100] Elizabeth Boone, "Recipe for Success," *Rough Notes*, April 1, 2002.

[101] The Progressive Corporation, 2001 10K.

[102] Insurance Information Institute Database, August 2, 2001.

[103] Insurance Information Institute Database, March 25, 2002.

[104] Chuck Salter, "Progressive Makes Big Claims," *Fast Company*, Issue 19, November 1998.

[105] Carol J. Loomis, "Sex. Reefer? And auto insurance!," *Fortune Magazine*, Vol. 132, No. 3, August 7, 1995.

[106] Chuck Salter, "Progressive Makes Big Claims," *Fast Company*, Issue 19, November 1998.

[107] Daniel Hays, "Progressive CEO to Arrest Prompts Inquiry," *National Underwriter Property & Casualty-Risk & Benefits Management Edition*, January 17, 2000.

[108] Carol J. Loomis, "Sex. Reefer? And auto insurance!," *Fortune Magazine*, Vol. 132, No. 3, August 7, 1995.

[109] Eric Torbenson, "Agile approach drives insurance success Series: Cover Story," *St. Petersburg Times*, September 22, 1997.

[110] Elizabeth Boone, "Recipe for Success," *Rough Notes*, April 1, 2002.

[111] William E. Sheeline, "Avoiding Growth's Perils," *Fortune*, August 13, 1990.

[112] Elizabeth Boone, "Recipe for Success," *Rough Notes*, April 1, 2002.

[113] Chuck Salter, "The Art of Being Progressive," *Fast Company*, Issue 19, November 1998.

[114] "Progressive," McDonal Investments, June 28, 2000.

[115] "Progressive Corporation: Topping the Curve," ABN-AMRO, July 2001.

[116] "Progressive Insurance Receives CIO-100 Award for Innovative Business Practices and Services," *PR Newswire*, August 15, 2001.

[117] "Progressive.com Named #1 Insurance Carrier Web Site by Gomez Fifth Consecutive Time," *PR Newswire*, November 15, 2001.

[118] Julie Gallagher, "Business-Savvy CIO Turns Tech-Savvy CEO – Glenn Renwick draws from both his business and technology experience to align business and IT," *Insurance and Technology*, July 1, 2001.

[119] Chuck Salter, "Progressive Makes Big Claims," *Fast Company*, Issue 19, November 1998.

[120] Chuck Salter, "Progressive Makes Big Claims," *Fast Company*, Issue 19, November 1998.

[121] Carol J. Loomis, "Sex. Reefer? And auto insurance!," *Fortune Magazine*, Vol. 132, No. 3, August 7, 1995.

[122] William E. Sheeline, "Avoiding Growth's Perils," *Fortune*, August 13, 1990.

[123] David Pilla, "Progressive's Lewis Honored As Insurance Leader of the Year, *Best's Insurance News*, January 19, 2006.

[124] Ronald Henkoff, "Service is Everybody's Business," *Fortune*, June 27, 1994.

[125] Interview with Ben Sheridan, March 30, 2006.

[126] Chuck Salter, "Progressive Makes Big Claims," *Fast Company*, Issue 19, November 1998.

[127] Steven Litt, "Innovation: a common thread for two movers and shakers," *The Plain Dealer*, June 13, 2002.

[128] Carrie Coolidge, "The Innovator," *Forbes*, January 10 2005.

[129] Patrick Barwise and Patrick Meehan, "The benefits of getting the basics right," *Financial Times*, October 8, 2004.

[130] Carol J. Loomis, "Sex. Reefer? And auto insurance!," *Fortune Magazine*, Vol. 132, No. 3, August 7, 1995.

[131] Andrea C. Poe, "Graduate Work," *HR Magazine*, October 1, 2003.

[132] Stanford Group Company Research Report, June 2, 2005.

[133] Steven Saint, "Bring a Friend into work (for good)," *The Gazette*, June 11, 2001.

[134] "Progressive Doubles Auto Claims Training Capacity, Opens Industry's First Motorcycle, ATV, RB and Boat...," *PR Newswire*, January 22, 2003.

[135] Jo-Ann Johnston, "Progressive Insurance Representatives Tune their Claims Skills," *KRTBN Knight-Ridder Business News: Tampa Tribune*, April 21, 2003.

[136] Judith N. Motti, "Progressive Puts Skills to Test," *InternetWeek*, March 8, 1999.

[137] The Progressive Corporation *2005 Annual Report*, pp. 10-11.

[138] Company website: http://investors.progressive.com/pdf/2006Handbook.pdf, p 20, accessed July 16, 2006.

[139] "Quality of Service from Auto Insurers Trumps Brand Recognition for Customer Retention, Says J.D. Power Survey," US Insurance News, September 10, 2007, accessed October 18, 2007 via http://www.usinsurancenews.com and "Nearly 20 Percent of Customers Consider Switching Auto Insurance Companies Following Their Most Recent Collision Claim," J.D. Power, January 9, 2007, accessed October 18, 2007 via http://www.jdpower.com/corporate/news/releases/pressrelease.aspx?ID=2007004..

[140] Company website: http://investors.progressive.com/pdf/2006Handbook.pdf, p 15, accessed July 16, 2006.

[141] Carol J. Loomis, "Sex. Reefer? And auto insurance!," *Fortune Magazine*, Vol. 132, No. 3, August 7, 1995.

GIOVANNI GAVETTI

REBECCA HENDERSON

SIMONA GIORGI

Kodak (A)

In February 2003, Daniel A. Carp, Kodak's chief executive officer and chairman, was reviewing 2002 data with the company's senior executives: film sales had dropped 5% from the already weak previous year and revenues were down 3%, sliding to $12.8 billion. The film industry was "under pressure unlike ever before", and Carp predicted a "fairly long downturn"[1] for traditional photography sales as more and more consumers were turning to digital cameras, which did not require film. The company had been investing heavily in digital imaging since the early 1980s, pioneering image-sensor technology in 1986 and entering the market with a variety of products during the 1990s.

In addition, Kodak was moving more of its manufacturing to China, where it could still boast film sales, and was planning to slash 2,200 jobs, or 3% of its work force, especially in the photo-finishing business. The picture for 2003 was not any brighter: Carp expected revenues to grow slightly to $13 billion and net income to be flat or down from the $770 million the company had earned in 2002.

A native of Wytheville, Virginia, Carp had graduated in management from MIT, and had begun his career at Kodak in 1970 as a statistical analyst. Since then he had held a variety of positions, including general manager of sales for Kodak Canada, general manager of the consumer electronics division, general manager of the European, African, and Middle Eastern regions in 1991, and president and chief operating officer in 1997. Carp was finally appointed CEO on January 1, 2000. After more than 30 years at the company, he realized this struggle was one of the toughest in the company's century-long history. How could he use digital imaging to revitalize Kodak?

Kodak's early days, 1880-1983

In 1880, after three years of photographic experiments, George Eastman, a young bank clerk, invented and patented a dry-plate formula and a machine for preparing large numbers of plates. In that same year, he leased the third floor of a building on State Street in Rochester, New York, and founded the Eastman Kodak Company. Although the company originally faced economic and technological challenges, it developed its first snapshot camera in 1888 and quickly became an American household name.

In 1904 Eastman articulated the company's competitive philosophy: "Nothing is more important than the value of our name and the quality it stands for. We must make quality our fighting argument."[2] Based in Rochester, "the Kodak town", as the first ads stated, the company operated its own laundry service, a bank, a cafeteria, and a blacksmith, among other services. There wasn't much that Kodak didn't provide for its employees: indoor golf courses, bowling alleys, and movie theaters. Kodak ran most of these services until the 1980s.[3]

From the very beginning, the founder of the company realized that success came from a user-friendly product, and, as he succinctly described it, his objective was "to make the camera as convenient as the pencil."[4] Marketing was regarded as an essential tool for the company's success; film advertisements started as early as 1885. Eastman himself coined the slogan "You press the button, we do the rest" when he introduced the first Kodak camera in 1888. Eastman identified four basic principles for his business: mass production at low cost, international distribution, extensive advertising, and focus on the customer. To these principles he added the policy to foster growth and development through continuous research.

In 1884, Eastman replaced glass photographic plates with a roll of film, expressing a profound belief in "the future of the film business."[5] During the black-and-white film era, Kodak's leadership stemmed not as much from its technical leadership as from its marketing campaigns and its relationships with retailers (both for shelf space for its film rolls and for photo-finishing with Kodak's paper). Although some competitors, like Ilford in the United Kingdom, had succeeded in setting new standards of quality during the war years, the perceived quality of the existing products was so high that consumers were not willing to pay for an enhanced product.[6]

The idea that money came from consumables, not from hardware, emerged early: cameras were relatively cheap and film fueled the company's growth. Especially with the advent of color film, which required conspicuous investments in R&D, many firms lagged behind. Kodak had been involved with the development of color film since 1921 and had spent over $60 million in research up to 1957, reaching a total of $121 million only on color film research by 1963.[7] In addition, Kodak's photofinishing process had become the industry standard and most rival brands, though of excellent quality when properly processed, tended to fare badly in the typical photo shop.[8] From the early 1960s attempts to entry the market had become extremely rare, especially because the film composition's balance between chemical and physical properties and the know-how embedded in manufacturing made the creation of compatible products a very expensive and risky option.

Over time the belief that all the money came from film led the company to pay little attention to equipment. A Kodak executive commented, "No matter what they said, they were a film company. Equipment was ok as long as it drove consumables. If a camera helped sell more film, Kodak would sell it, but there was little concern about what kind of cameras consumers wanted, or how to make them better."[9]

The role played by film was so pivotal that most corporate power centered on Kodak Park's massive film-making plant, and historically CEOs came out of manufacturing jobs at the Park. They were alike in many ways: most of Kodak's senior management received the same training, attending MIT's Sloan School of Business as a sort of finishing academy. Since a mistake in the massive manufacturing process would cost thousands of dollars, and the company's profitability was steadily more than satisfactory, the company avoided anything risky or innovative and developed a set of "procedures and policies to maintain the status quo."[10]

Kodak reached $1 billion in sales in 1962. In the 1960s the company started to introduce new products (126 cameras in 1960s, 110 in the early 1970s) that moved beyond consumer photography to medical imaging, and graphic arts. Most of these products exploited the traditional silver-halide technology and represented incremental improvements.

In 1969 Polaroid's basic patents on instant photography expired. Seven years later Kodak announced its first instant camera, and, thanks to its marketing and distribution capabilities, sold 16.5 million instant cameras between 1977 and 1985, severely threatening Polaroid. However, the company was forced to abandon this product line in 1985 because of a patent infringement suit by Polaroid. By 1976 Kodak controlled 90% of the film market and 85% of camera sales in the United States. Kodak's technological strengths and speed to market precluded the emergence of any serious competitor[11]. In 1981 Kodak's sales reached $10 billion, but growth began to decelerate thereafter because of increased competitive pressures, especially from the Japanese Fuji Photo Film Company. For an overview of the film market, see **exhibits 1, 2, 3, 4, 5** and **6**.

In 1981 Sony Corporation announced its plans to launch Mavica, a filmless digital camera that would display pictures on a television screen. Pictures could then be printed out on paper. Although CEO Colby Chandler contended that people "liked color prints" and that Kodak could quickly come out with its own digital camera, management became concerned over the longevity of silver-halide technology. A company's executive remembered, "It sent fear through the company." The reaction was, "Oh, my goodness, photography is dead."[12]

Diversification at Kodak, 1983 - 1993

Diversification in other businesses

Between 1983 and 1993 Kodak went through seven restructurings. Kodak acquired IBM's copier services business; Clinical Diagnostics, which produced in-vitro blood analyzers; Mass Memory, which sold Verbatim floppy disks; and other bioscience and lab research companies. In the late 1980s management looked further afield and chose to acquire Sterling Drug, a pharmaceutical company that sold popular products like Lysol and aspirin. The company believed that the pharmaceutical industry was related to its core "chemical" business: R&D played a pivotal role, and margins were high. Kodak paid $5.1 billion to acquire Sterling, of which $4.4 represented goodwill. Unfortunately, the stock price rose by only 2% from 1987 to 1993, and film market shares sunk by 5% between 1987 and 1992.[13]

Competition in the core imaging business: Fuji Photo Film Co.

"We were the imaging company of the world. We literally had no competition for so long, management hadn't become accustomed to it. Historically, if there was a competitor, Kodak would blow them away."
A former Kodak executive[14]

Fuji Photo Film Co., headquartered in Tokyo, was founded in 1934 as a comprehensive maker of photographic materials, producing film for movies and other applications, dry plates, and photo printing paper. In the 1960s Fuji started looking for alternatives to the development and production of silver-halide film and established a joint venture with Rank Xerox (Fuji Xerox).[15]

Fuji entered the U.S. market in 1965 as a private brand supplier. Although the company began to market film under its own brand name in 1972, its strategy consisted of following Kodak rather than attacking it directly. In 1976 Fuji was the first to introduce 400-speed color film, and more and more photo-finishers switched to its photographic paper and other supplies, which were 20% cheaper than Kodak's. In a case study of Fuji and the Japanese market, M.F. Winters, a Kodak market analyst, warned senior executives about the company's eroding market share, but the report was ignored, because "they didn't believe the American public would buy another film."[16]

At the beginning of the 1980s, Fuji had revenues of $2.4 billion, only one-fifth of Kodak's, but its net income over the previous five years had grown an average of 40% annually, more than twice Kodak's rate. With a 70% film market share in Japan, Fuji's other businesses included cameras, carbonless copying paper, copiers, and videotapes. Fuji signaled its ambitions to capture U.S. market share in 1981, when it won the sponsorship as the official film of the 1984 Olympics. Kodak had balked at the cost of officially sponsoring film supplies, and Fuji, taking advantage of the opportunity, boosted its U.S. market share to 12%. Peter Palermo, who was then Kodak's senior vice president of imaging, observed, "It was December seventh [Pearl Harbor Day] at Kodak."[17]

An important element in Fuji's success was its highly productive research laboratories in Ashigara. In 1986 Fuji began selling a disposable camera, which became a big hit in Japan. Kodak claimed that its labs had already developed similar products early in the 1980s, but the company had failed to patent them, some said because of their inconsistency with the traditional razor-blade model.

By 1985, Fuji's share of the U.S. market had grown to 11%, while 3M's Scotch brand had a 3.7% share. New labels, eager to gain a foothold in this highly profitable film market, included Konica, Agfa, dozens of private-label varieties, and Indian, English and Korean brands. Consumers were learning that they could get high-quality pictures with cheaper film (film prices were generally 20% lower than Kodak's), and retailers devoted more shelf display to private labels since they could make higher margins on their own products. By the end of 1993 the worldwide film market was still dominated by Kodak, but Fuji had gained a 21% market share.

Kodak's exploration of digital imaging, 1983-1989

In 1983 CEO Colby Chandler created a photographic and information management division to explore new technologies, especially digital imaging. In addition, the company hired John White, who had worked in the upper ranks of the Pentagon before getting into the software business, to push Kodak forward in this exploratory phase. White said:

> Kodak wanted to get into the digital business, but they wanted to do it in their own way, from Rochester and largely with their own people. That meant it wasn't going to work. The difference between their traditional business and digital is so great. The tempo is different. The kind of skills you need are different. Kay [Whitmore, President] and Colby [Chandler, CEO] would tell you they wanted change, but they didn't want to force the pain on the organization.[18]

The exploration of a broad range of technologies (e.g., communication, electronics, computer science) responded to the company's need to shape the new imaging business. The CEO was still foreseeing a silver-halide-based future, but recognized the need to "blend new technologies, to meet the expectations of a growing customer base."[19] The basic idea sounded simple: "anticipate customers' needs, create the products they want, then market those products better and more cost effectively than anyone else in the industry."[20] From Chandler's perspective the new digital world could be overcome by applying the same formula defined by George Eastman at the beginning of the century: focus on the customer, extensive advertising, and mass production at low cost. Still, he conveyed a sense of urgency in formulating his strategy in the 1984 annual report:

4

Kodak has historically evaluated future needs of a photographic market, conducted research to determine its size and growth potential, designed the goods, created manufacturing capacity and rolled out the new products. Today the pace of change has quickened. One Kodak strategy is to work with other major companies. Another proven Kodak approach is selective acquisition. Kodak is also increasing its involvement with several outstanding universities to conduct joint research in fields such as manufacturing productivity, biotechnology, microelectronics, and integrated circuitry.

In transforming itself, Kodak was abandoning its history as a stronghold of vertical integration. "One of the things we've learned is that one company can't do everything," Kodak president Kay R. Whitmore said. "We're prepared to acquire if it fits our strategic plan and gets us there sooner, or gives us a technical capacity we don't have in-house, or buys a market share that would be hard to build."[21]

In the mid-1980s Kodak built a research lab in Japan to study developments in electronics, in particular in digital cameras, because there was "a gut feeling that we ought to have a lab in the heartland of the consumer electronics revolution", said E.P. Przybylowicz, who operated as chief technical officer at the time. But it soon turned out to be "an impossible situation": the research lab had been put on a pay-as-you-go basis, and that meant that scientists had to look for financial support from individual business units, rather than from an overall corporate strategy.

The exploration of new technologies led Kodak to develop the 8mm Kodakvision video system together with TDK and Mitsushita; to acquire other companies, like the Datatape division of Bell and Howell, which manufactured high technology analog and digital recording equipment; and to devote internal resources to research. Relative to internal R&D, Chandler's stated strategy was to "continue support to extensive research in chemistry, optics, and increasingly in electronics."[22] But some executives still found it difficult to believe in something that was not as profitable as traditional film. "We're moving into an information-based company", Leo J. Thomas, senior vice president and director of Kodak research, stated, "[but] it's very hard to find anything [with profit margins] like color photography that is legal."[23]

In 1986 Kodak launched the world's first electronic image sensor with 1.4 million pixels (or picture elements), and the following year the electronic photography division was established. By 1989 Kodak had introduced more than 50 products that involved electronic image capture or conversion, such as printers and scanners (including products like Business Imaging Systems' Imagelink scanner 9000, Printer Products' XL 7700 digital continuous tone printer, Copy Products' Ektaprint 1392 printer, professional Photography's Premier image enhancement system and Motion Picture and Television's HDTV projection system). Within the information sector, four centers of excellence were established to develop image acquisition, storage system, software, and printer products. The same year the CEO declared his intent for the company to "be the world's best in chemical and electronic imaging" by "exploring and defining the best ways to manage the convergence of conventional imaging science with electronics."[24]

Although the company had been the first to introduce an image sensor, one of the core elements of a digital camera, the first widely announced digital product was the Photo CD. Kodak wanted to shape the new market creating the "film-based digital imaging."[25]

"Film-based digital imaging", 1990-1993

The Photo CD, developed in collaboration with Phillips, was designed to combine "the best of the photographic medium with the best attributes of electronic imaging."[26] The Photo CD started as a blank compact disc. A roll of film could be taken to a photofinisher, and images, rather than being printed, were then stored on the disc. Images could then be viewed on a TV screen with a special Photo CD player or on a computer screen with a CD-ROM. The project was expected to be a $600 million business by 1997 with $100 million earnings from operations, but there was little evidence that consumers were willing to pay $500 for a player that plugged into a TV, plus $20 per disc[27].

From the company's perspective new products had to rely on a hybrid film/electronic imaging technology because "for the foreseeable future" silver-halide technology was going to provide the highest-quality images attainable at the lowest price. But managing the alliance of chemical-based and electronic image was also a way to maintain leadership by shaping a Kodak-friendly new environment. Kay Whitmore, who had become chief executive officer in 1990, commented, "As this company did with black-and-white and color, we intend to set the standards and lead the way in film-based digital imaging."[28]

This blending of digital features and traditional photography allowed film to still play a pivotal role. Kodak planned to sell new hardware products improved by digital features, to license technology to computer manufacturers, to have more prints from discs at photofinishers, and to apply the knowledge acquired in digital imaging to the motion picture business and commercial products. But money still had to come from consumables, that is photographic film and paper, just "adding the flexibility offered by electronics."[29]

The first professional digital camera was introduced in 1991, but in Kodak's Annual Reports, management presented the Photo CD as the company's innovative offering. Unfortunately, the Photo CD did not prove to be a success: it had been targeted to the wrong market, the consumer segment, even though its invention team had suggested that its real potential lay in the commercial market. Scott Brownstein, who led the Photo CD team, said that senior managers at the time wanted a quick hit and did not "understand our real vision or strategy."[30] Brownstein and his group were looking for alliances with computer companies to make CD-ROMs compatible with the Photo CD, but when senior executives managed to get a meeting with Bill Gates, he remembered the lack of interest of Whitmore, who apparently fell asleep.[31] Later, when the Photo CD team managed to deal with the computer companies, they still had problems explaining the details to Whitmore. An industry observer commented:

> Kodak's strategy for digital imaging has been way out of focus for years. Product development was uncoordinated, and marketing was ineffectual. The Photo CD, a compact disc that stores photographs for viewing on TV screens or PC monitors, was a flop as a consumer product. Kodak introduced it in 1992 to consumers who didn't like the prices: $500 for a player that plugs into a TV, plus $20 per disk. And the computer industry adopted its software algorithms as the standard for manipulating color and images on CD-ROM. How did Kodak miss that? The entire digital revolution has been a trickle-down affair.[32]

On August 6, 1993, Kodak announced that CEO Kay Whitmore would step down. The members of the board were looking for a chief executive with "exceptional drive and energy" and in late 1993 they selected George M.C. Fisher, former CEO of Motorola. The first outsider ever to run the 116-year-old Kodak, Fisher, after receiving his Ph.D. in applied mathematics, had apprenticed at AT&T's Bell Labs, where he did work related to photography, such as conveying and compressing images. Fisher believed that Kodak was a company built on "imaging," not only on film, and that opportunities for growth could come from a focus on the core business and the exploitation of new digital technologies.

6

154

Back to the core business

Fisher's first step was to divest the company's health segment, with the exception of the health sciences unit, which included mostly X-ray film and other diagnostic imaging hardware and consumables. Kodak sold Sterling Drug, L&F Products, and Clinical Diagnostics in less than eight months, collecting $7.9 billion that it used largely to pay off debt. In December 1993 the company decided to spin off Eastman Chemical, which had been formed in 1920 to supply raw materials for Kodak's photographic business, but by 1993 only 8% of its sales derived from Kodak. As a result, the balance sheet improved, and S&P's rating on Kodak's debt raised from BBB+ to A+. In completing the divesture of the company's unrelated businesses, Fisher demonstrated his confidence in the future of the imaging segment, after a decade of pessimism. "People began to think electronics was going to take over the photography business. And if you are looking at the world from within the photography business, that would be a very scary event. But the fact of the matter is, I grew up in the electronics business and I looked at the photography and imaging business from the electronics side and it's not such a scary event. Electronics will add a lot to photography and a lot to imaging."[33]

Growing in the film business: Fisher's legacy in China

Fisher believed that scenarios about the future of silver-halide photography had been too pessimistic and that emerging markets, particularly China, represented an overlooked growth opportunity. He commented, "I think maybe people didn't properly understand that the world is a lot bigger than the United States and that something fundamental had changed in the last five years. About four billion people are now accessible as a market."[34]

Kodak had begun its push into China in 1993, and when Fisher joined Kodak, the company was third in film share and fourth in paper share, with only 30 employees. From his days at Motorola Fisher had established enormous credibility with officials in Beijing: from 1994 to 1997 Kodak negotiated with local officials and in March 1998 finally reached a deal that left Kodak committing $1.2 billion and that led to the creation of two joint ventures with the Chinese government. To improve its cost structure, by 2002 Kodak had moved facilities to China that manufactured digital, conventional, and single-use cameras, kiosks, and mini-labs. In addition to building its manufacturing presence, Kodak focused on creating a network of retail outlets that helped sales of film rolls. By the beginning of 2002 Kodak had 63% of the Chinese retail film market, with 7,000 Kodak Express film stores. An industry expert who toured Kodak's operations in China in 2000 observed, "Kodak's China operations represent the best of what an American industrial company can be in the emerging markets, in our opinion. It appears a true jewel for Kodak long term, and one that Mr. Fisher deserves full credit for discovering."[35] **Exhibit 19** reports on the company's retail presence in China.

Digital imaging in Fisher's era, 1993 – 1997

By the time Fisher arrived at Kodak, the company had already spent $5 billion on digital imaging R&D, but little had emerged from the labs. Product development and sales efforts were scattered over more than a dozen divisions, and at one point the company was engaged in developing 23 different digital scanner projects[36]. In 1994 Fisher separated the company's embryonic digital imaging operations from its traditional silver-halide photographic division, and created a digital and applied imaging division, in order to centralize the company's efforts in the area while building on Kodak's core capabilities in imaging technology and color science. Carl E. Gustin Jr., formerly with Digital Equipment Corporation and Apple Computer, was appointed general manager, and John Scully, former CEO of Apple Computer, was hired as a marketing and strategy consultant. In February

Fisher appointed Harry Kavetas, a former IBM executive credited with rejuvenating Big Blue's credit unit, as Kodak's chief financial officer.

Fisher saw considerable potential in the company's electronic imaging patent portfolio: he quickly pushed the introduction of the digital print station (a product sold to retailers that allowed customers to digitize their photos and to use them in many ways), new models of digital cameras, and thermal printers and paper to make prints from the cameras once the images were loaded into a personal computer. Fisher was determined to bring to market all those digital programs that had been languishing in the labs:

> Mr. Fisher unveiled a huge reorganization that would point Kodak back to the imaging business started by George Eastman in 1880. Yet, instead of dwelling on the future of the silver-halide photographic technology that has made Kodak the world's biggest photographic company, he talked mainly about digital imaging - a business that makes up a small fraction of Kodak's sales and has proved a consistent loss-maker.[37]

When Fisher joined the company he stressed that Kodak would focus on "profitable participation in the five links of the imaging chain: image capture, processing, storage, output, and delivery of images for people and machines anywhere."[38] In particular, Fisher, who had already turned Motorola into one of the world's finest manufacturers of pagers and cell phones, believed that "Kodak could be successful in the equipment business" because it possessed the capabilities to "do much besides make film."[39] His first step was to re-engineer the company from top to bottom, and "ten teams of senior managers - two of them led by Mr. Fisher - were charged with rethinking everything from product development to how to expand Kodak's markets:"[40]

> He wanted a 50% reduction in the cost of quality in two years. Each business would be required to calculate its customer satisfaction index and to show improvements. Every division had three years to reduce defects and improve reliability. Cycle times on everything from routine paperwork to manufacturing goods were to be improved by a factor of ten over three years.[41]

In his early days Fisher spent considerable time in meetings with Bill Gates and other leaders of the computer industry, with the aim of forming alliances and developing new products, because he thought that profitability on the hardware side could only come with the help of the computer and electronics industry. He hoped to "fill in the blanks" of Kodak's digital product line, which was marked by the initial failure of its consumer Photo CD product and digital camera for professionals, priced at $29,000.[42] Fisher believed that to be a winner in digital imaging Kodak had to become a high tech-company: "[Fisher] has devoted substantial energy to making Kodak more like Motorola, capable of producing new state-of-the-art products every few months. Company factories are churning out an impressive array of digital cameras, scanners, and other devices at a breakneck clip."[43]

But competition in the market for digital cameras was tough: when Kodak introduced the DC40 in 1995, there were two other models under $1,000, but by 1996 there were 25 different brands in the category. And not all executives believed in Fisher's new vision of the company. In fact competition from Hewlett Packard, Canon, Fuji and others was not the only difficulty that Fisher had to face. As one industry executive commented:

> The old-line manufacturing culture continues to impede Fisher's efforts to turn Kodak into a high-tech growth company. Fisher has been able to change the culture at the very top. But he hasn't been able to change the huge mass of middle managers, and they just don't understand this [digital] world.[44]

Fisher, who was used to dissent and open discussion in Motorola, where "they argued like cats and dogs, loudly, sometimes"[45], realized that Kodak executives tended to be very polite and things looked much easier than they actually were. Kodak's employees didn't like confrontations and venerated authority: "It was so hierarchically oriented that everybody looked to the guy above him for what needed to be done."[46] Fisher tried to introduce the Motorola-style of open discussion, but change was difficult. The razor-blade culture in Kodak was so deeply ingrained that even disposable cameras had been considered almost sacrilegious.

At an analysts' meeting in late 1997, after three quarters of sluggish sales and profits, Fisher admitted that 60% of the company's losses were "costs linked to digital cameras, scanners, thermal printers, writeable CDs and other products"[47] and announced a reversal of his hardware-based digital strategy:

We don't intend to be in the film business, in the computer business, in the digital imaging business. We're in the picture business. And our intention is to use whatever technology is available to us to truly help people do more with their pictures. Electronic imaging will not cannibalize film. One of the mistakes we at Kodak have made is that we've tried to do it all. We do not have to pursue all aspects of the digital opportunity and we see our opportunity in the output and service side.[48]

Analysts commented:

When the new management was brought on 3 years ago, one of its strategies for growth was to focus more on the hardware. This strategy has not been successful, considering the losses on digital cameras. Kodak continues to derive most of its profits from business units where more than 50% of revenue is generated from consumables and where the company has more than 50% market share.[49]

Toward a fully digital world, 1998 – 2003

Fisher established a new vision for the company's role in the digital age, a "network and consumables"–based business model:

We see a networked world in making, taking and processing pictures. We will stick ourselves in the middle of that world with services that people are willing to pay for, like creating photo albums online or simply sending photos from point A to point B. Or they'll use one of our 13,000 kiosks. People without computers can go to a kiosk and send photos halfway around the world. We will always sell film, paper and chemicals. But in the future, we will let people take pictures and scan them in digital form, and we will make money on the different media (CDs or the Internet, for example) or material for output - inkjet paper, thermal papers, and traditional silver halide paper.[50]

Fisher developed the idea of a "horizontal company", based on the outsourcing of most digital photographic equipment and on alliances (e.g., with Intel): "Traditionally, our business is chemically based, and we do everything. In the digital world, it is much more important to pick out horizontal layers where you have distinctive capabilities. In the computer world, one company specializes in microprocessors, one in monitors, and another in disk drives. No one company does it all."[51]

But on the film side, in 1998 the company was caught off guard by Fuji, which deeply cut prices to grab U.S. market share, where Kodak still enjoyed the highest margins. In one year Kodak lost more than four points in market share: Fisher observed that Fuji was "literally buying presence in this country, buying customers in this country, selling film at unbelievably low price because they could afford it and because they had an infinite source of money coming out of a protected market in Japan."[52] As a result of this price war, by the end of 1999 the company had to cut $1.2 billion in costs and 19,900 jobs, or about one-fifth of its payroll, the most severe cutback ever at Kodak.

In January 2000, one year before his contract was to expire, Fisher stepped down as chairman and handed over the post to a veteran insider, company president Daniel A. Carp, who had made his name as a brand builder rather than a technology guy. From Fisher, Carp inherited the idea of the horizontal company and the "network and consumables"–based business model:

> We see digitization in creating a film and a photo-finishing aftermarket that should fuel an explosion of pictures and use of digital and 35mm technology. At its core, Kodak's digital strategy is to create a profitable bridge between the old and new worlds of photography. Even as it hopes to jump-start sales of digital cameras, the company wants to transfer as many of its customers' traditional snapshots as possible to digital form. It figures there's big money to be made uploading traditional pictures onto the Internet and in expanding its share of the market for reprints, inkjet paper, and photo-editing software.[53]

Between 1999 and 2000, the digital strategy pursued by Fisher and Carp led the company to achieve a number two in digital cameras behind Sony, with a 25% market share, a running print-on-demand website, and promising joint ventures to popularize new distribution channels such as digital photo kiosks and the Internet.[54] The company was gradually changing its focus: "Just as the early Kodak pursued the holy trinity of film, paper and chemicals, and dominated all three, the new Kodak worships the digital trinity of image capture (cameras), services (online photo manipulation) and image output (digital kiosks, inkjet printers, paper and inks).[55]

On the output side, the Kodak network of 19,000 Picture Maker kiosks at retail stores was turning out to be quite successful. At $15,000 each, Carp said they were highly profitable and accounted for $200 million in sales; "with 95% of customers who used them coming back repeatedly, they produced steady photo paper sales."[56] Kodak also engaged with Hewlett Packard in an ongoing battle for the printing segment, investing a large portion of its R&D budget in inkjet printers, which drove sales of high-margin inkjet consumables and specialized paper.[57]

In fall 2000 another round of corporate restructuring brought digital and applied imaging and consumer imaging under one organization, a move that was expected to end the internal war between the film and the digital segments.[58] But in 2001 Kodak was still losing $60 on every digital camera it sold.[59] Still, Carp continued to invest in digital imaging, and the company actually boosted its advertising spending.[60] Kodak's commitment to building and consolidating its brand could be traced back to one of George Eastman's basic formulas for success: "advertise the product." In the 1970s the company had even moved to TV, sponsoring all-American programs like "The Adventures of Ozzie and Harriet" and "The Ed Sullivan show", and by 1995 it was using 177 advertising agencies (consolidated into four accounts by Fisher the following year).[61] In 2001 the company was trying to develop a more integrated marketing effort and message to the customer, with its "Where it all clicks" theme, and consumer imaging, digital and applied imaging and Kodak.com were all going to market with one ad campaign.[62]

The company also invested a considerable portion of its R&D dollars developing software for image manipulation, to enhance what could be done on a computer to a digital picture and at a retail store to traditional film. In October 2002 it launched in the Midwest the first mass-market product for digital film processing. With this new software, film was still developed traditionally, but instead of shining light through each negative onto photographic paper to create an image, digital processing scanned each negative, converting its image to a string of ones and zeros stored in a computer's memory. The computer then analyzed each image, looking for areas that had been exposed to too much or too little light. Using laser to paint each image pixel by pixel, the computer filled in light where needed and cut back on light where a flashbulb had supplied too much in the original negative. Carp commented, "This is the most important innovation for us since color. Using digital technology to enhance photos consumers take with existing analog cameras is an extension of Kodak's basic strategy of making it easier to take pictures."[63]

At the 2002 Kodak annual meeting, Carp outlined four strategic paths to move Kodak into the new millennium:[64]

- Expand the benefits of film. Kodak aimed to grow its share in the worldwide market by offering premium products (e.g., the Max HQ or the Max Versatility products), by leveraging its distribution, and by increasing its exposure through more targeted marketing campaigns. Kodak pricing of the low end of its film portfolio had narrowed over time, after the price war with Fuji between 1998 and 1999;

- Drive image output in all forms, to achieve higher margins at retailers. The company was planning the introduction of the Perfect Touch premium processing system and the expansion of its portfolio of digital mini-labs;

- Simplify the digital photo experience for consumers, with an emphasis on products such as the EasyShare digital camera platform, Picture Maker kiosks, and Picture CDs;

- Grow in emerging markets, in particular China and India, where the company already operated thousands of Kodak Express Stores.

Although the company optimistically outlined a scenario in 2002 in which the consumer digital business would break even in late 2003, by January 2003 digital cameras had not yet boosted the bottom line, while prices were plummeting: fourth quarter earnings were worse than analysts expected, and the company announced new layoffs.[65] However, despite financial problems, the company maintained control over a majority of photofinishing transactions in the United States, and had 15% of the U.S. digital camera market.[66] See **exhibits 18** and **20** for financial information about Kodak.

The Digital Imaging Industry

The digital imaging market began to expand in 1993 and 1994, with the introduction of a host of new products. In August 1994, there were 22 different models of filmless cameras on the market. One year later, only three models were priced under $1,000, but by 1996 25 different brands joined the category. In these early years there was a great deal of uncertainty about how market segments for digital cameras would evolve. Based upon quality and price, the market was generally separated into three levels. On the high end was studio photography, including magazine and catalog publishers, commercial photography studios, and in-house studios at corporations, hospitals, and government agencies. Leaf was an early leader in the studio camera market, but it quickly faced competition from companies such as Dicomed, Kanimage, Sony, and Kodak. In the mid-range segment, customers included photojournalists and professional photographers, who required a slightly lower resolution. This segment was very crowded, but Fuji and Kodak both had fairly popular offerings. The low end of the market included both consumer and business applications, such as real estate, insurance, and advertising as well as images displayed on computer screens or web sites. The first offering in the low-end market was Apple's QuickTake 100, priced at $749 in early 1994. Major competitors that followed included Logitech's Pixtura and Kodak's DC-40. All three cameras used an image sensor developed by Kodak in 1986.

Other digital products originally included 35 mm scanners, initially offered by Nikon, Polaroid, and Minolta; image-editing, dominated by Adobe's Photoshop; and printers, where the first players were Fuji, which offered a thermo-autochrome printer that garnered a great deal of attention, Epson, which had a color ink jet printer for the low-end priced under $700, and Kodak, which offered a widely acclaimed dye sublimation printer. It was difficult to determine clear leaders in each category, however.

By the end of the 1990s, the digital imaging industry was a portfolio of four major sub-markets, each with its own competitive dynamics: digital cameras, home printing, online services, and retail solutions (kiosks and mini-labs). The process of acquiring, digitizing, storing, printing, manipulating, transmitting, retrieving and projecting digital images had evolved over time in terms of ease of use and availability of options (**Figure A**).

Figure A   The Digital Imaging Chain

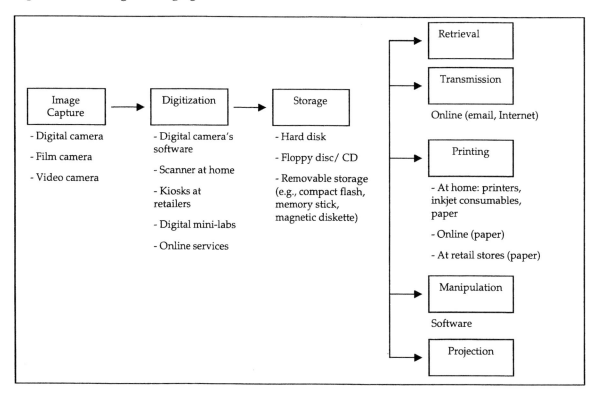

Source: Casewriter.

The digital camera markets began to expand rapidly in the late 1990s, and with 6 million units sold in 2001 (almost a 50% increase over year 2000) volumes were approaching early mass-market penetration, especially in the United States, where the installed base had reached 13 million households, 12.5% of the total. Digital cameras sales in September 2002 had increased 60% over the previous year, with a plummeting average price of $350. Although competition in the field was strong and largely based on price, features, and functionality (in an IDC study conducted in 2001, consumers were found to have relatively low brand awareness in digital cameras), the market was consolidating into a few major vendors like Sony, Kodak, Olympus, and Hewlett Packard. True profitability remained elusive for most, and since a lean cost structure played a pivotal role, vendors were moving manufacturing infrastructures to China. **Exhibits 7, 8, 9, 10, 11** and **12** show data about the traditional and digital cameras market.

In the film world, all images captured were processed at retail locations, however, in the digital world, users had multiple photo processing alternatives. Printing efforts focused on home/office printing, Internet photo service providers, and retail photofinishing. As concerned home printing, industry experts estimated that in 2002 almost 80% of digital prints were done in the office or at home, but that by 2005 home printing would decline to a 65% of all digital prints.[67] Four vendors dominated the inkjet-printers market: Hewlett Packard, Lexmark, Epson, and Canon. Much more profitable, however, was the consumable-side of the business: inkjet consumables, where Hewlett Packard enjoyed the lion's share, while Kodak had a small role thanks to its relationship with Lexmark, and high-grade inkjet paper. Hewlett Packard and Kodak dominated the specialty paper market with estimated EBIT margins of 25% after retail mark-up.

In 2000 more than a hundred companies were competing in online services, which mainly consisted of digitization, photo-finishing and storage, but by the end of 2002 three major players were still in the market: Kodak/Ofoto, Shutterfly, and Fuji. For instance, Ofoto, founded in 1999 and acquired two years later by Kodak, provided free online storage of photos and charged a fee for prints, enlargements, photo cards, albums, frames, and other photo-related merchandise, which were then delivered to the customers' doorstep. In addition, for less than $4 Ofoto's clients could have their traditional silver-halide pictures digitized and posted online. In 2002, online photo-finishing services accounted for 10% of all digital prints.[68] Prices had gone down with the elimination of service fees, but industry experts expected the model to be profitable in a few years since there was no retail markup. See **exhibits 13, 14** and **15** for more details on printing and photofinishing.

According to a report by International Data Corporation, in 2001 36% of the 31 million images captured were printed and 15% of them were processed at retailers, although digital mini-labs and kiosks were expected to capture the lion's share in the future.[69] Over the previous two decades, the photo processing industry had gone through dramatic changes. Early on, retailers had formed regional wholesale labs to sustain film processing and over the 1980s and the 1990s Kodak and Fuji promoted a massive consolidation that endowed the two players with almost total control of the market. Concurrently, new photo-processing units, designed to fit into retailers' shops, enabled local service of 24-hour and then one-hour processing. As a result, the amount of film sent to wholesale labs for processing declined.

Retailers offered two main processing solutions, mini-labs and kiosks, which were introduced in the mid-1990s to bridge between traditional inputs and new digital opportunities. With the advent of digital imaging, retailers turned to digital kiosks, which eliminated scanners from the system, and digital mini-labs, which could print digital files as easily and at the same quality as they could print silver-halide based photos. In addition, both digital mini-labs and kiosks provided for digital uploads from CDs, Zip discs, floppies, DVDs, and numerous flash cards. Once digitized, images could be archived on CDs or other media. The digital mini-labs market, which represented in 2002 almost 15% of the total mini-lab installed base, was dominated by Fuji with its Frontier products. Fuji, with more than 5,000 labs in place, had 60% of the U.S. digital mini-lab market and had signed deals to install machines in 2,500 Wal-Mart and about 800 Walgreen outlets. The two chains handled about 40% of the U.S. photo-processing market. Kodak lagged behind with about 100 digital mini-labs in service, because its 1997 agreement with Gretag ended in 2002 with the German imaging company's filing for bankruptcy. In the same year, Kodak joined forces with Noritsu Koki to close the gap, projecting to sell 1,000 mini-labs by the end of 2003.[70] **Exhibit 16** shows the evolution of the installed base of mini-labs and kiosks in the United States, while **exhibit 17** focuses on the competitive dynamics of the retail mini-lab market.

The Rochester-based company predominated in the offering of kiosks, with its 34,000 Picture Makers, providing retailers with a modular solution that consisted of three stations: Picture Maker Order Station, Digital Station, and Print Station. Each of these stations could be purchased individually and retailers could upgrade from one to the next without problems of compatibility.[71]

Appendix A presents an overview of Kodak's competitors in digital imaging.

Exhibit 1   U.S. Film Sales, 1983 - 2000 (in millions of rolls)

	35mm	APS	110/126	Disc	Instant	Other	Total Film
1983	224	-	177	82	95	16	594
1984	276	-	75	169	90	-	610
1985	339	-	74	165	80	9	667
1986	375	-	107	116	85	11	694
1987	430	-	117	124	93	17	781
1988	493	-	126	87	89	16	811
1989	567	-	117	62	92	6	843
1990	601	-	105	47	89	6	848
1991	629	-	83	28	89	10	837
1992	631	-	65	28	90	7	821
1993	687	-	61	15	91	6	860
1994	707	-	57	9	87	5	864
1995	704	-	50	6	88	19	867
1996	761	5	45	5	88	4	908
1997	744	30	60	3	90	2	928
1998	788	55	37	3	86	3	972
1999	856	80	23	0.3	80	5	1044
2000	844	104	21	0.1	84	3	1055

Source: Adapted from PMA Marketing Research.

Exhibit 2   Worldwide Film Revenues, 1994 - 2006E ($ millions)

	Color Negative	Color Reversal	Black and White
1994	11,600	980	860
1995	12,340	915	720
1996	13,530	905	640
1997	15,580	840	600
1998	15,265	835	560
1999	15,835	815	550
2000	15,897	810	550
2001	15,960	805	549
2002	15,618	784	538
2003E	15,231	764	527
2004E	14,853	744	516
2005E	14,463	724	504
2006E	14,082	705	493

Source: Adapted from Salomon Smith Barney, 2002

Exhibit 3 Worldwide Film Market Share, 1990 - 2002E (unit market share, in percent)

	Fuji	Kodak	Konica	Agfa	Others
1990	15	60	7	15	3
1991	17	58	7	15	3
1992	19	56	7	15	3
1993	21	54	7	15	3
1994	23	52	7	15	3
1995	25	50	7	15	3
1996	27	48	7	15	3
1997	29	46	7	15	3
1998	31	42	7	15	5
1999	33	40	7	15	5
2000	35	38	7	15	5
2001	37	36	7	15	5
2002E	39	34	7	15	5

Source: Adapted from Merrill Lynch and PhotoMarket

Exhibit 4 U.S. Film Revenues Share by Channel, 2000 - 2003E (in percent)

	2000	2001	2002	2003E
FDM*				
EK's share	68.2	65.2	65	64
Share of total market	44.7	44.2	45	45
Wal-Mart				
EK's share	53.3	50.7	51.4	29.9
Share of total market	28.3	29	29.9	29.7
Costco				
EK's share	61.5	100	100	100
Share of total market	7	6.8	7	7
Sam's Warehouse				
EK's share	68.5	100	100	91.6
Share of total market	6	6	5.4	5.5
Other warehouse				
EK's share	63	62	62.3	62.4
Share of total market	4	4	3	3
Specialty retailers				
EK's share	63	60.3	60.1	60.1
Share of total market	10	10	9.7	9.8

* Food, Drug, and Mass Merchandising Channel

Source: Adapted from Lehman Brothers, 2003

Exhibit 5 Film Revenues Change in the U.S. Food, Drug, and Mass Merchandising Channel, 2001 - 2002 (in percent)

	February-01*	March-01	April-02	May-02	June-02
Kodak	-12.8	-15.3	-19.8	-16.2	-15.4
Fuji	23.6	14.4	11.5	8.3	8.2
Polaroid	-15.5	-13.4	-14.2	-9.5	-21.1
Private Label	4.7	16.0	-4.3	-6.5	-9.8
Others	-42.8	-49.0	-53.7	-25.6	41.2

* Change in revenues over the 4 weeks ended February 2001, March 2001, April 2002, May 2002, and June 2002.

Source: Adapted from Morgan Stanley, July 2002

Exhibit 6 Average Price per Film Roll Change in the U.S. Food, Drug, and Mass Merchandising Channel, 2001 - 2002 (in percent)

	February-01*	March-01	April-02	May-02	June-02
Kodak	2.3	0.7	-1.4	-2.5	-1.7
Fuji	-2.7	-1.0	-2.0	-3.2	-0.4
Polaroid	-1.3	-6.4	-9.4	-14.6	-8.0
Private Label	-9.5	-5.4	-8.7	-12.2	-8.2
Others	-21.5	0.0	26.5	11.5	13.6

* Change in average price per roll over the 4 weeks ended February 2001, March 2001, April 2002, May 2002, and June 2002.

Source: Adapted from Morgan Stanley, July 2002

Exhibit 7 U.S. Camera Sales, 1983 - 2000 (in million units)

	35mm	Advanced Photo Sys.	110/126	Disc	Instant	OTU**	Other	Traditional tot.	Digital
1983	4.5	0	3.5	5.1	4	0	0.7	17.8	
1984	5.4	0	3.2	4.6	3.5	0	0.3	17	
1985	6.5	0	3.2	4.8	3	0	0.3	17.8	
1986	6.9	0	3.1	3	3.2	0	0.2	16.4	
1987	8	0	6	1.8	2.7	0	0.2	18.7	
1988	9	0	5.6	1	2.1	3	0.1	17.8	
1989	9.9	0	4.7	0.6	1.9	6	0.1	17.2	
1990	10.1	0	3.7	0.2	1.6	9	0	15.6	
1991	10.3	0	3	0.1	2.1	14	0	15.5	
1992	10.7	0	2.4	0	2.2	21.5	0.1	15.4	
1993	10.8	0	2.4	0	2.5	32.2	0.1	15.8	
1994	10.7	0	2.5	0	2.2	43.3	0.1	15.5	
1995	10.8	0	2.1	0	1.8	54.1	0.3	15	0.2
1996	10.6	1.1	1.6	0	1.7	71.7	0.2	15.1	0.4
1997	9.6	2.4	1.5	0	2	88.3	0.1	15.6	0.7
1998	9.9	3.1	1.3	0	1.9	110	0.1	16.4	1.2
1999	10.8	3.3	1.2	0	2.5	138	0.04	17.8	2.2
2000	11.4	3.3	0.8	0	4.2	161.8	0.02	19.7	4.5

Source: Adapted from PMA Marketing Association

Exhibit 8 Worldwide Camera Sales, 1997 - 2004E ($ in millions)

	1997	1998	1999	2000	2001	2002E	2003E	2004E
Digital	1,210	2,565	3,915	7,236	8,362	10,242	11,253	11,862
Traditional	16,000	16,250	16,750	14,740	14,070	12,864	11,539	9,809
Instant	413	450	788	1,013	962	904	841	774

Source: Adapted from Salomon Smith Barney 2003

Exhibit 9 Digital cameras sales by region, 1995 - 2000 (in millions of units)

	1995	1996	1997	1998	1999	2000
United States	0.2	0.4	0.7	1.2	2.2	4.5
Japan	0.1	0.5	1.0	1.5	1.8	3.6
Europe	0.0	0.1	0.4	0.6	1.1	2.3
Rest of the world	0.0	0.0	0.4	0.5	0.6	0.8

Source: Adapted from Salomon Smith Barney, 2001

Exhibit 10 U.S. Digital camera market share, 1998-2002 (units share)

	1998	1999	2000	2001	2002
Sony	59%	53%	28%	24%	34%
Kodak	17%	27%	13%	15%	13%
Olympus	9%	9%	18%	15%	20%
HP	5%	3%	4%	14%	5%
Fuji	1%	2%	5%	3%	4%
Canon	2%	1%	7%	5%	9%
Nikon	NA	NA	4%	4%	4%
Other	5%	6%	21%	20%	11%

Source: Adapted from Credit Suisse First Boston, 2002

Exhibit 11 Digital Camera Average Selling Price by mega-pixel resolution, 2000 - 2006E (in $)

	2000	2001	2002E	2003E	2004E	2005E	2006E
1MP	412	263	212	156	121	101	91
2MP	590	442	315	250	218	194	181
3MP	865	688	396	323	265	242	226
4MP	-	854	576	402	336	301	283
5MP	-	1,176	986	798	673	596	553
6+MP	-	-	1,201	1,002	833	754	668

Source: Adapted from IDC and Salomon Smith Barney, 2002

Exhibit 12 Worldwide Photography, Film, Processing, and Output Revenues ($ in millions)

	2000	2001	2002E	2003E	2004E	2005E	2006E
Cameras	22,988	23,394	24,101	23,615	22,443	20,556	19,373
Digital cameras	7,236	8,362	10,242	11,235	11,862	12,596	13,222
Traditional cameras	14,740	14,070	12,864	11,539	9,808	7,356	5,517
Instant cameras	1,013	962	904	841	774	704	634
Film	17,257	17,314	16,940	16,522	16,113	15,691	15,280
Paper	4,304	4,391	4,549	4,818	5,292	6,081	6,900
Paper	4,299	4,381	4,410	4,417	4,596	4,792	5,112
CD's	5	10	93	185	364	674	935
DVD's	0	0	46	163	332	615	853
Photofinishing	*36,545*	*37,389*	*36,939*	*35,936*	*34,996*	*34,114*	*33,290*
Amateur	27,244	27,890	27,725	27,183	26,680	26,214	25,785
Professional	9,301	9,499	9,214	8,753	8,316	7,900	7,505

Source: Adapted from Salomon Smith Barney, 2003

Exhibit 13 Worldwide Photofinishing Market Share by Region, 1995 - 2006E (in percent)

	1995	1996	1997	1998	1999	2000	2001	2002	2003E	2004E	2005E	2006E
United States	36.1	35.1	32.9	34.1	34.9	35	35	35.1	35	34.7	34.3	33.5
Japan	15.6	15.8	14.6	14	13.4	13.1	12.7	12.3	11.8	11.4	11	10.7
W. Europe	30.2	30.1	29	29	28.8	28.9	29.2	29.3	29.6	30	30.4	31
Other	18.1	19	23.5	22.9	22.9	23	23.1	23.3	23.6	23.9	24.3	24.8

Source: adapted from Photofinishing News and Salomon Smith Barney, 2002

Exhibit 14 Worldwide Digital and Film Image Capture and Print Volume, 2000 - 2006 (millions of units)

	2000	2001	2002	2003	2004	2005	2006	CAGR (%)
Digital								
Digital images captured	33,397	44,840	61,005	78,996	105,817	147,105	195,654	34.3
Digital images printed	14,363	19,062	24,851	31,764	35,680	41,307	48,376	20.5
Home / Office	12,369	15,085	19,387	23,823	25,088	27,121	29,781	14.6
Retail	1,350	3,015	4,075	5,597	7,528	9,973	12,975	33.9
Internet	645	962	1,389	2,344	3,063	4,213	5,620	42.3
Film								
Retail*	100,445	100,833	100,995	100,833	100,632	100,330	99,828	-0.2

* Retail film prints include onsite processing (mini-labs) and wholesale processing

Source: adapted from IDC, 2002

Exhibit 15   Worldwide Digital and Film Image Capture and Print Volume Revenue, 2000 - 2006 ($ in millions)

	2000	2001	2002	2003	2004	2005	2006	CAGR (%)
Digital								
Home / Office	6,833.8	8,482.4	10,901.5	13,629.1	14,352.6	15,648.7	17,183.6	15.2
Retail	899.6	2,010.2	1,996.7	2,238.8	2,634.9	2,992.0	3,892.5	14.1
Internet	316.0	365.4	486.2	703.2	919.0	1,263.8	1,686.1	35.8
Film								
Retail*	27,120.2	27,224.9	26,258.7	25,208.3	24,151.6	24,079.1	22,960.5	-3.3

* Retail film prints include onsite processing (mini-labs) and wholesale processing

Source: adapted from IDC, 2002

Exhibit 16   U.S. Kiosks and Mini-labs Installed Base and Share by Type, 2000 - 2006E (units)

	2000	2001	2002	2003E	2004E	2005E	2006E	CAGR (%)
Kiosks	21,343	24,385	29,159	36,915	49,378	68,549	96,381	31.6
Photo Printer (%)	100	78	68	24	16	15	11	-
Digital Printer (%)	0	22	32	58	56	54	51	-
Order Station (%)	0	0	0	18	28	31	38	-
Mini-labs	35,780	36,104	36,896	38,230	39,931	41,483	43,557	3.8
Digital (%)	6	11	21	31	40	48	62	-
Analog (%)	94	89	79	69	60	52	38	-

Source: Adapted from IDC, 2002

Exhibit 17   U.S. Retail Mini-lab Market Competitive Dynamics, 2002

Store name	Retail channel	Stores	Mini-labs	Manufacturers
Walgreen's	drug	3,520	3,380	Gretag, Fuji
CVS	drug	4,129	3,009	Gretag, Noritsu
WalMart	discount	4,414	2,300	Fuji
RiteAid	drug	3,497	2,075	Gretag, Noritsu
Eckerd Drug Store	drug	2,641	1,780	Gretag, Fuji, Noritsu
Ritz	photo	1,270	1,270	Fuji
Albertson's	supermarket	2,306	1,110	Gretag, Noritsu
Kmart	discount	1,831	766	Gretag, Agfa, Noritsu
Wolk Camera	photo	688	688	Fuji, Agfa, Noritsu
Winn Dixie	supermarket	1,153	581	Konica, Gretag
Kroger Co.	supermarket	3,211	561	Gretag, Fuji, Noritsu
Target	discount	1,053	400	Gretag
Fred Meyer	drug	385	385	Gretag, Fuji, Konica, Noritsu
Moto Photo	photo	282	282	Fuji, Agfa, Noritsu
Costco Wholesale	discount	365	273	Fuji, Noritsu
Longs	drug	437	268	Fuji, Noritsu
Safeway	supermarket	1,773	216	Gretag, Noritsu
H.E. Butt Grocery Co.	supermarket	300	181	Fuji, Gretag, Noritsu
Meijer	discount	152	143	Fuji
Kits Camera	photo	140	140	Fuji

Source: adapted from Noritsu Koki, UBS Warburg, December 2002

Exhibit 18   Kodak Financial Statements, 1993-2003E ($ millions)

	1993	1994	1995	1996	1997	1998	1999	2000	2001	2002E	2003E
Revenues	12,670	13,557	14,980	15,968	14,538	13,406	14,089	13,994	13,234	12,692	12,808
Photography	5,292	5,919	6,830	7,659	7,681	7,164	7,411	10,231	9,403	8,761	8,735
Professional	7,382	7,646	8,184	2,367	2,272	1,840	1,910	1,417	1,459	1,533	1,561
Health				1,627	1,532	1,526	2,120	2,220	2,262	2,279	2,390
Other				4,315	3,053	2,876	2,648	126	110	119	122
R&D	864	859	935	1,028	1,044	880	817	778	779	774	783
Operating Profit	1,248	1,309	1,941	2,203	1,771	2,065	2,454	2,170	1,233	1,211	1,316
Photography	931	878	1,254	1,324	1,072	1,080	1,304	1,430	787	663	777
Professional	317	431	687	319	284	330	396	233	165	194	205
Health				375	317	366	471	518	323	378	359
Other				185	98	289	283	-11	-42	-24	-25

Source: adapted from Salomon Smith Barney, 2002, and company's reports

21

Exhibit 19   Eastman Kodak: retail presence in China, 1994 - 2000 (number of stores)

	1994	1995	1996	1997	1998	1999	2000
Kodak	116	557	1,741	3,072	3,596	4,384	5,384
Fuji	223	1,124	1,986	2,800	3,000	3,000	3,000
Lucky	0	0	0	112	700	1,017	1,517

Source: adapted from Salomon Smith Barney, 2002, and company's reports

Exhibit 20   Eastman Kodak R&D Spending, 1977 - 2001 (in millions $)

	Sales	R&D	R&D / Sales
1977	5,967	351	5.88%
1978	7,013	389	5.55%
1879	8,028	459	5.72%
1980	10,815	520	4.81%
1981	10,337	615	5.95%
1982	10,815	710	6.56%
1983	10,170	746	7.34%
1984	10,600	838	7.91%
1985	10,631	976	9.18%
1986	11,550	1,059	9.17%
1987	13,305	992	7.46%
1988	17,034	1,147	6.73%
1989	18,398	1,253	6.81%
1990	18,908	1,329	7.03%
1991	19,419	1,337	6.89%
1992	20,183	1,419	7.03%
1993*	16,364	1,301	7.95%
1994**	13,557	859	6.34%
1995	14,980	935	6.24%
1996	15,968	1,028	6.44%
1997	14,538	1,230	8.46%
1998	13,406	922	6.88%
1999	14,089	817	5.80%
2000	13,994	784	5.60%
2001	13,234	779	5.89%

* Divesture of Eastman Chemical Company
** Divesture of non-imaging health businesses

Source: adapted from company's reports

170

Appendix A   Competition in Digital Imaging

Competitor	Overview
Canon, Inc.	Headquartered in Tokyo, Canon had 2002 estimated sales of $23.4 billion and a net income of $1,04 billion. Office equipment (copiers, business machines, information and telecommunication equipment), its largest business, accounted for 76% of sales, with an operating margin of 18%, the optical segment accounted for 7.5% of total sales, with negative margins of –5%, while the camera segment, which included film cameras, video cameras, and digital cameras, accounted for 16.5% of sales, with margins of 12%,[72] an increment of 1.5 points over year 2000.[73] In the camera segment, digital cameras generated 44% of sales, and had the best operating margin (14.1% versus 11.7% in film cameras and lenses and 5.4% in camcorders)[74]. In 2001, the company presented a "two-pronged product model strategy", the F series, which pursued photo quality, and the S series, which went after speed. In 2002 the company introduced the I series, with the aim of combining the two qualities with an emphasis on design. Since Canon brought out its 2002 models (IXY Digital 320, PowerShot S45, PowerShot G3), the company had surpassed Fuji Photo Film in digital cameras for a top domestic market share of 23%. The company's global market share in digital still cameras was 12%, while in traditional single-lens cameras it was more then 38%. Canon was one of the early pioneers in electronic photography, being the first to commercialize a still-video camera in 1986.
Fuji Photo Film Co.	Fuji business was divided into three divisions: *imaging solutions*, which included photographic film, photo printing paper, developing services, cameras and digital cameras, and which accounted for 32.7% of 2002 sales; *information solutions*, which included equipment for printing, medical diagnosis, IT systems, LCD components, and other electronic devices, generating 28.5% of sales; and *document solutions*, which included printers and copiers handled by Fuji Xerox, with 38.8% of sales. Operating margins for the three segments were respectively estimated to be 29%, 49%, and 22%.[75] The company's foray into digital cameras was the Fuji DS-100, released in 1993 at $3,200;[76] the DS-100 featured a 720x488 (350,000) pixel area array CCD and could store up to 21 images on a removable memory card. By 2000 the company had become one of the two leading digital camera manufacturers (the other being Olympus Optical), with sales of one million units, a leading domestic share, and a global share estimated at 20%. Fuji's strengths in digital cameras stemmed from high-picture quality, which was delivered by its in-house-developed charge-coupled devices (CCDs), thanks to a photodiode aligned in a unique honeycomb fashion, and cost competitiveness, achieved through in-house production of both CCDs and lens, which made up most of a camera's cost. In the digital camera business, Fuji's operating profit margin for 2001 was estimated at 5%, while its traditional mainstay business (color film, color paper, X-ray film, and photo-sensitive plates and film) generated over 15%.[77] Although R&D emphasis in the 1990s had been on developing digital imaging systems,[78] Fuji's strategy in digital imaging was similar to Kodak's in emphasizing the coexistence of film and digital. Both companies focused on the incremental effects of digital technology on traditional film-based halide technology. In 1999, at a panel discussion hosted by the Photo Imaging Manufacturer's and Distributor's Association, a Fuji executive stated that "right now, film has too large a price/performance advantage over digital to be replaced any time soon", and Harushi Yagi, managing director and general manager of the international marketing division, said of Fuji's unceasing R&D investment in traditional silver photography: "It is too early to predict whether digital products and services will really grow within the next few years, [but] we are certain that consumers will still enjoy photography, which after all they can nowadays get with excellent quality and at favorable prices."[79] In 2002 the company declared its plan to shift from a silver-halide-film-based company to a digital products maker, to compensate for an expected decline in demand for silver halide over the medium term,[80] with products such as digital cameras, mini-labs, and X-ray equipment. The weighting of digital products in overall sales was estimated to have surpassed 50% for the first time in 2001, with a contribution to operating profit of 50%. By contrast, Kodak's digital weighting remained a low 25%. An important part of Fuji's digital strategy was the installations of digital mini-labs to expand its market share in photographic film. Digital mini-labs, $100,000 computer and processing machines located behind store counters, handled inputs from conventional film, digital camera cards, digital media (including floppy disks, ZIP disks, and CDs), and prints, and offered a variety of services, including high-quality prints, variety prints (e.g., prints with text, frames, and greeting cards), and data writing, for storage on CD-R, floppy disk, MO disk, or ZIP disk.[81] The company introduced the Frontier in 1996 as the "core of a picture applications infrastructure in the digital era."[82] Fuji had a share of more than 60% of

	the U.S. market for digital mini-labs, with installations of 5,000 machines at the end of March 2003, while Kodak had only 100 mini-labs in service.[83] Shipments of Fuji's digital mini-labs benefited from its acquisition of Wal-Mart's photo-finishing division in 1997, and from the replacement of existing Kodak's products by customers like the leading drug chain Walgreen's.
Hewlett Packard Co.	The new Hewlett Packard, merged with Compaq Computer Corporation, had combined revenues of approximately $81.7 billion in fiscal year 2001, with operations in more than 160 countries. The company's offerings were categorized into four core business groups: the imaging and printing group (printer hardware, all-in-ones, digital-imaging devices such as cameras and scanners, and associated supplies and accessories); the enterprise systems group, which provided the key technology components of IT infrastructure; services, and the personal systems group (desktop PCs, notebooks, workstations, thin clients, smart handheld and personal devices). In January 2002, at the International Consumer Electronics Show, CEO Carly Fiorina dedicated most of her speech to the power of digital imaging, arguing that it was the next big thing in the computing and communications industries.[84] Hewlett Packard's imaging and printing research teams had been working so fast to get ahead in this emerging line of business that they filed for 2,500 related patents in 2001 alone. By 2002 the company had gained a 7.5% global market share in digital cameras. Hewlett Packard's success in digital imaging was based on the aggressive pricing of cameras and printers, with the aim of increasing sales of high-margin inkjet consumables.
Nikon	In 2000 Nikon reorganized its two sales groups, consumer and industrial products, into four new categories: imaging products (film cameras, digital cameras, interchangeable camera lenses), precision equipment (IC steppers, LCD steppers), instruments (microscopes, measuring instruments, inspection instruments), and others (e.g., binoculars, telescopes). In the 1990s, Nikon's share in traditional film cameras had maintained a stable market share of 20% on a unit base[85]. In 2000 it held a 30% market share for SLR cameras and a 6% market share for compact and digital cameras, which had been profitable since 1999 (but with margins lower than on traditional cameras). In the 1990s, Nikon had targeted the more profitable higher-end segment, but from the beginning of the 2000s it started its expansion into the more popular 2-megapixel cameras. Analysts had compared Nikon's strategy in digital imaging with Canon's, because of its aim to "link digital cameras sales to peripherals, printing paper, ink, and other consumables, graphic engines, and CMOS sensors."[86] From 2000 to 2002, digital still cameras had been performing well, with an increasing contribution to sales of the imaging business (from 32% of the group sales in 2000 to 47% in 2002[87]), but with top players shipping three million to four million cameras per year, Nikon's scale of operation was still comparatively small.[88]
Sony Corp.	The company had sales of $19 billion for third quarter 2002, up 1.2% from the previous year, and an operating profit of $1.5 billion. The electronic segment of the world's largest supplier of audio-video equipment recorded sales of $12 billion, down 4.6% from the previous year, because of the PCs' negative performance, but a rising operating profit. Digital cameras and camcorders fueled profitability.[89] Sony, which first demonstrated its Mavica digital camera in 1982, initially focused its marketing efforts on high-end pre-press and professional photography applications. But during the 1990s success came from its original Mavica, which stored images on 3.5-inch floppy disks, more familiar to Americans than the image-storage chips used by most Japanese vendors[90]. In 1999 Sony enjoyed an 80% market share in the low-end segment, which on its own accounted for 46% of the digital mix sales. Industry experts believed that Sony's breakout performance with technically lower quality products highlighted two key strengths of the company, its brand and its customer orientation, which was reflected in its products' ease of use[91]. By 2002 Sony's bestseller model was still the Mavica. The company boasted the number-one position in 2001 in the United States with a 23% share, and a number-two position in both Europe (with a share of 16%, second to Canon) and Japan (17% share versus Fuji's 25%). Sony maintained EBITDA margins of more than 10% on its digital photo products: the greatest profit driver in the digital camera world is the CCD business, with EBITDA margins of more than 20% and a 60% worldwide market share.

Endnotes

[1] *BusinessWeek*, "Daniel Carp, Kodak: Not a Pretty Picture," Feb. 3, 2003.

[2] Eastman Kodak (1988), *Focus on the future: a guide to Kodak's business units and products*

[3] Company's website.

[4] Company's website.

[5] A. Swasy (1997), *Changing Focus: Kodak and the Battle to Save a Great American Company*, Times Business, Random House.

[6] J. Sutton (1999), *Technology and Market Structure*, The MIT Press, Cambridge, MA.

[7] J. Sutton (1999), *Technology and Market Structure*, The MIT Press, Cambridge, MA.

[8] J. Sutton (1999), *Technology and Market Structure*, The MIT Press, Cambridge, MA.

[9] A. Swasy, *Changing Focus.*

[10] A. Swasy, *Changing Focus.*

[11] Salomon Brothers, *Eastman Kodak Company: A Changing Image*, Nov. 30, 1994.

[12] A. Swasy, *Changing Focus.*

[13] Salomon Brothers, *Eastman Kodak Company: A Changing Image*, Nov. 30, 1994.

[14] A. Swasy, *Changing Focus.*

[15] HSBC, *Fuji Photo Film*, Oct. 22, 2002.

[16] A. Swasy, Changing Focus.

[17] A. Swasy, Changing Focus.

[18] A. Swasy, Changing Focus.

[19] Eastman Kodak, *Annual Report 1984.*

[20] Eastman Kodak, *Annual Report 1985.*

[21] *Wall Street Journal,* "Kodak Facing Big Challenges in Bid to Change," May 22, 1985.

[22] Eastman Kodak, *Annual Report 1983.*

[23] *Wall Street Journal,* "Kodak Facing Big Challenges in Bid to Change," May 22, 1985.

[24] Eastman Kodak, *Annual Report 1989.*

[25] Eastman Kodak, *Annual Report 1991.*

[26] Eastman Kodak, *Annual Report 1991*.

[27] *Fortune*, "Getting digital imaging in focus," May 1, 1995.

[28] Eastman Kodak, *Annual Report 1991*.

[29] Eastman Kodak, *Annual Report 1991*.

[30] A. Swasy, *Changing Focus*.

[31] A. Swasy, Changing Focus.

[32] *Fortune*, "Getting digital imaging in focus," May 1, 1995.

[33] A. Swasy, *Changing Focus*.

[34] A. Swasy, Changing Focus.

[35] Salomon Smith Barney (J. Rosenzweig), *Eastman Kodak*, Sept. 26, 2000, p. 4.

[36] *BusinessWeek*, "Kodak's new focus," Jan. 30, 1995.

[37] *The Economist*, "Picture imperfect," May 28, 1994.

[38] *PR Newswire*, "Kodak's CEO unveils new corporate strategy," May 3, 1994.

[39] *Fortune*, "Digital imaging had better boom before Kodak film busts," May 1, 1995.

[40] *The Economist*, "Picture imperfect," May 28, 1994.

[41] A. Swasy, *Changing Focus*.

[42] *Forbes*, "George Fisher," June 5, 1995.

[43] *BusinessWeek*, "Can George Fisher Fix Kodak?," Oct. 20, 1997.

[44] *BusinessWeek*, "Can George Fisher Fix Kodak?," Oct. 20, 1997.

[45] A. Swasy, *Changing Focus*.

[46] *BusinessWeek*, "Kodak's new focus," Jan. 30, 1995

[47] *Electronics*, "Kodak changes digital strategy," Nov. 17, 1997

[48] *Denver Post,* "Kodak's chief outlines photo giant's challenges," Nov. 9, 1997.

[49] Credit Suisse First Boston (G.Huskey), *Eastman Kodak Co.*, May 21, 1998

[50] *Money*, "Keeping Kodak focused," Jan. 1999.

[51] *Money*, "Keeping Kodak focused," Jan. 1999.

[52] *Denver Post*, "Kodak's chief outlines photo giant's challenges," Nov. 9, 1997.

[53] *Forbes*, "Razors with no blades," Oct. 18, 1999.

[54] *The Economist*, "Business: Develop or Die," Sept. 30, 2000.

[55] *Forbes*, "Kodak's Digital Moment, " Aug. 21, 2000

[56] *Forbes*, "Razors with no blades."

[57] Salomon Smith Barney (J. Rosenzweig), *Eastman Kodak*, Feb. 14, 2002.

[58] *Rochester Business Journal*, "Kodak's CEO wraps up year of challenge," Dec. 8, 2000.

[59] CNBC/Dow Jones Business Video, Eastman Kodak President & CEO, interview by Mark Haines and Rick Schottenfeld, 1 May 2001.

[60] Salomon Smith Barney (J. Rosenweig), *Eastman Kodak*, Feb. 2001.

[61] A. Swasy, *Changing Focus.*

[62] Salomon Smith Barney (J. Rosenweig), *Eastman Kodak*, Feb. 2001.

[63] *Knight Ridder Tribune Business News*, "Kodak Launches Digital Film Processing Technology," Oct. 6, 2002.

[64] Salomon Smith Barney (J. Rosenzweig, S. Crane), *Kodak*, May 15, 2002.

[65] *The Wall Street Journal,* "Kodak Posts Disappointing Net, Plans New Layoffs," Jan. 23, 2003.

[66] Credit Suisse First Boston, *Pixels & Profits*, Oct. 2002.

[67] International Data Corporation, *The battle for digital images: worldwide photo printer forecast, 2001-2006*, IDC #28366, November 2002.

[68] Lyra Research.

[69] International Data Corporation, *The Image Bible, 2002-2006*, IDC #28258, November 2002.

[70] *BusinessWeek*, "Big Yellow's digital dilemma," Mar. 24, 2003.

[71] International Data Corporation, *The battle for digital images: U.S. kiosk and minilab forecast, 2002-2006*, IDC #28574, December 2002.

[72] HSBC, *Canon*, Mar. 27, 2002.

[73] Morgan Stanley, *Canon*, F2002 earnings preview, Jan. 28, 2003.

[74] HSBC, *Canon*, Mar. 27, 2002, HSBC estimates and assumptions.

[75] HSBC, *Fuji Photo Film*, Oct. 22, 2002

[76] J. Leonard, E.Olmsted Teisberg, "Digital Imaging in 1995: Opportunities in the Descent to the Desktop," HBS Case, April 1996.

[77] HSBC, *Fuji Photo Film*, Feb. 2000.

[78] MorningStar Inc., *Fuji Photo Film – Co report*, Jan. 14, 1994

[79] International Contact, *The Bigger Picture, the real business, Fuji film at PMA,* April/May 1999.

[80] HSBC, *Fuji Photo Film,* Oct. 22, 2002.

[81] *BusinessWeek,* "Big Yellow's digital dilemma," Mar. 24, 2003.

[82] Fuji Photo Film, *Annual Report 1999.*

[83] *BusinessWeek,* "Big Yellow's digital dilemma," Mar. 24, 2003.

[84] *Wireless Week,* "Digital imaging: Just a click away," July 1, 2002.

[85] Commerzbank, *Nikon,* July 2001.

[86] Commerzbank, *Nikon,* July 2001.

[87] UBS Warburg, *Nikon,* Jan.2003.

[88] Morgan Stanley, *Nikon,* May 14, 2002.

[89] DAIWA, *Sony,* Feb. 2003

[90] *BusinessWeek,* "Fuji: Beyond Film, " Nov. 22, 1999.

[91] Credit Suisse First Boston, *Pixels and Profits,* Oct. 29, 1999.

9-708-480

REV: SEPTEMBER 8, 2008

DAVID B. YOFFIE

MICHAEL SLIND

Apple Inc., 2008

In January 2007, three decades after its incorporation, Apple Computer shed the second word in its name and became Apple Inc.[1] With that move, the company signaled a fundamental shift away from its historic status as a vendor of the Macintosh personal computer (PC) line. Mac sales remained vital to Apple's future, but they now accounted for less than half of its total revenue. A year and a half later, in June 2008, the company posted results that ratified the success of its leap beyond the PC business: In its third quarter, Apple earned a net profit of $1.07 billion on $7.46 billion in revenue, for a 38% increase on year-ago quarterly sales. Annual results were also impressive. Sales in the 2007 fiscal year topped $24 billion, up 24% from the previous year. (See **Exhibit 1a**—Apple Inc.: Selected Financial Information, plus **Exhibit 1b** and **Exhibit 1c**.) Investors, meanwhile, sent Apple's stock to new heights: Despite a sharp drop in early 2008, its share price had risen more than 15-fold since 2003 and now hovered near its all-time high. (See **Exhibit 2**—Apple Inc.: Daily Closing Share Price.)

Non-PC product lines drove much of Apple's financial performance. The company's iPod line of portable music players, together with its iTunes Store, had upended the music business. With the iPhone, a multifunction handheld device released in June 2007, Apple aimed to do the same for the mobile phone market. The launch of the iPhone 3G, in July 2008, involved major changes to the offering—a revamped pricing model, a new retail channel advanced, and a platform for third-party applications, along with 3G network service—that promised to make it still more competitive.

"Apple Inc." was thriving to a degree that was seemingly far beyond the capacity of "Apple Computer." Yet critical aspects of the company's strategic profile had changed rather little. Although Mac sales had surged in recent years, for example, Apple's share of the worldwide PC market consistently failed to rise above a 3% ceiling. (See **Exhibit 3**—Apple Inc.: Worldwide PC Share.) CEO Steve Jobs, therefore, faced a new variation on an old question: Was Apple's recent success just another temporary "up" in its up-and-down history, or had he finally established a sustainable strategy for the company?

Apple's History

Steve Jobs and Steve Wozniak, a pair of 20-something college dropouts, founded Apple Computer on April Fool's Day, 1976.[2] Working out of the Jobs family's garage in Los Altos, California, they built a computer circuit board that they named the Apple I. Within several months, they had made 200

Professor David B. Yoffie and Research Associate Michael Slind prepared this case. This case was developed from published sources. This case derives from earlier cases, including "Apple Computer 2002," HBS No. 702-469, by Professor David B. Yoffie and Research Associate Yusi Wang, and "Apple Computer, 2006," HBS No. 706-496, by Professor David B. Yoffie. HBS cases are developed solely as the basis for class discussion. Cases are not intended to serve as endorsements, sources of primary data, or illustrations of effective or ineffective management.

sales and taken on a new partner—A.C. "Mike" Markkula, Jr., a freshly minted millionaire who had retired from Intel at the age of 33. Markkula, who was instrumental in attracting venture capital, was the experienced businessman on the team; Wozniak was the technical genius; and Jobs was the visionary who sought "to change the world through technology."

Jobs made it Apple's mission to bring an easy-to-use computer to market. In April 1978, the company launched the Apple II, a relatively simple machine that people could use straight out of the box. The Apple II sparked a computing revolution that drove the PC industry to $1 billion in annual sales in less than three years.[3] Apple quickly became the industry leader, selling more than 100,000 Apple IIs by the end of 1980. In December 1980, Apple launched a successful IPO.

Apple's competitive position changed fundamentally in 1981, when IBM entered the PC market. The IBM PC, which used Microsoft's DOS operating system (OS) and a microprocessor (also called a CPU) from Intel, seemed bland and gray alongside the graphics- and sound-enhanced Apple II. But the IBM PC was a relatively "open" system that other producers could clone. By contrast, Apple relied on proprietary designs that only Apple could produce. As IBM-compatibles proliferated, Apple's revenue continued to grow, but its market share dropped sharply, falling to 6.2% in 1982.[4]

In 1984, Apple introduced the Macintosh, marking a breakthrough in ease of use, industrial design, and technical elegance. Yet the Mac's slow processor speed and a lack of compatible software limited its sales. Between 1983 and 1984, Apple's net income fell 17%, leaving the company in crisis. In April 1985, Apple's board removed Jobs from an operational role. Several months later, Jobs left Apple to found a new company named NeXT. Those moves left John Sculley, the CEO whom Apple had recruited from Pepsi-Cola in 1983, alone at the helm. Sculley had led Pepsi's successful charge against Coca-Cola. Now he hoped to help Apple compete against dominant players in its industry.

The Sculley Years, 1985–1993

Sculley sought to make Apple a leader in desktop publishing as well as education. He also moved aggressively to bring Apple into the corporate world. Apple's combination of superior software, such as Aldus (later Adobe) PageMaker, and peripherals, such as laser printers, gave the Macintosh unmatched capabilities in desktop publishing. Sales exploded, turning Apple into a global brand. By 1990, Apple's worldwide market share stabilized at about 8%. In the education market, which contributed roughly half of Apple's U.S. sales, the company held a share of more than 50%. Apple had $1 billion in cash and was the most profitable PC company in the world.

Apple controlled the only significant alternative, both in hardware and in software, to the then-prevailing IBM-compatible standard. The company practiced horizontal and vertical integration to a greater extent than any other PC company, with the exception of IBM. Apple typically designed its products from scratch, using unique chips, disk drives, and monitors, as well as unusual shapes for its computers' chassis. The company also developed its own proprietary OS, which it bundled with the Mac; its own application software; and many peripherals, including printers.

Analysts generally considered Apple's products to be more versatile than comparable IBM-compatible machines. IBM-compatibles narrowed the gap in ease of use in 1990, when Microsoft released Windows 3.0. But in many core software technologies, such as multimedia, Apple retained a big lead. In addition, since Apple controlled all aspects of its computer, it could offer customers a complete desktop solution, including hardware, software, and peripherals that allowed customers to "plug and play." By contrast, users often struggled to add hardware or software to IBM-compatible PCs. As a result, one analyst noted, "The majority of IBM and compatible users 'put up' with their machines, but Apple's customers 'love' their Macs."[5]

This love affair with the Mac allowed Apple to sell its products at a premium price. Top-of-the-line Macs went for as much as $10,000, and gross profit hovered around an enviable 50%. However, senior executives at Apple realized that trouble was brewing. As IBM-compatible prices dropped, Macs appeared overpriced by comparison. As Sculley explained, "We were increasingly viewed as the 'BMW' of the computer industry. Our portfolio of Macintoshes were almost exclusively high-end, premium-priced computers.... Without lower prices, we would be stuck selling to our installed base." Moreover, Apple's cost structure was high: Apple devoted 9% of sales to research and development (R&D), compared with 5% at Compaq, and only 1% at many other IBM-clone manufacturers. These concerns led Dan Eilers, then vice president of strategic planning at Apple, to conclude: "The company was on a glide path to history."[6]

Sculley was a marketer by training. Nonetheless, in March 1990, he took on the post of chief technology officer (CTO). As CEO and CTO, Sculley strove to move Apple into the mainstream by offering "products and prices designed to regain market share."[7] That meant becoming a low-cost producer of computers with mass-market appeal. He also sought to maintain Apple's technological lead by bringing out "hit products" every 6 to 12 months. In October 1990, Apple shipped the Mac Classic, a $999 computer that was designed to compete head-to-head with low-priced IBM clones. One year later, the company launched the PowerBook laptop to rave reviews. And in 1993, Apple introduced the Newton, a high-profile "personal digital assistant" (PDA). Despite Sculley's high hopes for the Newton, it ultimately failed.

In 1991, meanwhile, Sculley made a bold move to forge an alliance with Apple's foremost rival, IBM. Apple and IBM formed a joint venture, named Taligent, with the goal of creating a revolutionary new OS. At the time, it cost around $500 million to develop a next-generation OS; subsequent marginal costs were close to zero. The two companies also formed a joint venture, named Kaleida, to create multimedia applications. Apple committed to switching from the Motorola microprocessor line to IBM's new PowerPC chip, while IBM agreed to license its technology to Motorola in order to guarantee Apple a second source. Sculley believed that the PowerPC could help Apple to leapfrog the Intel-based platform. Meanwhile, Apple undertook another cooperative project, this one involving Novell and Intel. Codenamed Star Trek, it was a highly secretive effort to rework the Mac OS to run on Intel chips. A working prototype was ready in November 1992.

Under Sculley, Apple worked to drive down costs—by shifting much of its manufacturing to subcontractors, for example. But these efforts were not enough to sustain Apple's profitability. Its gross margin dropped to 34%—14 points below the company's 10-year average. In June 1993, the Apple board "promoted" Sculley to chairman and appointed Michael Spindler, the company president, as the new CEO. Five months later, Sculley left Apple for good.

The Spindler and Amelio Years, 1993–1997

As head of Apple, Spindler tried to reinvigorate its core markets: education (K-12) and desktop publishing, in which the company held 60% and 80% shares, respectively.[8] Meanwhile, Spindler killed the plan to put the Mac OS on Intel chips and announced instead that Apple would license a handful of companies to make Mac clones. Those companies would pay roughly $50 per copy for a Mac OS license. International growth became a key objective for Apple during the Spindler years. (In 1992, 45% of its sales came from outside the United States.) Spindler also moved to slash costs, cutting 16% of Apple's workforce and reducing R&D spending. Yet despite Spindler's efforts, Apple lost momentum: A 1995 *Computerworld* survey of 140 corporate buyers found that none of the Windows users would consider buying a Mac, while more than half the Apple users expected to buy an Intel-based PC.[9] (See **Exhibit 4**—Shipments and Installed Base of PC Microprocessors.) Like Sculley, moreover, Spindler had hoped that a revolutionary new OS would turn the company around, but prospects for a breakthrough faded. At the end of 1995, Apple and IBM parted ways on Taligent and Kaleida. After spending more than $500 million, neither side wanted to switch to a new technology.[10] Then, in its first fiscal quarter of 1996, Apple reported a $69 million loss and announced further layoffs.[11] Two weeks later, Gilbert Amelio, an Apple director, replaced Spindler as CEO.

Amelio sought to push Apple into high-margin segments such as servers, Internet access devices, and PDAs. Soon after he arrived, he proclaimed that Apple would return to its premium-price differentiation strategy. In addition, while Amelio saw the pressing need for a new OS, he canceled development of the much-delayed next-generation Mac OS. In December 1996, Amelio announced that Apple would acquire NeXT Software and develop a new OS based on work done by NeXT. He also announced that the founder of NeXT, Steve Jobs, would return to Apple as a part-time adviser. Meanwhile, Amelio led the company through three reorganizations and several deep payroll cuts.[12] Despite these austerity moves, Apple lost $1.6 billion on his watch, and its worldwide market share dropped from 6% to 3%.[13] The Apple board forced Amelio out, and in September 1997 Steve Jobs became the company's interim CEO.

Steve Jobs and the Apple Turnaround

Steve Jobs moved quickly to shake things up. In August 1997, he announced that Microsoft had agreed to invest $150 million in Apple and had also reaffirmed its commitment to develop core products, such as Microsoft Office, for the Mac through August 2002. Jobs also brought the Macintosh licensing program to an abrupt end. Since the announcement of the first licensing agreement, clones had reached 20% of Macintosh unit sales, while the value of the Mac market had fallen 11%.[14] Convinced that clones were cannibalizing Apple's sales, Jobs refused to license the latest Mac OS. In addition, Jobs consolidated Apple's product range, reducing the number of its lines from 15 to 3.

Jobs's first real coup was the launch of the iMac, in August 1998. The iMac lacked a floppy-disk drive but incorporated a low-end CPU, a CD-ROM drive, and a modem, all housed in a distinctive translucent case that came in multiple colors. It also supported "plug-and-play" peripherals, such as printers, that were designed for Windows-based machines. (Previous Macs had required peripherals that were built for the Apple platform.) Roughly three years after its launch, the iMac had sold about 6 million units, compared with sales of 300 million PCs during the same time frame.

Under Jobs, Apple continued its restructuring efforts. It outsourced the manufacturing of Mac products to Taiwanese contract assemblers and revamped its distribution system, eliminating relationships with thousands of smaller outlets and expanding its presence in national chains. In November 1997, Apple launched a website to sell its products directly to consumers for the first time. Internally, Jobs worked to streamline operations and to reinvigorate innovation. Under his watch, Apple pared down its inventory significantly and increased its spending on R&D. (See **Exhibit 5**—PC Manufacturers: Key Operating Measures.)

Another priority for Jobs was to reenergize Apple's image. The company began promoting itself as a hip alternative to other computer brands. For Jobs, Apple was not just a technology company; it was a cultural force. Not coincidentally, perhaps, Jobs retained his position as CEO of Pixar, an animation studio that he had cofounded in 1986. In collaboration with Disney, Pixar produced such major films as *Toy Story* and *Monsters, Inc.*[15] (In 2006, Disney bought Pixar. Jobs, who had become Disney's largest shareholder, assumed a seat on the Disney board.[16])

The Macintosh Business in the 21st Century

In 2008, the sale of Macintosh computers remained a pivotal business for Apple, notwithstanding the company's name change. "We think PCs are more important than they were five years ago," Jobs said in 2007.[17] That year, Mac sales accounted for 43% of Apple's total revenue.[18]

Apple put a high premium on creating machines that offered a cutting-edge, tightly integrated user experience. Apple charged premium prices as well. Its top-of-the-line model, the Mac Pro, cost $2,799. While it had a sleek metal case and featured high-end graphics capability, it did not come with a monitor. For $599 to $1,799, users could buy an Apple Cinema Display to accompany the Mac Pro. At the low end of its product line, Apple offered the Mac mini; ranging in price from $599 to $799, the mini required users to purchase a keyboard, a mouse, and a monitor separately. Notebook models accounted for the lion's share of Mac sales. They included the MacBook ($1,099 to $1,499), the MacBook Pro ($1,999 to $2,799), and ultra-thin MacBook Air ($1,799 to $2,598).[19]

In marketing its Mac products, Apple highlighted features that differentiated them from other PCs while also emphasizing their interoperability with other machines. Attractive Apple design factors ("Design that turns heads"), ease of use ("It just works"), security ("114,000 Viruses? Not on a Mac"), and high-quality bundled software ("Awesome out of the box") were among the qualities that distinguished the Macintosh line. At the same time, Apple trumpeted the Mac as an "Everything-ready" device that worked well with other devices.[20] Over time, the Mac had become a less closed system, incorporating standard interfaces such as the USB port. Owners of a Mac mini could use a non-Mac keyboard, for example, and users of a non-Mac PC could attach it to an Apple display.[21]

Technology and Innovation

Under Jobs, the seeds of earlier efforts to engineer Macintosh products for the Intel platform at last came to fruition. In June 2005, Apple announced that it would abandon its longstanding use of PowerPC chips in favor of Intel microprocessors.[22] Apple began shipping two products built with Intel Core Duo chips in January 2006, and the entire Macintosh line ran on Intel chips by early 2007.[23]

Driving the leap to Intel was Jobs's frustration with the PowerPC chip line. The makers of that line, IBM and Freescale Semiconductor (a spin-off from Motorola), had failed to match Intel's performance, especially in low-power applications. High energy use drained batteries, created excess heat, and blocked advances in laptop performance. The latter point was crucial. Portable machines made up an increasingly large share of Apple's PC revenue—61% in 2007, up from 45% just two years earlier.[24] Intel's dual-core technology, which in effect allowed two chips to occupy one piece of silicon, enabled Apple to build laptops that were both faster and less power-hungry.[25] With "Intel inside," the Mac also became a machine that could easily run Windows and other third-party operating systems: By loading a software package such as VMware Fusion or Parallels Desktop, Macintosh users could operate both Windows- and Mac-based applications.[26] That capability offset a longstanding disadvantage to choosing a Mac—the relative lack of Macintosh software.

On the operating system front, Apple introduced a fully overhauled OS in 2001. Called Mac OS X and based on UNIX, the new operating system offered a more stable environment than previous Mac platforms.[27] Apple issued upgrades of OS X every 12 to 18 months, with the aim of generating not only extra revenue, but also new interest in the Mac and greater loyalty among existing Mac users. In October 2007, it launched its sixth major OS X release, called Leopard. Just two months later, Jobs called Leopard the "most successful" OS X release ever: With sales totaling 4 million copies, it had already reached 20% of the Macintosh installed base.[28]

Proprietary, Apple-developed applications made up a growing segment of the company's efforts to support the Macintosh line. Instead of relying on independent software vendors (ISVs), Apple built programs such as those in the iLife suite (iPhoto, iTunes, iWeb) on its own. In 1998, when Adobe Systems rejected Jobs's request to create a video-editing program for the Mac, Apple launched an internal project to create Final Cut Pro.[29] Such moves required Apple to assume significant development costs.[30] Meanwhile, the company continued to depend on the cooperation of key ISVs—especially Microsoft. In 2003, after Apple developed the Web browser Safari, Microsoft announced that it would no longer develop Internet Explorer for the Mac. Apple did receive assurances in 2005 that Microsoft would develop its Office suite for Macintosh for at least another five years.[31] Full interoperability with Office products was critical to Apple's market viability. Microsoft benefited from this arrangement as well. By one estimate, it raised up to $1 billion by selling Office to Mac users. (In January 2008, Microsoft released Office:Mac 2008.) All the same, Jobs hedged his bets by developing iWork productivity applications, including Pages, Keynote, and Numbers.[32]

Distribution and Sales

Apple opened its first retail store in McLean, Virginia, in May 2001.[33] As of June 2008, it operated 215 stores, and its retail division accounted for 19% of total revenues. Although most of the stores were in the United States, the chain also included outlets in Australia, Canada, China, Italy, Japan, and the United Kingdom.[34] Observers viewed Apple's retail strategy as a huge success: One analyst said that the company had become "the Nordstrom of technology."[35] By mid-2008, its stores had logged more than 350 million visits; during a single quarter in 2007, they drew 31 million visitors.[36] The Apple retail experience gave many of those visitors their first exposure to the Macintosh product line, and the company estimated that "new to Mac" consumers bought half of the 1.4 million Macs sold in Apple stores during the 2007 fiscal year.[37] (Apple boosted its presence in other retail venues as well. In late 2006, for example, it entered a partnership with Best Buy, and by the end of 2007 customers could shop for Mac products in 270 Best Buy outlets.[38]) A key factor in bringing people into the stores, most analysts believed, was the popularity of the iPod. More generally, observers speculated that an iPod "halo effect" had benefited Apple's Mac business.[39]

Macintosh sales were indeed robust. In the fiscal year 2007, Mac revenues came to $10.3 billion, for a year-over-year increase of 40%. Unit sales exceeded 7 million, up from 5.3 million in the previous year.[40] (See **Exhibit 6**—Apple Inc.: Unit Sales by Product Category.) Mac sales thus grew three times as fast as the overall PC market, which increased by about 14% in 2007.[41] By mid-2008, Apple had become the third-largest PC maker within the U.S. market, with a market share of 8.5%.[42] Yet Apple's share of the worldwide PC market had edged up only slightly in recent years; it remained in the 2% to 3% range, where it had languished for nearly a decade.[43]

The Evolving Personal Computer Industry

From its earliest days in the mid-1970s, the industry had experienced explosive growth. Although Apple pioneered the first usable "personal" computing devices, IBM was the company that brought PCs into the mainstream. IBM's brand name and product quality helped it to capture the lion's share of the market in the early 1980s, when its customers included almost 70% of the Fortune 1000. IBM's dominance of the PC industry started to erode in the late 1980s, as buyers increasingly viewed PCs as commodities. IBM tried to boost its margins by building a more proprietary PC, but instead it lost more than half of its market share. By the early 1990s, "Wintel" (the Windows OS combined with an Intel processor) had replaced "IBM-compatible" as the industry standard. Throughout the 1990s, thousands of manufacturers—ranging from Compaq and Dell to no-name clone makers—built PCs around building blocks from Microsoft and Intel.

In 2008, by one estimate, the number of PCs in use around the world would top 1 billion.[44] In 2007, worldwide PC shipments totaled 269 million units.[45] The U.S. market and the Asia/Pacific market (which excluded Japan) each accounted for about 26% of total shipments, Latin America for 9%, and Japan 5%. The largest regional market, EMEA (Europe, Middle East, and Africa), absorbed 34% of worldwide PC shipments.[46] Annual PC unit growth had averaged roughly 15% from the mid-1980s through 2000. After leveling off sharply early in the following decade, growth resumed at a 10% to 15% rate annual over the next several years. A rising share of that growth occurred in Asia and in other emerging markets. In the United States, where an estimated 60% of households already owned a PC, the PC market grew by only about 3% per year.[47]

Revenue growth, meanwhile, did not keep pace with volume growth—largely because of strong downward pricing pressure. By one estimate, the average selling price (ASP) for a PC declined from $1,699 in 1999 to $1,034 in 2005, or by a compound annual rate of 8% per year.[48] During that period, prices for key components (CPUs, memory, and hard disk drives) dropped even faster, by an average annual rate of 30%.[49] PC pricing then leveled off somewhat, partly because consumer demand shifted toward powerful machines that could run media and gaming applications, and partly because demand shifted from desktop units to more-expensive notebook models. In 2007, the ASP for notebook PCs was about $1,000, while the desktop ASP ran at roughly $700.[50] For PC vendors, the upshot of these pricing trends was persistently low profitability: The average profit margin on a PC in 2007 was less than 5%.[51]

PC Manufacturing

The PC was a relatively simple device. Using a screwdriver, a person with relatively little technological sophistication could assemble a PC from four widely available types of components: a microprocessor (the brains of the PC), a motherboard (the main circuit board), memory storage, and peripherals (the monitor, keyboard, mouse, and so on). Most manufacturers also bundled their PCs with an operating system. While the first PC was a desktop machine, by 2008 there was a wide range of forms, including laptops, notebooks, sub-notebooks, workstations (more powerful desktops), and servers (computers that acted as the backbone for PC networks).

In 2008, using off-the-shelf components, it cost roughly $400 to produce a mass-market desktop computer that would retail for $500. The largest cost element was the microprocessor, which ranged in price from $50 to more than $500 for the latest CPU. The other main components of a basic machine—motherboard, hard drive, memory, chassis, power, and packaging—together cost between $120 and $250. A keyboard, mouse, modem, CD-ROM and floppy drives, and speakers totaled $50 to $140; a basic monitor cost about $75; and Windows Vista and labor added about $70 and $30, respectively, to the final cost. A PC maker could push its retail price down to $300 by using a less powerful CPU, cutting back on hard drive capacity and memory, and offering lower-quality peripherals. Alternatively, by tailoring a machine for computer gaming enthusiasts, a manufacturer could build a PC whose sale price topped $3,000.[52]

As components became increasingly standardized, PC makers cut spending on research and development. In the early 1980s, the leading PC companies spent an average of 5% of sales on R&D. By the early 2000s, Dell Computer—then the industry leader—devoted less than 1% of its revenue to that purpose. Rather than invest heavily in R&D, companies such as Dell looked to innovations in manufacturing, distribution, and marketing to give them a competitive edge. Many firms, for example, turned to contract manufacturers to produce both components and entire PCs. At first, these contractors focused on handling simple manufacturing tasks at flexible, high-volume plants in low-cost locations. Over time, they moved into more complex areas, such as design and testing.

Buyers and Distribution

PC buyers fell into five categories: home, small- and medium-sized business (SMB), corporate, education, and government. In 2007, home buyers purchased about 42% of the world's computers, while SMB customers accounted for roughly 32% of the PC market, large corporations for 12%, education for 8%, and government for 6%.[53] (In recent years, the home share of the market had risen by a few percentage points; the business share had gone down slightly, partly because of slowing corporate PC upgrade cycles.[54]) The criteria that guided PC purchases varied by market segment. Business customers made decisions according to a combination of service and price. Education buyers focused on a combination of price and software availability. The consumers who made up the home market, traditionally very sensitive to cost, had begun in recent years to value stylish product design, as well as mobility and wireless networking capability.

In the 1980s, most PC buyers were business managers with relatively little technological sophistication. In general, they bought no more than a few PCs at a time, placed great emphasis on receiving service and support, and preferred to buy established brands through full-service dealers. In the early 1990s, however, as customers became more knowledgeable about PCs, alternative channels emerged. Corporate information technology managers and purchasing departments, often operating under tight budgets, began to buy large numbers of PCs directly from vendors or their distributors. Superstores (Wal-Mart, Costco) and electronics retailers (Best Buy, Circuit City) catered to the consumer and SMB markets. Web-based retailers, which sold PC merchandise at steep discounts, also saw a sharp increase in demand. By the early 2000s, the so-called "white box" channel—which featured generic machines assembled by local entrepreneurs—had become the largest channel for PC sales. Although branded PC makers had recaptured a portion of overall market share in recent years, white-box PCs still made up 37% of worldwide shipments as of 2006, and their share of key emerging markets remained particularly large.[55]

PC Manufacturers

In 2007, the four top PC vendors—Hewlett-Packard, Dell, Acer, and Lenovo—accounted for more than 50% of worldwide PC shipments. Below this top tier were various PC brands, but none of them could claim more than a 5% share.[56] (See **Exhibit 7**—PC Manufacturers: Worldwide Market Shares.) Even as these companies continued to consolidate the PC market, their fortunes were very much in flux. (See **Exhibit 8**—Apple Competitors: Selected Financial Information.)

Hewlett-Packard (HP), following a rough period in the wake of its acquisition of Compaq Computer in 2002, had staged an impressive comeback. In 2006, HP overtook IBM to become the world's largest technology company (with sprawling operations in imaging and printing, software and services, and data storage); it also surpassed Dell as the world's leading PC maker. Under CEO Mark Hurd, HP rebuilt its PC business around the company's strong presence in retail channels (where sales via 110,000 outlets worldwide made up 40% to 45% of its PC revenue) and around a "decommoditization" strategy. That strategy (exemplified by the slogan "The Computer Is Personal Again") emphasized product design, stepped-up R&D spending, and aggressive consumer marketing.[57] Dell, meanwhile, had stumbled. In the early 2000s, it had been the leading PC vendor, in terms of both market share and profitability. Its distinctive business model, which combined direct sales and build-to-order manufacturing, made for significant cost savings and enabled its products to become the favorite of corporate IT managers. In 2007, more than 80% of its revenues came from the corporate market. Yet Dell did not adapt quickly to the changing needs of the PC marketplace. In January 2007, three years after handing control of the company to a successor, founder Michael Dell returned as CEO and initiated a far-reaching transformation plan. Under his new strategy, the company doubled its investment in design and began releasing consumer-friendly products, including a notebook PC that came in eight colors. More important, it moved into retail distribution for the first time since 1994. By January 2008, Dell had made deals to sell its PCs through Wal-Mart, Best Buy, and Staples, as well as through major chains in Europe, China, and Japan. Boosting international sales was another high priority for Dell, which had long focused on the U.S. market.[58]

Two Asian companies, Acer and Lenovo, focused much of their activity on emerging markets. But they also benefited from acquisitions of high-profile U.S. PC brands. With its purchase in August 2007 of Gateway, the number-three U.S. PC brand, Taiwan-based Acer became the third-largest PC vendor in the world. As part of that deal, Acer also acquired Packard-Bell, a PC maker with a strong presence in Europe (where Acer also was a leading brand). Given the strength of all three brands in retail channels, Acer was poised to target the growing consumer market. Similarly, its emphasis on producing notebook PCs (worldwide, it sold almost as many notebooks as Dell) aligned the company with current trends.[59] China-based Lenovo vaulted into the front ranks of PC vendors in 2005, when it acquired IBM's PC business for $1.75 billion. Although Lenovo would retain the right to use the IBM logo on ThinkPad notebooks and ThinkCentre desktop PCs until 2010, it was phasing out its reliance on the IBM brand, whose reach did not extend far beyond the slow-growing corporate market. Lenovo's greatest asset was its position in China, where it commanded a 35% market share. Under its CEO (a former Dell executive named William Amelio), Lenovo pursued a broad global strategy, operating headquarters both in Beijing and in Raleigh, North Carolina.[60]

Suppliers, Complements, and Substitutes

Suppliers to the PC industry fell into two categories: those that made products (such as memory chips, disk drives, and keyboards) with many sources; and those that made products—notably microprocessors and operating systems—that had just a few sources. Products in the first category were widely available at highly competitive prices. Products in the second category were supplied chiefly by two firms: Intel and Microsoft.

Microprocessors   Microprocessors, or CPUs, were the hardware "brains" of a PC. In 2006, microprocessor sales totaled $33.2 billion.[61] For many years, Intel was the dominant producer of PC-compatible CPUs. But that market became more competitive in the 1990s, when companies like AMD (Advanced Micro Devices) and Transmeta challenged Intel with directly competitive products. Still, Intel remained the market leader by virtue of its powerful brand and its large manufacturing scale. In 2007, despite inroads by AMD into Intel's share of the microprocessor market, Intel continued to supply more than 80% of all PC CPUs.[62] Since 1970, CPU prices (adjusted for changes in computing power) had dropped by an average of 30% per year.[63]

Operating systems   An OS was a large piece of software that managed a PC's resources and supported its applications. After the launch of the IBM PC, Microsoft dominated the PC OS market, in part because it offered an open standard that multiple PC makers could incorporate into their products. During the 1980s, Microsoft sold a relatively crude OS called MS-DOS. In 1990, Microsoft started to challenge Apple's technical supremacy by introducing Windows 3.0, an OS that featured a Macintosh-like graphical interface. Although Windows was generally inferior to the Mac OS, users—and corporate IT managers, in particular—eagerly adopted it. During the 1990s, Microsoft issued a new, highly profitable release of Windows every few years. Windows XP, released in October 2001, sold 17 million copies in its first eight weeks on the market. Developed at a cost of $1 billion, XP initially garnered Microsoft between $45 and $60 in revenue per copy, according to analysts' estimates.[64] The latest edition of Windows, Vista, fared less well in its early going. Released in January 2007 after numerous delays, Vista received low marks for its sluggish performance, and users were reluctant to upgrade to it from XP. In response to user complaints, Dell even revised its Vista-only offer on new PCs and began offering PCs with XP preloaded on them.[65] Meanwhile,

9

Microsoft reportedly aimed to issue its next upgrade, Windows 7, in 2010.[66] In 2007, 85% to 90% of all PCs in the world ran on some version of Windows.[67]

Application software   The value of an OS corresponded directly to the quantity and quality of application software that was available on that platform. The Apple II, for example, was a hit among business users because it supported VisiCalc, the first electronic spreadsheet. Other important application segments included word processing, presentation graphics, desktop publishing, database management, personal finance, and Internet browsing. Throughout the 1990s and into the next decade, the number of applications available on PCs exploded, while average selling prices (ASPs) for PC software collapsed. Microsoft was the largest vendor of software for Wintel PCs and, aside from Apple itself, for Macs as well.[68] However, ISVs wrote the majority of PC applications.

Alternative technologies   By 2008, PCs were far easier to use than they had been two decades earlier. They had also begun to enter the price range of consumer electronics (CE) products. As a result, the "digital convergence" of PC and CE products had become a significant factor in the PC marketplace. Various alternative devices—ranging from handheld PDAs to smartphones, from TV set-top boxes to game consoles—had begun to supplement or even to replace PCs. Advanced game devices like Sony PlayStation3, for example, allowed consumers to not only run traditional video games, but also to play DVDs and CDs, surf the Web, and play games directly online.

Beyond Macintosh

A fast-increasing portion of Apple's core operations involved non-Macintosh business areas that were less than a decade old (iPod, iTunes) or, indeed, less than a year old (Apple TV, iPhone). These product lines set Apple on a path toward becoming a full-fledged digital convergence company.

The iPod Phenomenon

Apple launched the iPod, a portable digital music player based on the MP3 compression standard, in November 2001.[69] Thanks to its sleek design, it soon became "an icon of the Digital Age," in the words of one writer.[70] In 2008, Apple offered a full line of iPod devices, ranging in price from $49 to $499. At the low end was the 1GB iPod shuffle, which randomly played up to 240 songs. Apple also offered the iPod nano, which stored up to 2,000 songs or up to 8 hours of video content; the iPod classic, whose 160GB version could hold 40,000 songs or 200 hours of video; and the iPod touch, which stored up to 7,000 songs and offered many new features, including WiFi connectivity.[71] ASPs for products in the iPod line ran $50 to $100 higher than that of other MP3 players.[72]

The economics of the iPod were stellar by CE industry standards, with gross margins that ranged from 30% to 35%.[73] In 2007, analysts estimated that Apple paid a bill of materials (BOM) of $127 for an 80GB iPod classic, which retailed for $249. The largest expense in the BOM was for the hard drive, which cost $78.[74] In the case of the iPod nano, which used flash memory instead of a hard drive, margins were higher: An 8GB nano (which retailed for $199) had a BOM of $83, with flash components accounting for $48 of that sum. As the cost of flash memory dropped, Apple built an increasing share of its iPod line around flash drives.[75] Maintaining relationships with key suppliers—ranging from Samsung, which manufactured the iPod's video-audio chip, to Toshiba, which made many of its hard disk drives—was crucial to Apple's strategy for the device. Forging deals with flash manufacturers was especially important. In November 2005, the company agreed to pay $500 million up-front to Intel and Micron to secure "a substantial portion" of the output from a new flash-memory joint venture. It made similar deals with Hynix, Samsung, and Toshiba.[76] In mid-2007, Apple was on track to command roughly 25% of all flash production for use either in iPod products or in the iPhone, which also relied on flash memory.[77]

As of mid-2008, Apple had sold more than 150 million iPods. According to most estimates, the device commanded 70% or more of the U.S. market for portable music players.[78] Rivals in the MP3 player market included Creative, Samsung, and Sony. The most prominent challenge to the iPod came from Microsoft, which introduced its Zune line of music players in late 2006. At the hardware level, Zune players roughly matched comparable iPod models and included features—wireless music-sharing capability, an FM tuner—that the iPod lacked. According to some reviewers, though, Zune software and the Zune Marketplace content store were inferior to iTunes offerings.[79] Most iPod competitors had converged on the use of Microsoft's WMA standard.[80] (See **Exhibit 9**—iPod Competitors: Comparison of Models and Prices for MP3 Players.)

Initially, the iPod could sync only with Macs. But in August 2002 Apple introduced an iPod for Windows.[81] In other ways, too, the company's approach to developing and marketing the iPod was less closed than its longtime approach to deploying the Macintosh. In this regard, the iPod accessory market was particularly important. By 2007, that market—consisting of 1,000-plus advertised items—generated more than $1 billion in sales. For every $3 dollars spent on an iPod, according to one analyst, consumers spent another $1 on iPod add-on products. And Apple, through a program that licensed its "Made for iPod" logo, earned an estimated 5% of the retail price of such items.[82]

The iTunes System

One key element of the iPod system was the iTunes Music Store, an online service that Apple launched in April 2003. For 99 cents per song, visitors could download music offered by all five major record labels and by thousands of independent music labels. Users could play a downloaded song on their computer, burn it onto their own CD, or transfer it to an iPod. Initially available only to Mac users, the iTunes store became Windows-compatible in October 2003. Within three days of the launch of that service, PC owners had downloaded 1 million copies of free iTunes software and had paid for 1 million songs.[83] By mid-2007, users had downloaded more than 500 million copies of the Windows version of iTunes.[84] The first legal site that allowed music downloads on a pay-per-song basis, iTunes became the dominant online store of its kind. By June 2008, it had sold more than 5 billion songs, and it claimed a 70% share of the worldwide digital music market. It was also the largest U.S. music retailer of any kind, having surpassed Wal-Mart and Best Buy in music sales earlier that year.[85]

The introduction of iTunes had a galvanic impact on iPod sales. Before the advent of iTunes, Apple sold an average of 113,000 iPods per quarter; by the quarter that ended December 2003, iPod sales had shot up to 733,000 units—and then continued to rise.[86] (See **Exhibit 10**—iPod and iTunes: Quarterly Unit Sales.) In 2007, combined iPod and iTunes sales accounted for 45% of total revenue at Apple.[87] The direct impact of iTunes on Apple's profitability was far less impressive. Of the 99 cents that Apple collected per song, as much as 70 cents went to the music label that owned it, and about 20 cents went toward the cost of credit card processing. That left Apple with only about a dime of revenue per track, from which Apple had to pay for its website, along with other direct and indirect costs.[88] In essence, Jobs had created a razor-and-blade business, only in reverse: Here, the variable element served as a loss leader for a profit-driving durable good.[89]

Central to the iTunes model was a set of standards that guarded both the music labels' intellectual property and the proprietary technology inside the iPod. An Apple-exclusive "digital rights management" (DRM) system called FairPlay protected iTunes songs against piracy by limiting to five the number of computers that could play a downloaded song. FairPlay enabled Jobs to coax music executives into supporting the initial iTunes venture. It also helped fuel iPod sales, since no competing MP3 player could play FairPlay-protected songs.[90] Observers called iTunes a "Trojan horse" that allowed iPod-specific standards to invade users' music libraries and, in effect, to lock out other music players.[91] The iPod, meanwhile, could play content recorded in most standard formats.

Despite the success of iTunes, Apple had a tense relationship with music companies, which balked at its dominance of the digital music market and objected in particular to its fixed pricing structure. In July 2007, after Apple refused to renegotiate its flat 99-cent-per-song price, Universal Music Group declined to renew its annual contract with iTunes and instead opted to license content to Apple on an at-will basis. Other big labels, yielding to the power of the iTunes market share, renewed their iTunes contracts largely on Apple's terms.[92] At the same time, they pursued other outlets for selling digital music. Napster, Rhapsody, Wal-Mart.com, and Zune Marketplace, among other online music stores, each had distribution deals with all four remaining major labels (EMI, Sony BMG, Universal, and Warner Brothers). These stores sold individual song downloads at 99 cents or less per track, and a few of them also offered subscription plans that allowed unlimited listening for $5.99 to $14.99 per month. Most of these services used Microsoft's WMA format. Meanwhile, mobile telephony companies such as AT&T and Verizon also sold digital music, mainly through subscription services.[93] In April 2008, the social network site MySpace announced plans to open an online music store in partnership with major music labels.[94]

A new competitive threat to iTunes emerged in September 2007, when Amazon.com began distributing DRM-free copies of music from the four big labels. To secure rights to that music, Amazon agreed to use variable pricing, with song prices ranging from 89 cents to more than $1 apiece.[95] By mid-2008, most major online music retailers—including Napster, Rhapsody, and Wal-Mart—offered DRM-free songs, variable pricing, or both.[96] Apple, for its part, had signed a deal with EMI in May 2007 that allowed it to sell DRM-free songs under its new "iTunes Plus" offering. Other labels, however, had so far refused to license their content to Apple for DRM-free distribution.[97]

The Apple TV "Hobby"

Starting in 2005, Apple moved to adapt its digital music model to digital video. That year, it created a video iPod device that could play movies, TV shows, and music videos.[98] By 2008, all iPods other than the shuffle model could play video files, and users could download TV shows (for $1.99 or more per episode) and movies (for $9.99 or more apiece) from iTunes.[99] In addition, Apple launched a video rental offering in early 2008. Fees ($2.99 to $3.99 for a 24-hour rental) were comparable to those of other rental services, and the movie selection included titles from all six major film studios.[100] By mid-2008, iTunes users were buying or renting more than 50,000 movies per day, and iTunes had become "the world's most popular online movie store."[101] Nonetheless, as Jobs conceded, Apple's digitial video business fell short of the standard set by its music offerings.[102] Lack of cooperation from content providers was largely to blame: In August 2007, for example, NBC Universal announced that it would stop licensing its TV shows for sale on iTunes.[103]

In a related effort, Apple took steps to bring digital video content directly into consumers' living rooms. In March 2007, the company released the Apple TV, a device that enabled users to stream movies and TV shows to a television set—after downloading that content from iTunes via PC. High pricing and limited functionality kept early sales of the device low. In July 2007, Jobs referred to the Apple TV as "a hobby," suggesting that it was of lower priority than Apple's three main businesses (Macintosh, iPod-iTunes, iPhone).[104] But in January 2008 he released "Apple TV, take two," which featured increased memory, lower pricing, and improved functionality. Apple TV users could now acquire content for their TV directly from iTunes, while bypassing their PC entirely.[105]

The iPhone Gamble—Version 1.0

Apple and its distribution partner, the mobile operator AT&T Mobility (formerly called Cingular Wireless), began selling the iPhone in late June 2007. The iPhone was Apple's bid to unite the iPod with a mobile phone service. But the company's real goal for the product, Jobs said, was to "reinvent the phone."[106] The iPhone was a multifunction communication device—"the Internet in your pocket," in Jobs's words—that shared many qualities with smartphones.[107] It featured e-mail capability, Web access, and text messaging; a calendar, an address book, and other PDA functions; and a 2-megapixel camera.[108] The entire system ran on a specially adapted version of Apple's OS X platform.[109]

Buyers of the iPhone, during its first year of availability, paid $399 for an 8-GB model and $499 for a 16-GB model. In a departure from standard industry practice, AT&T did not cushion those prices with a subsidy.[110] The iPhone therefore stood out in a worldwide market where handsets that cost $300 or more accounted for only 5% of total sales.[111] (In the U.S. market, where operator subsidies were particularly generous, an estimated 80% of handset transactions were for less than $100 apiece.[112]) Service plans for the iPhone, available exclusively from AT&T, required a two-year contract and started at $59.99 per month. While that fee was $20 per month more than AT&T's standard wireless package, it covered both voice and data service.[113]

AT&T, the largest U.S. mobile operator, made concessions to Apple that no handset maker had previously received in a carrier distribution agreement.[114] (Verizon Wireless, the second-largest operator, reportedly turned down a similar deal with Apple.[115]) In exchange for a five-year exclusivity period in the U.S. market, AT&T gave Apple near-complete control over the development, and branding of the iPhone.[116] Apple also barred AT&T from distributing the iPhone through third parties, such as Best Buy and Radio Shack. Most important, instead of subsiding iPhone sales, AT&T agreed to share service revenue with Apple. According to reports, Apple received 10% of all subscription fees paid by iPhone users, or an average of about $10 per month per subscriber.[117]

Before July 2008, data service for the iPhone relied on AT&T's relatively slow Edge network (also known as a 2G or 2.5G service). A 3G (third-generation) network was the fastest available wireless solution; Jobs initially opted against equipping the iPhone for such a network because 3G usage severely taxed the device's battery charge.[118] Meanwhile, iPhone users could also tap into WiFi hot-spots, which generally offered much faster service than the Edge network.[119]

When Jobs first announced the iPhone, in January 2007, he said that Apple aimed to sell 10 million units of the device by the end of 2008.[120] By June 2008, consumers had bought about 6 million iPhones. As impressive as that figure was, it left Apple with a likely share of the worldwide mobile handset market of less than 1%. (Consumers in 2007 bought an estimated 1.1 billion handsets.[121]) The iPhone's position within the smartphone market was somewhat better. Jobs, for example, cited data showing that the iPhone gained a 19.5% share of the U.S. smartphone market during its first quarter of availability.[122] (Worldwide, users bought about 120 million smartphones in 2007.[123])

Unit sales told only part of the iPhone story, however. As many as 1 million of the 3.7 million iPhones sold by the end of 2007 fell into the worldwide "gray market," in which consumers bought unlocked iPhones from unauthorized resellers and used them on unsanctioned mobile networks. Most of those units ended up in China, Russia, and other markets with no legal iPhone distribution. (As of June 2008, Apple had signed agreements to distribute the iPhone only in the United States and in five European countries. Deals were slow in coming, partly because Apple demanded a share of service revenue that ran as high as 40%.) Even so, by an estimate made in early 2008, the resulting loss of service-share revenue was on track to cost Apple $1 billion over a three-year period.[124]

The iPhone Gamble—Version 2.0

In July 2008, just a year after launching the iPhone, Apple reinvented it.[125] The new offering, called the iPhone 3G, came not only with faster network service, but also with an entirely new pricing model and with a new platform for adding third-party applications to the device.

As the product name implied, a key difference between the iPhone 3G and its predecessor was that it supported 3G network coverage. The device's battery life had improved enough to allay Jobs's concerns. In tests, the 3G service enabled downloading of data that was two or three times as fast as the Edge service. All the same, users complained about the limitations of AT&T's 3G coverage area.[126] In August 2008, users also began reporting frequent connection failures while using the 3G network; one report suggested that the iPhone's 3G chipset, rather than AT&T service, was to blame.[127]

The iPhone 3G was also cheaper than the first iPhone—at least with respect to the initial purchase price for the device. U.S. consumers could buy an 8-GB iPhone 3G for $199 or a 16-GB model for $299. Those prices reflected a subsidy from AT&T. To take advantage of it, users had to join one of AT&T's service plans, which now started at $69.99 per month ($10 higher than before). AT&T still required users to enter a two-year contract.[128] Meanwhile, the carrier also signaled that at some point it would offer an unsubsidized iPhone for $599 (8-GB) to $699 (16-GB).[129]

A restructured agreement between Apple and AT&T—one that was closer to the U.S. mobile industry norm for such deals—underlay the reduction in consumer pricing for the iPhone. Apple gave up its claim to a share of iPhone subscription revenue, and in exchange it received from AT&T a fixed premium for each iPhone sold.[130] According to one report, AT&T paid Apple an average of $466 for every iPhone bought by a consumer (an average that covered sales of both 8-GB model and 16-GB models). That figure, the same report suggested, included a $100 bounty that AT&T paid to Apple each time an iPhone buyer signed up for AT&T service through an Apple retail outlet.[131] AT&T, as part of its revised agreement with Apple, was also able to extend its period of exclusivity for selling the iPhone by one year.[132] In another notable step away from the initial iPhone deal, Apple opened up a new retail channel for the device: Best Buy announced in August 2008 that Apple had agreed to let it begin selling iPhones in its nearly 1,000 stores.[133]

The chief benefits of the iPhone 3G essentially matched those of the first iPhone, and they reflected Apple's prowess in designing user interface (UI) technology. Unlike most mobile phones, the iPhone had no embedded keyboard. Instead, it featured a 3.5-inch "multi-touch" widescreen display that took up most of its surface area. Critics raved about this UI, which allowed users to manipulate content on the screen by tapping, pinching, and dragging their finger on it. The device also featured "accelerometer" technology, which enabled it to sense when users were moving and to adjust its screen orientation accordingly. Its screen quality, meanwhile, marked a big step forward for iPod video functionality.[134] Partnerships with Google and YouTube allowed Apple to provide customized search, mapping, and video features. In addition, users could buy music for the iPhone directly from the device, via the iTunes Wi-Fi Music Store.[135]

In conjunction with launching the iPhone 3G, Apple introduced a new benefit for iPhone users: a platform for third-party applications. An updated software package, called iPhone 2.0, enabled users to install programs distributed through Apple's new online App Store. Users could visit the store and download applications directly from their iPhone. Offerings ranged from popular games (Scrabble, Sodoku) to business programs developed by Oracle and salesforce.com. The first iPhone did not support such applications. But now even users of the older model, as well as iPod touch owners, could download iPhone 2.0 software (for a $10 fee) and equip their device for the new platform. As of July 2008, the App Store distributed more than 800 different programs—90% of them priced at less than $10.[136] By mid-August 2008, customers had downloaded more than 60 million applications, and sales came to an average of $1 million per day. Jobs speculated that the App Store might become "a $1 billion marketplace at some point in time." Apple, which had to approve each application before it went on sale, kept 30% of the retail price for every product and let developers keep the rest.[137]

Drawbacks to the iPhone included its low storage capacity, in comparison with other music players, and its lack of memory expandability; its relatively low-resolution camera, which lacked

14

video capability; and a level of GPS functionality (introduced in the iPhone 3G) that fell short of what other smartphones offered. Its battery lasted as little as five hours during routine 3G use (or ten hours during 2G use); more important, the battery was non-replaceable and had a predicted life of roughly one year. To attract enterprise customers, the second iteration of the iPhone added features that the first iPhone lacked, such as advanced email security and support for the Microsoft Exchange email platform. Yet the iPhone 3G, while it could display Microsoft Office documents, lacked the ability to run or synchronize with them. For high-volume email users, its lack of a physical QWERTY keyboard and its failure to provide a cut-and-paste tool were also serious limitations.[138]

Apple launched the iPhone 3G simultaneously in 22 markets (including Australia, Japan, Mexico, and many European countries), and the device would be available in roughly 70 markets worldwide (including India, as well as numerous Latin American countries) by the end of 2008.[139] On the whole, pricing structures and distribution agreements in those markets matched those in the U.S. market, with carriers subsidizing iPhone sales. By moving away from the revenue-sharing model, Apple was able to sign deals with carriers rapidly. The company also moved away from offering iPhone exclusivity to carriers. As yet, Apple had no deal to sell the device in China, the world's largest mobile phone market. Negotiations with China Mobile, that country's dominant carrier, broke down in early 2008 over Apple's demand for a share of service revenue, but they resumed later that year.[140]

The economics of the iPhone 3G tilted strongly in Apple's favor. Falling component costs and design improvements, for example, reduced the iPhone's cost structure. According to one analysis, the cost of materials for an 8-GB model was about $174, while materials for the first iteration of that model had cost $227.[141] Meanwhile, lower consumer pricing and wider international distribution helped fuel promising early sales for the iPhone 3G. Over the first weekend of its availability, worldwide shipments of the device totaled 1 million units. At that pace, Apple was on track to exceed its initial goal of selling 10 million units before 2009.[142]

In 2008, would-be "iPhone killer" products were rapidly appearing on the market. Mobile operators, in collaboration with handset makers, rushed to offer touchscreen devices: Sprint-Nextel distributed the Samsung Instinct, for example, while Verizon Wireless sold the LG Dare; both products hit the U.S. market in July 2008.[143] Blackberry (which had a market-leading 45% share of the U.S. smartphone market) released a 3G device called the Bold in May and would release an advanced touchscreen phone called the Thunder by the end of the year.[144] Other iPhone competitors included the Palm Centro; the Nokia N95; and the Diamond Touch, a 3G touchscreen handset that HTC Corp. introduced in May 2008.[145] Most of these devices ran on closed platforms such as Windows Mobile OS or Nokia's Symbian OS. Meanwhile, Google had created an open mobile OS called Android; mobile operators and handset makers could use it at no cost and without restriction.[146] In August 2008, T-Mobile announced that it would distribute an HTC-made Android phone in the U.S. market sometime before the end of the year. Called "the Dream," that device would feature a touchscreen UI, would support 3G service, and would retail for $150 (with a two-year contract).[147]

"New Rules"?

Apple underwent profound changes during the first decade of the 21st century—from its migration to a new microchip architecture to its expansion into whole new business lines. Steve Jobs, noted one analyst at mid-decade, "has created a fusion of fashion, brand, industrial design and computing. . . . [I]f he is to successfully revamp Apple, [Jobs] will ultimately win not by taking on PC rivals directly, but by changing the rules of the game."[148] Could Apple truly "change the rules" of the game in computing and in next-generation devices? And could it retain its innovative edge even after Jobs—the man who had "changed the rules" for the company, again and again—was no longer at its helm? Those questions animated discussion of Apple Inc. and its future.

Exhibit 1a   Apple Inc.: Selected Financial Information, 1981–2008 (in millions of dollars, except for number of employee and stock-related data)

	1981	1986	1991	1996	1998	2000	2002	2004	2005	2006	2007	1Q08–3Q08
Net sales	334	1,902	6,309	9,833	5,941	7,983	5,742	8,279	13,931	19,315	24,006	24,584
Cost of sales	170	891	3,314	8,865	4,462	5,733	4,021	5,871	9,738	13,525	15,568	15,859
Research and development	21	128	583	604	310	380	447	489	534	712	782	811
Selling, general, and administrative	77	610	1,740	1,568	908	1,546	1,557	1,910	2,393	3,145	3,745	3,573
Operating income (loss)	66	274	447	(1,383)	261	620	46	349	1,650	2,453	4,409	4,833
Net income (loss)	39	154	310	(816)	309	786	65	276	1,335	1,989	3,498	3,698
Cash, cash equivalents, and short-term investments	73	576	893	1,745	2,300	4,027	4,337	5,464	8,261	10,110	15,386	20,774
Accounts receivable, net	42	263	907	1,496	1,035	955	707	1,050	1,312	2,845	4,029	3,245
Inventories	104	109	672	662	78	33	45	101	165	270	346	545
Net property, plant, and equipment	31	222	448	598	348	313	621	707	817	1,281	1,832	2,177
Total assets	255	1,160	3,494	5,364	4,289	6,803	6,298	8,050	11,551	17,205	25,347	31,709
Total current liabilities	70	138	1,217	2,003	1,520	1,933	1,658	2,680	3,484	6,443	9,299	9,218
Total shareholders' equity	177	694	1,767	2,058	1,642	4,107	4,095	5,076	7,466	9,984	14,532	19,622
Cash dividends paid	—	—	57	14	—	—	—	—	—	—	—	—
Employees	2,456	5,600	14,432	13,398	9,663	11,728	12,241	13,426	16,820	20,186	23,700	NA
International sales/sales	27%	26%	45%	52%	45%	46%	43%	41%	41%	41%	41%	NA
Gross margin	49%	53%	47%	10%	25%	28%	30%	29%	30%	35%	35%	35%
R&D/sales	6%	7%	9%	6%	5%	5%	8%	6%	4%	4%	3%	3%
SG&A/sales	23%	32%	28%	16%	15%	19%	27%	23%	17%	16%	16%	15%
Return on sales	12%	8%	5%	NA	5%	10%	1%	3%	10%	10%	15%	15%
Return on assets	24%	15%	10%	NA	7%	12%	1%	3%	12%	14%	14%	12%
Return on equity	38%	25%	19%	NA	22%	19%	2%	5%	18%	24%	24%	19%
Stock price low	$1.78	$2.75	$10.28	$4.22	$3.28	$7.00	$6.80	$10.64	$31.65	$50.57	$83.27	110.15
Stock price high	$4.31	$5.47	$18.19	$8.75	$10.75	$36.05	$13.06	$34.22	$74.98	$91.81	$199.83	198.08
P/E ratio at year-end	27.7	16.8	21.9	NA	17.5	6.1	79.6	90.7	46.1	37.4	50.4	31.5
Market value at year-end	1,223.7	2,578.3	6,649.9	2,598.5	5,539.7	4,996.2	5,146.4	25,892.5	60,586.6	72,900.8	173,426.9	147,618.9

Sources: Standard & Poor's Compustat® data; Datastream.

Notes: Apple's fiscal year ends in September. All data here reflect fiscal-year results, except for share price data, which reflect calendar-year results. All data for the 1Q08–3Q08 period pertain to the nine months ending June 30, 2008.

NA = Not Available or Not Applicable.

Exhibit 1b Apple Inc.: Net Sales Data by Product Category, 2002–2008 (in millions of dollars)

	2002	2003	2004	2005	2006	2007	1Q08–3Q08
Power Macintosh[a]	1,380	1,237	1,419	NA	NA	NA	NA
iMac[b]	1,448	1,238	954	NA	NA	NA	NA
Desktops[c]	NA	NA	NA	3,436	3,319	4,020	4,240
PowerBook	831	1,299	1,589	NA	NA	NA	NA
iBook	875	717	961	NA	NA	NA	NA
Portables[d]	NA	NA	NA	2,839	4,056	6,294	6,416
Total Macintosh Net Sales	4,534	4,491	4,923	6,275	7,375	10,314	10,656
iPod	143	345	1,306	4,540	7,676	8,305	7,493
Other music products[e]	4	36	278	899	1,885	2,496	2,508
iPhone and related products	NA	NA	NA	NA	NA	123	1,038
Peripherals and other hardware[f]	527	691	951	1,126	1,100	1,260	1,231
Software[g]	307	362	502	NA	NA	NA	NA
Service and other net sales	227	282	319	NA	NA	NA	NA
Software, service, and other sales[h]	NA	NA	NA	1,091	1,279	1,508	1,658
Total Net Sales	5,742	6,207	8,279	13,931	19,315	24,006	24,584

Source: Apple financial statements; casewriter calculations.

Note: Apple's fiscal year ends in September. All data here reflect fiscal-year results.

NA = Not Available or Not Applicable.

[a]Includes Xserve product line.

[b]Includes eMac product line.

[c]Includes iMac, eMac, Mac Mini, Mac Pro, Power Mac, and Xserve product lines.

[d]Includes MacBook, iBook, MacBook Pro, and PowerBook product lines.

[e]Includes sales from iTunes Music Store, iPod-related services, and iPod-related accessories.

[f]Includes sales of Apple-branded and third-party displays, wireless connectivity and networking solutions, and other hardware accessories.

[g]Includes sales of Apple-branded operating system, application software, and third-party software.

[h]Includes sales of Apple-branded operating system, application software, third-party software, AppleCare Services, and Internet services.

Exhibit 1c   Apple Inc.: Operational Data by Segment, 2002–2008 (in millions of dollars)

	2002	2003	2004	2005	2006	2007	*1Q08–3Q08*
Americas							
Net sales	3,131	3,181	4,019	6,658	9,415	11,596	*11,001*
Operating income	278	323	465	970	1,899	2,949	NA
Depreciation, amortization, and accretion	4	5	6	6	6	9	NA
Segment assets	395	494	563	705	896	1497	NA
Europe							
Net sales	1,251	1,309	1,799	3,073	4,096	5,460	*5,899*
Operating income	122	130	280	465	627	1,348	NA
Depreciation, amortization, and accretion	4	4	4	4	4	6	NA
Segment assets	165	252	259	289	471	595	NA
Japan							
Net sales	710	698	677	924	1,211	1,082	*1,189*
Operating income	140	121	115	147	208	232	NA
Depreciation, amortization, and accretion	2	3	2	3	3	3	NA
Segment assets	50	130	114	165	181	159	NA
Retail							
Net sales	283	621	1,185	2,278	3,246	4,115	*4,597*
Operating income (loss)	(22)	(5)	39	396	600	875	NA
Depreciation, amortization, and accretion	16	25	35	43	59	88	NA
Segment assets	141	243	351	589	651	1,085	NA
Other[a]							
Net sales	367	398	599	998	1,347	1,753	*1,898*
Operating income	44	51	90	118	235	388	NA
Depreciation, amortization, and accretion	2	2	2	2	3	3	NA
Segment assets	67	78	124	133	180	252	NA

Source: Apple financial statements; casewriter calculations.

Note: Apple's fiscal year ends in September. All data here reflect fiscal-year results.

NA = Not Available or Not Applicable.

[a]"Other" segments include the Asia-Pacific region and Apple's FileMaker business.

Exhibit 2   Apple Inc.: Daily Closing Share Price, December 1980–August 2008

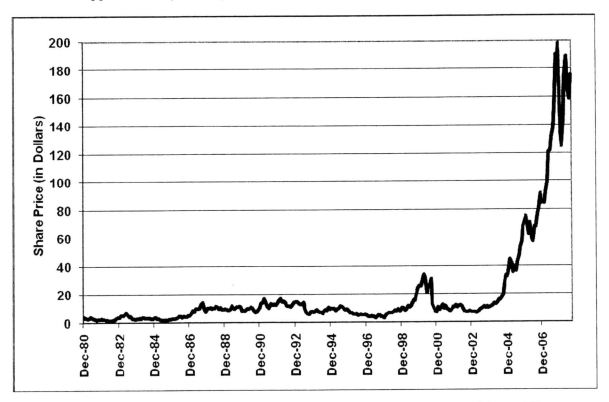

Source: Thomson Datastream, accessed January 2008; OneSource Global Business Browser, accessed August 2008.

Exhibit 3   Apple Inc.: Worldwide PC Share, 1980–2007

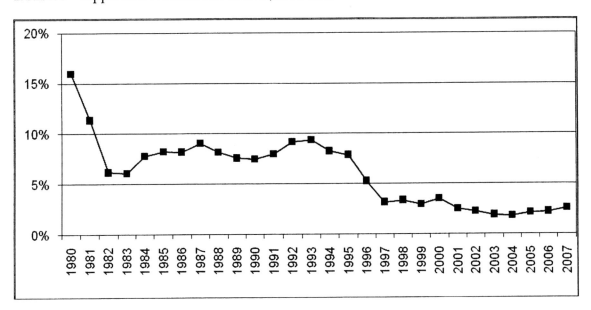

Source: Adapted from InfoCorp., International Data Corp., Gartner Dataquest, and Merrill Lynch data.

Exhibit 4   Shipments and Installed Base of PC Microprocessors, 1992–2007 (in millions of units)

Total Shipments	1992	1994	1996	1998	2000	2002	2003	2004	2005	2006	2007
Intel Technologies											
PC units shipped	30.6	47.8	76.0	105.0	156	126	152	170	200	230	261
PC installed base	122.2	211.4	347.5	542.5	839	1,111	1,263	1,433	1,633	1,863	2,124
Mac units shipped	NA	NA	NA	NA	NA	NA	NA	NA	NA	5.7	7.6
Motorola (680X0)											
Units shipped	3.9	3.9	0.8	0.2	NA	NA	NA	NA	NA	NA	NA
Installed base	16.5	24.9	26.8	27.5	NA	NA	NA	NA	NA	NA	NA
PowerPC											
Units shipped	0	0.8	4.0	3.5	4.7	3.1	3.3	3.5	4.7	NA	NA
Installed base	0	0.8	7.8	14.1	22.2	29.4	32.9	36.2	40.9	NA	NA

Source: Adapted from Gartner Dataquest, InfoCorp., International Data Corp., Merrill Lynch, and Credit Suisse data.

Notes: Between 5% and 10% of total microprocessor shipments go into non-PC end products. In any given year, roughly 30% to 45% of microprocessors in the total installed base involve older technologies that are probably no longer in use. The figures for PowerPC shipments exclude microprocessors destined for Sony PlayStation and Xbox 360 machines. Figures for "Mac units shipped" cover Macintosh calendar year sales.

NA = Not Available or Not Applicable.

Exhibit 5   PC Manufacturers: Key Operating Measures, 1997–2007

	1997	2000	2003	2004	2005	2006	2007
Gross Margin (%)							
Apple	21%	28%	29%	29%	30%	30%	35%
Dell	23%	21%	19%	19%	18%	17%	19%[a]
Hewlett-Packard	38%	31%	29%	27%	25%	26%	24%
R&D/Sales							
Apple	12.1%	4.8%	7.6%	5.9%	3.8%	3.7%	3.3%
Dell	1.2%	1.5%	0.8%	0.9%	0.8%	0.9%	1.0%[a]
Hewlett-Packard	7.2%	5.4%	5.0%	4.4%	4.0%	3.9%	3.5%

Source: Compiled from company financial reports; Hoover's, Inc., www.hoovers.com.

Note: All information is on a fiscal-year basis. The fiscal year ends in September for Apple, in January for Dell, and in October for Hewlett-Packard.

[a]For Dell, 2007 figures cover the three quarters ending November 2, 2007.

Exhibit 6   Apple Inc.: Unit Sales by Product Category, 2004–2008 (in thousands of units)

	2004	Y/Y Change	2005	Y/Y Change	2006	Y/Y Change	2007	3Q08– 3Q08
Desktops[a]	1,625	55%	2,520	(3%)	2,434	12%	2,714	*2,776*
Portables[b]	1,665	21%	2,014	42%	2,869	51%	4,337	*4,328*
Total Macintosh Unit Sales	3,290	38%	4,534	17%	5,303	33%	7,051	*7,104*
Net Sales per Unit Sold	$1,496	(7%)	$1,384	1%	$1,391	5%	$1,463	*$1,500*
iPods	4,416	409%	22,497	75%	39,409	31%	51,630	*43,776*
Net Sales per Unit Sold	$296	(32%)	$202	(3%)	$195	(17%)	$161	*$171*
iPhones	NA	NA	NA	NA	NA	NA	1,389	*4,735*

Source: Apple financial statements; casewriter calculations.

Note: Apple's fiscal year ends in September. All data here reflect fiscal-year results.

    NA = Not Available or Not Applicable.

[a]Includes iMac, eMac, Mac Mini, Mac Pro, Power Mac, and Xserve product lines.

[b]Includes MacBook, iBook, MacBook Pro, and PowerBook product lines.

Exhibit 7   PC Manufacturers: Worldwide Market Shares, 2000–2007

	2000	2001	2002	2003	2004	2005	2006	2007
Hewlett-Packard[a]	7.8%	6.9%	16.0%	16.2%	15.8%	15.6%	16.5%	18.8%
Dell	11.4%	12.9%	15.1%	16.7%	17.9%	18.1%	16.6%	14.9%
Acer	—	—	—	3.1%	3.6%	4.7%	5.8%	7.9%
Lenovo[b]	—	—	—	—	2.3%	6.2%	7.1%	7.5%
Toshiba	3.0%	2.8%	3.2%	3.1%	3.6%	3.5%	3.9%	4.1%
Fujitsu Siemens	5.1%	4.5%	4.2%	4.1%	4.0%	4.1%	—	—
IBM[b]	7.1%	6.2%	5.9%	5.8%	5.9%	—	—	—
Compaq[a]	13.0%	11.2%	—	—	—	—	—	—
Packard Bell NEC	4.5%	3.5%	3.3%	—	—	—	—	—
Apple	3.5%	2.5%	2.3%	1.9%	1.9%	2.2%	2.3%	2.6%
Total shipments	128.5 million	121.8 million	136.9 million	154.7 million	177.5 million	208.6 million	235.4 million	269.0 million

Source: "PC Market Still Strong in Q4 With Solid Growth Across Regions, According to IDC" (press release), International Data Corp., January 16, 2008; IDC data, as cited in Scott H. Kessler, "Computers: Hardware" (industry survey), Standard & Poor's, April 26, 2007, p. 7, and in previous editions of that survey; Apple Inc. annual financial reports; and casewriter estimates.

Note: Market share data for Apple are derived from Macintosh unit sales, as reported in the company's annual reports. The sampling of market shares for other companies comes mainly from annual listings of the top five PC makers, as measured by IDC. Absence of a figure indicates that a company placed below the top five in a given year.

[a]Hewlett-Packard acquired Compaq in mid-2002. The 2002 market share figure for HP incorporates Compaq sales for the first part of that year.

[b]Lenovo acquired IBM's PC business in mid-2005. The 2005 market share figure for Lenovo incorporates IBM sales for the first part of that year.

Exhibit 8   Apple Competitors: Selected Financial Information, 2000–2007 (in millions of dollars)

	2000	2002	2004	2005	2006	2007
Acer						
Total revenues	1,164	3,107	6,746	9,898	11,343	5,878[a]
Cost of sales	1,052	2,643	5,878	8,790	10,114	5,258[a]
R&D	3	7	13	14	12	NA
SG&A	70	412	689	810	944	462[a]
Net income	31	250	210	264	314	230[a]
Total assets	413	3,191	3,908	5,217	5,781	6,194[a]
Total current liabilities	173	938	1,883	3,106	3,373	3,902[a]
Total stockholders' equity	165	1,929	1,908	2,001	2,271	2,150[a]
Gross margin	10%	15%	13%	11%	11%	11%[a]
R&D/sales	0%	0%	0%	0%	0%	NA
SG&A/sales	6%	13%	10%	3%	8%	8%[a]
Return on sales	3%	8%	3%	3%	3%	4%[a]
Market value at year-end	286	1,860	3,423	5,603	4,829	4,573
Dell						
Total revenues	31,888	35,404	49,205	55,908	57,420	61,133
Cost of sales	25,205	28,844	39,856	45,227	47,433	49,462
R&D	482	319	463	463	498	693
SG&A	3,675	3,505	4,761	5,499	6,346	7,538
Net income	2,177	2,122	3,043	3,572	2,583	2,947
Total assets	13,435	15,470	23,215	23,109	25,635	27,561
Total current liabilities	6,543	8,933	14,136	15,927	17,791	18,526
Total stockholders' equity	5,622	4,873	6,485	4,129	4,439	3,735
Gross margin	21%	19%	19%	19%	17%	19%
R&D/sales	2%	1%	1%	1%	1%	1%
SG&A/sales	12%	10%	10%	9%	11%	12%
Return on sales	7%	6%	6%	6%	4%	5%
Market value at year-end	45,630	68,968	104,689	70,488	56,995	54,927
Hewlett-Packard						
Total revenues	48,782	56,588	79,905	86,696	91,658	104,286
Cost of sales	33,709	40,134	58,540	64,718	67,727	79,670
R&D	2,646	4,105	3,543	3,492	3,643	3,801
SG&A	10,029	12,345	14,530	14,674	14,857	15,837
Net income	3,697	(903)	3,497	2,398	6,198	7,264
Total assets	34,009	70,710	76,138	77,317	81,981	88,699
Total current liabilities	15,197	24,310	28,588	31,460	35,850	39,260
Total stockholders' equity	14,209	36,262	37,564	37,176	38,144	35,526
Gross margin	31%	29%	27%	25%	26%	24%
R&D/sales	5%	7%	4%	4%	4%	4%
SG&A/sales	21%	22%	18%	17%	16%	15%
Return on sales	8%	-2%	4%	3%	7%	7%
Market value at year-end	62,431	52,973	63,327	81,242	112,070	129,929

[a]For Acer, 2007 figures (except for "market value at year-end") cover the half-year ending June 30, 2007.

[b]For Lenovo (see p. 23), 2007 figures (except for "market value at year-end") cover the two quarters ending September 30, 2007.

Exhibit 8 (continued)

	2000	2002	2004	2005	2006	2007
Lenovo						
Total revenues	3,491	2,978	2,894	13,329	14,590	8,358[b]
Cost of sales	3,051	2,189	2,437	11,463	12,337	7,107[b]
R&D	15	40	49	192	227	(120)[b]
SG&A	284	221	NA	1,338	1,613	(874)[b]
Net income	110	130	144	22	161	172[b]
Total assets	1,276	866	1,158	5,057	5,449	6,653[b]
Total current liabilities	648	321	445	3,199	3,526	4,473[b]
Total stockholders' equity	617	537	667	1,049	1,134	1,335[b]
Gross margin	13%	16%	16%	14%	15%	15%[b]
R&D/sales	0%	2%	2%	1%	2%	NA
SG&A/sales	8%	8%	NA	10%	11%	NA
Return on sales	3%	5%	5%	1%	1%	2%[b]
Market value at year-end	4,696	2,501	2,236	3,923	3,463	8,049
Intel						
Total revenues	33,726	26,764	34,209	38,826	35,382	38,334
Cost of sales	9,429	8,389	9,591	15,777	17,164	18,430
R&D	4,006	4,054	4,778	5,145	5,873	5,755
SG&A	8,986	8,543	9,466	5,688	6,096	5,401
Net income	10,535	3,117	7,516	8,664	5,044	6,976
Total assets	47,945	44,224	48,143	48,314	48,368	55,651
Total current liabilities	8,650	6,595	8,006	9,234	8,514	8,571
Total stockholders' equity	37,322	35,468	38,579	36,182	36,752	42,762
Gross margin	72%	69%	72%	59%	51%	52%
R&D/sales	12%	15%	14%	13%	17%	15%
SG&A/sales	27%	32%	28%	15%	17%	14%
Return on sales	31%	12%	22%	22%	14%	18%
Market value at year-end	202,321	103,836	147,895	150,484	116,762	155,881
Microsoft						
Total revenues	22,956	28,365	36,835	39,788	44,282	51,122
Cost of sales	2,334	4,177	5,899	5,316	6,660	9,287
R&D	3,775	4,307	7,779	6,184	6,584	7,121
SG&A	8,925	10,604	18,560	16,946	19,051	21,905
Net income	9,421	7,829	8,168	12,254	12,599	14,065
Total assets	52,150	67,646	92,389	70,815	69,597	63,171
Total current liabilities	9,755	12,744	14,969	16,877	22,442	23,754
Total stockholders' equity	41,368	52,180	74,825	48,115	40,104	31,097
Gross margin	90%	85%	84%	87%	85%	82%
R&D/sales	16%	15%	21%	16%	15%	14%
SG&A/sales	39%	37%	50%	43%	43%	43%
Return on sales	41%	28%	22%	31%	28%	28%
Market value at year-end	231,290	276,412	290,720	278,358	293,538	333,054

Sources: Standard & Poor's Global Vantage and company financial reports. (In the case of Dell, Intel, and Lenovo, 2007 data come from company financial reports. All other data come from S&P Global Vantage. Variations may result from differences in how S&P Global Vantage and some companies tabulate reported data.)

Notes: All information is on a fiscal-year basis, except for "market value at year-end," which is on a calendar-year basis. The fiscal year ends in December for Acer, in January for Dell, in October for Hewlett-Packard, in March for Lenovo, in December for Intel, and in June for Microsoft.

NA = Not Available or Not Applicable.

23

199

Exhibit 9   iPod Competitors: Comparison of Models and Prices for MP3 Players (August 2008)

	1 GB – 2 GB	4 GB – 16 GB	30 GB – 160 GB	8 GB – 32 GB (multi-touch)
Apple	iPod shuffle (1 GB) $49 iPod shuffle (2 GB) $69	iPod nano (4 GB) $149 iPod nano (8 GB) $199	iPod classic (80 GB) $249 iPod classic (160 GB) $349	iPod touch (8 GB) $299 iPod touch (32 GB) $499
Creative	Zen Stone (1 GB) $35 MuVo V100 (2 GB) $30	Zen (4 GB) $90 Zen (16 GB) $180	Zen (32 GB) $250 Zen X-Fi (32 GB) $280	NA
iRiver	T60 (1 GB) $70 T60 (2 GB) $90	E100 (4 GB) $100 CLIX (8 GB) $240	NA	NA
SanDisk	Sansa Clip (1 GB) $40 Sansa Express (2 GB) $70	Sansa Fuze (4 GB) $80 Sansa View (16 GB) $200	Sansa View (32 GB) $350	NA
Sony	Walkman (1 GB) $45 Walkman (2 GB) $60	Walkman (4 GB) $100 Walkman (16 GB) $300	NA	NA
Microsoft	NA	Zune (4 GB) $130 Zune (8 GB) $180	Zune (30 GB) $200 Zune (80 GB) $250	NA

Source: Company websites, accessed August 2008.

Note: Pricing information reflects retail prices as listed on each company's website or, in a few cases, on Amazon.com.

Exhibit 10   iPod and iTunes: Quarterly Sales (of iPod Units and iTunes Songs), 2001–2008

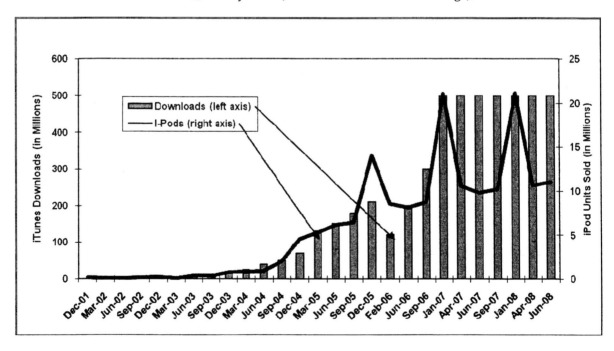

Source: Compiled from Apple financial reports, Apple press releases, and casewriter estimates.

Note: Because Apple does not report iTunes song downloads on regular quarterly basis, some information in this chart reflects casewriter adjustments to reported data.

24

200

Endnotes

[1] "Jobs Says Apple to Rename Itself Apple Inc.," *Dow Jones News Service*, January 9, 2007, accessed via Factiva.

[2] This discussion of Apple's history is based largely on Jim Carlton, *Apple: The Inside Story of Intrigue, Egomania, and Business Blunders* (New York: Times Business/Random House, 1997); David B. Yoffie, "Apple Computer 1992," HBS No. 792-081 (Boston: Harvard Business School Publishing, 1992); and David B. Yoffie and Yusi Wang, "Apple Computer 2002," HBS No. 702-469 (Boston: Harvard Business School Publishing, 2002). Unless otherwise attributed, all quotations and all data cited in this section are drawn from those two cases.

[3] Carlton, *Apple*, p. 10.

[4] Data from Gartner Dataquest, cited in Carlton, *Apple*, p. 11.

[5] Yoffie, "Apple Computer 1992."

[6] Ibid.

[7] Ibid.

[8] Ibid, p. 273.

[9] David B. Yoffie, "Apple Computer 1996," HBS No. 796-126 (Boston: Harvard Business School Publishing, 1996).

[10] Charles McCoy, "Apple, IBM Kill Kaleida Labs Venture," *The Wall Street Journal*, November 20, 1995.

[11] Louise Kehoe, "Apple Shares Drop Sharply," *The Financial Times*, January 19, 1996.

[12] Dawn Kawamoto and Anthony Lazarus, "Apple Lays Off Thousands," CNET News.com, March 14, 1997.

[13] Jim Carlton and Lee Gomes, "Apple Computer Chief Amelio Is Ousted," *The Wall Street Journal*, July 10, 1997.

[14] Laurie J. Flynn, "Apple Sending Clone Makers Mixed Signals," *The New York Times*, August 11, 1997.

[15] "Steve Jobs" (executive profile), Apple Computer website, http://www.apple.com/pr/bios/jobs.html, accessed April 2006.

[16] "$7.4 Billion Seals Disney-Pixar Deal," *Hollywood Reporter*, January 31, 2006, accessed via Factiva.

[17] Cliff Edwards and Peter Burrows, "Apple: Back to the iMac," BusinessWeek Online, August 9, 2007, accessed via Factiva.

[18] "Apple Computer: Annual Financials," Hoover's, Inc., www.hoovers.com.

[19] All product and price information for Macintosh computers is drawn from the Apple Inc. website, http://www.apple.com/getamac/whichmac.html, accessed January 2008 and August 2008.

[20] See "Get a Mac," Apple website, http://www.apple.com/getamac, accessed January 2008.

[21] On interoperability of Mac and non-Mac devices, see pages on the Apple website devoted to the Mac Mini (http://www.apple.com/macmini) and to Apple displays (http://www.apple.com/displays), both accessed February 2008.

[22] "Apple's Intel Switch," CNet News.com, June 15, 2005, accessed via Factiva.

[23] Nick Turner and Patrick Seitz, "Apple's Intel Machines Ahead of Schedule," *Investor's Business Daily*, January 11, 2006, p. A4; Thomas Clayburn and Darrell Dunn, "Apple Bets Its Chips," *InformationWeek*, "January 16, 2006, p. 26; Daniel Drew Turner, "Apple Shows New Intel Notebooks, Software," *eWeek*, January 10, 2006; "Apple, Inc.," Hoover's, Inc., www.hoovers.com, accessed January 2008.

24 Apple Inc., Form 10-K for the fiscal year ending September 29, 2007, p. 42.

25 Stephen Fenech, "Apple's New Core: New Macs with Intel Dual Processors Revealed," *Daily Telegraph* (London), January 18, 2006, p. 11.

26 See "Everything-Ready," Apple website, http://www.apple.com/getamac/everything-ready.html, accessed February 2008.

27 "A Talk with Apple's Mr. Marketer," BusinessWeek Online, January 22, 2002, accessed via Factiva.

28 Jacqui Cheng, "Macworld.Ars: Macworld 2008 Keynote Live on Ars" (live weblog reporting of Steve Jobs's keynote address to MacWorld 2008), Ars Technica, January 15, 2008, http://arstechnica.com/news.ars/post/20080115-macworld-ars-macworld-2008-keynote-live-on-ars.html, accessed January 2008.

29 Ibid.

30 Brent Schlender, "How Big Can Apple Get?" *Fortune*, February 21, 2005, p. 66, accessed February 2008.

31 Thomas Claburn and Darrell Dunn, "Apple Bets Its Chips," *InformationWeek*, January 15, 2006, p. 26; Nick Wingfield and Don Clark, "With Intel Inside, Macs May Be Faster, Smaller," *The Wall Street Journal*, June 7, 2005, p. B1.

32 Arik Hesseldahl, "What's Behind Apple's iWork?" BusinessWeek Online, August 10, 2007, accessed via Factiva; Walter S. Mossberg, "New Office for Mac Speeds Up Programs, Integrates Formats," *The Wall Street Journal*, January 3, 2008, p. B1, accessed via Factiva.

33 "Apple to Open 25 Stores in 2001" (press release), Apple Computer, May 15, 2001, http:/www.apple.com/pr/library/2001/may/15retail.html, accessed February 2005.

34 "Apple's First Retail Store in Australia Opens in Sydney on Thursday, 19 June," Apple, Inc., June 18, 2009, http://www.apple.com/pr/library/2008/06/18retail.html, accessed July 2008; "Apple Reports Record Third-Quarter Results," Apple, Inc., July 21, 2008, http://www.apple.com/pr/library/2008/07/21results.html, accessed July 2008.

35 Katie Hafner, "Inside Apple Stores, a Certain Aura Enchants the Faithful," *The New York Times*, December 27, 2007, p. C1, accessed via Factiva.

36 "Apple's First Retail Store in Australia Opens in Sydney"; Arik Hesseldahl, "Apple Forecasts: Not Just Hype," BusinessWeek Online, December 11, 2007, accessed via Factiva.

37 Ibid.

38 Randall Stross, "A Window of Opportunity for Macs, Soon to Close," *The New York Times*, September 26, 2007, p. C4, accessed via Factiva.

39 Chris Whitmore, Sherri Scribner, and Joakim Mahlberg, "Beyond iPod" (analysts' report), Deutsche Bank, September 21, 2005, p. 31; Megan Graham-Hackett, "Computers: Hardware" (industry survey), Standard & Poor's, December 8, 2005, p. 8; Arik Hesseldahl, "Apple's Growing Army of Converts," BusinessWeek Online, November 10, 2005, accessed Factiva.

40 Apple Inc., Form 10-K for the fiscal year ending September 29, 2007, p. 42

41 Kevin Allison, "Apple Ushers in New Mac Generation," *Financial Times*, August 13, 2007, p. 20, accessed via Factiva; "PC Market Still Strong in Q4 with Solid Growth Across Regions, According to IDC" (press release), International Data Corp., January 16, 2008, http://www.idc.com/getdoc.jsp?containerId=prUS21041708, accessed January 2008.

42 Matt Hartley, "Mac Division Could Steal iPhone's Thunder," *The Globe and Mail* (Toronto), July 21, 2008, p. B3, accessed via Factiva.

43 See Exhibit 3 in this case.

[44] Siobhan Chapman, "Worldwide PC Numbers to Hit 1B in 2008, Forrester Says," CIO website, http://www.cio.com/article/118454/Worldwide_PC_Numbers_to_Hit_B_in_Forrester_Says, accessed February 2008.

[45] "PC Market Still Strong in Q4 with Solid Growth Across Regions, According to IDC."

[46] "Gartner Says Worldwide PC Market Grew 13 Percent in 2007" (press release), Gartner, Inc., January 16, 2007, http://www.gartner.com/it/page.jsp?id=584210&format=print, accessed January 2008.

[47] Scott H. Kessler, "Computers: Hardware" (industry survey), Standard & Poor's, April 26, 2007, pp. 1–2, 7–8, 14.

[48] IDC (International Data Corp.) data, as cited in Graham-Hackett, "Computers: Hardware," p. 7.

[49] Bill Shope and Elizabeth Borbolla, "IT Hardware: Top Issue for 2006 and Industry Primer" (analysts' report), JP Morgan, January 30, 2006, pp. 28–29.

[50] David Wong, Amit Chandra, and Lindsey Matherne, "Chip/Computer/Cellphone Data" (research report), Wachovia Capital Markets LLC, December 10, 2007, pp. 33–34.

[51] Michelle Kessler, "Computer Industry Sits at Critical Crossroads," USA Today, March 5, 2007, p. B1, accessed via Factiva.

[52] Component costs and wholesale prices are based on casewriter communications with a computer industry insider. Retail pricing is based on a survey of online PC vendors.

[53] Wong, et al., "Chip/Computer/Cellphone Data." p. 35.

[54] Kessler, "Computers: Hardware," pp. 19–20.

[55] Erica Ogg, "Trouble on the Horizon for 'White Box" PC Makers," CNet News.com, October 30, 2007, accessed via Factiva; Bruce Einhorn, "Grudge Match in China," BusinessWeek, April 2, 2007, p. 42, accessed via Factiva.

[56] Kessler, "Computers: Hardware," p. 7; "PC Market Still Strong in Q4 with Solid Growth Across Regions, According to IDC."

[57] Bob Keefe and Dan Zehr, "Five Years After Maligned Merger, Hewlett-Packard Prospers," The Atlanta Journal-Constitution, April 29, 2007, p. C1, accessed via Factiva; Damon Darlin, "Design Helps H.P. Profit More on PCs," The New York Times, May 17, 2007, p. C1, accessed via Factiva; Christopher Lawton, "Hard Drive: How H-P Reclaimed Its PC Lead over Dell," The Wall Street Journal, June 4, 2007, p. A1, accessed via Factiva; Louise Lee, "BW's Businessperson of the Year," BusinessWeek Online, January 3, 2008, accessed via Factiva.

[58] Jennifer L. Schenker, "Dell Steps Up Consumer Pursuit," BusinessWeek Online, June 8, 2007, accessed via Factiva; Steve Lohr, "Can Michael Dell Refocus His Namesake?" The New York Times, September 9, 2007, p. C1, accessed via Factiva; Christopher Helman, "The Second Coming," Forbes, December 10, 2007, p. 78, accessed via Factiva; Christopher Lawton, "Dell Treads Carefully into Selling PCs in Stores," The Wall Street Journal, p. B1, accessed via Factiva.

[59] Jason Dean and Jane Spencer, "Taiwan's Acer Rebounds, Takes on Global PC Titans," The Wall Street Journal Asia, April 5, 2007, p. 1, accessed via Factiva; Jason Dean and Loretta Chao, "Acer's Gateway Purchase Vaults It Ahead of Lenovo," The Wall Street Journal Asia, August 28, 2007, p. 1, accessed via Factiva; Arik Hesseldahl, "Acer's Gateway to the U.S. Market," BusinessWeek Online, August 29, 2007, accessed via Factiva; Bruce Einhorn, "Acer Chief Promises No Gateway Layoffs," BusinessWeek Online, October 30, 2007, accessed via Factiva.

[60] Bruce Einhorn, "IBM Shrinks Its Lenovo Stake," BusinessWeek Online, February 7, 2007, accessed via Factiva; Bruce Einhorn, Olga Kharif, and Dexter Roberts, "Grudge Match in China," BusinessWeek Online, April 2, 2007, accessed via Factiva; Jane Spencer, "Can Durability Trump Price in Laptop War?" The Wall Street Journal, May 17, 2007, p. B1, accessed via Factiva.

[61] Clyde Montevirgen and Karan Kawaguchi, "Semiconductors" (industry survey), Standard and Poor's, May 31, 2007, p. 19

[62] Kessler, "Computers: Hardware," pp. 14, 18.

[63] Montevirgen and Kawaguchi, "Semiconductors," p. 25.

[64] David B. Yoffie, Dharmesh M. Mehta, and Rudina I. Suseri, "Microsoft in 2005," HBS Case No. 705-505, (Boston: Harvard Business School Publishing, 2006).

[65] Stross, "A Window of Opportunity for Macs, Soon to Close"; Claudine Beaumont, "As Windows Wilts, Apple Blossoms," *The Daily Telegraph* (London), December 15, 2007, p. 12, accessed via Factiva.

[66] Todd Bishop, "Gates Picks Challenging Year to Leave Microsoft," *Seattle Post-Intelligencer*, December 21, 2007, p. C1, accessed via Factiva.

[67] Kessler, "Computers: Hardware," p. 14.

[68] Hesseldahl, "What's Behind Apple's iWork?"

[69] For a general overview of the origin and impact of the iPod, see Rob Walker, "The Guts of the New Machine," *The New York Times Magazine*, November 30, 2003, p. 78.

[70] Peter Burrows and Ronald Glover, with Heather Green, "Steve Jobs' Magic Kingdom," *BusinessWeek*, February 6, 2006, p. 62.

[71] All product and price information for the current line of iPod devices is drawn from the Apple Inc. website, http://www.apple.com/ipod/whichipod/, accessed August 2008.

[72] Robert Semple, Stephanie Sun, and Thompson Wu, "Apple Computer Inc." (analysts' report), Credit Suisse, June 5, 2007, p. 6.

[73] Arik Hesseldahl, "Apple's Cheap to Build Nano," BusinessWeek Online, September 19, 2007, accessed via Factiva.

[74] Arik Hesseldahl, "Are iPod's Hard Drive Days Numbered?" BusinessWeek Online, October 11, 2007, accessed via Factiva.

[75] Hessedahl, "Apple's Cheap to Build Nano'; Hessedahl, "Are iPod's Hard Drive Days Numbered?"; "Apple Lowers Costs of iPod Nano Parts," Reuters News, September 28, 2007, accessed via Factiva.

[76] Arik Hesseldahl, "Unpeeling Apple's Nano," BusinessWeek Online, September 22, 2007, accessed via Factiva.

[77] "Samsung, Hynix to Boost Output of Flash Memory Chips for Apple," Nikkei Report, May 31, 2007, accessed via Factiva; Ben Charny and Roger Cheng, "Higher Demand Could Make Flash a Flash in the Pan," Dow Jones Newswires, July 18, 2007, accessed via Factiva; Yun-Hee Kim, "Apple Price Cut, Products to Boost Flash Makers," Dow Jones Newswires, September 13, 2007, accessed via Factiva; Hessedahl, "Are iPod's Hard Drive Days Numbered?"

[78] Yinka Adegoke, "Apple Seen Having Upper Hand in Music Negotiations," Reuters News, April 20, 2007, accessed via Factiva; Ben Cherny and Roger Cheng, "Pressure from IPhone, Rivals Weighs on Latest IPod Debut," Dow Jones Newswires, September 4, 2007, accessed via Factiva; Ricki Morell, "MP3 Options, From Apple to Zune," *The Boston Globe*, June 8, 2008, p. G2, accessed via Factiva; Chris Sorensen, "A Pod-Forsaken Future?" *Toronto Star*, June 14, 2008, p. B1, accessed via Factiva.

[79] Walter S. Mossberg and Katherine Boehret, "Singing a New Zune," *The Wall Street Journal*, November 14, 2007, p. D1, accessed via Factiva; Andy Ihnatko, "Zune's in Tune This Year," *Chicago Sun-Times*, November 15, 2007, p. 60, accessed via Factiva; Rich Karpinski, "Microsoft Updates Zune, Targeting iPod—Eventually iPhone Too?" Penton Insight (online), May 6, 2008, accessed via Factiva.

[80] Saul Hansell, "Gates vs. Jobs: The Rematch," *The New York Times*, November 14, 2004, p. 3-1, accessed via Factiva; Bill Shope, Elizabeth Borbolla, and Mark Moskowitz, "Apple Computer: iPod Economics II" (analysts' report), JP Morgan, May 26, 2005, p. 20.

[81] "Apple Unveils New iPods" (press release), Apple Computer, July 18, 2002, accessed via Factiva; John Markoff, "Oh, Yeah, He Also Sells Computers," *The New York Times*, April 24, 2004, p. C1, access via Factiva.

[82] Damon Darlin, "Add-Ons Have Become a Billion-Dollar Bonanza," *The New York Times*, February 3, 2006, p. C1, accessed via Factiva; Nick Wingfield and Don Clark, "Apple Goes Hi-Fi," *The Wall Street Journal*, March 1, 2006, p. B1, accessed via Factiva; Peter Burrows, "Welcome to Planet Apple," *BusinessWeek*, July 9, 2007 p. 88, accessed via Factiva.

[83] Chris Taylor, "The 99¢ Solution," *Time*, November 17, 2003, p. 66, accessed via Factiva.

[84] Aaron Ridadela, "Apple Reignites the Browser Wars," BusinessWeek Online, June 13, 2007, accessed via Factiva.

[85] Burrows, "Welcome to Planet Apple"; May Wong, "Apple Bets on Online Movie Rentals," Associated Press Newswires, January 16, 2008, accessed via Factiva; "iTunes Store Top Music Retailer in the US," Apple, Inc., April 3, 2008, http://www.apple.com/pr/library/2008/04/03itunes.html, accessed July 2008; "iTunes Store Tops Over [SIC] Five Billion Songs Sold," Apple, Inc., June 19, 2008, http://www.apple.com/pr/library/2008/06/19itunes.html, accessed July 2008.

[86] Ibid, p. 7.

[87] "Apple Computer: Annual Financials," Hoover's, Inc., www.hoovers.com.

[88] Shope, et al., "Apple Computer: iPod Economics II," p. 26; Ronald Grover and Peter Burrows, "Universal Music Takes on iTunes," *BusinessWeek*, October 22, 2007, p. 30, accessed via Factiva.

[89] Ibid, pp. 8–10.

[90] Ibid, pp. 10–13.

[91] Taylor, "The 99¢ Solution"; Walker, "The Guts of the New Machine."

[92] Adegoke, "Apple Seen Having Upper Hand in Music Negotiations"; Alex Veiga, "Apple Inc. Seeking End to Music Copy Restrictions in iTunes Talks," Associated Press Newswires, May 7, 2007, accessed via Factiva; Jeff Leeds, "Apple Faces a Rebellion over iTunes," *The New York Times*, July 2, 2007, p. C1, accessed via Factiva; Grover and Burrows, "Universal Music Takes on iTunes."

[93] Ethan Smith and Vauhina Vara, "Music Service from Amazon Takes on iTunes," *The Wall Street Journal*, May 17, 2007, p. D1, accessed via Factiva; Frank Ahrens and Mike Musgrove, "Music-Selling Rivals Take Aim at iTunes," *The Washington Post*, August 22, 2007, p. D1, accessed via Factiva; Adrian McCoy, "A Road Map to Download Services," *Pittsburgh Post-Gazette*, October 18, 2007, p. A6, accessed via Factiva.

[94] Jessica E. Vascellaro and Ethan Smith, "Big Record Labels, MySpace Challenge Apple iTunes Store," *The Wall Street Journal*, April 4, 2008, p. B1, accessed via Factiva; Jeff Leeds and Brad Stone, "MySpace Will Expand Music Site," *The International Herald Tribune*, April 5, 2008, p. 12, accessed via Factiva.

[95] Smith and Vara, "Music Service from Amazon Takes on iTunes"; Jeff Leeds, "Free Song Promotion Is Expected from Amazon," *The New York Times*, January 14, 2008, p. C1, accessed via Factiva.

[96] Vito Pilieci, "Wal-Mart, iTunes Moves Worry Music Industry," *Vancouver Sun*, March 4, 2008, p. D4, accessed via Factiva; Mylene Mangalindan, "Slow Slog for Amazon's Digital Media," *The Wall Street Journal*, April 23, 2008, p. B1, accessed via Factiva; Tim Anderson, "How Apple Is Changing DRM," *The Guardian* (London), May 15, 2008, p. 1, accessed via Factiva; Jamie Lendino, "Rhapsody's New DRM-Free MP3 Store Matches the Competition," *PC Magazine*, June 30, 2008, accessed via Factiva; Arik Hesseldahl, "Taking the Wraps off the New Rhapsody," BusinessWeek.com, July 1, 2008, accessed via Factiva.

[98] Don Fernandez, "Apple Makes Leap to Video," *The Atlanta Journal-Constitution*, October 13, 2005, p. A1, accessed via Factiva.

[99] "Which iPod Are You?" Apple website, http://www.apple.com/ipod/whichipod, accessed August 2008.

[100] Jefferson Graham, "Now Showing at an iPod Near You; Apple to Rent Movies Through iTunes Store," *USA Today*, January 16, 2008, p. B2, accessed via Factiva.

[101] "iTunes Store Tops Over [SIC] Five Billion Songs Sold."

[102] Connie Cuglielmo, "Apple Unveils 'World's Thinnest' Laptop, Film Rentals," Bloomberg.com, January 15, 2008, http://www.bloomberg.com/apps/news?pid=20601087&sid=aJxgkqbGItZk&refer=home, accessed January 2008; Ellen Lee, "Macworld Announcements Make Ripples, Not Waves," *The San Francisco Chronicle*, January 19, 2008, p. C1, accessed via Factiva.

[103] Brooks Barnes, "NBC to End ITunes Sales of Its Shows," *The New York Times*, August 31, 2007, p. C1, accessed via Factiva.

[104] Scott Woolley, "The iFlop: Steve Jobs Tried to Design—and Dictate—the Future of Television; Here's How He Failed," *Forbes*, October 1, 2007, p. 46, accessed via Factiva; Walter S. Mossberg, "All Things Digital—iPod, iPhone, iTunes, Apple TV: Where Steve Jobs Sees Them All Heading," *The Wall Street Journal*, June 18, 2007, p. R4, accessed via Factiva.

[105] "Apple Introduces New Apple TV Software and Lowers Price to $229" (press release), January 15, 2008, Apple website, http://www.apple.com/pr/library/2008/01/15appletv.html, accessed February 2008; Lee, "Macworld Announcements Make Ripples, Not Waves."

[106] Donna Fuscaldo and Mark Boslet, "Jobs Says Apple to Rename Itself Apple Inc.," Dow Jones News Service, January 9, 2007, accessed via Factiva.

[107] Mossberg, "All Things Digital."

[108] Rachel Konrad, "Apple CEO Unveils New Name, Long-Awaited Phone; Shares Jump," Associated Press Newswires, January 9, 2007, accessed via Factiva; "Breakthrough Internet Device" and other iPhone pages on the Apple website, http://www.apple.com/iphone/features/index.html#internetl, accessed October 2007.

[109] Arik Hesseldahl, "Apple's iPhone Rings a Lot of Bells," BusinessWeek Online, January 11, 2007, accessed via Factiva.

[110] Li Yuan and Pui-Wing Tam, "Apple Storms the Cellphone Field," *The Wall Street Journal*, January 10, 2007, p. A3, accessed via Factiva; Leslie Cauley, "iWeapon: AT&T Plans to Use Its Exclusive iPhone Rights to Gain the Upper Hand in the Battle for Wireless Supremacy," *USA Today*, May 22, 2007, p. B1, accessed via Factiva.

[111] Nick Wingfield and Li Yuan, "Apple's iPhone: Is It Worth It?" *The Wall Street Journal*, January 10, 2007, p. D1, accessed via Factiva.

[112] Jeffrey Bartash, "No Margin for Error for Handset Firms," Dow Jones New Service, January 10, 2007, accessed via Factiva.

[113] "iPhone: Individual Plans," AT&T website, http://www.wireless.att.com/cell-phone-service/specials/iPhoneCenter.html, accessed October 2007.

[114] Cauley, "iWeapon."

[115] Amol Sharma, Nick Wingfield, and Li Yuan, "Apple Coup: How Steve Jobs Played Hardball in iPhone Birth," *The Wall Street Journal*, February 17, 2007, p. A1, accessed via Factiva.

[116] Cauley, "iWeapon."

[117] Sharma, Wingfield, and Yuan, "Apple Coup"; Nick Wingfield and Daniel Thomas, "Why iPhone Faces Tough Sell in Europe," *The Wall Street Journal*, September 19, 2007, p. B5, accessed via Factiva; Olga Kharif and Peter Burrows, "On the Trail of the Missing iPhones," *BusinessWeek*, February 11, 2008, p. 25, accessed via Factiva.

[118] May Wong, "Apple's iPhone Stirs Rivals, Who Question 'Revolutionary' Claim," Associated Press Newswires, February 1, 2007, accessed via Factiva; Roger Cheng, "Risks Abound As Apple, AT&T Ready iPhone Launch," Dow Jones Newswires, June 6, 2007, accessed via Factiva; Erik Pfanner, "iPhone Introduced to Europe, Where Standards Differ," *The New York Times*, September 19, 2007, p. C2, accessed via Factiva.

[119] David Pogue, "Apple Waves Its Wand at the Phone," *The New York Times*, January 11, 2007, p. C1, accessed via Factiva.

[120] John Markoff, "Apple, Hoping for Another iPod, Introduces Innovative Cellphone," *The New York Times*, January 10, 2007, p. A1, accessed via Factiva.

[121] Ryan Kim, "Pushing the Apple," *The San Francisco Chronicle*, January 22, 2007, p. C1, accessed via Factiva.

[122] Scott Morrison, "Apple Sells 4 Million iPhones, Topping Expectations," Dow Jones Newswires, January 15, 2008, accessed via Factiva.

[123] Wong, "Apple's iPhone Stirs Rivals."

[124] Kharif and Burrows, "On the Trail of the Missing iPhones"; Peter Burrows, "Inside the iPhone Gray Market," BusinessWeek.com, February 13, 2008, accessed via Factiva; David Barboza, "Iphone on Gray Market Merry-Go-Round," *The International Herald Tribune*, February 19, 2008, p. 11, accessed via Factiva; Arik Hesseldahl and Jennifer L. Schenker, "iPhone 2.0 Takes on the World," BusinessWeek.com, June 9, 2008, accessed via Factiva; Jeremiah Marquez, "Asia Underground Market Awaits iPhone," Associated Press Newswires, July 11, 2008, accessed via Factiva; Maria Kiselyova and Sophie Taylor, "Apple in No Rush to Bring iPhone to Russia, China," Reuters News, July 17, 2008, accessed via Factiva; Paul Sonne, "iPhones Hot Even in Places Apple Has Yet to Reach," Associated Press Newswires, July 18, 2008, accessed via Factiva.

[125] John Markoff, "In Line for an iPhone, and Then Prevented from Turning It On," *The New York Times*, July 12, 2008, p. C1, accessed via Factiva.

[126] Rob Pegoraro, "The iPhone, Rehashed," *The Washington Post*, July 17, 2008, p. D3, accessed via Factiva.

[127] Leslie Cauley, "Dropped Calls Plague iPhone 3G," *USA Today*, August 15, 2008, p. B3, accessed via Factiva.

[128] Nick Wingfield, "Will Masses Embrace Apple's $199 Handset?" The Wall Street Journal, June 10, 2008, p. B1, accessed via Factiva; "iPhone 3G: On the Nation's Fastest Network," AT&T Mobility, http://www.wireless.att.com/cell-phone-service/specials/iPhone.jsp, accessed August 2008.

[129] Leslie Cauley, "'We're All About Wireless': AT&T's Stephenson's iPhone Deal with Apple Is Part of Global Strategy," *USA Today*, August 1, 2008, p. B1, accessed via Factiva.

[130] Ibid.

[131] Philip Elmer-DeWitt, "What AT&T Pays Apple for the iPhone," Fortune.com, June 19, 2008, http://apple20.blogs.fortune.cnn.com/2008/06/19/what-att-pays-apple-for-the-iphone, accessd August 2008.

[132] Cauley, "'We're All About Wireless.'"

[133] Andrew LaVallee, "Best Buy to Sell iPhone," *The Wall Street Journal*, August 13, 2008, p. B6, accessed via Factiva.

[134] Pogue, "Apple Waves Its Wand at the Phone"; Charles Arthur, "The Hands-On Revolution," *The Guardian*, January 18, 2007, accessed via Factiva; Lev Grossman, "The Apple of Your Ear," *Time*, January 22, 2007, p. 48, accessed via Factiva.

[135] Natali T. Del Conte, "Apple Announces iPod Touch with Wi-Fi," PC Magazine website, September 5, 2007, accessed via Factiva.

[136] Sascha Segan, "iPhone 2.0: The New App Store Turns Any iPhone or iPod Touch into a True Smart Phone," *PC Magazine,* July 10, 2008, accessed via Factiva; Walter S. Mossberg and Katherine Boehret, "A Shopping Trip to the App Store for Your iPhone," *The Wall Street Journal,* July 23, 2008, p. D1, accessed via Factiva; Jeong Ho Yoon, "App Store and Apple's 3rd Party Application Strategy," ROA Group White Papers, July 31, 208, accessed via Factiva; Brian Caulfield, "Phone Apps for Adults," *Forbes,* August 11, 2008, p. 48b, accessed via Factiva.

[137] "Apple Chief Says iPhone Sales Take Off," Reuters News, August 11, 2008, accessed via Factiva.

[138] Joe Nocera, "Cute iPhone; Too Bad About the Battery," *The International Herald Tribune,* July 12, 2008, p. 11, accessed via Factiva; Sinead Carew, "Fans Drool over iPhone, but Ask for More," Reuters News, July 18, 2008, accessed via Factiva; Paul Taylor, "Apple Fails Blackberry Test," *Financial Times,* July 18, 2008, p. 10, accessed via Factiva; Galen Gruman, "Why iPhone 2.0 Won't Yet Rule the Roost in the Enterprise," InfoWorld Daily News, July 24, 2008, accessed via Factiva.

[139] Thomas Ricker, "The Lucky 22: Countries Receiving iPhone 3G on July 11th," Engadget (web log post), June 9, 2008, http://www.engadget.com/2008/06/09/the-lucky-22-countries-receiving-iphone-3g-on-july-11th, accessed August 2008.

[140] Hesseldahl and Schenker, "iPhone 2.0 Takes on the World"; Dominic White and James Quinn, "Rivals Beware: Now the Apple Revolution Has Really Started," *The Daily Telegraph* (London), June 17, 2008, p. 7, accessed via Factiva; Kiselyova and Taylor, "Apple in No Rush to Bring iPhone to Russia, China"; Chi-Chu Tschang, "Apple Struggles to Win Fans in China," BusinessWeek.com, July 22, 2008, accessed via Factiva.

[141] Arik Hesseldahl, "Inside the Latest iPhone," BusinessWeek.com, June 24, 2008, accessed via Factiva; Arik Hesseldahl, "Tearing Down the iPhone 3G," BusinessWeek.com, July 16, 2008, accessed via Factiva.

[142] Adrian Bathgate and Christine Kearney, "New iPhone Snapped Up in Asia, Europe; Snags in US," Reuters News, July 14, 2008, accessed via Factiva; Therese Poletti, "Even with Glitches, iPhone Sales Surge at Launch," Dow Jones News Service, July 15, 2008, accessed via Factiva.

[143] Hiawatha Bray, "No, It's not the New iPhone: Sprint Nextel's Instinct Has Some Fine Features, But Overall Apple Wins Again," *The Boston Globe,* July 3, 2008, p. E1, accessed via Factiva; "LG 'Dares' Apple iPhone Hold," Korea Times, July 3, 2008, accessed via Factiva.

[144] Matt Hartley, "RIM's Bold Move into the Future," *The Globe and Mail* (Toronto), August 18, 2008, p. B1, accessed via Factiva; Brian Deagon, "Bold, Thunder, Flip: Blackberry Maker Begins Key Rollouts," *Investor's Business Daily,* August 21, 2008, accessed via Factiva.

[145] Even Koblentz, "Apple's iPhone 3G Is Poised to Re-Invigorate the Smartphone Market, But Is the Industry Prepared to React?" *Wireless Week,* July 1, 2008, p. 16, accessed via Factiva; "The HTC Diamond Touch Looks Like the Perfect iPhone Killer, Except for One Fatal Flaw," *The Guardian* (London), July 10, 2008, p. 4, accessed via Factiva; Jennifer Dudly-Nicholson, "Smartphone War," *The Courier-Mail,* August 20, 2008, p. H19, accessed via Factiva.

[146] Miguel Helft and John Markoff, "Google Enters the Wireless World," *The New York Times,* November 5, 2007, http://www.nytimes.com/2007/11/05/technology/05cnd-gphone.html, accessed November 2007.

[147] "HTC to Launch World's First Android Phones in U.S. in Sept.," Taiwan Economic News," August 14, 2008, accessed via Factiva; Laura M. Holson and Miguel Helft, "Smartphone Is Expected Via Google," *The New York Times,* August 15, 2008, p. C1, accessed via Factiva.

[148] Markoff, "Oh, Yeah, He Also Sells Computers."

MICHAEL Y. YOSHINO

PERRY L. FAGAN

The Renault-Nissan Alliance

We are not merging, we are creating a binational company.

—Louis Schweitzer, chairman and CEO of Renault SA[1]

We are managing the apparent contradiction between synergy and identity.

—Carlos Ghosn, president and CEO of Nissan Motors[2]

On Wednesday, May 29, 2002, the board of directors of Renault-Nissan BV (RNBV) met for the first time to discuss the state of the alliance between Renault SA and Nissan Motors—two of the world's largest automakers. RNBV was a 50/50 joint venture company established in March of that year to oversee the strategy of the alliance and all activities undertaken jointly by Renault and Nissan.[3] The new company would "steer alliance strategy and supervise common activities on a global level, while respecting the identity and culture of each company and not interfering in operations."[4] Louis Schweitzer, Renault's chairman and CEO, held the position of president of the RNBV board; while Nissan CEO Carlos Ghosn held the position of vice president (see **Exhibit 1**). Renault and Nissan would continue to run their operations under their respective management teams.

"The creation of RNBV is the next natural step in the evolution of the [a]lliance," declared Yoshikazu Hanawa, Nissan's chairman. "It demonstrates that a Japanese and a French company, deeply rooted in their own culture and identity, have been able to cooperate successfully, without losing their uniqueness."[5]

In 1999 Renault had invested $5.4 billion in Nissan—for 36.8% of the company—at a time when Nissan was a struggling automaker rumored to be days away from bankruptcy. The investment was a bold bid by Renault to gain additional scale and global reach, and marked the largest ever investment by foreigners in a Japanese industrial company. Shortly before the RNBV board meeting,

---

[1] David Gauthier-Villars, "Car Making: What Makes Carlos Ghosn Tick?" *Far Eastern Economic Review*, September 14, 2000, p. 60.

[2] As quoted in "Halfway down a long road," *The Economist*, August 18, 2001.

[3] The companies established a foundation in the Netherlands, which would hold options on preferred stock issued by Renault-Nissan BV. This structure was intended to protect the two companies from potential takeover bids.

[4] Source: Renault-Nissan joint press release, October 30, 2001.

[5] Ibid.

Professor Michael Y. Yoshino and Senior Research Associate Perry L. Fagan prepared this case. HBS cases are developed solely as the basis for class discussion. Cases are not intended to serve as endorsements, sources of primary data, or illustrations of effective or ineffective management.

Renault and Nissan had executed a cross-shareholding agreement wherein Renault raised its stake in Nissan to 44.4%, and Nissan acquired a 15% stake in Renault for roughly 2.2 billion euros.[6] The transaction, which had been written into the original alliance agreement, took place a year earlier than expected.[7]

Executives at both companies believed much had been accomplished in the first three years of the alliance. Nissan, under Ghosn's leadership, had improved its finances dramatically and was rapidly reemerging as a major player in the global auto industry. Nissan's profit accounted for 47% of Renault's profit for the fiscal year 2001. In 2001 the two companies sold a combined five million automobiles (Nissan sold 2.6 million while Renault sold 2.4 million; see **Exhibit 2**). The alliance share of the world market came to more than 9.2% (4.4% for Renault and 4.8% for Nissan), positioning the alliance among the world's top five automakers. Moreover, the alliance partners were in line with their initial forecast of $3.3 billion in cost savings and synergies promised by 2002, according to their internal reporting.

As the board prepared to meet, Schweitzer and Ghosn believed the alliance faced difficult challenges ahead. To what extent would the two companies be able to realize further savings and synergies, particularly in the areas of manufacturing and additional sales? How should the RNBV board address issues that had surfaced as employees of the two firms worked together across disparate corporate and national cultures, functions, and geographies? Ultimately, would the two firms be able to strike a balance between deepening their alliance while "respecting the identity and culture of each company and not interfering in operations?"

History of the Alliance

Renault, the oldest automaker in France, had been nationalized by Charles de Gaulle in 1945. The company had been profitable in all years but one during the 1990s, but its profit margins generally had been slim. In 1996 the firm lost $900 million, including a $700 million restructuring charge. In the late 1990s Renault's financial performance had been buoyed by a strong European car market, several popular new models, and extensive cost-cutting.

Renault sold about 85% of its cars in Western Europe—a third of them in France alone—and maintained a marginal presence outside its home region. The company had withdrawn from the U.S. market in 1987 and had only a tiny presence in Asia. As a result, Renault was principally a maker of small- to medium-size cars, with little participation in the markets for premium cars and light trucks (including sport utility vehicles).

To address this imbalance Schweitzer began looking for potential partners. An early attempt to merge with Swedish automaker Volvo had failed in 1993. "[After that] we were looking towards internationalization, but there were no European partners that made sense," Schweitzer recalled. "To look for an American partner made no sense because they were so much larger. The Asian financial

---

[6] The shares acquired by Nissan were ordinary shares. However, under French self-control law the shares did not confer voting rights on Nissan. Under Japanese rules, 15% was the minimum level that allowed the consolidation of the partners' financial results by the equity method. Meanwhile, the French government took advantage of suitable market conditions to reduce its stake from 44% to 26%.

[7] Renault raised its stake in Nissan effective March 1, 2002, while Nissan raised its stake in Renault through two capital increases on March 29 and May 28, 2002.

2

crisis [of 1997] created opportunities [for us]."[8] "We felt [finding a partner] was a matter of survival," added a company veteran.

Schweitzer, 58, a 16-year Renault veteran who was described as "cerebral," "soft-spoken" and "diplomatic," had previously served as chief of staff to Laurent Fabius, French prime minister in the early 1980s, and before that as a director of the country's budget department.

Schweitzer reportedly met with executives from some of Asia's leading auto companies to discuss the possibility of a cooperation agreement, with Nissan emerging as the favorite.

At the time Nissan was a company on the verge of collapse, weighed down by flagging sales (Nissan had been losing market share for 27 years in the Japanese market), and poor returns (the firm had only one profitable year in the period 1992–1999). Moreover, Nissan was saddled with $20 billion in debt and was under pressure from its banks to find a financial partner. Analysts blamed Nissan's poor performance on bland styling, infrequent model changes, high manufacturing and parts costs, and bureaucratic decision-making. Within Japan Nissan was famous for its bureaucratic management style, which earned its head office located in the Ginza district of Tokyo the nickname "Ginza Kasumigaseki." (Kasumigaseki was the district in which all of Japan's government ministries were located.[9]) Talks were also underway between Nissan and several other suitors, including German-American rival DaimlerChrysler.

Due Diligence

According to Schweitzer, Renault approached the Nissan alliance carefully, in part because of lessons it had learned in the wake of its failed merger with Volvo Schweitzer explained:

> In the Volvo deal, we weren't sensitive enough about the feelings within Volvo. We remembered this when we started [discussions] with Nissan. Before taking a stake in Nissan, we did a lot of homework. We arrived at an analysis where we felt that this was a good company with management problems.

> There was a major effort to build a good understanding of the state of the company, the technical, engineering and the financial sides. We had looked into it for six to eight months. We had many meetings from July 1998 up to March 1999. During these meetings with top management, we wanted to get people to know each other before agreeing. In many marriages today, people go for marriage without knowing each other well. There was a good personal relationship before we started.[10]

In March 1999, Schweitzer and Hanawa signed the Renault-Nissan Alliance and Equity Participation agreement (see **Exhibit 3**). Renault took a 36.8% stake in Nissan for $5.4 billion. In addition, Renault obtained warrants to purchase 540 million shares to be newly issued by Nissan at 400 yen per share, granting Renault the right to increase its stake up to 39.9% of Nissan at any time,

---

[8] As quoted in Tim Burt and David Owen, "Renault's Global Gamble: The French carmaker's strategy of buying into financially troubled Asian and east European manufacturers to achieve competitive scale could backfire," *Financial Times* (London), May 30, 2000, p. 26.

[9] Robert Ashton, David Moorcroft and Clive Wiggins, "Nissan Motor: More that just a cost-cutting story," Commerzbank Securities, November 6, 2001, p. 17.

[10] Scott Miller, "Renault Steers Forward. After a Failed Marriage to Volvo, Schweitzer Gets It Right with Nissan. Car Makers Overcome Culture Clash via a Common Strategy," *The Wall Street Journal*, February 15, 2001, p. 31.

and up to 44.4% from May 29, 2003, through May 28, 2004. Nissan was given the right to purchase Renault shares under terms to be decided later.[11]

In June Schweitzer dispatched to Tokyo his second-in-command, Carlos Ghosn (pronounced "Ghone"), 48, who had joined Renault as executive vice president in October 1996 after 18 years at Michelin Tire Company. Ghosn, a bushy-browed Brazilian born to a French mother and a Brazilian father, spoke five languages and was a graduate of the prestigious French École Polytechnique. At Renault the energetic Ghosn earned the nickname "Le Cost Killer" for implementing a sweeping cost reduction program, which included controversial plant closings.

"If I didn't have Mr. Ghosn, I would not have done the deal with Nissan," said Schweitzer."

Upon his arrival at Nissan, Ghosn took over as chief operating officer. He brought with him two Renault veterans: Thierry Moulonguet to serve as Nissan deputy chief financial officer, and Patrick Pelata to serve as executive vice president of Nissan's Strategy and Planning Group.

Ghosn explained the rationale for the Renault investment: "On paper, the deal made sense for both sides: Nissan's strength in North America filled an important gap for Renault, while Renault's cash reduced Nissan's mountain of debt. The capabilities of the two companies were also complementary: Renault was known for innovative design and Nissan for the quality of its engineering."[12] (See **Exhibit 4**.)

However, the financial markets gave the alliance a decidedly cool reception in the days following the announcement. "We were called 'the marriage of the poor,'" recalled a Nissan executive. Another report dubbed the relationship the "alliance of the weak."[13] (See **Exhibits 5 and 6**.)

"As many people know, Renault was not Nissan's number one choice for partner," Ghosn explained. "DaimlerChrysler was the preferred counterpart, which on paper was not that surprising, given its financial muscle and reputation at the time. In the end, DaimlerChrysler dropped out [of negotiations with Nissan], believing that Nissan was too risky. In the words of one Chrysler executive, bailing out Nissan would have been like putting $5 billion into a steel container and throwing it into the ocean."[14] (See **Exhibit 7**.)

Moulonguet recalled the atmosphere in the boardroom the first time Renault executives met their counterparts at Nissan: "[It was] that of a company close to the end of the road." He remembered the first words a senior Nissan executive said to him were: "Please teach us how to make a profit."[15]

The Alliance in Practice

On the ground, the work of the alliance was performed by 11 "cross-company teams" (CCTs), which had been studying and realizing synergies across the major functional areas of both firms since

---

[11] For a discussion of the financial aspects of the Renault investment in Nissan, see Jeremy Cott and Thomas R. Piper, "Nissan Motor Company," HBS Case No. 200-067 (Boston: Harvard Business School Publishing, June 2, 2000).

[12] Carlos Ghosn, "Saving the Business Without Losing the Company," *Harvard Business Review*, January 2002.

[13] Yumiko Ono, "Lesson for Today: When in Japan, Bow to Shareholders—Nissan's Brazilian-Born President Feels the Heat for His Oversight," *The Asian Wall Street Journal*, June 21, 2000, p. 1.

[14] Ghosn, p. 11.

[15] David Ibison, "A blueprint for revival: Nissan's new deal: French-led management has rewritten the rule book on how to operate an alliance with a Japanese company," *Financial Times* (London), November 6, 2000, p. 22.

4

March 1999—in products, platforms, technology and markets. Teams were active in powertrains, vehicle engineering, purchasing, manufacturing and logistics, product planning, and sales and marketing. In addition, there were teams focused on markets and regions, including Mexico.

Each CCT consisted of approximately 10 members drawn from the ranks of middle managers, mostly people with line responsibilities. Their small size made it difficult for each team to cover all the issues in depth. Some teams formed sub-teams consisting of CCT members and other managers selected by the CCT. The sub-teams focused on particular issues facing the broader team. For example, the manufacturing team had four sub-teams, which reviewed capacity, productivity, fixed costs, and investments. All together, some 500 people from the two companies worked in the CCTs and sub-teams, supported by each company's line organization, including various functional task teams (FTTs).

Each CCT had a "pilot"—typically a manager with operating experience and credibility within the organization. CCT membership was not a full-time assignment, even for the pilot. Members had these responsibilities in addition to their regular jobs at Renault or Nissan. The amount of time devoted to the alliance was difficult to determine: for pilots, estimates ranged between 20% and 80% of their time; for members, around 20%.

Joint annual planning sessions were held for CCTs in each area. The purpose of these meetings was to set the goals to be achieved by the team in the coming year, and to identify the resources and personnel required to fulfill the objectives.

Ghosn recalled the evolution of the CCTs:

> At a certain point in the negotiations between the two companies, there was a discussion about how they would work together. Renault's negotiators assumed that the best way forward would be to set up a series of joint ventures, and they wanted to discuss all legal issues surrounding a joint venture: who contributes what and how much, how the output is shared, and so forth. The Nissan team pushed back; they wanted to explore management and business issues, not legal technicalities. As a result, negotiations were stalled.
>
> Schweitzer asked me if I could think of a way to resolve that impasse. I recommended abandoning the joint venture approach. If you want people to work together, the last thing you need is a legal structure that gets in the way. My solution was to introduce informal cross-company teams.
>
> Today the cross-company teams and the cross-functional teams [CFTs, working separately inside Nissan and Renault] have complementary roles: the company CFTs serve as guardians of each company's revival plan, while the CCTs feed the alliance.[16]

The Alliance Coordination Bureau

CCTs met each month to prepare a report on their progress to the Alliance Coordination Bureau (CB), headed by two executives: Pierre Martin in Paris, and Robert Ferraris in Tokyo. Martin explained the role of the CB: "We compare the original forecasts to the progress made by the CCTs, try to understand the variances, and we promote additional ideas in order to compensate." Martin and Ferraris and their respective staffs (which were small) typically stayed in close day-to-day

---

[16] Ghosn, p. 9.

contact with the CCTs, and were often asked for assistance in resolving communication or other difficulties encountered during the teams' work.

In addition to the reporting function, the CB performed three other functions—namely, (1) providing specialized technical advice such as legal, accounting, etc., (2) trying to resolve company-wide policy issues that went beyond a single CCT, such as how to determine the fees for certain services provided, etc.; and (3) trying to resolve specific conflicts within the CCTs in a given area.

The CB reported the results of the CCTs to the governing body of the alliance. Prior to the creation of RNBV, Martin and Ferraris reported CCT activity to the Alliance Board (AB) (see **Exhibit 8**). The AB, consisting of the chairmen, CEOs and executive vice presidents of the partner companies, had met once per month (most of the time face-to-face) for an entire day. The meeting location alternated between Paris and Tokyo.

An engineering steering committee met one day before each AB meeting to discuss critical engineering issues (for example, deciding on a common engine) and to develop joint recommendations to the AB. The membership included the executive vice presidents in charge of development and manufacturing from both partners, and two or three other senior executives. These discussions were characterized as "detailed" and "often controversial."

After AB meetings CCTs met again to discuss the governing body's decisions. Martin explained: "We try to ensure that the decisions taken by the AB are correctly cascaded down to the teams and put into action. "Our job at the CB," said Ferraris, "is to make sure decisions are being taken on time and that decision-making is transparent. We are building a commitment culture, with personal commitments and team commitments."

In addition to the monthly meetings, the partners had held two Alliance Conventions, attended by leading CCT members and others involved in the alliance (about 160 people) for one full day to review progress and to share best practices and experiences. The meeting was attended by Schweitzer and Ghosn, as well as all senior executives from both companies. The location of the annual meeting alternated between Paris and Tokyo.

By mid-2002 joint projects between Renault and Nissan that had been identified by CCTs were underway in six major areas: joint purchasing, R&D, manufacturing, joint distribution, joint information systems, and platform sharing.

Joint Purchasing

Renault and Nissan executives reported that their joint purchasing efforts were impacting both companies, resulting in significant savings. Jean-Baptiste Duzan, senior vice president of purchasing and chairman and CEO of the 100-person Renault-Nissan Purchasing Organization (RNPO), said that under the alliance, Renault had adopted Nissan's quality management system and Nissan was following Renault's use of modules in vehicle design.

Renault and Nissan formed RNPO as a 50/50 joint venture on April 2, 2001, to purchase parts, materials, and services for the two companies. RNPO was a virtual organization—comprised of employees of both Renault and Nissan in France, Japan, and the United States. Three general managers reported to Saikawa, executive general manager: in powertrain components (gasoline-engine and diesel-engine management systems, catalysts, turbochargers, starters, alternators, and batteries); vehicle parts (harnesses, glass, fuel systems and engine cooling systems, seats, safety systems, brakes, wheels, tires, suspension, steering parts); and materials and services (paint, energy, travel, consulting, and information technology).

Under each general manager were two global supplier account managers (GSAMs), one each in Paris and Tokyo. GSAMs were "the core of the operation," according to Hiroto Saikawa, RNPO's executive general manager.[17] They were responsible for purchasing strategy and sourcing nominations and decisions, plus the performance review and assessment of suppliers. Assisting each GSAM was a deputy (DGSAM). RNPO's policy was to pair GSAMs and DGSAMs in such a way that if a GSAM was from Renault, he or she would work in France while the DGSAM would come from Nissan and be based in Tokyo. GSAMs from Nissan based in Tokyo would likewise be paired with a DGSAM from Renault based in Paris. "The 'mirror effects' of the alliance are very helpful," said Ferraris. "You get to talk to someone who does the same job as you. This is highly unusual in business."

By mid-2002, RNPO accounted for around 30% of the companies' purchases. Duzan hoped to reach 44% by the end of the year, and 70% eventually. "There is no doubt we are on track," he said. "All financial objectives have been achieved. It works. It is a real common organization. We are already buying more than 100% of the previous Renault total. We can do more. We can go further, much further."

Duzan believed that the quality of Renault's products had improved measurably under RNPO: "We have not reached the Nissan level, but we are on the curve," he explained. "When we say common suppliers, it means common standards. We can only choose the supplier together if we agree on everything—including quality."[18]

Yasuhiro Yamauchi, pilot of the purchasing CCT, believed that in the purchasing area Nissan had learned much from Renault, particularly in how to manage the supplier selection process. "In the past, at Nissan suppliers were already determined and they worked together to get to the target price during the development process. This was an approach commonly used in Japan," explained Yamauchi. After joining forces with Renault, Nissan began telling potential suppliers its target price and if it could not meet it, it would be eliminated right from the start. "The approach creates a lot of 'constructive' tension," Yamauchi said.

Yamauchi saw challenges for the purchasing team stemming from differences in measurement criteria and incentives at Renault and Nissan. "For example, commitments and targets are used only within Nissan, but not in Renault, where targets are expressed only as opportunities," he said. "This is a problem and should be evaluated."

Another difficulty lay in reaching consensus on which parts should be common and purchased jointly by RNPO. The selection of parts could be quite complex and required the active participation and support of the engineering groups of the partner companies. Renault was reportedly much more aggressive in trying to increase the number of common parts to be purchased jointly, while Nissan's engineers were viewed as more cautious. Some engineers at Nissan argued that the difference stemmed from the fact that Renault's most important market was Europe, whereas Nissan's were Japan and the United States. Nissan engineers believed that the market requirements in Japan and the United States were different from those in Europe, and were often more rigorous. Therefore, despite the obvious cost savings from joint purchasing, Nissan remained more cautious than Renault in increasing the range of common parts.

---

[17] As quoted in Colin Whitbread, "Renault and Nissan learn from each other," *Automotive News Europe*, May 20, 2002, p. 8.

[18] Ibid.

Some speculated that another reason Nissan was not as aggressive in pushing for common parts was that it did not enjoy as strong a position relative to the engineering group as its counterpart at Renault. "Nissan has long been an engineering-dominated company and culture," said a Nissan manager.

Finally, some employees felt the benefits of joint purchasing had been one-sided, with Nissan receiving the bulk of the benefit while its contribution to Renault had been limited. The willingness of each partner to contribute to the effort would be critical going forward.

R&D

The two companies intended to work together in basic research and development. As a first step, in March 2001 the companies launched a joint program for basic fuel-cell technologies that was expected to cost about 85 billion yen. Analysts expected the companies to realize significant cost savings by sharing basic research and development.

Manufacturing

Despite Nissan's poor performance for decades, it had excellent manufacturing capability. Nissan operated the most productive auto plants in North America and Europe, and had always been near the top of surveys of reliability. In Europe, Nissan produced 101 vehicles per employee a year at its plant in Sunderland, England, in 2000. In contrast, Renault produced 77 vehicles per employee a year at its most productive plant. Several years before the alliance, Renault had begun benchmarking Nissan's manufacturing capability and had sent people to Nissan's plant in the United Kingdom, considered the most productive in Europe.

Nissan managers believed Renault had a lot to learn about engineering, production processes, and product quality. As part of the alliance teams of Nissan, engineers and executives had been dispatched to help upgrade technical standards at Renault. "If you have a very productive [manufacturing] system, as we do at Nissan," explained Ghosn, "that means you have very good practices. So these practices are being analyzed by Renault and transported from Nissan to Renault. Also, the level of reliability of Nissan cars is very high. Renault has benchmarked this and has said there are a lot of practices in terms of the management of quality that they would like to adopt."

Inside manufacturing plants, Nissan advisors were working with Renault line-workers to improve their dexterity and basic skills. With Nissan's help, Renault had created dexterity schools teaching, among other skills, the proper use of a screwdriver, how best to paint a car, and how to work with the right or left hand. "We have come to recognize that in manual work there is skill. We learned this from Nissan," said a Renault executive.

In April 2002, a newspaper report offered this view of Nissan's contribution at the plant level:

Anyone walking through a Renault plant can see the early signs of Nissan's influence there. Wearing green overalls as they do at Nissan, Japanese production experts gather up groups of 10 or so gray-clad Renault laborers to lecture them on basic assembly-line technique. One group meets only a couple of meters from the workers' stations on the line; painted lines on the concrete floor mark the boundaries of the classroom. Speaking through an interpreter, a serious-looking Japanese tells the French that he noticed some of them were using two hands to hold drills that screw on door panels. That won't do. Holding the drill out for all to see, he shows them how to grip with one hand. Now, he says, they can use their free hand to hold screws.[19]

The Nissan influence was also visible at the individual workstations on the assembly line. So-called "standard operating papers" (SOPS), which explained how to perform particular tasks, were posted next to work schedules and absentee rates on bulletin boards near the line, where workers could take breaks. SOPs were written by senior assembly-line workers with guidance from engineers, and were designed to be understandable to factory-floor workers.

Prior to the alliance, at Renault these instructions were sent straight from the engineering department to the line and were often complex and technical. For example, workers connecting dashboard wires were previously given elaborate schematic diagrams to decipher. Under the Nissan method, they were instead given an easy-to-follow one-page guide with hand-drawn sketches showing which wires to connect first, how to reach them, and what tools to use. Experiments at eight Renault plants to test the effectiveness of the SOPs had reportedly gone well, and the SOPs were about to be adopted company-wide.

"We were a bit concerned about how some of our guys, who have been doing their jobs for years, would react to this kind of basic instruction," said Jean-Marc Calloud, director for industrial strategy and performance development at Renault. "But we know a lot of this makes sense. This not only has helped us reduce the number of errors on the line, but it has been a real morale booster for assembly-line leaders who now have more important jobs."[20]

Nissan's approach to manufacturing was also raising quality at Renault's purchasing department:

Before the alliance, Renault factory workers would report defective parts to Renault's purchasing department, which often as not would make a quick phone call to the supplier to find out what went wrong. Now the quality department of Renault's purchasing operation has explained to all its suppliers that every time production at a factory is stopped because of bad parts, they will get calls from senior staff and detailed letters. Exceed a given number of bad-parts incidents, suppliers have been told, and they will lose Renault's business. For the first time in years, Renault has gone three months without having to halt production because of bad parts. Renault expected the number of defects per million parts would fall to the level of the Nissan Sunderland plant by 2003.[21]

Nissan also introduced Renault to its *Kaizen*, or continuous improvement process, and to "synchronous production" techniques, showing Renault managers how to organize upstream logistics so parts could be delivered in the right order at the right time. This helped Renault reduce in-process inventories.

"There is little that we did not know before," said Philippe LeBorne, director of the Industrial System Performance Deployment group at Renault, and copilot of the manufacturing and logistics CCT. "But what is new is Nissan's ability to be practical and operational. In the French mind, nobody liked standards and standardization as it was supposed to imply a loss of freedom. But things are changing now and people understand that standardization is, on the contrary, the right frame in which to put their ideas and to progress." Ferraris added: "Japanese are very concrete. Details,

[19] Scott Miller and Todd Zaun, "Nissan Intends to Return a Favor to a French Ally," *The Asian Wall Street Journal*, April 5–7, 2002.

[20] Ibid.

[21] Ibid.

details, details. French like a macro, general idea and abstract concepts. The two are very complementary. Americans are more organized, more structured. They are somewhere between the Japanese and French."

Kuniaki Okumi, pilot of the manufacturing/logistics CCT, agreed:

One of Renault's problems was it lacked the concept of standard procedures. At Nissan all the manufacturing processes are carefully analyzed and standardized; thus, it is easy to judge whether a particular worker is performing his job right. A reason for this difference is that Renault has much smaller number of models; thus, they can fill a 20,000-unit line with one model, where at Nissan we require a number of different models to fill a line. It is very difficult for workers to work on a line making multiple models.

Okumi also noted that Nissan's effort to assist Renault in manufacturing involved worldwide efforts. Nissan's United States division was particularly helpful in this regard, he said.

A Renault executive explained: "It is always the same with the Japanese. They set up standards and formats and stick to them. It works."

While most of the benefits of the alliance in manufacturing seemed headed to Renault, Nissan, for its part, identified cost management and factory ergonomics as areas where it could learn from Renault. According to Okumi, Nissan had adopted Renault's cost-management system and it had become a part of Nissan's annual budgetary system. He explained: "In the past, Nissan's approach was to reduce a certain percentage from the prior year's cost base. Now it is done on a per-unit basis, rather than on the total cost. Managers must commit to a given numerical target, and it cannot be debated. This is a commitment and you must achieve it. In the past, the people thought of all sorts of reasons why the goals could not be achieved. Now, not only there is a commitment, but there is a stretch target, so even one who achieves the commitment must keep working to achieve the stretch target."

Looking ahead, LeBorne saw significant challenges for the alliance in manufacturing: "To make further progress we will need to build common policies in quality, design, and technology, which is in process. Not to be able to do it would be a weakness of the alliance, because if we want to use our industrial system as a common alliance system, be able to build a Nissan or Renault car, and to do it in the most efficient way, that is imperative. Achieving this convergence is not an easy thing, but that is, for me, a key point."

Okumi saw another issue: "Because the benefits of the alliance in manufacturing have been perceived to be one way, from Nissan to Renault, I have had a difficult time persuading very busy people at Nissan to contribute to the alliance. Most of them were busy trying to help Nissan's turnaround, including plant closings, transferring production lines and creation of new models, etc. They were just too busy."

Sharing Factories: Mexico and Brazil

In December 2000, Renault and Nissan began producing the Renault *Scénic* at Nissan's plant in Cuernavaca, Mexico, marking Renault's return to the Mexican market. (It had withdrawn from Mexico in 1986.) The two companies began producing Renault's *Clio* in December 2001.[22]

"The improvement in Nissan's manufacturing position [in Mexico] has been dramatic," proclaimed Ghosn. He continued:

> At the Cuernavaca plant, the capacity utilization rate has risen from 55% at the end of 1998 to nearly 100%. For Renault's part, the arrangement greatly accelerated its reentry into Mexico. In fact, Renault was able to begin selling cars in Mexico even before the first *Scénic* rolled off the production line. Because the Mexican government recognized Renault as a partner of the Nissan group, Renault was able to immediately export cars to Mexico without having to obtain separate government approval. What's more, Renault could use Nissan's local dealers as distributors.[23]

Mr. Patrice Ratti, who managed the Mexico project on the Renault side and was head of the firm's Mexico subsidiary, remarked: "Only 16 months after the decision, we have been able to produce a Renault car within a Nissan factory using the same paint line and final assembly line as Nissan cars; with a second, one year later. The two projects were done on time and within the cost target." Nissan was also helping Renault to build a network of dealers in Mexico, working with local advertising agencies, and was helping Renault set up financing programs.

"In terms of cooperation, Mexico was easy in a sense that Renault depended almost entirely on Nissan to reenter the market," said Ichiro Yoshizawa, pilot of the Mexico CCT. "Reentry on its own would have been nearly impossible for Renault. In fact, the discussion of possible collaboration in Mexico had begun before the discussion of a potential alliance even started. So, we hit the ground running, as soon as the alliance was formed."

Both Ratti and Yoshizawa said they were proud of the fact that Mexico produced the first tangible benefits of the alliance.

Brazil

On December 20, 2001, Schweitzer and Ghosn opened a new Renault light commercial vehicle (LCV) assembly plant built at Renault's industrial complex in Brazil.[24] The new Renault facility was the first new plant that had been planned and built to be shared by the two companies. The opening of the plant marked the arrival of Nissan as a local Brazilian manufacturer. The new plant assembled the Renault *Master* van and, beginning in April 2002, Nissan's *Frontier* pickup. The *Frontier* was the first Nissan vehicle assembled in a Renault plant. Renault and Nissan had reportedly invested a total of $236 million in the project. Nissan expected sales in Brazil to increase to approximately 4,000 units in 2002.

---

[22] However, because both models were designed before the Renault-Nissan alliance, they shared no common engineering with the Nissan cars already being built in the factory, and were thus built on a partly separate production line.

[23] Ghosn, p. 9.

[24] The Renault complex comprised two assembly plants—a powertrain plant and supplier operations. Renault had a network of 160 dealers in Brazil. Renault's share of the passenger-car market in Brazil was 5.4% in the first 11 months of 2001, placing it fifth in the market behind Ford, with 6.4%.

The companies planned to use factory sharing as a way to help each other enter new markets, particularly in South America and Asia. In addition, in late 2002 Nissan would assemble an LCV derived from a Renault model to be sold by Nissan, Renault, and General Motors in Europe.

Joint Distribution

During 2000, Nissan started to merge its back-office operation in Europe with that of Renault. Nissan claimed that this step would reduce back-office costs by 20%. In Europe, Renault dealers were also gaining the right to sell Nissan cars. Meanwhile, Renault acquired all of Nissan's European financing subsidiaries, and a joint distribution organization was being established. The companies would keep their respective brands and customer-service organizations separate, however.

In Japan, as well as in other parts of Asia, Nissan began offering Renault models at its dealerships. Renault planned to increase its annual sales in Japan from 2,175 in 2000, to 15,000 in 2004, to 30,000 by the end of the decade. However, Japanese consumers viewed non-Japanese cars with skepticism, with foreign brands accounting for only 5% of the total market for cars (and that 5% included mostly the premium German brands Mercedes-Benz, BMW, and Porsche).

"We tried putting some Renault cars in a Tokyo showroom, but Japanese customers did not like the designs at all," said the head of a Tokyo Nissan dealership in September 2000. "The interiors of Renault cars look cheap and shoddy, and I will not try very hard to sell them if I am forced to put them in my showroom."[25] One Nissan executive, upon reading these comments, said he doubted the dealer's comment was representative of all comments.

Outside of Japan, Renault had entered the Australian market through a Nissan-owned distributor that planned to help Renault gain 5% market share by 2007. Similar actions had been taken in Taiwan and Indonesia, and other markets in Southeast Asia were being considered.

Nissan hoped to use the alliance with Renault to gain greater access to markets in South America. Renault was already an established presence there, but its market share remained small. Poor road quality in many areas and the need to transport relatively large groups of people meant that the small, light cars produced by Renault were often not as well-suited to customer's needs as were the rugged pickup trucks and four-wheel-drive vehicles offered by Nissan. The two companies hoped to roughly double their current market share of 7% (most of which was Renault's) by 2010.

The companies developed plans to re-badge Renault's *Master* and *Trafic* LCVs for sale in Europe starting, respectively, in March and September 2002.[26] Nissan began to sell Renault's *Master* under the name "Interstar" from March 2002. Nissan Motor Iberica in Spain started to produce part of Renault's *Trafic* and to sell some vehicles under the Nissan "Primaster" name. Other vehicles under consideration included the marketing of Renault-badged versions of some of Nissan's truck-based products in emerging markets.

---

[25] Benjamin Fulford, "Renaissance at Nissan," *Forbes*, October 2, 2000, p. 80.

[26] Re-badging was a process wherein one company's nameplate was attached to a slightly repackaged existing model developed and produced by another company. It allowed a company to quickly and cheaply round out its product range under its own brand. However, often the designs and product characteristics of a car produced by one company did not reflect the designs and product attributes of another. As a result, re-badged vehicles rarely sold in large volumes. Nissan had previously tried such arrangements with its *Terrano II* SUV, supplied to Ford for sale under the *Maverick* name in Europe, and the Ford *Windstar* minivan, supplied to Nissan and sold under the name *Quest*.

Joint Information Systems

Senior managers at the two companies believed that harmonizing information systems worldwide would be essential to building a strong alliance. In July 2002, the companies established the Renault-Nissan Information Services (RNIS) to aid the integration of logistics, production, and distribution systems worldwide. Renault and Nissan were working to merge their manufacturing processes and production methods over the next several years.

Platform Sharing

At the time the two companies signed the alliance agreement, Nissan had three times as many platforms as Renault (24 versus 8). Nissan had managed to reduce the number of platforms by about 10, and planned to reduce the number further in the coming years by eliminating low-volume platforms. "A platform is the part of the car the customer doesn't see," explained a Renault manager. Cars built on the same platform shared the basic floorplan that was the core of the car body, and employed a common range of engines, gear boxes, and other parts. Renault and Nissan planned to build all of their cars on the same 10 platforms.

The first two platforms under joint development were the B (subcompact) and C (compact) platforms (see **Exhibit 9**), which the companies estimated would account for more than 50% of production volumes by 2006.

The first model, based on the smaller B platform, the Nissan *March*, was launched in Japan in spring 2002. Early sales were promising. The *March* would appear in Europe later in 2002 as the *Micra*. Another Nissan model, the *Cube*, would launch in Japan in summer 2002, with roughly 90% shared components. Renault's redesigned *Clio* and *Twingo* models (based on the new platform) were expected to debut in Europe in late 2004. All in all, each model would share with the other models on the same platform a minimum of 50% of platform components. However, each member of the alliance retained full control over its own designs in order to preserve brand identity.

Joint work on the larger C platform began in February 2001. The first model on this platform, Renault's redesigned *Megane*, was expected in late 2002. Other models planned for this platform included the Renault *Scénic*, the Nissan *Sunny* and *Sentra*, and the next-generation *Primera*. For different models within the same regional area, the commonality was expected to be 80% of platform components.

Analysts estimated that if Renault-Nissan's expectations were met, the B and C platforms would rank among the largest three platforms in use by any auto manufacturer worldwide.

Managing Two Cultures

According to executives at the two companies, both Schweitzer and Ghosn paid personal attention to the smooth day-to-day functioning of the alliance. In July 1999 Schweitzer appointed Tsumoto Sawada, former executive vice president of Nissan responsible for engineering and manufacturing, as senior vice president at Renault and advisor to Schweitzer. Nissan management reportedly welcomed the appointment as an indication of Schweitzer's commitment to make the alliance work. Sawada was highly regarded within Nissan and, as the executive responsible for engineering, had overseen the most powerful group at the company. Sawada described his role at Renault:

I have no line responsibility. My main responsibility is to provide advice to Mr. Schweitzer and to his senior executives about how best to work with Nissan. One thing I can say unequivocally is that Messrs. Schweitzer and Ghosn are determined to make the alliance a success. They pay a lot of attention to making sure that the alliance works. I try to serve as a link between Nissan and Renault. Having worked for Nissan for forty years, I know most of the key people and I can talk with them quite openly. My primary responsibility is to make sure that there are few surprises between the partners.

Reflecting on the three years of experience in the alliance, Sawada had the following to say:

Alliance is like a marriage. The partners must make constant efforts to make a marriage a productive and happy one. It is a "give and take." At any point in time, seldom the contributions and benefits between the two companies are balanced. This is particularly true for a particular function, such as purchasing or manufacturing. We must take a long-term view. That is, of course, easier said than done. It takes time. Like a marriage, tensions and conflicts are unavoidable. I have learned that it is important to detect the problems early and deal with them quickly. The worst thing is to let the problem fester.

An executive at Nissan noted that in the course of negotiation, Schweitzer and Nissan chairman Hanawa developed close personal ties, which had served the alliance well. An executive familiar with the relationship between the two men stated: "These two men trust one another and they can talk about problems quite candidly." He went on to note, "Every time they get together, Schweitzer asks Hanawa how the people at Nissan feel about the alliance, and wants to know the real feelings of the ranks and file. It is not just a perfunctory question, but he is truly interested."

Another Nissan executive said: "From time to time, Ghosn protected us from what we thought were arbitrary demands from Renault. For example, in some areas, Renault people insisted on changing our approaches or systems to conform to their own. Sometimes, they were quite arbitrary. This was particularly true in the early days of the alliance. Ghosn was very careful in making sure to focus on activities that were important. He really means it when he says he wants to protect Nissan's identity."

Schweitzer, for his part, believed that managing the alliance successfully would mean the transfer of management technologies and best practices between the two companies, and not the merging of cultures, which, in his view, were inherently local. "We're establishing common goals. And we're looking for a good balance between the traditional Japanese bottom-up and the traditional French top-down management techniques." He continued:

I do not believe that in a car company you can separate the car, the brand, and the corporation. If you try to merge them without looking at these, you destroy brand value and brand identity. I also believe strongly that the best way to make a relationship work is by doing things together, achieving things together. Traditional mergers . . . run the risk of looking inward more than outward. When it is [a partnership] 13,000 kilometers away, with different languages, and where people look different and behave differently, you are always reminded that you are different. You have to accept this as a fact and not try to ignore it. We sent a management team to Nissan. We said to the people we were sending that you aren't representing Renault. You are sent by Renault to work for Nissan.[27]

---

[27] Christine Tierney, Anna Bawden, and Irene M. Kunii, "The Renault-Nissan pairing pays off," *Business Week*, October 23, 2000, p. 26.

Speaking English

The two firms officially adopted English as the language of the alliance. Only a limited number of executives at both companies spoke the language, however. "The language barrier was what we expected to be the most difficult barrier, and it has been," said Schweitzer."[28] English was a second language for both partners. "This turns out to be important," said an observer. "It tends to put both parties on an equal footing."

All Nissan employees, from receptionists to top executives, received intensive English training. "Having to speak English is very helpful, as it is not our native tongue; so we have to simplify our thoughts down to core issues," said Moulonguet. "[For example,] it turns out there are not two different ways to talk about important financial data."[29] Ghosn described English as a "utilitarian, non-proprietorial form of communication."[30]

English also was employed for internal e-mail, which was encouraged by Ghosn and Schweitzer. "E-mail is written speech," Schweitzer observed. "It makes written communication clearer. I don't think the alliance would be possible without it."

Teams based in Paris and Tokyo coordinated cross-company communications from within the CB. Martin explained:

> We have constant communication to explain the common activities of the alliance. I want to emphasize how important this is. Keep in mind that maybe 30–40% of Nissan employees are working in Japan. Therefore, their only direct contact with Renault is to know Renault in Japan. On the other side, 45% of Renault people are working in France. Similarly, their only direct contact with Nissan is to know the commercial activity of Nissan in France.

> If you consider the fact that the current market share of Nissan is 1.2% in France, and the fact that Renault is only selling 2,000–3,000 cars [annually] in Japan, you can imagine that the direct image those people have may not be the best one. So it is very important to provide to anyone working in Renault a correct and complete image of what is Nissan, and at the same time to provide to Nissan people a correct image of what is Renault.

Employee Perceptions

Schweitzer and Ghosn believed that the motivation of rank-and-file employees was critical to the success of the alliance. Ghosn said: "In the alliance our principle is not to impose things. You have to create the eagerness in each company to boost their performance. And when this eagerness is strong enough, then Nissan people will go by themselves to see what Renault is doing, and vice-versa. Everything which is imposed has limits. Everything which comes from eagerness and motivation from people, has no limits."

During January–February 2000, nearly 4,000 employees from each company worldwide were surveyed to gauge their views on the alliance. During November and December of the same year, the survey was repeated.

---

[28] Scott Miller, "Renault Steers Forward. After a Failed Marriage to Volvo, Schweitzer Gets It Right with Nissan. Car Makers Overcome Culture Clash via a Common Strategy," *The Wall Street Journal*, February 15, 2001, p. 31.

[29] Fulford, p. 80.

[30] Oliver Morgan, "Nissan's boy from Brazil puts accent on profits: 'Le Cost Killer' has closed plants but Sunderland is safe for now," *The Observer*, May 27, 2001, p. 7.

The second survey showed that both Renault and Nissan employees expressed a "strong commitment" to the alliance (Renault 83%, Nissan 68%), and their "personal contribution" remained at what the companies described as "a good level" (Renault 53%, Nissan 57%).

However, many employees expressed a strong desire for more information about the alliance, particularly managerial staff. (63% of Renault employees felt that they were sufficiently informed compared to 68% from the first survey; while at Nissan the result was 27% compared to 32%.) Renault personnel were reportedly more informed about the firms' common product-development strategy, and Nissan employees were more informed about the cost-reduction policy. In addition, the survey revealed that each team's familiarity with the other company had improved. It also underscored the need to clarify the relationship between each company's individual strategy and the alliance's strategy.

The results of the survey showed that the effects of the alliance were generally visible to employees. More employees at both companies, regardless of position, sector, or country of residence, reported witnessing the concrete effects of the alliance (up by 16% for Renault and by 38% for Nissan). Many reportedly felt that the objectives that had been set were in the process of being achieved (between 80% and 90% for Renault; between 60% and 69% for Nissan).

Renault employees reported being less worried about a potential loss of corporate identity than their Nissan counterparts, whose concern increased slightly over the first survey. Nissan employees were more confident than before that the alliance would work (64% compared to 57% from the first survey). The majority of employees surveyed reportedly rejected the notion that the alliance would disproportionately favor one or other of the partners.

Opinion was divided on the long-term future of the alliance, however. In both companies, most people thought it was important for the alliance to be continued. The majority of employees believed that Nissan's financial results would have a positive impact on the alliance. Finally, employees from both companies preferred to keep independent management structures (67% for Renault and 47% for Nissan) and to retain their brand image (89% for Renault and 82% for Nissan).[31]

According to employees at both firms, some of the CCTs had had rocky beginnings, but many said that the working relationships had become a lot smoother after three years of collaboration. Employees also stressed the importance of personal relationships between Nissan and Renault personnel, and their ability to communicate freely via e-mail. However, some reported that the inevitable turnover in personnel often complicated the relationships on the teams.

Finally, employees at both companies, particularly Nissan, reported feeling stressed by the additional work created by the alliance. This included not only CCT members but also others who had to help implement the decisions. Having to work cross nationally and use a foreign language was a stressful experience. Equally serious was the fact that the successful implementation of many actions (such as purchasing and manufacturing) involved the cooperation of many employees for whom the alliance was not their primary responsibility. This was particularly difficult for Nissan employees, because they were in the midst of their financial turnaround. Ghosn's emphasis on personal commitments to objectives—and the serious consequences if those commitments were not kept—only added to the tension at Nissan.

"Why is the alliance successful?" asked Schweitzer. "Because both sides wanted it. Both needed it. This need must be continually felt so that they stay together. People must feel every day that they are better off together."

---

[31] Survey data drawn from common internal Renault-Nissan documents.

"The way people see themselves at Nissan has changed," said Ghosn. "This is no longer an uncertain company with an uncertain future, but a strong company in a balanced alliance with Renault."[32]

A third survey was planned for September 2002, targeting a similar number of people.

More Synergies?

Going forward, each of the partners had distinct goals. Renault sought to improve profitability and to increase sales. Meanwhile, under Ghosn, Nissan had launched its next three-year operating plan, the "Nissan 180" plan. Nissan 180's targets included: 1) a global sales increase of one million units by 2004, 2) a consolidated operating margin of 8%; and 3) the complete elimination of net automotive interest-bearing debt by 2004. Schweitzer and Ghosn hoped to use the alliance to help each company succeed.

Schweitzer believed that a fundamental challenge in realizing additional synergies lay in developing closer ties between both companies' engineering departments. "The heart of the matter lies in the engineering department," he said. "Engineers tend to be rather proud and to think the way they do things is the right one. Engineering departments must be managed differently than other departments. I do not think it makes sense to try to merge them." "We will not merge engineering departments," agreed Georges Douin, executive vice president for strategic product planning and international operations. One major question that needed to be addressed, then, was how best for the engineering groups in the two companies to cooperate. The same was true for the firms' research functions.

An automotive analyst saw another challenge facing the two companies:

> The most serious issue now confronting Nissan is generating significant improvements to its model lineup via its alliance with Renault. The real test of the alliance's achievements is whether the partners are able to make products superior to those of their rivals, rather than just how much they are able to reduce costs.

> Reducing costs via component and platform standardization should only be a means to lowering the cost burden necessary to create high-caliber products. If Nissan's products created in the alliance are merely competitive with its rivals' soon-to-be superceded models, then the alliance has not resulted in any improvement to the company' competitiveness.[33]

---

[32] Tim Burt, "The ice-breaker sees open waters," *Financial Times* (London), March 21, 2001, p. 16.

[33] Noriyuki Matsushima and Shotaro Noguchi, "Nissan Motor (7201): Will the new March still be selling in October?" NikkoSalomonSmithBarney Equity Research Japan, March 12, 2002, pp. 12–13.

17

Exhibit 1   RNBV Board Members

President. Louis Schweitzer, Chairman and Chief Executive Officer, Renault, joined Renault in 1986 and became chief financial officer and head of strategic planning in 1988, then executive vice president in 1989. He was appointed president and chief operating officer in December 1990, and had been chairman and chief executive officer since May 1992.

Vice President. Carlos Ghosn, President and Chief Executive Officer, Nissan, joined Renault in October 1996 after his career at Michelin. In December he was appointed executive vice president in charge of advanced research, car engineering and development, car manufacturing, powertrain operations and purchasing. He joined Nissan as chief operating officer in June 1999, and became president in June 2000. In June 2001 he assumed the positions of president and chief executive officer.

Members

Pierre-Alain De Smedt, Executive Vice President, Renault. After a long career at Volkswagen Auto Group, where he was also chairman of SEAT, he joined Renault in 1999 as executive vice president, engineering, manufacturing and purchasing. He was also responsible for the Mercosur division.

Georges Douin, Executive Vice President, Renault. He joined Renault in 1967, and after a career in engineering and technology, was appointed senior vice president, product and strategic planning, and international operations in July 1997. He was appointed executive vice president in 1998.

François Hinfray, Executive Vice President, Renault. He joined Renault in 1989 as director in charge of European affairs. In October 1998 he became executive vice president, sales and marketing. He was also responsible for the light commercial vehicles division.

Norio Matsumura, Executive Vice President, Nissan, joined Nissan in April 1966. He became vice president of Nissan Europe N.V. in January 1992, chairman of Nissan Motor Espanã, S.A. in January 1995, executive vice president in charge of overseas operations in May 1999, and president of Nissan North America in April 2000. Since April 2001 he served as executive vice president in charge of global sales and marketing, North American operations, general overseas market operations, and Nissan's global parts business.

Nobuo Okubo, Executive Vice President, Nissan, joined Nissan in April 1964. Since May 1999 he had served as executive vice president in charge of engineering research and development, after a career in design, development, product planning and environmental and safety engineering.

Tadao Takahashi, Executive Vice President, Nissan. He joined Nissan in April 1968, and had spent most of his career in manufacturing. In April 2002 he was appointed executive vice president in charge of manufacturing, industrial machinery and the marine division.

Source: Company documents.

Exhibit 2   Renault-Nissan Alliance Worldwide Sales (passenger cars and LCVs)

	2001	2000	Change 2001/2000 (%)
Worldwide Sales			
Renault Group	**2,409,226**	**2,356,208**	**+2.3%**
Renault	2,286,565	2,293,726	-0.3
RSM[a]	70,648	12,349	+472.1
Dacia[a]	52,013	50,133	+3.8
Nissan Group	**2,580,351**	**2,632,876**	**-2.0%**
Nissan	2,505,221	2,548,185	-1.7
Infiniti	7,130	84,691	-11.3%
Renault-Nissan Alliance	**4,989,577**	**4,989,084**	**+0.0%**
Sales in Western Europe			
Renault	**1,904,421**	**1,873,990**	**+1.6%**
France	792,779	784,143	+1.1
Germany	220,310	219,522	+0.4
Spain	216,723	214,055	+1.2
Italy	186,622	187,223	-0.3
United Kingdom	198,363	174,717	+13.5
Nissan	**454,378**	**508,931**	**-10.7%**
France	34,038	36,905	-7.8
Germany	65,434	76,963	-15.0
Spain	73,902	82,826	-10.8
Italy	66,616	66,602	0.0
United Kingdom	97,963	89,809	+9.1
Renault-Nissan Alliance	**2,358,799**	**2,382,921**	**-1.0%**
France	826,817	821,048	+0.7
Germany	285,744	296,485	-3.6
Spain	290,625	296,881	-2.1
Italy	253,238	253,825	-0.2
United Kingdom	296,326	264,526	+12.0
Sales in North America			
Nissan (including Infiniti)	**759,972**	**799,491**	**-4.9%**
United States	703,308	752,087	-6.5
Canada	56,664	47,404	+19.5%
Spain	216,723	214,055	+1.2
Sales in Japan			
Renault Nissan	**2,774**	**2,010**	**+38.0%**
Nissan	**731,615**	**729,739**	**+0.3%**
Renault-Nissan Alliance	**734,389**	**731,749**	**+0.4%**

Exhibit 2 (continued)

	2001	2000	Change 2001/2000 (%)
Sales in Latin and South America[b]			
Renault	**148,000**	**146,843**	**+0.8%**
Brazil	70,387	56,558	+24.5
Argentina	35,346	60,780	-41.8
Mexico	3,136	--	+++
Nissan	**227,364**	**213,088**	**+6.7%**
Brazil	1,554	211	+636.5
Argentina	1,397	1,000	+39.7
Mexico	190,537	173,066	+10.1
Renault-Nissan Alliance	**375,364**	**359,931**	**+4.3%**
Brazil	71,941	56,769	+26.7
Argentina	36,743	61,780	-40.5
Mexico	193,673	173,066	+11.9
Sales in Middle East and Africa			
Renault	**63,735**	**58,757**	**+8.5%**
Nissan	**149,523**	**131,600**	**+13.6%**
Renault-Nissan Alliance	**213,258**	**190,357**	**+12.0%**
Sales in Other Areas[c]			
Renault	**290,296**	**274,608**	**+5.7%**
Nissan	**257,499**	**250,027**	**+3.0%**
Renault-Nissan Alliance	**547,795**	**524,635**	**+4.4%**

Source: Renault-Nissan.

[a]Sales on the local market. Full consolidation of RSM, effective September 2000.

[b]Latin American countries include: Argentina, Brazil, Mexico (first year of trading for Renault), Chile, Paraguay, Peru, Uruguay, Venezuela, Colombia, the Commonwealth of Puerto Rico, and other countries.

[c]Other areas include: Asia and Oceania, Eastern Europe, and the U.S. Pacific Islands.

Exhibit 3   Alliance with Renault

Transaction Summary

- Renault will purchase 1,464 million newly issued shares of Nissan at ¥400. The investment amounts to ¥5,857 million, representing 36.8% ownership.

- Renault will purchase a five-year bond with warrants issued by Nissan for ¥216 billion, which allows Renault to purchase an additional 540 million shares to obtain 44.4% ownership.

- Renault will purchase 22.5% interest in Nissan Diesel, the fourth-largest truck manufacturer and affiliate of Nissan, for ¥9.3 billion.

- Renault will purchase Nissan's European financing subsidiaries for ¥38 billion.

- Renault will make a minority investment of ¥5 billion in Nissan's South African subsidiary.

Management

- Renault will take key positions in Nissan's top management. C. Ghosn will be Chief Operating Officer, P. Pelata will be Executive Vice President in charge of Product Planning and Strategy, and T. Moulonguet will be deputy CFO and Managing Director [and would later become Executive Vice President and CFO].

- Global Alliance Committee will be established and chaired by Renault's CEO and Nissan's President. Other members include five senior executives each from Renault and Nissan.

Operations

- Integrate platforms. Number of platforms (initially Renault 8, Nissan 24) will be reduced to 10.

- Use common parts for powertrains and transmissions. Number of parts (currently Renault 7, Nissan 20) will be reduced to 8.

- Joint development of small diesel engines.

- Renault will reenter Mexican market using Nissan manufacturing and sales infrastructure.

- Nissan will enter South American market using Renault manufacturing and sales infrastructure.

- Nissan will supply CVT and 4WD systems to Renault.

- Joint marketing in markets outside Japan and France.

Source: Company documents.

Exhibit 4   Market Shares of Major Auto Manufacturers, 1998

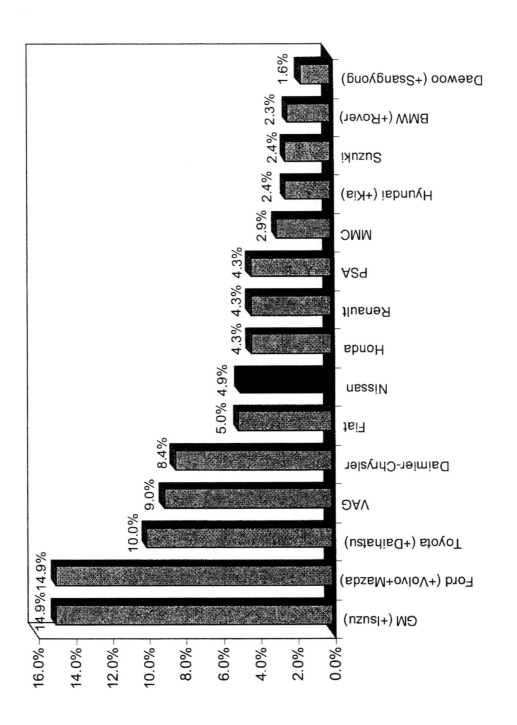

Source: Renault-Nissan (based on production figures from CCFA, December 1998).

Exhibit 5   Nissan Motor Stock Price Performance (January 1995–May 2002)

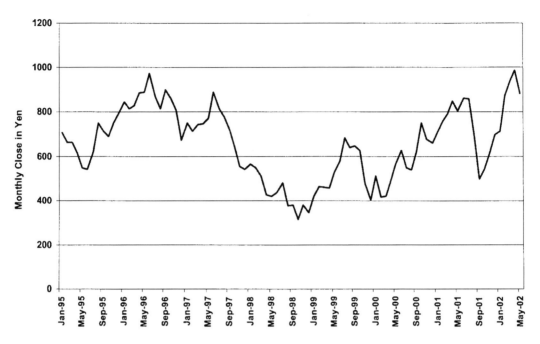

Source: Thomson Financial Datastream.

Exhibit 6   Renault Stock Price Performance (January 1995–May 2002)

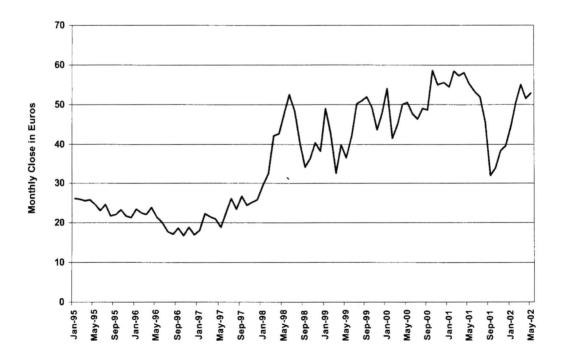

Source: Thomson Financial Datastream

Exhibit 7   Major Global Automaker Groups

Group	Members	Parent Holding	CY 2000 Sales (millions)	Overview
GENERAL MOTORS GM $43.78 FIA.MI €17.15 7269.T ¥1326 7270.T ¥606 7202.T ¥117 N/A	***TOTAL*** General Motors Fiat Auto Suzuki Motor Fuji Heavy Industries Isuzu Motors Daewoo Motors	 20.0% 20.1% 21.1% 48.5% 67.0%	***14.23*** 8.59 2.65 0.85 0.58 0.58 0.97	Largest single automaker and largest group: indifferent product and strategic confusion invites competitive assault and market share losses in U.S. and Europe; except Isuzu, all alliances relatively new; Asian network reflects admission GM unable to go it alone in region; benefits yet to emerge; Fiat alliance promises £1b synergies by 2005, but prospects uncertain given direct competition with Opel and Fiat's continued difficulties.
FORD MOTOR I $16.18 7261.T ¥215	***TOTAL*** Ford Motor Mazda Motor	 33.4%	***8.40*** 7.35 1.05	As GM, suffering from Japanese onslaught in U.S. and revival in indigenous makers in Europe; Premier Automotive Group collection of wholly owned luxury brands represents unique strategy but profitability as yet uncertain; Mazda turnaround fizzled after initial mid-1990s restructuring gains; second attempt still fails to clarify Mazda position with group.
TOYOTA MOTOR 7203.T ¥3060 7262.T ¥566 7205.T ¥459	***TOTAL*** Toyota Motor Daihatsu Motor Hino Motors	 51.2% 36.6%	***6.22*** 5.51 0.66 0.05	Overwhelming strength in Japan and biggest threat to Big 3 in U.S.; excellent financial standing and strong technologies for future; conservative management focused on equity partnerships with Japanese only and less explicit commitment to shareholder value; staid product image possible future Achilles heel.
DAIMLERCHRYSLER DCXGn.F €39.95 7211.T ¥254	***TOTAL*** DaimlerChrysler Mitsubishi Motors	 37.3%	***6.41*** 4.75 1.67	Mercedes-Benz brand still unchallenged; Chrysler unit's losses resulted from aging product line-up and onslaught by Japanese makers; embarking on aggressive restructuring at struggling Mitsubishi, which possesses credible Asian truck operation; South Korea's Hyundai Motor also tied to group by smaller stakes.
VOLKSWAGEN VOWG.F €45,10			***5.16***	Primarily European-led product and platform-sharing strategy across large number of brands largely successful in past decade; emerging signs of realignment of brand strategy following upcoming succession handover; commitment to shareholder value questioned by group.
RENAULT-NISSAN RENA.PA €36.66 7201.T ¥557	***TOTAL*** Renault Nissan Motor	 36.8%	***5.07*** 2.44 2.63	Good product and geographical fit between two parts; Carlos Ghosn's restructuring gains at Renault in late-90s repeated with success so far at Nissan; Renault also hoping to revive Romanian Dacia and South Korean Samsung Motors.
HONDA MOTOR 7267.T ¥4670			***2.54***	Able to punch above weight in absence of alliance distractions; highly profitable, especially in dynamic U.S. car business and global bike business; appears able to withstand consolidation trend for foreseeable future.
PEUGEOT CITROEN PEUP.PA €45.85			***2.88***	As Honda, thriving without distraction of equity alliances, although as yet uncertain whether recent primarily Euro-centric product revival can sustain strong momentum.
BMW BMWG.F €35.1			***1.01***	Management stability and share price benefited from strategic U-turn resulting in sales of Rover mass-market operation and focus on purely premium brands.

Source: Company data from Commerzbank Securities.

Exhibit 8 Implementation of the Alliance Pre-RNBV

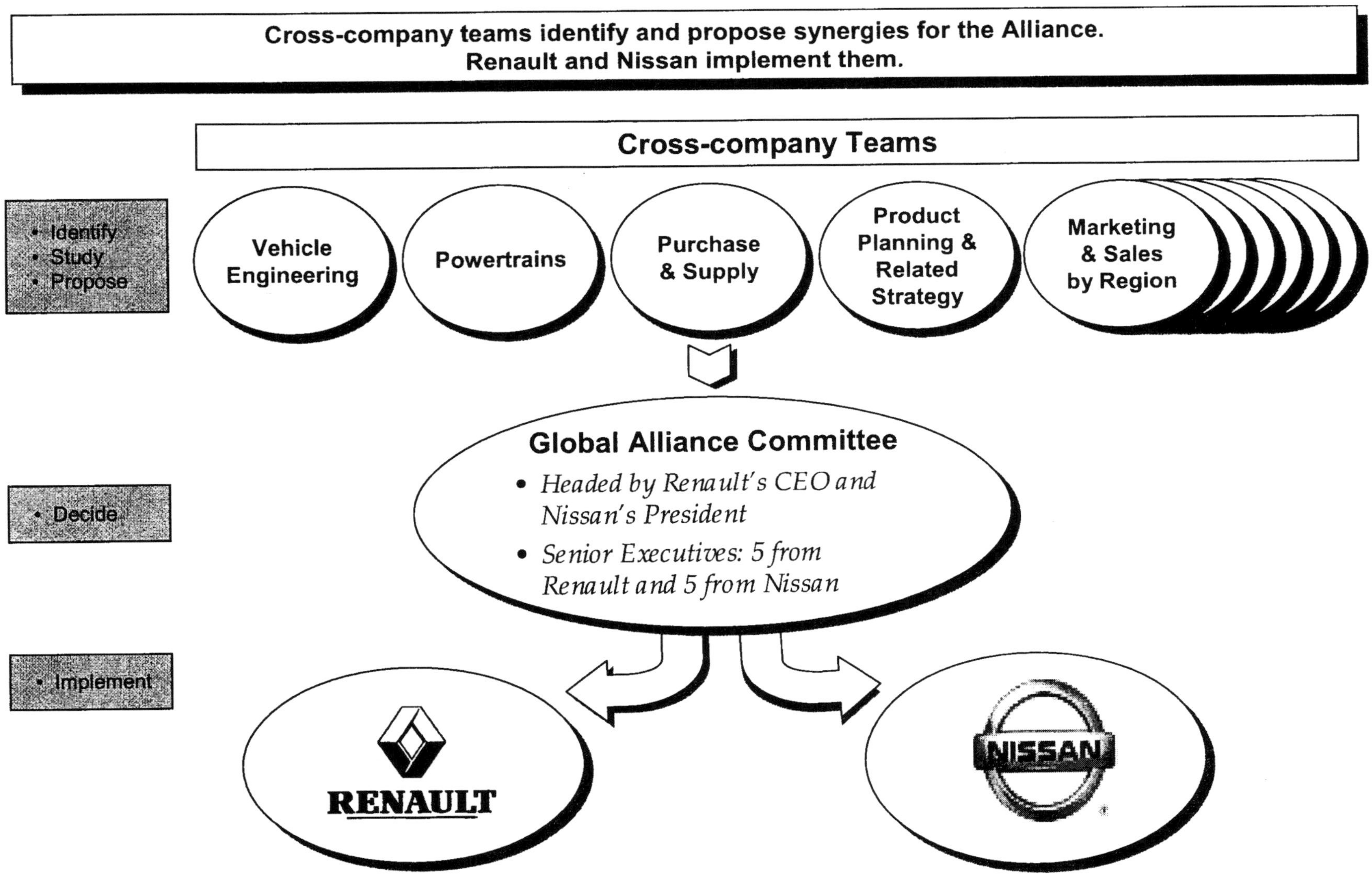

Cross-company teams identify and propose synergies for the Alliance. Renault and Nissan implement them.

Cross-company Teams

- Vehicle Engineering
- Powertrains
- Purchase & Supply
- Product Planning & Related Strategy
- Marketing & Sales by Region

Global Alliance Committee

- *Headed by Renault's CEO and Nissan's President*
- *Senior Executives: 5 from Renault and 5 from Nissan*

NISSAN

RENAULT

- Identify
- Study
- Propose

- Decide

- Implement

Source: Company documents.

233

Exhibit 9   Fit of Renault and Nissan Product Range by Platform (# units in thousands)

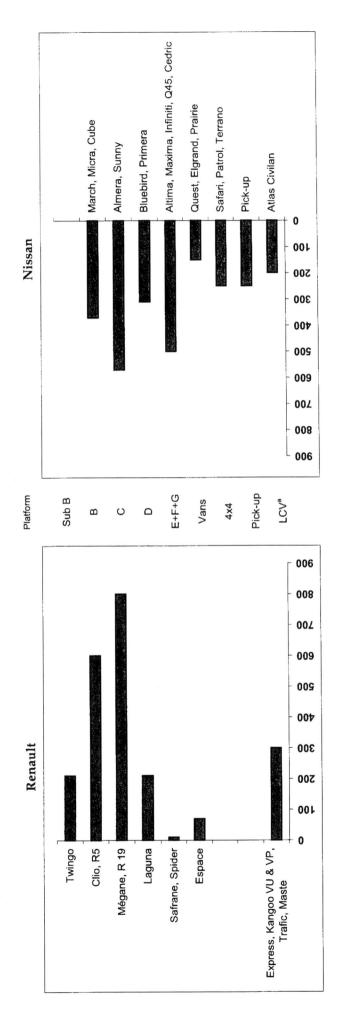

Source: Company documents.

[a]Light Commercial Vehicles

PANKAJ GHEMAWAT

JOSÉ LUIS NUENO

ZARA: Fast Fashion

Fashion is the imitation of a given example and satisfies the demand for social adaptation. . . . The more an article becomes subject to rapid changes of fashion, the greater the demand for cheap products of its kind.

—Georg Simmel, "Fashion" (1904)

Inditex (Industria de Diseño Textil) of Spain, the owner of Zara and five other apparel retailing chains, continued a trajectory of rapid, profitable growth by posting net income of €340 million on revenues of €3,250 million in its fiscal year 2001 (ending January 31, 2002). Inditex had had a heavily oversubscribed Initial Public Offering in May 2001. Over the next 12 months, its stock price increased by nearly 50%—despite bearish stock market conditions—to push its market valuation to €13.4 billion. The high stock price made Inditex's founder, Amancio Ortega, who had begun to work in the apparel trade as an errand boy half a century earlier, Spain's richest man. However, it also implied a significant growth challenge. Based on one set of calculations, for example, 76% of the equity value implicit in Inditex's stock price was based on expectations of future growth—higher than an estimated 69% for Wal-Mart or, for that matter, other high-performing retailers.[1]

The next section of this case briefly describes the structure of the global apparel chain, from producers to final customers. The section that follows profiles three of Inditex's leading international competitors in apparel retailing: The Gap (U.S.), Hennes & Mauritz (Sweden), and Benetton (Italy). The rest of the case focuses on Inditex, particularly the business system and international expansion of the Zara chain that dominated its results.

The Global Apparel Chain

The global apparel chain had been characterized as a prototypical example of a buyer-driven global chain, in which profits derived from "unique combinations of high-value research, design, sales, marketing, and financial services that allow retailers, branded marketers, and branded manufacturers to act as strategic brokers in linking overseas factories"[2] with markets. These attributes were thought to distinguish the vertical structure of commodity chains in apparel and other labor-intensive industries such as footwear and toys from producer-driven chains (e.g., in automobiles) that were coordinated and dominated by upstream manufacturers rather than downstream intermediaries (see **Exhibit 1**).

Production

Apparel production was very fragmented. On average, individual apparel manufacturing firms employed only a few dozen people, although internationally traded production, in particular, could feature tiered production chains comprising as many as hundreds of firms spread across dozens of countries. About 30% of world production of apparel was exported, with developing countries generating an unusually large share, about one-half, of all exports. These large cross-border flows of apparel reflected cheaper labor and inputs—partly because of cascading labor efficiencies—in developing countries. (See **Exhibit 2** for comparative labor productivity data and **Exhibit 3** for an example.) Despite extensive investments in substituting capital for labor, apparel production remained highly labor-intensive so that even relatively large "manufacturers" in developed countries outsourced labor-intensive production steps (e.g., sewing) to lower-cost labor sources nearby. Proximity also mattered because it reduced shipping costs and lags, and because poorer neighbors sometimes benefited from trade concessions. While China became an export powerhouse across the board, greater regionalization was the dominant motif of changes in the apparel trade in the 1990s. Turkey, North Africa, and sundry Eastern European countries emerged as major suppliers to the European Union; Mexico and the Caribbean Basin as major suppliers to the United States; and China as the dominant supplier to Japan (where there were no quotas to restrict imports).[3]

World trade in apparel and textiles continued to be regulated by the Multi-Fiber Arrangement (MFA), which had restricted imports into certain markets (basically the United States, Canada, and Western Europe) since 1974. Two decades later, agreement was reached to phase out the MFA's quota system by 2005, and to further reduce tariffs (which averaged 7% to 9% in the major markets). As of 2002, some warned that the transition to the post-MFA world could prove enormously disruptive for suppliers in many exporting and importing countries, and might even ignite demands for "managed trade." There was also potential for protectionism in the questions that nongovernmental organizations and others in developed countries were posing about the basic legitimacy of "sweatshop trade" in buyer-driven global chains such as apparel and footwear.

Cross-Border Intermediation

Trading companies had traditionally played the primary role in orchestrating the physical flows of apparel from factories in exporting countries to retailers in importing countries. They continued to be important cross-border intermediaries, although the complexity and (as a result) the specialization of their operations seemed to have increased over time. Thus, Hong Kong's largest trading company, Li & Fung, derived 75% of its turnover from apparel and the remainder from hard goods by setting up and managing multinational supply chains for retail clients through its offices in more than 30 countries.[4] For example, a down jacket's filling might come from China, the outer shell fabric from Korea, the zippers from Japan, the inner lining from Taiwan, and the elastics, label, and other trim from Hong Kong. Dyeing might take place in South Asia and stitching in China, followed by quality assurance and packaging in Hong Kong. The product might then be shipped to the United States for delivery to a retailer such as The Limited or Abercrombie & Fitch, to whom credit risk matching, market research, and even design services might also be supplied.

Branded marketers represented another, newer breed of middlemen. Such intermediaries outsourced the production of apparel that they sold under their own brand names. Liz Claiborne, founded in 1976, was a good example.[5] Its eponymous founder identified a growing customer group (professional women) and sold them branded apparel designed to fit evolving workplace norms and their actual shapes (which she famously described as "pear-shaped"), that was presented in collections within which they could mix and match in upscale department stores. Production was

2

outsourced from the outset, first domestically, and then, in the course of the 1980s, increasingly to Asia, with a heavy reliance on OEM or "full-package" suppliers. Production was organized in terms of six seasons rather than four to let stores buy merchandise in smaller batches. After a performance decline in the first half of the 1990s, Liz Claiborne restructured its supply chain to reduce the number of suppliers and inventory levels, shifted half of production back to the Western Hemisphere to compress cycle times, and simultaneously cut the number of seasonal collections from six to four so as to allow some reorders of merchandise that was selling well in the third month of a season.

Other types of cross-border intermediaries could be seen as forward or backward integrators rather than as pure middlemen. Branded manufacturers, like branded marketers, sold products under their own brand names through one or more independent retail channels and owned some manufacturing as well. Some branded manufacturers were based in developed countries (e.g., U.S.-based VF Corporation, which sold jeans produced in its factories overseas under the Lee and Wrangler brands) and others in developing countries (e.g., Giordano, Hong Kong's leading apparel brand). In terms of backward integration, many retailers internalized at least some cross-border functions by setting up their own overseas buying offices, although they continued to rely on specialized intermediaries for others (e.g., import documentation and clearances).

Retailing

Irrespective of whether they internalized most cross-border functions, retailers played a dominant role in shaping imports into developed countries: thus, direct imports by retailers accounted for half of all apparel imports into Western Europe.[6] The increasing concentration of apparel retailing in major markets was thought to be one of the key drivers of increased trade. In the United States, the top five chains came to account for more than half of apparel sales during the 1990s, and concentration levels elsewhere, while lower, also rose during the decade. Increased concentration was generally accompanied by displacement of independent stores by retail chains, a trend that had also helped increase average store size over time. By the late 1990s, chains accounted for about 85% of total retail sales in the United States, about 70% in Western Europe, between one-third to one-half in Latin America, East Asia, and Eastern Europe, and less than 10% in large but poor markets such as China and India.[7]

Larger apparel retailers had also played the leading role in promoting quick response (QR), a set of policies and practices targeted at improving coordination between retailing and manufacturing in order to increase the speed and flexibility of responses to market shifts, which began to diffuse in apparel and textiles in the second half of the 1980s.[8] QR required changes that spanned functional, geographic, and organizational boundaries but could help retailers reduce forecast errors and inventory risks by planning assortments closer to the selling season, probing the market, placing smaller initial orders and reordering more frequently, and so on. QR had led to significant compression of cycle times (see **Exhibit 4**), enabled by improvements in information technology and encouraged by shorter fashion cycles and deeper markdowns, particularly in women's wear.

Retailing activities themselves remained quite local: the top 10 retailers worldwide operated in an average of 10 countries in 2000—compared with top averages of 135 countries in pharmaceuticals, 73 in petroleum, 44 in automobiles, and 33 in electronics—and derived less than 15% of their total sales from outside their home markets.[9] Against this baseline, apparel retailing was relatively globalized, particularly in the fashion segment. Apparel retailing chains from Europe had been the most successful at cross-border expansion, although the U.S. market remained a major challenge. Their success probably reflected the European design roots of apparel—somewhat akin to U.S.-based fast food chains' international dominance—and the gravitational pull of the large U.S. market for U.S.-based retailers. Thus, The Gap, based on its sales at home in the United States, dwarfed H&M and

Inditex combined. The latter two companies were perhaps the most pan-European apparel retailers but had yet to achieve market shares of more than 2%–3% in more than two or three major countries.

Markets and Customers

In 2000, retail spending on clothing or apparel reached approximately €900 billion worldwide. According to one set of estimates, (Western) Europe accounted for 34% of the total market, the United States for 29%, and Asia for 23%.[10] Differences in market size reflected significant differences in per capita spending on apparel as well as in population levels. Per capita spending on apparel tended to grow less than proportionately with increases in per capita income, so that its share of expenditures typically decreased as income increased. Per capita spending was also affected by price levels, which were influenced by variations in per capita income, in costs, and in the intensity of competition (given that competition continued to be localized to a significant extent).

There was also significant local variation in customers' attributes and preferences, even within a region or a country. Just within Western Europe, for instance, one study concluded that the British sought out stores based on social affinity, that the French focused on variety/quality, and that Germans were more price-sensitive.[11] Relatedly, the French and the Italians were considered more fashion-forward than the Germans or the British. Spaniards were exceptional in buying apparel only seven times a year, compared with a European average of nine times a year, and higher-than-average levels for the Italians and French, among others.[12] Differences between regions were even greater than within regions: Japan, while generally traditional, also had a teenage market segment that was considered the trendiest in the world on many measures, and the U.S. market was, from the perspective of many European retailers, significantly less trendy except in a few, generally coastal pockets. There did, however, seem to be more cross-border homogeneity within the fashion segment. Popular fashion, in particular, had become less of a hand-me-down from high-end designers. It now seemed to move much more quickly as people, especially young adults and teenagers, with ever richer communication links reacted to global and local trends, including other elements of popular culture (e.g., desperately seeking the skirt worn by the rock star at her last concert).

Attempts had also been made to identify the strategic implications of the changing structure of the global apparel chain that were discussed above. Some implications simplified to "get big fast"; others, however, were more sophisticated. Thus, an article by three McKinsey consultants identified five ways for retailers to expand across borders: choosing a "sliver" of value instead of competing across the entire value chain; emphasizing partnering; investing in brands; minimizing (tangible) investments; and arbitraging international factor price differences.[13] But Inditex, particularly its Zara chain, served as a reminder that strategic imperatives depended on how a retailer sought to create and sustain a competitive advantage through its cross-border activities.

Key International Competitors

While Inditex competed with local retailers in most of its markets, analysts considered its three closest comparable competitors to be The Gap, H&M, and Benetton. All three had narrower vertical scope than Zara, which owned much of its production and most of its stores. The Gap and H&M, which were the two largest specialist apparel retailers in the world, ahead of Inditex, owned most of their stores but outsourced all production. Benetton, in contrast, had invested relatively heavily in production, but licensees ran its stores. The three competitors were also positioned differently in product space from Inditex's chains. (See **Exhibit 5** for a positioning map and **Exhibit 6** for financial and other comparisons.)[14]

4

The Gap

The Gap, based in San Francisco, had been founded in 1969 and had achieved stellar growth and profitability through the 1980s and much of the 1990s with what was described as an "unpretentious real clothes stance," comprising extensive collections of T-shirts and jeans as well as "smart casual" work clothes. The Gap's production was internationalized—more than 90% of it was outsourced from outside the United States—but its store operations were U.S.-centric. International expansion of the store network had begun in 1987, but its pace had been limited by difficulties finding locations in markets such as the United Kingdom, Germany, and Japan (which accounted for 86% of store locations outside North America), adapting to different customer sizes and preferences, and dealing with what were, in many cases, more severe pricing pressures than in the United States. By the end of the 1990s, supply chains that were still too long, market saturation, imbalances and inconsistencies across the company's three store chains—Banana Republic, The Gap, and Old Navy—and the lack of a clear fashion positioning had started to take a toll even in the U.S. market. A failed attempt to reposition to a more fashion-driven assortment—a major fashion miss—triggered significant writedowns, a loss for calendar year 2001, a massive decline in The Gap's stock price, and the departure, in May 2002, of its long-time CEO, Millard Drexler.

Hennes and Mauritz

Hennes and Mauritz (H&M), founded as Hennes (hers) in Sweden in 1947, was another high-performing apparel retailer. While it was considered Inditex's closest competitor, there were a number of key differences. H&M outsourced all its production, half of it to European suppliers, implying lead times that were good by industry standards but significantly longer than Zara's. H&M had been quicker to internationalize, generating more than half its sales outside its home country by 1990, 10 years earlier than Inditex. H&M also had adopted a more focused approach, entering one country at a time—with an emphasis on northern Europe—and building a distribution center in each one. Unlike Inditex, H&M operated a single format, although it marketed its clothes under numerous labels or concepts to different customer segments. H&M also tended to have slightly lower prices than Zara (which H&M displayed prominently in store windows and on shelving), engaged in extensive advertising like most other apparel retailers, employed fewer designers (60% fewer than Zara, although Zara was still 40% smaller), and refurbished its stores less frequently. H&M's price-earnings ratio, while still high, had declined to levels comparable to Inditex's because of a fashion miss that had reduced net income by 17% in 2000 and because of a recent announcement that an aggressive effort to expand in the United States was being slowed down.

Benetton

Benetton, incorporated in 1965 in Italy, emphasized brightly colored knitwear. It achieved prominence in the 1980s and 1990s for its controversial advertising and as a network organization that outsourced activities that were labor-intensive or scale-insensitive to subcontractors. But Benetton actually invested relatively heavily in controlling other production activities. Where it had little investment was downstream: it sold its production through licensees, often entrepreneurs with no more than $100,000 to invest in a small outlet that could sell only Benetton products. While Benetton was fast at certain activities such as dyeing, it looked for its retailing business to provide significant forward order books for its manufacturing business and was therefore geared to operate on lead times of several months. Benetton's format appeared to hit saturation by the early 1990s, and profitability continued to slide through the rest of the 1990s. In response, it embarked on a strategy of narrowing product lines, further consolidating key production activities by grouping them into "production poles" in a number of different regions, and expanding or focusing existing outlets while starting a program to set up much larger company-owned outlets in big cities. About 100 such Benetton megastores were in operation by the end of 2001, compared with a network of approximately 5,500 smaller, third-party-owned stores.

Inditex

Inditex (Industria de Diseño Textil) was a global specialty retailer that designed, manufactured, and sold apparel, footwear, and accessories for women, men, and children through Zara and five other chains around the world. At the end of the 2001 fiscal year, it operated 1,284 stores around the world, including Spain, with a selling area of 659,400 square meters. The 515 stores located outside of Spain generated 54% of the total revenues of €3,250 million. Inditex employed 26,724 people, 10,919 of them outside Spain. Their average age was 26 years, and the overwhelming majority were women (78%).

Just over 80% of Inditex's employees were engaged in retail sales in stores; 8.5% were employed in manufacturing; and design, logistics, distribution, and headquarters activities accounted for the remainder. Capital expenditures had recently been split roughly 80% on new-store openings, 10% on refurbishing, and 10% on logistics/maintenance, roughly in line with capital employed. Operating working capital was negative at most year-ends, although it typically registered higher levels at other times of the year given the seasonality of apparel sales. (See **Exhibit 7** for these and other historical financial data.) Plans for 2002 called for continued tight management of working capital and €510–560 million of capital expenditures, mostly on opening 230–275 new stores (across all chains). The operating economics for 2001 had involved gross margins of 52%, operating expenses equivalent to 30% of revenues, of which one-half were related to personnel, and operating margins of 22%. Net margins on sales revenue were about one-half the size of operating margins, with depreciation of fixed assets (€158 million) and taxes (€150 million) helping reduce operating profits of €704 million to net income of €340 million. Despite high margins, top management stressed that Inditex was *not* the most profitable apparel retailer in the world—that stability was perhaps a more distinctive feature.

The rest of this section describes the pluses and minuses of Inditex's home base, its foundation by Amancio Ortega and subsequent growth, the structure of the group in early 2002, and recent changes in its governance. (A timeline, **Exhibit 8**, summarizes key events over this period chronologically.)

Home Base

Inditex was headquartered in and had most of its upstream assets concentrated in the region of Galicia on the northwestern tip of Spain (see **Exhibit 9**). Galicia, the third-poorest of Spain's 17 autonomous regions, reported an unemployment rate in 2001 of 17% (compared with a national average of 14%), had poor communication links with the rest of the country, and was still heavily dependent on agriculture and fishing. In apparel, however, Galicia had a tradition that dated back to the Renaissance, when Galicians were tailors to the aristocracy, and was home to thousands of small apparel workshops. What Galicia lacked were a strong base upstream in textiles, sophisticated local demand, technical institutes and universities to facilitate specialized initiatives and training, and an industry association to underpin these or other potentially cooperative activities. And even more critical for Inditex, as CEO José Maria Castellano put it, was that "Galicia is in the corner of Europe from the perspective of transport costs, which are very important to us given our business model."

Some of the same characterizations applied at a national level, to Inditex's home base of Spain compared, for example, to Italy. Spanish consumers demanded low prices but were not considered as discriminating or fashion-conscious as Italian buyers—although Spain had advanced rapidly in this regard as well as in many others, since the death of long-time dictator General Francisco Franco in 1975 and the country's subsequent opening up to the world. On the supply side, Spain was a relatively productive apparel manufacturing base by European standards (see **Exhibit 2**), but lacked Italy's fully developed thread-to-apparel vertical chain (including machinery suppliers), its dominance of high-quality fabrics (such as wool suiting), and its international fashion image. For this reason, and because rivalry among them had historically been fierce, Italian apparel chains had been quick to move overseas. Spanish apparel retailers had followed suit in the 1990s, and not just Inditex. Mango, a smaller Spanish chain that relied on a franchising model with returnable merchandise, was already present in more countries around the world than Inditex.

Early History

Amancio Ortega Gaona, Inditex's founder, was still its president and principal shareholder in early 2002 and still came in to work every day, where he could often be seen lunching in the company cafeteria with employees. Ortega was otherwise extremely reclusive, but reports indicated that he had been born in 1936 to a railroad worker and a housemaid and that his first job had been as an errand boy for a La Coruña shirtmaker in 1949. As he moved up through that company, he apparently developed a heightened awareness of how costs piled up through the apparel chain. In 1963, he founded Confecciones Goa (his initials reversed) to manufacture products such as housecoats. Eventually, Ortega's quest to improve the manufacturing/retailing interface led him to integrate forward into retailing: the first Zara store was opened on an upmarket shopping street in La Coruña, in 1975. From the beginning, Zara positioned itself as a store selling "medium quality fashion clothing at affordable prices." By the end of the 1970s, there were half a dozen Zara stores in Galician cities.

Ortega, who was said to be a gadgeteer by inclination, bought his first computer in 1976. At the time, his operations encompassed just four factories and two stores but were already making it clear that what (other) buyers ordered from his factories was different from what his store data told him customers wanted. Ortega's interest in information technology also brought him into contact with Jose Maria Castellano, who had a doctorate in business economics and professional experience in information technology, sales, and finance. In 1985, Castellano joined Inditex as the deputy chairman of its board of directors, although he continued to teach accounting part-time at the local university.

Under Ortega and Castellano, Zara continued to roll out nationally through the 1980s by expanding into adjoining markets. It reached the Spanish capital, Madrid, in 1985 and, by the end of the decade, operated stores in all Spanish cities with more than 100,000 inhabitants. Zara then began to open stores outside Spain and to make quantum investments in manufacturing logistics and IT. The early 1990s was also when Inditex started to add other retail chains to its network through acquisition as well as internal development.

Structure

At the beginning of 2002, Inditex operated six separate chains: Zara, Massimo Dutti, Pull & Bear, Bershka, Stradivarius, and Oysho (as illustrated in **Exhibit 10**). These chains' retailing subsidiaries in Spain and abroad were grouped into 60 companies, or about one-half the total number of companies whose results were consolidated into Inditex at the group level; the remainder were involved in textile purchasing and preparation, manufacturing, logistics, real estate, finance, and so forth. Given internal transfer pricing and other policies, retailing (as opposed to manufacturing and other activities) generated 82% of Inditex's net income, which was roughly in line with its share of the group's total capital investment and employment.

The six retailing chains were organized as separate business units within an overall structure that also included six business support areas (raw materials, manufacturing plants, logistics, real estate, expansion, and international) and nine corporate departments or areas of responsibility (see **Exhibit 11**). In effect, each of the chains operated independently and was responsible for its own strategy, product design, sourcing and manufacturing, distribution, image, personnel, and financial results, while group management set the strategic vision of the group, coordinated the activities of the concepts, and provided them with administrative and various other services.

Coordination across the chains had deliberately been limited but had increased somewhat, particularly in the areas of real estate and expansion, as Inditex had recently moved toward opening up some multichain locations. More broadly, the experience of the older, better-established chains, particularly Zara, had helped accelerate the expansion of the newer ones. Thus Oysho, the lingerie chain, drew 75% of its human resources from the other chains and had come to operate stores in seven European markets within six months of its launch in September 2001.

Top corporate managers, who were all Spanish, saw the role of the corporate center as a "strategic controller" involved in setting the corporate strategy, approving the business strategies of the individual chains, and controlling their performance rather than as an "operator" functionally involved in running the chains. Their ability to control performance down to the local store level was based on standardized reporting systems that focused on (like-for-like) sales growth, earnings before interest and taxes (EBIT) margin, and return on capital employed. CEO Castellano looked at key performance metrics once a week, while one of his direct reports monitored them on a daily basis.

Recent Governance Changes

Inditex's initial public offering (IPO) in May 2001 had sold 26% of the company's shares to the public, but founder Amancio Ortega retained a stake of more than 60%. Since Inditex generated substantial free cash flow (some of which had been used to make portfolio investments in other lines of business), the IPO was thought to be motivated primarily by Ortega's desire to put the company on a firm footing for his eventual retirement and the transition to a new top management team.

Also in 2001, Inditex made progress toward implementing a social strategy involving dialogue with employees, suppliers, subcontractors, nongovernmental organizations, and local communities. Immediate initiatives included approval of an internal code of conduct, the establishment of a corporate responsibility department, social audits of supplier and external workshops in Spain and Morocco, pilot developmental projects in Venezuela and Guatemala, and the joining, in August 2001, of the Global Compact, an initiative headed by Kofi Annan, Secretary General of the United Nations, that aimed to improve global companies' social performance.

Zara's Business System

Zara was the largest and most internationalized of Inditex's chains. At the end of 2001, it operated 507 stores in countries around the world, including Spain (40% of the total number for Inditex), with 488,400 square meters of selling area (74% of the total) and employing €1,050 million of the company's capital (72% of the total), of which the store network accounted for about 80%. During fiscal year 2001, it had posted EBIT of €441 million (85% of the total) on sales of €2,477 million (76%

of the total). While Zara's share of the group's total sales was expected to drop by two or three percentage points each year, it would continue to be the principal driver of the group's growth for some time to come, and to play the lead role in increasing the share of Inditex's sales accounted for by international operations.

Zara completed its rollout in the Spanish market by 1990, and began to move overseas around that time. It also began to make major investments in manufacturing logistics and IT, including establishment of a just-in-time manufacturing system, a 130,000-square-meter warehouse close to corporate headquarters in Arteixo, outside La Coruña, and an advanced telecommunications system to connect headquarters and supply, production, and sales locations. Development of logistical, retail, financial, merchandising, and other information systems continued through the 1990s, much of it taking place internally. For example, while there were many logistical packages on the market, Zara's unusual requirements mandated internal development.

The business system that had resulted (see **Exhibit 12**) was particularly distinctive in that Zara manufactured its most fashion-sensitive products internally. (The other Inditex chains were too small to justify such investments but generally did emphasize reliance on suppliers in Europe rather than farther away.) Zara's designers continuously tracked customer preferences and placed orders with internal and external suppliers. About 11,000 distinct items were produced during the year—several hundred thousand SKUs given variations in color, fabric, and sizes—compared with 2,000–4,000 items for key competitors. Production took place in small batches, with vertical integration into the manufacture of the most time-sensitive items. Both internal and external production flowed into Zara's central distribution center. Products were shipped directly from the central distribution center to well-located, attractive stores twice a week, eliminating the need for warehouses and keeping inventories low. Vertical integration helped reduce the "bullwhip effect"—the tendency for fluctuations in final demand to get amplified as they were transmitted back up the supply chain. Even more importantly, Zara was able to originate a design and have finished goods in stores within four to five weeks in the case of entirely new designs, and two weeks for modifications (or restocking) of existing products. In contrast, the traditional industry model might involve cycles of up to six months for design and three months for manufacturing.

The short cycle time reduced working capital intensity and facilitated continuous manufacture of new merchandise, even during the biannual sales periods, letting Zara commit to the bulk of its product line for a season much later than its key competitors (see **Exhibit 13**). Thus, Zara undertook 35% of product design and purchases of raw material, 40%–50% of the purchases of finished products from external suppliers, and 85% of the in-house production *after* the season had started, compared with only 0%–20% in the case of traditional retailers.

But while quick response was critical to Zara's superior performance, the connection between the two was not automatic. World Co. of Japan, perhaps the only other apparel retailer in the world with comparable cycle times, provided a counterexample. It, too, had integrated backward into (domestic) manufacturing, and had achieved gross margins comparable to Zara's.[15] But World Co.'s net margins remained stuck at around 2% of sales, compared with 10% in the case of Zara, largely because of selling, general, and administrative expenses that swallowed up about 40% of its revenues, versus about 20% for Zara. Different choices about how to exploit quick-response capabilities underlay these differences in performance. World Co. served the relatively depressed Japanese market, appeared to place less emphasis on design, had an unprofitable contract manufacturing arm, supported about 40 brands with distinct identities for use exclusively within its own store network (smaller than Zara's), and operated relatively small stores, averaging less than 100 square meters of selling area. Zara had made very different choices along these and other dimensions.

Design

Each of Zara's three product lines—for women, men, and children—had a creative team consisting of designers, sourcing specialists, and product development personnel. The creative teams simultaneously worked on products for the current season by creating constant variation, expanding on successful product items and continuing in-season development, and on the following season and year by selecting the fabrics and product mix that would be the basis for an initial collection. Top management stressed that instead of being run by maestros, the design organization was very flat and focused on careful interpretation of catwalk trends suitable for the mass market.

Zara created two basic collections each year that were phased in through the fall/winter and spring/summer seasons, starting in July and January, respectively. Zara's designers attended trade fairs and ready-to-wear fashion shows in Paris, New York, London, and Milan, referred to catalogs of luxury brand collections, and worked with store managers to begin to develop the initial sketches for a collection close to nine months before the start of a season. Designers then selected fabrics and other complements. Simultaneously, the relative price at which a product would be sold was determined, guiding further development of samples. Samples were prepared and presented to the sourcing and product development personnel, and the selection process began. As the collection came together, the sourcing personnel identified production requirements, decided whether an item would be insourced or outsourced, and set a timeline to ensure that the initial collection arrived in stores at the start of the selling season.

The process of adapting to trends and differences across markets was more evolutionary, ran through most of the selling season, and placed greater reliance on high-frequency information. Frequent conversations with store managers were as important in this regard as the sales data captured by Zara's IT system. Other sources of information included industry publications, TV, Internet, and film content; trend spotters who focused on venues such as university campuses and discotheques; and even Zara's young, fashion-conscious staff. Product development personnel played a key role in linking the designers and the stores, and were often from the country in which the stores they dealt with were located. On average, several dozen items were designed each day, but only slightly more than one-third of them actually went into production. Time permitting, very limited volumes of new items were prepared and presented in certain key stores and produced on a larger scale only if consumer reactions were unambiguously positive. As a result, failure rates on new products were supposed to be only 1%, compared with an average of 10% for the sector. Learning by doing was considered very important in achieving such favorable outcomes.

Overall, then, the responsibilities of Zara's design teams transcended design, narrowly defined. The teams also continuously tracked customer preferences and used information about sales potential based, among other things, on a consumption information system that supported detailed analysis of product life cycles, to transmit repeat orders and new designs to internal and external suppliers. The design teams thereby bridged merchandising and the back end of the production process. These functions were generally organized under separate management teams at other apparel retailers.

Sourcing & Manufacturing

Zara sourced fabric, other inputs, and finished products from external suppliers with the help of purchasing offices in Barcelona and Hong Kong, as well as the sourcing personnel at headquarters. While Europe had historically dominated Zara's sourcing patterns, the recent establishment of three companies in Hong Kong for purposes of purchasing as well as trend-spotting suggested that sourcing from the Far East, particularly China, might expand substantially.

About one-half of the fabric purchased was "gray" (undyed) to facilitate in-season updating with maximum flexibility. Much of this volume was funneled through Comditel, a 100%-owned subsidiary of Inditex, that dealt with more than 200 external suppliers of fabric and other raw materials. Comditel managed the dyeing, patterning, and finishing of gray fabric for all of Inditex's chains, not just Zara, and supplied finished fabric to external as well as in-house manufacturers. This process, reminiscent of Benetton's, meant that it took only one week to finish fabric.

Further down the value chain, about 40% of finished garments were manufactured internally, and of the remainder, approximately two-thirds of the items were sourced from Europe and North Africa and one-third from Asia. The most fashionable items tended to be the riskiest and therefore were the ones that were produced in small lots internally or under contract by suppliers who were located close by, and reordered if they sold well. More basic items that were more price-sensitive than time-sensitive were particularly likely to be outsourced to Asia, since production in Europe was typically 15%–20% more expensive for Zara. About 20 suppliers accounted for 70% of all external purchases. While Zara had long-term ties with many of these suppliers, it minimized formal contractual commitments to them.

Internal manufacture was the primary responsibility of 20 fully owned factories, 18 of them located in and around Zara's headquarters in Arteixo. Room for growth was provided by vacant lots around the principal manufacturing complex and also north of La Coruña and in Barcelona. Zara's factories were heavily automated, specialized by garment type, and focused on the capital-intensive parts of the production process—pattern design and cutting—as well as on final finishing and inspection. Vertical integration into manufacturing had begun in 1980, and starting in 1990, significant investments had been made in installing a just-in-time system in these factories in cooperation with Toyota—one of the first experiments of its kind in Europe. As a result, employees had had to learn how to use new machines and work in multifunctional teams.

Even for the garments that were manufactured in-house, cut garments were sent out to about 450 workshops, located primarily in Galicia and across the border in northern Portugal, that performed the labor-intensive, scale-insensitive activity of sewing. These workshops were generally small operations, averaging about 20–30 employees (although a few employed more than 100 people apiece), which specialized by product type. As subcontractors, they generally had long-term relations with Zara. Zara accounted for most if not all of their production; provided them with technology, logistics, and financial support; paid them prearranged rates per finished garment; carried out inspections onsite; and insisted that they comply with local tax and labor legislation.

The sewn garments were sent back from the workshops to Zara's manufacturing complex, where they were inspected, ironed, folded, bagged, and ticketed before being sent on to the adjoining distribution center.

Distribution

Like each of Inditex's chains, Zara had its own centralized distribution system. Zara's system consisted of an approximately 400,000-square-meter facility located in Arteixo and much smaller satellite centers in Argentina, Brazil, and Mexico that consolidated shipments from Arteixo.

All of Zara's merchandise, from internal and external suppliers, passed through the distribution center in Arteixo, which operated on a dual-shift basis and featured a mobile tracking system that docked hanging garments in the appropriate barcoded area on carousels capable of handling 45,000 folded garments per hour. As orders were received from hand-held computers in the stores (twice a week during regular periods, and thrice weekly during the sales season), they were checked in the

11

distribution center and, if a particular item was in short supply, allocation decisions were made on the basis of historical sales levels and other considerations. Once an order had been approved, the warehouse issued the lists that were used to organize deliveries.

Lorena Alba, Inditex's director of logistics, regarded the warehouse as a place to move merchandise rather than to store it. According to her, "The vast majority of clothes are in here only a few hours," and none ever stayed at the distribution center for more than three days. Of course, the rapidly expanding store network demanded constant adjustment to the sequencing and size of deliveries as well as their routing. The most recent revamp had been in January 2002, when Zara had started to schedule shipments by time zone. In the early morning while European store managers were still stocktaking, the distribution center packed and shipped orders to the Americas, the Middle East, and Asia; in the afternoon, it focused on the European stores. The distribution center generally ran at half its rated capacity, but surges in demand, particularly during the start of the two selling seasons in January and July, boosted utilization rates and required the hiring of several hundred temporary workers to complement close to 1,000 permanent employees.

Shipments from the warehouse were made twice a week to each store via third-party delivery services, with shipments two days a week to one part of the store network and two days a week to the other. Approximately 75% of Zara's merchandise by weight was shipped by truck by a third-party delivery service to stores in Spain, Portugal, France, Belgium, the United Kingdom, and parts of Germany. The remaining 25% was shipped mainly by air via KLM and DHL from airports in Santiago de Compostela (a major pilgrimage center in Galicia) and Porto in Portugal. Products were typically delivered within 24–36 hours to stores located in Europe and within 24–48 hours to stores located outside Europe. Air shipment was more expensive, but not prohibitively so. Thus, one industry participant suggested that air freight from Spain to the Middle East might cost 3%–5% of FOB price (compared with 1.5% for sea freight) and, along with a 1.5% landing charge, a 1% finance charge, miscellaneous expenses, and (generally) a 4% customs duty, bring the landed markup on FOB price to 12% or so. In the case of the United States, a 20%–25% landed markup seemed a better approximation because of tariffs of up to 12% as well as other added cost elements.

Despite Zara's historical success at scaling up its distribution system, observers speculated that the centralized logistics model might ultimately be subject to diseconomies of scale—that what worked well with 1,000 stores might not work with 2,000 stores. In an attempt to increase capacity, Zara was beginning construction of a second distribution center, at Zaragoza, northeast of Madrid. This second major distribution facility, to be started up in summer 2003, would add 120,000 square meters of warehouse space at a cost of €88 million close to the local airport and with direct access to the railway and road network as well.

Retailing

Zara aimed to offer fresh assortments of designer-style garments and accessories—shoes, bags, scarves, jewelry and, more recently, toiletries and cosmetics—for relatively low prices in sophisticated stores in prime locations in order to draw masses of fashion-conscious repeat customers. Despite its tapered integration into manufacturing, Zara placed more emphasis on using backward vertical integration to be a very quick fashion follower than to achieve manufacturing efficiencies by building up significant forward order books for the upstream operations. Production runs were limited and inventories strictly controlled even if that meant leaving demand unsatisfied. Both Zara's merchandising and store operations helped to reinforce these upstream policies.

Merchandising   Zara's product merchandising policies emphasized broad, rapidly changing product lines, relatively high fashion content, and reasonable but not excessive physical quality:

"clothes to be worn 10 times," some said. Product lines were segmented into women's, men's, and children's, with further segmentation of the women's line, considered the strongest, into three sets of offerings that varied in terms of their prices, fashion content, and age targets. Prices, which were determined centrally, were supposed to be lower than competitors' for comparable products in Zara's major markets, but percentage margins were expected to hold up not only because of the direct efficiencies associated with a shortened, vertically integrated supply chain but also because of significant reductions in advertising and markdown requirements.

Zara spent only 0.3% of its revenue on media advertising, compared with 3%–4% for most specialty retailers. Its advertising was generally limited to the start of the sales period at the end of the season, and the little that was undertaken did not create too strong a presence for the Zara brand or too specific an image of the "Zara Woman" or the "Zara Girl" (unlike the "Mango Girl" of Spanish competitor Mango). These choices reflected concerns about overexposure and lock-in as well as limits on spending. Nor did Zara exhibit its merchandise at the ready-to-wear fashion shows: its new items were first displayed in its stores. The Zara name had nevertheless developed considerable drawing power in its major markets. Thus by the mid-1990s, it had already become one of the three clothing brands of which customers were most aware in its home market of Spain, with particular strengths among women between ages of 18 and 34 from households with middle to middle-high income.

Zara's drawing power reflected the freshness of its offerings, the creation of a sense of scarcity and an attractive ambience around them, and the positive word of mouth that resulted. Freshness was rooted in rapid product turnover, with new designs arriving in each twice-weekly shipment. Devout Zara shoppers even knew which days of the week delivery trucks came into stores, and shopped accordingly. About three-quarters of the merchandise on display was changed every three to four weeks, which also corresponded to the average time between visits given estimates that the average Zara shopper visited the chain 17 times a year, compared with an average figure of three to four times a year for competing chains and their customers. Attractive stores, outside and inside, also helped. Luis Blanc, one of Inditex's international directors, summarized some of these additional influences:

> We invest in prime locations. We place great care in the presentation of our storefronts. That is how we project our image. We want our clients to enter a beautiful store, where they are offered the latest fashions. But most important, we want our customers to understand that if they like something, they must buy it now, because it won't be in the shops the following week. It is all about creating a climate of scarcity and opportunity.[16]

For the customers who did walk in through the door, the rapid turnover obviously created a sense of "buy now because you won't see this item later." In addition, the sense of scarcity was reinforced by small shipments, display shelves that were sparsely stocked, limits of one month on how long individual items could be sold in the stores, and a degree of deliberate undersupply.

Of course, even though Zara tried to follow fashions instead of betting on them, it did make some design mistakes. These were relatively cheap to reverse since there was typically no more than two to three weeks of forward cover for any risky item. Items that were slow to sell were immediately apparent and were ruthlessly weeded out by store managers with incentives to do so. Returns to the distribution center were either shipped to and sold at other Zara stores or disposed of through a small, separate chain of close-out stores near the distribution center. The target was to minimize the inventories that had to be sold at marked-down prices in Zara stores during the sales period that ended each season. Such markdowns had a significant impact on apparel retailers' revenue bases: in the United States, for example, women's apparel stores averaged markdowns of 30%-plus of (potential) revenues in the mid-1990s.[17] Very rough estimates for Western Europe indicated markdowns that were smaller but still very significant. Zara was estimated to generate 15%–20% of its sales at marked-down prices, compared with 30%–40% for most of its European peers. Additionally, since Zara had to move less of its merchandise during such periods, the percentage markdowns on the items affected did not have to be as large—perhaps only half as much as the 30% average for other European apparel retailers, according to Zara's management.

Store operations   Zara's stores functioned as both the company's face to the world and as information sources. The stores were typically located in highly visible locations, often including the premier shopping streets in a local market (e.g., the Champs Elysées in Paris, Regent Street in London, and Fifth Avenue in New York) and upscale shopping centers. Zara had initially purchased many of its store sites, particularly in Spain, but had preferred long-term leases (for 10 to 20 years) since the mid-1990s, except when purchase was necessary to secure access to a very attractive site. Inditex's balance sheet valued the property that it owned (mostly Zara stores) at about €400 million on the basis of historical costs, but some analysts estimated that the market value of these store properties might be four or five times that amount.

Zara actively managed its portfolio of stores. Stores were occasionally relocated in response to the evolution of shopping districts and traffic patterns. More frequently, older, smaller stores might be relocated as well as updated (and typically expanded) in new, more suitable sites. The average size of the stores had gradually increased as Zara improved the breadth and strength of its customer pull. Thus, while the average size of Zara stores at the beginning of fiscal year 2001 was 910 square meters, the average size of the stores opened during the year was 1,376 square meters. In addition, Zara invested more heavily and more frequently than key competitors in refurbishing its store base, with older stores getting makeovers every three to four years.

Zara also relied on significant centralization of store window displays and interior presentations in using the stores to promote its market image. As the season progressed and product offerings evolved, ideas about consistent looks for windows and for interiors in terms of themes, color schemes, and product presentation were prototyped in model window and store areas in the headquarters building in Arteixo. These ideas were principally carried to the stores by regional teams of window dressers and interior coordinators who visited each store every three weeks. But some adaptation was permitted and even planned for in the look of a store. For example, while all Zara in-store employees had to wear Zara clothes while working in the stores, the uniforms that the sales assistants were required to wear might vary across different Zara stores in the same city to reflect socioeconomic differences in the neighborhoods in which they were located. Uniforms were selected twice a season by store managers from the current season's collection and submitted to headquarters for authorization.

The size, location, and type of Zara store affected the number of employees in it. The number of sales assistants in each store was determined on the basis of variables such as sales volume and selling area. And the larger stores with the full complement of stores-within-stores—women's, men's, and children's—typically had a manager for each section, with the head of the women's section also serving as store manager. Personnel were selected by the store manager in consultation with the section manager concerned. Training was the responsibility of the section manager and was exclusively on-the-job. After the first 15 days, the trainee's suitability for the post was reviewed. Personnel assessment was, once again, the job of the store manager.

In addition to overseeing in-store personnel, store managers decided which merchandise to order and which to discontinue, and also transmitted customer data and their own sense of inflection points to Zara's design teams. In particular, they provided the creative teams with a sense of latent demand for new products that could not be captured through an automated sales-tracking system. The availability of store managers capable of handling these responsibilities was, according to CEO Castellano, the single most important constraint on the rate of store additions. Zara promoted

14

approximately 90% of its store managers from within and had generally experienced low store manager turnover. Once an employee was selected for promotion, his or her store, together with the human resources department, developed a comprehensive training program that included training at other stores and a two-week training program, with specialized staff, at Zara's headquarters. Such off-site training fulfilled important socialization goals as well, and was followed up by periodic supplemental training.

Store managers received a fixed salary plus variable compensation based primarily on their store's performance, with the variable component representing up to one-half of the total, which made their compensation very incentive-intensive. Since prices were fixed centrally, the store managers' energies were primarily focused on volume and mix. Top management tried to make each store manager feel as if she were running a small business. To this end, clear cost, profit, and growth targets for each store were set, as were regular reporting requirements—with stores' volume metrics being tracked particularly closely at the top of the (relatively flat) managerial hierarchy.

Zara's International Expansion

At the end of 2001, Zara was by far the most internationalized as well as the largest of Inditex's chains. Zara operated 282 stores in 32 countries outside Spain (55% of the international total for Inditex) and had posted international sales of €1,506 million (86% of Inditex's international sales) during the year. Of its international stores, 186 were located in Europe, 35 in North America, 29 in South America, 27 in the Middle East, and 5 in Japan. Overall, international operations accounted for 56% of Zara's stores and 61% of its sales in 2001, and had been steadily increasing its shares of those totals. The profitability of Zara's operations was not disaggregated geographically but, according to top management, was roughly the same in (the rest of) Europe and the Americas as in Spain. Approximately 80% of the new Zara stores slated to be opened in 2002 were expected to be outside Spain, and Inditex even cited the weight of Zara in the group's total selling area as the principal reason Inditex's sales were increasingly international. But over a longer time frame, Zara faced several important issues regarding its international expansion.

Market Selection

Zara's international expansion began in 1988 with the opening of a store in Oporto in northern Portugal. In 1989, it opened its first store in New York and in 1990, its first store in Paris. Between 1992 and 1997, it entered about one country per year (at a median distance of about 3,000 kilometers from Spain), so that by the end of this period, there were Zara stores in seven European countries, the United States, and Israel. Since then, countries had been added more rapidly: 16 countries (at a median distance of 5,000 kilometers) in 1998–1999, and eight countries (at a median distance of less than 2,000 kilometers) in 2000–2001. Plans for 2002 included entry into Italy, Switzerland, and Finland. Rapid expansion gave Zara a much broader footprint than larger apparel chains: by way of comparison, H&M added eight countries to its store network between the mid-1980s and 2001, and The Gap added five. (**Exhibit 14** tracks aggregate store additions across all of Inditex's chains.)

Inditex's management sometimes described this pattern of expansion as an "oil stain" in which Zara would first open a flagship store in a major city and, after developing some experience operating locally, add stores in adjoining areas. This pattern of expansion had first been employed in Spain and had been continued in Portugal. The first store opened in New York was intended as a display window and listening post, but the first store in Paris anchored a pattern of regional—and then national—expansion that came to encompass about 30 stores in the Paris area and 67 in France by the end of 2001. Castellano explained the approach:

> For us it is cheaper to deliver to 67 shops than to one shop. Another reason, from the point of view of the awareness of the customers of Inditex or of Zara, is that it is not the same if we have one shop in Paris compared to having 30 shops in Paris. And the third reason is that when we open a country, we do not have advertising or local warehouse costs but we do have headquarters costs.

Similarly, Zara's entry into Greece in 1993 was a springboard for its expansion into Cyprus and Israel.

Zara had historically looked for new country markets that resembled the Spanish market, had a minimum level of economic development, and would be relatively easy to enter. To study a specific entry opportunity, a commercial team from headquarters conducted both the macro and micro analysis. Macro analysis focused on local macroeconomic variables and their likely future evolution, particularly in terms of how they would affect the prospects for stores (e.g., tariffs, taxes, legal costs, salaries, and property prices/rents). Micro analysis, performed onsite, focused on sector-specific information about local demand, channels, available store locations, and competitors. The explicitly competitive information that was gathered included data on levels of concentration, the formats that would compete most directly with Zara, and their potential political or legal ability to resist/retard its entry, as well as local pricing levels. According to Castellano, Zara—unlike its competitors—focused more on market prices than on its own costs in forecasting its prices in a particular market. These forecasts were then overlaid on cost estimates, which incorporated considerations of distance, tariffs, taxes, and so forth, to see whether a potential market could reach profitability quickly enough (often within a year or two of opening the first store).

The actual application of this template for market analysis varied somewhat from country to country. The opening of the first store in New York for informational purposes was an early example. Germany provided a more recent case: while Zara usually conducted market analysis at the country level, it had made an exception by separately analyzing seven large German cities. Sometimes, specific opportunities or constraints overshadowed market-level analysis. Castellano characterized the early entry into Greece in such terms: "The obvious next step [after France] was to open in Belgium. But Greece offered, to us at least, a unique real estate opportunity. From the point of view that it was not a very competitive market there in the early 1990s, we decided to open in Greece. But now our strategy is to be in all the advanced countries [of Europe]."

Market Entry

If the commercial team's evaluation of a particular market was positive, the logical next step was to assess how to enter it. In contrast to Spain, where all of Zara's stores were company-owned and managed, three different modes of market entry were used internationally: company-owned stores, joint ventures, and franchises. Zara usually employed just one of these modes of market participation in a particular country, although it did sometimes shift from one to another. Thus, it had entered Turkey via franchising in 1998, but had acquired ownership of all its Turkish stores in 1999.

Zara had originally expanded internationally through company-owned stores and, at the end of 2001, operated 231 such stores in 18 countries outside Spain. Zara typically established company-managed stores in key, high-profile countries with high growth prospects and low business risk. Company-owned stores did, however, entail the greatest commitment of resources, including management time. As a result, Zara had used two other modes of market entry, franchises and joint ventures, in about half the countries it had entered since 1998.

Zara first used franchising to enter Cyprus in 1996 and, at the end of 2001, had 31 franchised stores in 12 countries.[18] Zara tended to use franchises in countries that were small, risky, or subject to significant cultural differences or administrative barriers that encouraged this mode of market participation: examples included Andorra, Iceland, Poland, and the Middle Eastern countries that the chain had entered (where restrictions on foreign ownership ruled out direct entry). Franchise contracts typically ran for five years, and franchisees were generally well-established, financially strong players in complementary businesses. Franchisees were usually given exclusive, countrywide franchises that might also encompass other Inditex chains, but Zara always retained the right to open company-owned stores as well. In return for selling its products to franchisees and charging them a franchise fee that typically varied between 5% and 10% of their sales, Zara offered franchisees full access to corporate services, such as human resources, training, and logistics, at no extra cost. It also allowed them to return up to 10% of purchased merchandise—a higher level than many other franchisers permitted.

Zara used joint ventures in larger, more important markets where there were barriers to direct entry, most often ones related to the difficulty of obtaining prime retail space in city centers. At the end of 2001, 20 Zara stores in Germany and Japan were managed through joint ventures, one in each country. Interests in both ventures were split 50:50 between Zara and its partners: Otto Versand, the largest German catalog retailer and a major mall owner, and Bigi, a Japanese textile distributor. The agreements with these partners gave Zara management control, so that it grouped stores in both countries with its owned stores as "company-managed." Nevertheless, the split ownership did create some potential complexities: thus, the agreement with Otto Versand contained put and call options under which Zara might be required to buy out its partner's interest or elect to do so.

In addition, Zara had been presented with opportunities to acquire foreign chains but had rejected them because of overlapping store networks, physical and cultural impediments to retrofitting its model on to them, and the difficulty of meeting profitability targets after paying acquisition premia. Some of Inditex's smaller chains, in contrast, *had* been acquired and, partly because of that heritage, relied much more heavily on franchising. Overall, nearly one-third of the international stores of Inditex's other chains were franchised.

Marketing

While management stressed that Zara used the same business system in all the countries in which it operated, there was some variation in retailing operations at the local level. The first store(s) opened in each market—often a flagship store in a major city—played a particularly critical role in refining the marketing mix by affording detailed insights into local demand. The marketing mix that emerged there was applied to other stores in the country as well.

Pricing was, as described earlier, market-based. However, if a decision was taken to enter a particular market, customers effectively bore the extra costs of supplying it from Spain. Prices were, on average, 40% higher in Northern European countries than in Spain, 10% higher in other European countries, 70% higher in the Americas, and 100% higher in Japan. (**Exhibit 15** provides more information, for a representative product.) Zara had historically marked local currency prices for all the countries in which it operated on each garment's price tag, making the latter an "atlas" as its footprint expanded. (See **Exhibit 16** for an old, multi-country price tag.) As key Western European markets switched to the euro at the beginning of 2002, Zara simplified its price tags to list only the prices in the local markets in which a particular garment might be sold, even though this complicated logistics.

The higher prices outside Spain did imply a somewhat different positioning for Zara overseas, particularly in emerging markets. Castellano explained the situation with an example:

In Spain, with the prices we have and the information available to the public, about 80% of Spanish citizens can afford Zara. When we go to Mexico, for cultural reasons, for informational reasons, for economic reasons—because the average income in Mexico is $3,000 compared to $14,000—our targeted customer base is narrower. Who buys from us in Mexico? The upper class and the middle class. That is the class that knows fashion, that is accustomed to buying in Europe, or in the United States, in New York or Miami. In Mexico we are targeting 14 million inhabitants, compared to 35–36 million in Spain [out of populations of 100 million and 40 million, respectively]. But 14 million is more than enough to put in a network of stores there.

Differences in positioning also affected the stores in which products were sold and Zara's overall image. For example, in South America, Zara products had to present a high-end rather than a mid-market image, and it was emphasized that they were "made in Europe." The image presented was never one of "made in Spain," however. Thus, according to a survey by *Vogue*, young Parisiennes—who voted Zara to be their favorite apparel chain—generally thought it was of French origin.[19]

Zara's promotion policies and product offerings varied less internationally than did its prices or positioning. Advertising and other promotional efforts were generally avoided worldwide except during the sales periods, which were typically biannual, in line with Western European norms. And while product offerings catered to physical, cultural, or climate differences (e.g., smaller sizes in Japan, special women's clothes in Arab countries, different seasonality in South America), 85%–90% of the basic designs sold in Zara stores tended to be common from country to country. This commonality was facilitated by the frequent interactions between the creative team in La Coruña and local store managers. Furthermore, the 10%–15% of products that did vary from country to country were selected from the same broad menu of offerings: Zara did not develop products to meet just one country's requirements. Management thought that the implementation of this relatively standardized strategy had become easier over time as tastes converged across national boundaries. Residual differences permitted products that did not sell well in one market to be sold in others.

Management

Zara's international activities were organized primarily under a holding company created in 1988, Zara Holding, B.V., of the Netherlands. Zara Holding's transactions with international franchisees were denominated in euros (Inditex's official currency). Sales in other currencies to subsidiaries in the Americas roughly offset dollar-denominated purchases from the Far East.

Under Zara Holding were the country operations, which exercised managerial control of the downstream portions of the value chain, particularly the real estate and personnel costs associated with store operations. Country management teams typically consisted of a country general manager, a real estate manager, a human resource manager, a commercial manager, and an administrative and financial manager. Such management teams sometimes served clusters of neighboring countries (e.g., Belgium and Luxembourg) if individual countries were too small. Country general managers played a particularly important role bridging between top management at headquarters and store managers at the local level: they were key conduits, for example, in propagating best practices through the organization. A committee of subsidiaries that met every two to three months was of particular help in this regard. Country managers each received four to six months of training at headquarters. The country managers in key European markets were all locals, but some in the Americas were expatriates.

Corporate as well as country managers' ability to control local store operations was enhanced by the use of standardized reporting systems. Persistently subpar performance generally triggered extensive analysis followed by attempts to fix the problem(s) identified rather than market exit. However, a Pull & Bear franchised store in China had shut down during 2000 and, in early 2002, the prospects for the Argentine operation—struggling because of 35% tariffs and advance tax payment requirements even before the country's acute macroeconomic crisis—looked grim.

Growth Options

Inditex's plans for 2002 called for the addition of 55 to 65 Zara stores, 80% of them outside Spain.[20] But the geographic focus of Zara's store additions over a longer timeframe remained to be determined. Since Zara had accounted for two-thirds of the total selling area added by Inditex across all its chains in 2001, decisions about Zara's expansion would have important group-level implications. The growth options for Zara within its home market of Spain seemed somewhat limited. Zara still had only a 4% share there, but Inditex's total share amounted to 6%. And the experience of H&M—which had undergone like-for-like sales declines after its share in its home market, Sweden, hit 10%—hinted that there might be relatively tight constraints on such an approach. Also of possible relevance was H&M's entry into Spain in 2001.

Castellano and his top management team saw the rest of Europe as offering the brightest prospects for significant, sustained growth over the medium term. Italy was thought to be a case in point. Italy was the largest single apparel market in Europe, partly because Italians spent more than €1,000 per capita on apparel (versus less than €600 per capita for Spaniards). Italian consumers visited apparel stores relatively frequently and were considered relatively fashion-forward. Apparel retailing in Italy was dominated by independent stores, which accounted for 61% of the market there (vs. 45% in Spain and 15%–30% in France, Germany, and the United Kingdom). Relatedly, concentration levels were lower in Italy than in any of the four other major European markets. (See **Exhibit 17** for data on European markets along some of these and other dimensions.)

Both of Zara's attempts to enter the Italian market had been orchestrated through joint ventures, because of the planning and retailing regulations that made it hard to secure the location and the multiple licenses required to open a new store. An initial joint venture agreement with Benetton, formed in 1998, failed to overcome this difficulty and was later dissolved. Over roughly the same timeframe, Benetton apparently secured a large bank loan and launched an aggressive campaign, particularly in Italy, to open up directly managed megastores of its own that were much larger than the third-party stores that it had traditionally licensed. In 2001, Inditex formed a 51:49 joint venture with Percassi, an Italian group specializing in property and fashion retail premises and one of Benetton's largest licensees, to enable expansion in Italy. This second joint venture resulted in the opening of Zara's first store in Milan in April 2002—at 2,500 square meters, the largest Zara store in Europe and a major media event. Inditex and Percassi reportedly planned to add 70–80 Zara stores in Italy over the next 10 years.

Of course, expansion within Europe was only one of several regional options. Zara could conceivably also deepen its commitment to a second region by investing significantly in distribution and even production there. North America and Asia seemed to be the two other obvious regional possibilities. South America was much smaller and subject to profitability pressures that were thought likely to persist; the Middle East was more profitable on average, but even smaller. However, the larger regions presented their own challenges. The U.S. market, the key to North America, was subject to retailing overcapacity, was less fashion-forward than Europe, demanded larger sizes on average, and exhibited considerable internal variation. Benetton had had to retreat after a disastrous attempt to expand in the United States in the 1980s. And in early 2002, H&M had slowed down its ambitious expansion effort there because of higher-than-expected operating costs and weak demand—despite the fact that its prices there were pegged at levels comparable to those that it posted in its large markets in North Europe. Asia appeared to be even more competitive and difficult to penetrate than North America.

Outlook

While the issues surrounding Zara's future geographic focus were important, top management had to consider some questions that reached even farther. One immediate set concerned the non-Zara chains that had recently proliferated, but at least some of which were of subcritical scale. Could Inditex cope with the complexity of managing multiple chains without compromising the excellence of individual chains, especially since its geographic scope was also relatively broad? Looking farther out, should it start up or acquire additional chains? The questions were sharpened by Inditex's revenue growth rate requirements, which top management pegged at 20%+ per annum. While like-for-like sales growth had averaged 9% per year recently, it might fall to 7% or even 5%, so a 15% annual increase in selling space seemed to be a minimal requirement. And, of course, margins had to be preserved as well—potentially a challenge given some of the threats to the sustainability of Inditex's competitive advantages. A roundtable video of Inditex's top management sheds additional light on some of these issues as well as others discussed in this case.

Exhibit 1 Buyer-Driven vs. Producer-Driven Global Chains

	Buyer-Driven Global Chains (e.g., Apparel)	Producer-Driven Global Chains (e.g., Automobiles)
Upstream Structure	Fragmented, locally owned, dispersed, and often tiered production	Global oligopolies
Downstream Structure	Relatively concentrated intermediaries	Relatively fragmented intermediaries
Key Cross-Border Links	Retailers, branded marketers, and branded manufacturers	Producers
Rent Concentration	Downstream	Upstream
Types of Rents	Relational Trade policy Brand name	Technology Organizational
Typical Industries	Labor-intensive consumer products	Capital- and technology-intensive products

Source: Casewriter compilation of data from Gary Gereffi, "International Trade and Industrial Upgrading in the Apparel Commodity Chain," *Journal of International Economics* 48 (June 1999): 37–70.

Exhibit 2 Average Labor Costs and Productivity in Apparel ($/hour, 1998)

	Labor Cost	Value Added
EU Countries		
Germany	18	23
Spain	7	11
Italy	14	20
Portugal	4	6
UK	11	13
Major Suppliers		
Turkey	2	12
China	0.4	na
India	0.4	2
Egypt	0.7	2
Other Major Markets		
US	10	20
Japan	14	na

Source: Casewriter compilation of data from: Werner Stengg, "The Textile and Clothing Industry in the EU," Enterprise Papers No. 2, June 2001; and http://europa.eu.int/comm/enterprise/textiles/statistics.htm, accessed December 17, 2002.

Exhibit 3 Landed Costs of a Large Men's Shirt in Spain: Illustrative

Manufactured in Spain			Manufactured in Asia	
Fabric Costs	€17.20	€25.32	Purchasing costs	
Other input costs	€13.25	€1.49	Transportation costs	
Labor Costs	€11.79	€2.28	Rehandling costs	
Total	€42.24	€29.09	Total	

Source: Confidential industry sources.

Exhibit 4 Cycle Time Compression through Quick Response

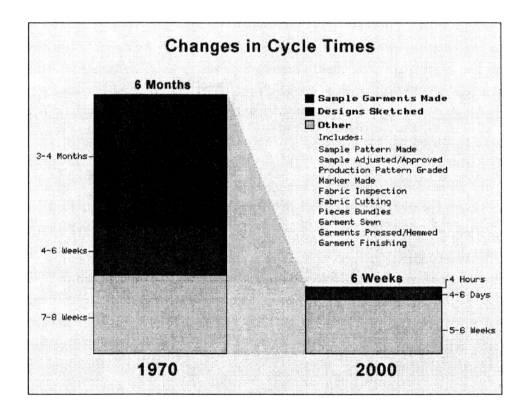

Source: Inditex.

Exhibit 5   A Product Market Positioning Map

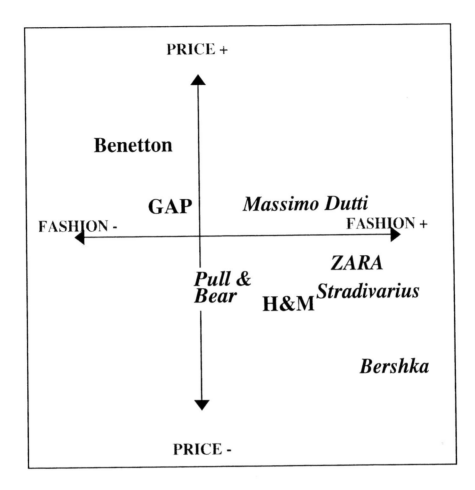

Source: Adapted from Morgan Stanley Dean Witter, "Inditex," 1998.

Note: Zara, Massimo Dutti, Pull & Bear, Bershka, and Stradivarius were separate Inditex chains, as described in the
         Inditex/Structure section of this case.

Exhibit 6　　Key Competitors and Inditex, 2001

	Gap	H&M	Benetton	Inditex
Operating Results (€ Millions)				
Net Operating Revenues	15,559	4,269	2,098	3,250
Cost of Goods Sold	10,904	2,064	1,189	1,563
Gross Margin	4,656	2,204	909	1,687
Operating Expenses	4,276	1,615	624	982
Operating Profits	379	589	286	704
Non-operating Expenses	108	-28	43	209
Pre-tax Income	272	617	243	495
Income Tax	280	206	92	150
Minority Interests	0	0	2	5
Net Income	-9	410*	148	340
Financial Position (€ Millions, except where noted otherwise)				
Current Assets	3,436	1,468	1,558	854
Property, Plant, and Equipment	4,695	661	720	1,228
Other Noncurrent Assets	435	54	543	523
Total Assets	8,566	2,183	2,821	2,605
Current Liabilities	2,320	432	956	834
Noncurrent Liabilities	2,850	101	625	285
Total Liabilities	5,170	532*	1,580	1,119
Equity--Book Value	3,396	1,650	1,241	1,486
Equity--Market Value[a]	12,687	15,564	2,605	13,433
One Year Change in Market Value (%)[b]	-60%	8%	-20%	47%
Other Statistics				
Employees	166,000	22,944	6,672	26,724
Number of Countries of Operation	6	14	120	39
Sales in Home Country (%)	87%	12%	44%	46%
Sales in Home Continent (%)	NA	96%	78%	77%
Number of Store Locations[c]	3,097	771	5,456	1,284
Stores in Home country (%)	87%	15%	40%	60%
Stores in Home Continent (%)	92%	96%	80%	86%
Average Store Size (sq. meter)	632	1,201	279	514

Sources: Compiled from annual reports; analyst reports; Bloomberg; Standard & Poor's Compustat® data via Research Insight℠; J. P. Morgan, "Hennes & Mauritz," company report, February 10, 1999, p. 89, Compustat.

* Totals off due to rounding.

[a]On May 22, 2002.

[b]In-home currency.

[c]Includes franchised stores.

24

Exhibit 7 Inditex Historical Financials (millions of euros)

Year	2001	2000	1999	1998	1997	1996
Net Operating Revenues	3,249.8	2,614.7	2,035.1	1,614.7	1,217.4	1,008.5
Cost of Goods Sold	1,563.1	1,277.0	988.4	799.9	618.3	521.0
Gross Margin	1,686.7	1,337.7	1,046.7	814.8	599.1	487.5
Operating Expenses	982.3	816.2	636.2	489.2	345.5	285.4
Operating Profits	704.4	521.5	410.5	325.6	253.6	202.1
Non-Operating Expenses	209.3	152.7	118.1	96.7		
Pre-Tax Income	495.1	368.8	292.4	228.9		
Income Tax	149.9	106.9	86.2	76.1		
Minority Interest	4.8	2.7	1.5	-0.2		
Net Income	340.4	259.2	204.7	153.0	117.4	72.7
Net Margin	10.47%	9.91%	10.06%	9.48%	9.64%	7.21%
Inventories	353.8	245.1	188.5	157.7		
Accounts Receivable	184.2	145.2	121.6	75		
Cash and Cash Equivalents	315.7	210	171.8	158.8		
Total Current Assets	853.7	600.3	481.9	391.5	274.0	190.3
Property, Plant, and Equipment	1,336.8	1,339.5	1,127.4	880.4	635.7	
Other Non Current Assets	414.5	167.8	163.6	54.4	67.5	
Total Assets	2,605	2,107.6	1,772.9	1,326.3	977.2	820.3
Asset Turnover	1.25	1.24	1.15	1.2	1.2	1.2
ROA	13.07%	12.30%	11.54%	11.54%	12.01%	8.86%
Accounts Payable	426.3	323.0	276.1	215.6	131.4	
Other Current Liabilities	407.9	347.3	275.6	229.1	141.5	
Total Current Liabilities	834.2	670.3	551.7	444.7	272.9	234.1
Non Current Liabilities	284.5	1,437.7	1,221.3	881.6	704.3	586.2
Total Liabilities	1,118.7	2,108	1,773	1,326.3	977.2	820.3
Equity	1,486.2	1,170.9	893.2	673.4	529.9	414.9
Leverage	1.75	1.80	1.98	1.97	1.84	1.98
ROE	22.9%	22.1%	22.9%	22.7%	25.0%	20.0%

Source: Inditex.

Exhibit 8 Inditex Timeline

Year	No. of Stores	Event
1963		• Establishment of Confecciones Gao, S.A. Beginning of the company's activities
1975	2	• Opening of 1st Zara store in La Coruña
1976	2	• Establishment of Goasam as the owner of the Zara chain stores • Purchase of 1st computer
1985	37	• Reorganization of group structure with Inditex at the apex
1988	71	• Formation of Zara B. V. in the Netherlands as holding company for international activities
1989	88	• International rollout begins with opening of a Zara store in Portugal
1990	105	• Opening of fully automated 130,000-square-meter central warehouse • Joint venture with Toyota (Japan) introduces just-in-time system at one of the factories
1991	218	• Establishment of commercial office in Bejing to handle purchase of supplies in Asia • Diversification into new segments • Acquisition of 65% of Massimo Dutti • Implementation of telecommunications system between headquarters and the supply, production, and sales centers • Launch of the Pull & Bear chain
1993	369	• Preparation/implementation of expansion plan for Zara in the French market
1995	508	• Acquisition of all of the share capital of Massimo Dutti
1996	541	• Expansion of central warehouse to cope with the increase in the number of points of sale
1998	748	• Creation of the Amancio Ortega Foundation • Alliance with Otto Versand to enter the German market • Launch of the Bershka chain, targeting the younger female market
1999	922	• Acquisition of Stradivarius makes it the fifth chain of the Group
2000	1,080	• Opening of new Inditex headquarters complex in Arteixo, near La Coruña
2001	1,284	• Initial public offering of 26% of Inditex's shares • Launch of the Oysho lingerie chain
2002		• Alliance with Percassi results in opening of first Italian store

Source: Inditex.

26

Exhibit 9 Map of Spain

Source: Adapted from *The Encyclopedia of World Geography* (New York: Barnes and Noble, 1996).

Exhibit 10   Inditex Chains

Zara

- 500 stores in 30 countries
- Created in 1975
- Continuous innovation based on customer desires
- For women, men, and youth, from infants to age 45
- Web link: www.zara.com

Massimo Dutti

- 200 stores in 12 countries
- Acquired by Inditex in 1995
- Fashion variety, from sophisticated to sporty
- For men & women, ages 25-45
- Web link: www.massimodutti.com

Bershka

- Founded by Inditex in 1998
- 170 stores in 8 countries
- Trendy clothing for a younger female target audience, ages 13-23
- Stores are designed as a social hot-spot, highlighting fashion, music, and street art
- Web link: www.bershka.com

Pull and Bear

- 225 stores in 9 countries
- Founded by Inditex in 1991
- Casual clothing at affordable prices
- For men and women, ages 14-28
- Web link: www.pullbear.com

Stradivarius

- Acquired in 1999
- 100 stores in 7 countries
- Youthful urban fashion
- For young men & women, ages 15-25
- Web link: www.e-stradivarius.com

Oysho

- Inditex's newest chain
- 25 stores in 6 European countries
- Latest trends in lingerie
- Quality products at reasonable prices
- Web link: www.oysho.com

Source: Inditex.

Exhibit 11   Inditex Management Structure

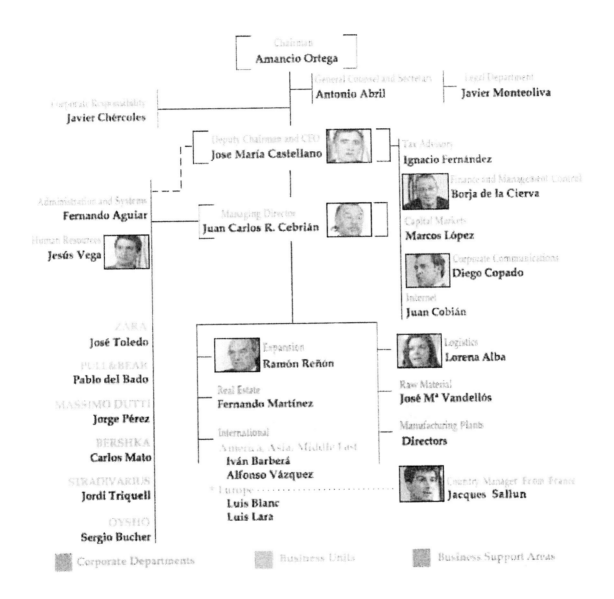

Source: Inditex.

263

Exhibit 12   Zara's Business System

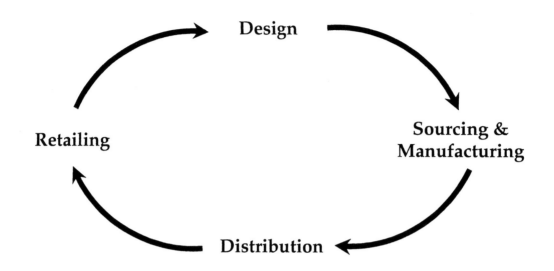

Source: Casewriter.

Exhibit 13   Product Precommitments: Zara vs. Traditional Industry

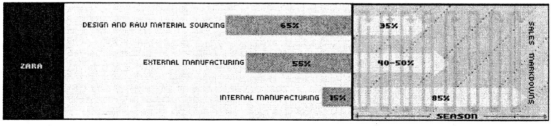

Source: Inditex.